Buff Facings and Gilt Buttons

Facings

The facings for General Officers, and for Officers of the Adjutant General's Department, the Quartermaster General's Department, the Commissary General's Department, and the Engineers—buff. The Coat for all officers to be edged throughout with the facing designated.

Buttons

For General Officers and Officers of the General Staff—bright gilt, rounded at the edge, convex, raised eagle in the centre, with stars surrounding; large size, one inch in exterior diameter; small size, half an inch.

Article XLVII,
Confederate Army Regulations, 1863

Buff Facings
and
Gilt Buttons

*Staff and Headquarters Operations in the
Army of Northern Virginia, 1861–1865*

J. Boone Bartholomees, Jr.

University of South Carolina Press

Published in Columbia, South Carolina, by the
University of South Carolina Press

Manufactured in the United States of America

02 01 00 99 98   5 4 3 2 1

Library of Congress Cataloging-in-Publication Data

Bartholomees, J. Boone, 1947–
    Buff facings and gilt buttons : staff and headquarters operations in the
Army of Northern Virginia, 1861–1865 / J. Boone Bartholomees Jr.
        p.   cm.
    Includes bibliographical references (p.) and index.
    ISBN 1-57003-220-3
    1. Confederate States of America. Army of Northern Virginia—Staffs.
2. United States—History—Civil War, 1861–1865—Regimental histories.
3. Virginia—History—Civil War, 1861–1865—Regimental histories.   I.
Title.
E470.2.B326 1998
973.7'455—ddc21   98-19676

CONTENTS

PREFACE

Jay Luvaas and Len Fullenkamp unknowingly forced me to write this book. Jay recently retired as the professor of military history at the U.S. Army War College at Carlisle Barracks, Pennsylvania, and Len is the director of military history there. They shared an office and, among other things, ran a program of staff rides for military groups to local (and not so local) Civil War battlefields. When I joined the faculty of the war college, I also became a member of the History Guild—an informal band Len uses to track historians and people with an interest in military history. Len and I taught military history together at West Point, and I was filling one of the surprisingly few historian positions at the college, so joining the guild was automatic. I quickly discovered that one of the major duties of guild membership is leading staff rides. Jay, the father of the modern staff ride, took me and other volunteers to stomp around Gettysburg (the closest battlefield to Carlisle and the most frequent staff-ride location) and later Antietam. He patiently and expertly walked us through the battles and the administrative intricacies of one-way roads, places to eat lunch, and public latrine locations. Eventually, he declared me fit to lead staff rides. Chris Hockensmith (Jay and Len's secretary) started calling immediately to see if I was available on such-and-such a day to take such-and-such a group to Gettysburg.

Staff rides are fun and I enjoy doing them, but a person would be crazy to take a busload of army officers to Gettysburg or Antietam without significant preparation. Army officers generally have an interest in military history, and the ones willing to come long distances to study an old battlefield often have a passion for the subject. Some are true buffs of the variety about whom Ted Ropp always warned his graduate students. In any case, they have little patience for novice historians with superficial knowledge of their subject. The Civil War was not my specialty

vii

in graduate school, although I am eclectic and do not limit myself to one period. I knew enough to be dangerous but not effective. I needed to study Gettysburg—and I did. However, after leading a few staff rides, I found I had to read up on more than just the battle. Staff-ride participants ask all kinds of great questions about intelligence, medicine, logistics, and other specialized subjects. Most of the questions, at least those not directly about leadership or a point of fact, concern some aspect of staff work. I went to the library looking for books about Civil War staff operations. There were books about specific aspects of the staff—like quartermaster, ordnance, or medical—but nothing in general, and nothing that treated staff and headquarters operations as a whole. I expanded my research. Soon, what began as a casual attempt to prepare for staff rides became a full-blown project.

The Civil War is a treasure trove for historians. Thousands of books have been written about that war; nevertheless, subjects remain untouched, and there are hundreds of different ways to approach, organize, and interpret the available material. I quickly found I had to limit the scope of my subject and research to something manageable or this project would become my life's work. Staff functions at the national level in Washington and Richmond did not serve my immediate purpose, and historians have worked on those topics. Similarly, I was not interested in researching a single aspect of the staff. I wanted to study field staff work broadly but in a digestible manner. I decided to look at all the elements of the staff but to limit myself by concentrating on a single army. Having served on several staffs from battalions to the Department of the Army, I am convinced they have individual styles—almost organizational personalities. What is true of the Army of Northern Virginia may not be true of the Army of Tennessee and almost certainly is not true of the Army of the Potomac or the Army of the Cumberland. Since the purpose was to improve my knowledge of Gettysburg and Antietam, studying either the Army of Northern Virginia or the Army of the Potomac was only logical. I first got interested in military history reading *Lee's Lieutenants* as a boy, and I guess I never lost my romantic attachment to the Army of Northern Virginia. I picked it to study, although I have not been a stickler about the name. I included P. G. T. Beauregard's staff at First Manassas, Joseph E. Johnston's staff of the Confederate Army of the Potomac, Thomas J. Jackson's staff in the Shenandoah Valley, James Longstreet's staffs both when he took First Corps to join the Army of Tennessee and during his independent command of the Department of Virginia and North Carolina, and the Second Corps staff during the period in 1864 when it was technically the Valley Army under Jubal A. Early.

With the subject somewhat limited, I next had to decide about sources. My formal historical training prejudiced me toward primary documents as the only legitimate source of good history. Preliminary investigation showed that researching even a small percentage of the extant Army of Northern Virginia documents would be impossible. The U.S. Army Military History Institute, fortuitously collocated at Carlisle with the war college, has a good collection on the Civil War. Other than documents at the institute, I reluctantly but consciously limited myself to published primary and secondary sources. This study cannot, therefore, be definitive. It is only a start, but I believe it is a major start. There may be materials at the National Archives; the Museum of the Confederacy; the Southern Historical Collection in Chapel Hill, North Carolina; the collections of the National Park Service at the various battlefields; or any of a hundred other places that would significantly change my interpretation. I sincerely hope somebody has the interest to look. Recognizing the research limitations, I still believe I have something to contribute to understanding this subject. I have examined traditional material from a unique perspective, that of an experienced staff officer looking at earlier staff officers. A friend who read a draft commented that much of the material was familiar, but he had never considered it in quite the way I did. I suspect others will have the same reaction.

This book is not for everybody. It assumes a basic knowledge of the Civil War and the Army of Northern Virginia. I have made no attempt to explain the war, give biographical sketches of personalities, or detail the conduct or outcome of battles. I assume anybody who tackles a book like this is familiar with such subjects. I occasionally give dates of battles parenthetically as chronological reference points. Examples to support general assertions are illustrative rather than exhaustive. Quotations retain the spelling, punctuation, and emphasis of the original.

I want to thank Professors Theodore Ropp, I. B. Holley, and Richard L. Watson, who mentored me through my graduate studies; Jay and Len and hundreds of staff-ride participants who unconsciously started me on this project; the staff of the U. S. Army Military History Institute, particularly Louise Arnold-Friend in the library and Richard Sommers, Dave Keough, and Pam Cheney in the manuscript division, for patient assistance; and especially my family, Sharon, Jay, Sara, and Dorothy, who (at least while living at home) put up with evenings and weekends of having husband and father closeted in his basement office staring at the computer waiting for the muse to strike.

INTRODUCTION

Anyone who reads even casually about military operations during the American Civil War encounters frequent mention of an otherwise anonymous class of soldier—the men who comprised the staffs of the opposing armies. Those officers bear uninspiring titles—assistant adjutant general, inspector of artillery, medical director—that imply duties of an administrative nature. Despite their prosaic appellations, they pop up with disturbing frequency in otherwise stirring narratives, rushing about chaotic battlefields, delivering orders, rallying troops, and conducting reconnaissance. Occasionally, they figure in romantic episodes. There are stories about staff officers slipping across the lines into enemy territory to rescue damsels in distress, escorting fallen leaders off the field, and dancing with beautiful ladies at impromptu balls. Some left well-known memoirs that constitute important sources in the historiography of the Civil War; others slipped into obscurity with only brief mention in the footnotes of musty tomes. Staff officers were military administrators, responsible for minor but important tasks; however, they were much more than that. Staff officers were a critical element of Civil War armies. They were the nineteenth-century representatives of a band as old as organized warfare. Their direct organizational descendants in today's armed forces—still innocuous and still bearing prosaic, administrative-sounding titles—perform duties their Civil War predecessors would appreciate. Who were these men? What were they doing, or think they were doing? What should they have been doing? How did they operate? What did they contribute?

Military staffs are ancient institutions. The armies of ancient Egypt had officers with titles that indicate staff organization. There were quartermasters, scribes, overseers of arsenals, caravan leaders, and specialists in desert and frontier warfare. Such positions expanded over time as the army grew larger and more complex. Military scribes and quartermasters of the pharaohs' armies about 1400 B.C.E. took written tests on calculating the ration requirement for division-sized units. King Uzziah of Judah (ruled 786–56 B.C.E.) had a chief of staff who commanded in his absence; an adjutant general (*sofer*) who kept the army's rolls, was responsible for all clerical work, and whose Hebrew title also implied responsibility for intelligence; and a staff officer (*shoter*) responsible for enforcing headquarters orders and overseeing parts of the logistics system. Ancient Assyria had an effective, centralized national remount system, called the *musarkisus,* capable of supplying three thousand horses a month to its armies. Running such systems is the province of staffs. Alexander the Great had a personal staff to perform special duties, act as a council, and provide a talent pool for high military and administrative positions. The Macedonian general also had staff sections including commissary departments and baggage trains, engineers and siege experts, scientists and surveyors, and clerks and historians. Roman armies had aides for officers, clerks and bookkeepers, doctors, military engineers, and veterinarians. Specialists from provincial headquarters performed intelligence and escort services and the mundane work of Roman justice (torture and execution). Roman military staffs kept documents and records of medical exams, unit strengths, daily watchwords, duty rosters, arrivals and departures—to say nothing of a dossier on every man that included records of his service, pay, savings, and detached duties.[1] More significant, all those ancient armies campaigned across difficult terrain at great distances from their bases over extended periods. Such operational capability does not just happen—it requires planning, preparation, and coordination. Alexander was a military genius; Egyptian pharaohs considered themselves gods. But even geniuses and gods (at least mortal gods) cannot be everywhere or know everything. They need help administering and fighting large armies. Staffs were the solution—they developed early and lasted long.

The West lost the tradition of military staffs—along with other more significant elements of civilization—with the fall of Rome. However, as Europe emerged from the Dark Ages it rediscovered the utility of large, effective armies, and the necessity of administrative and logistical staffs to support them. Between 1500 and 1800, battlefield staff functions gradually separated from administration. Specialized groups of guides, aides, and adjutants general rose in various armies toward the end of the seventeenth century. When institutionalized and trained, they proved invaluable on the battlefield. After 1760, when armies began articulating into self-contained operational and even strategic units (divisions and later corps), general staffs emerged to coordinate their activities. By the end of the eighteenth century, modern armies depended on their staffs and the office furniture, files, and printed forms those officers hauled around with them on campaign. Still, when bullets began to fly, techniques of command and control differed little from those used by the ancient Egyptians. Despite all the hoopla historians make over flags, banners, drums, bugles, gongs, bells, and pyrotechnics, command on the battlefield above the unit level was mainly a matter of face-to-face communication or handwritten, hand-delivered notes. The experience of the Napoleonic Wars convinced the Prussians they needed a rationalized, systematized staff comprised of officers specially trained for the task. They developed the concepts that evolved into today's staff doctrine.

Contemporary European observers, coming from an environment of trained and efficient staffs, were harsh on American Civil War staff work. They found little to admire in the hastily organized bodies that supported American commanders, especially early in the war. The critique of a French observer of Union staff work during the advance to Williamsburg in 1862 is typical of the attitude:

> There is no special branch of the service whose duty it is to regulate, centralize and direct the movements of the army. In such a case as this of which we are speaking, we should have seen the General Staff Officers of a French army taking care that nothing should impede the advance of the troops, stopping a file of wagons here and ordering it out of the road to clear the way, sending for a detail of men there to repair the roadway or to draw a cannon out of the mire, in order to communicate to every corps commander the orders of the General-in-Chief.
>
> Here nothing of the sort is done. The functions of the adjutant-general are limited to the transmission of the orders of the general. He has nothing to do with seeing that they are executed. The general has no one to bear his orders but aides-de-camp who have the best intentions in the world, and are excellent at repeating mechanically a verbal order, but to whom nobody pays much attention if they undertake to exercise any initiative whatever.[2]

Even later European observers, who saw more competent staffs at work, found few American staff activities beyond medical/sanitary practices and railroad repair techniques to recommend to their readers at home. Twentieth-century authorities have been equally harsh on American staff work, especially in the Confederate armies. T. Harry Williams found Lee's staff to be little more than glorified clerks and messengers, while Grant's associates were more modern and expert. Jeffry Wert thinks Lee had an unprofessional general staff that was too small and included many men of limited ability. Wert concluded an article about the

Army of Northern Virginia staff with the observation that they did little to help Lee; however, the general never thought to demand more.[3]

American Civil War staffs did not equal their European counterparts in either training or efficiency, but they were not all as abominable as either contemporary or modern critics imply. In 1866 and 1870 the German general staff mobilized, armed, equipped, moved, deployed, and fought large armies with an ease and efficiency that must have amazed ex-Confederates. The Germans amazed the Austrian and French general staffs just as much. It is significant that while the Prince de Joinville's comments above criticize American staffs for failing to supervise execution, there is no mention of them failing to plan. Historians who look in vain for evidence of operations and planning staffs on the Prussian model measure against a standard uncommon at the time. While they certainly were not modern, staffs in the Army of Northern Virginia met most of the tests we demand from staffs today.

Modern doctrine assigns certain critical functions and characteristics to staffs. The U.S. Army's *Field Manual 101–5: Command and Control for Commanders and Staff* says a staff assists a commander by:

- Securing and providing information, data, and advice.
- Preparing detailed plans and orders according to the commander's decisions and guidance.
- Transmitting orders, directions, and so forth, to the command.
- Notifying the commander of matters which require his action or of which he needs to know.
- Making a continuous study of the situation.
- Preparing tentative plans for possible future contingencies for the commander's consideration.
- Supervising, within its authority, execution of the commander's orders as he may prescribe.
- Carrying out as necessary, the commander's intentions.[4]

A historian of the military staff, James D. Hittle, found "certain characteristics that must be possessed by a staff system before it can be considered to exist and function according to the modern understanding of the term." He listed those characteristics as: "A regular education system for training staff officers, delegation of authority from the commander, supervision of the execution of orders issued by or through the staff, and a set method of procedure by which each part performs certain specified duties."[5]

Army of Northern Virginia staffs routinely did most of the activities listed in *FM 101–5*. Staff officers did not commonly prepare plans in advance for the commander's decision or prepare plans for future contingencies, but even those events occurred occasionally. As to Hittle's characteristics of a modern staff, the Army of Northern Virginia could check off every one except the first. Given time and less pressing immediate requirements, the Confederacy might have established a staff school. Jefferson Davis was well aware of the contemporary European staff system, with its emphasis on education and training. In a letter to the Confederate Congress he recognized the importance of a well-trained general staff and expressed regret that the Confederate States could not afford the luxury of such education.[6] However, in that one important respect the Confederate staff failed to meet either Hittle's or the European standard. The failure to provide operational or contingency planning was a much more serious deficiency, but observers at the time did not commonly recognize it. The operational-planning failure reflected an ancient tradition of what staffs did rather than anticipate the more modern doctrine that would grow from the Prussian model.

Thus, the staff system of the Army of Northern Virginia demonstrates one of the peculiar traits of the Civil War. That war occurred on a cusp of military history—it had elements both ancient and modern, and it reflected the struggle of soldiers trying to reconcile the two. Civil War military institutions had their roots firmly planted in the traditions and doctrine of the past while they confronted modern problems. The story of the disconnection between linear tactics that would have been recognizable to either Alexander or Frederick the Great and deadly rifled muskets is familiar. The story of ill-trained and ill-prepared staffs trying to coordinate all the intricate details of a vast, semimodern army operating in a huge theater of war with doctrine and procedures that would soon be (if they were not already) outmoded is less familiar. That is the story of staff work in the Army of Northern Virginia.

Chapter 1

STAFF ORGANIZATION

FORMATION OF THE CONFEDERATE STAFF

The Confederate States of America organized its army from the top down. Jefferson Davis signed the law establishing the general staff agencies, defined as the Adjutant and Inspector General Department, the Quartermaster General Department, the Subsistence Department, and the Medical Department, on February 26, 1861. The law described the composition of the departments, set the rank of their chiefs at colonel, restricted general staff officers from command of line units, and assigned responsibility for paying the army to the Quartermaster Department. After providing for the high-level administration of its forces, the Confederate Congress could begin organizing the troops that were already forming in the rebellious states. An act passed two days after the establishment of the general staff authorized the president to assume control of military operations throughout the Confederacy and made provisions for accepting state and volunteer forces into national service in the Provisional Army of the Confederate States. The president, with the advice and consent of Congress, would appoint general officers and, by extension, supporting staffs for the provisional forces.[1]

Simply accepting state and volunteer units for national service did not provide an efficient mechanism for mustering, equipping, or managing the fledgling army. The Confederate Congress soon expanded and refined procedures for administering the rebellious nation's military forces. On March 6, 1861, President Davis signed two laws to flesh out the Confederate military establishment. The first authorized accepting for twelve months up to one hundred thousand volunteers, who would furnish their own uniforms and horses and be armed by their states to the extent possible. Once inspected and accepted into Confederate service, the president could organize the units into brigades and divisions and apportion generals and staff officers. Thereafter such troops would "be regarded in all respects as a part of the army of said Confederate States." Section 9 of the law provided staff support to volunteer units accepted into Confederate service as follows:

> When volunteers or militia are called into the service of the Confederate States in such numbers that the officers of the quartermaster, commissary and medical departments, which may be authorized by law for the regular service, are not sufficient to provide for the supplying, quartering, trans-porting, and furnishing them with the requisite medical attention, it shall be lawful for the President to appoint, with the advice and consent of Con-gress, as many additional officers of said departments as the service may require, not exceeding one commissary and one quartermaster for each brigade, with rank of major, and one assistant quartermaster with rank of Captain, one assistant commissary with rank of Captain, one surgeon and one assistant surgeon for each regiment . . . the said officers to be allowed the same pay and emoluments as shall be allowed officers of the same grade in the regular service, and to be subject to the rules and articles of war, and to continue in service only so long as their services may be re-quired in connection with the militia and volunteers.[2]

The second law established the regular army of the Confederate States of America. The statute authorized recruiting line units "and the staff de-partments already established by law." Although the Confederacy re-cruited few regular line regiments, the law was significant for the staff departments. It organized a hundred-man "company of sappers, miners, and pontoniers" that would become the Corps of Engineers and autho-rized a colonel as the chief engineer. It established a rudimentary Corps of Artillery and assigned the ordnance staff function to that branch. The law created four brigadier generals (later changed to full generals) and authorized each an aide-de-camp. It fixed the pay of staff officers, except those in the Medical Department, at the pay of a cavalry officer of equal rank (ten to twenty dollars more per month than infantry officers, de-pending on grade), gave aides a thirty-five dollar monthly bonus, and es-tablished a sliding pay scale for surgeons and assistant surgeons based on time in service and grade. Promotion and date of rank would be strictly by seniority and regiment in the line and by corps of service for general staff, artillery, and engineer officers.[3]

This series of laws, frequently adjusted and refined but never sub-stantially altered, provided the legal basis for the Confederate armies throughout the war and (particularly important for this study) the legal basis for the military staffs that would support those armies. Organiza-tions changed as the armies in the field grew larger, more complex, and more experienced. Authorizations for staff officers at various headquarters fluctuated. New staff sections (like the Signal Corps) were added as they emerged. Pay rates and provisions for indirect compensation—for example, rations and forage—changed. Congress debated minor tweaks and fundamental restructuring. In 1864, after President Davis vetoed their first attempt, the legislators finally passed a major staff reorganization bill to regularize the staffs of the field armies. However, the Adjutant and Inspector General Department anticipated Congress and established the field structure for its department and the Medical Department in a general order published before Congress could act. The president, who had a hand in drafting the general order, liked it better than the subsequent law; he simply ignored those provisions of the law with which he disagreed.[4] Thus, despite many adjustments, the basic legal skeleton of Confederate staffs remained remarkably fixed throughout the war.

The Confederate War Department used regulations and general orders to flesh out the bones of the army and staff provided by Congress. The original regulations and Articles of War of the Confederacy in 1861 were lifted directly from their U.S. counterparts of 1857 by the simple expedient of substituting the word *Confederate* for *United* throughout. Even the 1862 version contained little unique material—the authors only rewrote two inconsequential articles. By 1863 the regulations had matured and contained more altered or original material, but they still largely duplicated the basic U.S. regulations of 1857. The same is true for versions issued in 1864. Confederate regulations have a curious peacetime flavor and contain provisions that were overly prescriptive, excessively detailed, unrealistic, or inappropriate under wartime conditions. For example, consider what soldiers of the Army of Northern Virginia must have thought about the following provisions from their regulations as late as 1863: "Dirty clothes will be kept in an appropriate part of the knapsack; no article of any kind to be put under the bedding"; "The bread will be thoroughly baked, and not eaten until it is cold. The soup must be boiled at least five hours, and the vegetables always cooked sufficiently to be perfectly soft and digestible"; or the requirement to forward to the adjutant general the complete results of scheduled artillery practice periods in April, June, and October.[5] Despite such anomalies, the regulations spelled out for the general staff, in more or less detail, the theoretical duties and responsibilities of their positions.

DEFINING THE STAFF

The statutes that authorized staffs and the regulations that explained their duties do not neatly delineate the staff of the Army of Northern Virginia. There existed, and continues to exist, a problem in defining the staff. Law designated a general staff, but its members were not the only staff officers. There were men in every headquarters from army to regiment who spent all or part of their time doing staff work. Some of these men, although not formally included in the general staff, were obviously staff officers and were considered such at the time. Others had no official position and thus ambiguous status but performed duties that included staff work. Some officers served a dual role as commanders and staff officers and normally claimed the more prestigious title of commander even if their primary activities were in the staff arena. Also, there were the ever-present but almost historically invisible clerks, orderlies, and couriers who populated every headquarters. To even approach understanding how the staff functioned in the Army of Northern Virginia requires consideration of each of these categories to try to fit them into the jigsaw puzzle that was a nineteenth-century military staff.

The appellation "staff officer" was rife with implications, but contemporaries were not precise about or did not agree on the definition of the term. Some Confederates with excellent credentials did not even consider all members of the officially established general staff to be true staff officers. Brigadier General G. Moxley Sorrel, a Georgian who compiled an outstanding record as a staff officer and chief of staff for Lieutenant General James Longstreet before assuming command of a brigade late in the war, named only four primary officers and two other late arrivals as members of Robert E. Lee's staff. Sorrel went on to say, "There were possibly one or two lieutenants for personal aids, but this was Lee's staff. . . . Of course it does not include the important administrative officers like [Lieutenant Colonel Robert G.] Cole, chief commissary; [Lieutenant Colonel James L.] Corley, chief quartermaster; Doctor [Lafayette] Guild, medical director, and his chief of ordnance and other organizations."[6] On the same subject, Sorrel also remarked, "I suppose that at this date there are some hundreds of men in the South who call themselves members of Lee's staff, and so they were if teamsters, sentry men, detailed quartermasters (commissary men), couriers and orderlies, and all the rest of the following of a general headquarters of a great army are to be considered. But by the staff we usually confine ourselves to those responsible officers immediately about a general, and Lee had selected carefully. Four majors (afterwards lieutenant-colonels and colonels) did his principal work."[7]

Colonel Walter H. Taylor, Lee's assistant adjutant general throughout the war and one of the four officers Sorrel mentioned as part of Lee's true staff, made the same distinction but included more men on his roster. He listed two assistant adjutants general, four aides, and a military secretary as Lee's personal staff. Taylor recognized others who did staff work in the Army of Northern Virginia only as "chiefs of the several departments of the service attached to [Lee's] staff." According to Taylor's interpretation, by the end of the war Lee's staff consisted of only one assistant adjutant general and two aides-de-camp.[8]

Sorrel and Taylor limited the staff to men who served the commander directly, an imprecise usage common at the time; however, most contemporaries defined the staff more liberally. For example, in his official reports on battles, where it was customary to praise the staff in one of the concluding paragraphs, Lee did not limit himself to the four officers Sorrel mentioned. While thanking his staff in the report on the Seven Days' Battles (June 25–July 1, 1862), Lee listed seven assistant adjutants general and aides who were "continuously with me in the field" and eight others (chiefs of artillery, quartermaster, commissary, ordnance, and engineers; medical director; and inspector general) who "attended unceasingly to their several departments." This was not simply a case of Lee taking liberties with a term to spread praise—it reflected his official position on the composition of the staff. In a letter to Jefferson Davis commenting on a Senate bill to reorganize field army staffs, Lee discussed all the above positions except chiefs of artillery and engineers and added a request for a separate chief of staff with an assistant. In other correspondence, Lee expressed a desire to have a brigadier general serve on his staff as the Army of Northern Virginia chief of engineers.[9]

To really muddy the definitional waters, Sorrel, who insisted on a strict interpretation of Lee's staff, named seventeen people and Colonel E. Porter Alexander, "an officer who might also be numbered on the staff," as comprising Lieutenant General James Longstreet's staff in November 1862. Including Alexander (the corps chief of artillery), Sorrel's list encompassed every position Lee mentioned, several assistants, a signal officer, and a chief of staff. As further demonstration of confusion, Colonel William Gilham, instructor of tactics and commandant of cadets at the Virginia Military Institute, listed a slightly different staff when he reissued for Confederate use the manual for volunteers and militia he originally published as a major in the U.S. Army. That popular book described a staff closer to Lee's than to Sorrel's original list, but it omitted the chief of artillery and included instead a paymaster.[10] By 1862, when the Rebel version of Gilham's manual went into its second printing, the Confederate Congress had already decided to handle paymaster responsibilities in the Quartermaster Department rather than to establish a separate bureau. The good colonel must have disagreed with Congress, lacked the time to edit his manual beyond the obligatory change of

United to *Confederate,* or decided that including a paymaster as a separate entity on the staff did not really matter.

To impose order where none existed, it is convenient to classify staff positions as coordinating, special, or personal. This is a modern paradigm; however, with a simple substitution of the term *general staff* for *coordinating staff,* a Confederate would have understood the concept. Civil War military vocabulary used the terms *general staff* and *personal staff* in recognizably modern form, although the correlation is not perfect. *Personal staff* referred to officers assigned to the general personally and in practice often included general staff officers while excluding officers traditionally or legally included today. Personal staff officers took their rank, position, and authority from their general and moved with him when he was promoted or reassigned. The designation "special staff" was not used in the mid-nineteenth century, although the Confederate War Department came close to coining the term in a letter answering a congressional inquiry when it called those staff bureaus that were neither general nor personal "the offices of the chiefs of special services." Contemporary usage must have made some distinction between general staff and special staff, since some field returns contain separate entries for categories titled "general staff" and "staff."[11] Using the modern three-part classification system while redesignating the coordinating staff as general staff to retain historical terminology as much as possible, the Confederate general staff consisted of officers from the Adjutant and Inspector General Department and quartermaster, commissary of subsistence, and medical officers. We would call aides-de-camp, judge advocates general, and chaplains personal staff, while the artillery, engineer, ordnance, signal, and provost marshal officers in the headquarters were special staff.

Sorrel raised another definitional issue when he dismissed "teamsters, sentry men, detailed quartermasters (commissary men), couriers and orderlies, and all the rest of the following of a general headquarters of a great army" from consideration as members of the staff.[12] Many such men worked at the various headquarters of the Army of Northern Virginia. Some, like clerks and quartermaster sergeants, did actual staff work, prepared staff papers, or served as assistants to staff officers. Others, like couriers and some signalmen, did not do true staff work but worked at headquarters and directly supported the staff. Similarly, the teamsters, servants, and orderlies at headquarters did the daily housekeeping chores necessary to keep a headquarters operating efficiently. Finally, there were hundreds of soldiers involved in general support of the army in the various trains comprising the field logistics system—blacksmiths, forage masters, armorers, wagon masters, teamsters, provost guards, and hospital orderlies, among others. Most of those soldiers had no claim to being on a staff, but some did. Modern armies typically assign staff and headquarters-support soldiers to a specific headquarters unit (usually a very large company) and soldiers performing logistic and general support to various specialized units of a support command. There is evidence that the Army of Northern Virginia briefly used the concept of a headquarters battalion, at least for accounting purposes, but forcing the modern doctrine of a support command on any Confederate army would be artificial and inaccurate. Distinguishing among staff, staff or headquarters support, and general support soldiers is impossible in all but isolated cases. Recognizing the deviation from the standards of the Civil War, this study will ignore General Sorrel's warning that only the officers nearest a general who took their orders directly from him comprised the staff; this work considers as staff (or at least as headquarters functionaries) all soldiers whose duty placed them with a brigade or higher headquarters and most of the key personnel in the trains of the army.

SIZE OF THE STAFF

Inextricably related to the issue of defining the staff is the problem of estimating its size. A prominent historian called Confederate unit staffs large and attributed their size to the reliance on messengers as the primary means of field communications. General Longstreet might have concurred. He commented about dispatching the scout Harrison on his mission at the outset of the Gettysburg campaign, "He wanted to know where he could find us, and was told that the head-quarters of the First Corps were large enough for any intelligent man to find." Conversely, some contemporaries who served on those staffs thought they were too small. One of General Thomas J. "Stonewall" Jackson's staff officers blamed his general's poor performance in the Seven Days' Battles at least partially on poor staff work. "Here again, as had happened before, and happened more than once afterwards, his [Jackson's] staff was not large enough, and it was impossible for them to do the work required of them." A famed Confederate staff officer and artilleryman, E. Porter Alexander, also thought Lee had "a staff insufficient to keep him in touch with what was taking place."[13] There is some truth in both assertions—Army of Northern Virginia staffs were large, but they may have been too small.

The Confederate army had an aversion to large staffs, at least philosophically. A huge retinue trailing behind a commander was showy and ostentatious; a small one, somehow manly. A staff officer wrote in 1863,

"I was much amused to see Stuart pass through Martinsburg with a large cavalcade of staff and couriers and two buglers blowing furiously. Lee, [A. Powell] Hill, Ewell and Longstreet respectively passed the point at which I was standing, each with one or two persons with them and not even a battleflag to make their rank."[14] While commenting on a staff re-organization bill then under consideration in Congress, Lee suggested it was "important & indeed necessary to simplify the mechanism of our army as much as possible." He recommended keeping authorizations for staffs small, since it was easier to build up than down if the original num-ber was incorrect.[15] Commenting on the same bill, Jefferson Davis criti-cized Congress for providing too many staff officers: "They would encourage love of ostentation and feed a fondness for vain display, which should rather be discouraged than fostered. . . . The experience of this war has demonstrated that the most efficient commanders, those who have attracted the respect, gratitude, and admiration of their coun-try, have avoided the large retinue of personal staff which this bill would seem to sanction as proper or desirable."[16] The last sentence is a thinly veiled reference to Lee, who had a well-known aversion to large staffs. The postwar assertions by Sorrel and Taylor about the small size of an Army of Northern Virginia staff exaggerate that foible to the point of in-credibility—an exaggeration reflecting the hobby of ex-Confederates of inflating the Lee legend at every opportunity, but even legends often grow from some factual basis. People with no particular attachment to Lee remarked at the time on his modest habits and small staff. For ex-ample, Major John Tyler, temporarily with the Army of Northern Vir-ginia before returning west to resume service as Major General Sterling Price's aide, wrote to Price, "In Lee's army everything is reduced down to the smallest compass. Your own headquarters establishment is more numerous and bulky. He rides with only two or three members of his staff and never takes with him an extra horse or servant, although he is upon the lines usually from daybreak until dark. He is almost unap-proachable, and yet no man is more simple, or less ostentatious, hating all pretensions."[17] Tyler was an acute observer. Lee certainly was not os-tentatious, and in important respects he did have a small staff.

The Lee style of staff organization deserves special consideration be-cause of its impact as a model for staffs throughout the Army of North-ern Virginia. First, it worked well for Lee because of his position and leadership style. Blessed with competent subordinate commanders at least through the early years of the war and arguably throughout, Lee could afford to issue orders and leave their execution to his subordinates. Actually, at least in regard to tactical employment on the battlefield, the Army of Northern Virginia commander probably did not supervise closely enough, leaving too much in the hands of his corps commanders. Such a leadership style does not require a large operational staff. Second, Lee's staff was much larger than it appeared. Contemporary observers who commented in disbelief on the small size and humble accommodations of the Army of Northern Virginia headquarters only saw the tip of a much larger iceberg. The army headquarters operated from multiple sites—only the element immediately with Lee was small. Alexander said that fifteen officers, including Lee, were paroled from the army staff at Appomattox, but he ignored a significant group of individuals who also served with Lee's headquarters. Besides the fifteen officers Alexander mentioned, fifty-seven other staff officers, seven ordnance officers listed separately, and a topographical engineer who turned himself in after the army dispersed (for a total of eighty) received paroles from the Army of Northern Virginia Headquarters. Even the tabular summary of paroles in the *Official Records* shows sixty-nine officers in the general headquarters. There is no composite roster of enlisted men paroled from the army headquarters. One parole list included twenty-one soldiers detailed to and employed by a single assistant quartermaster captain, another had nine clerks and couriers from the quartermaster and commissary staff, and a third listed four soldiers from the medical purveyor's office. The *Official Records* reflect 212 enlisted men in the general headquarters at the time of parole, a number that included staff and escort. Colonel Taylor kept extracts of strength reports that show that the Army of Northern Virginia headquarters carried as many as 223 enlisted soldiers on its rolls during the period December 1863–April 1864. If one considers at least part of the army provost guard and signal detachment as part of the headquarters, up to twenty-seven officers and 341 soldiers could be added to that figure. Including Brigadier General William N. Pendleton's artillery headquarters, essentially a staff compartment of the army headquarters by 1864, could increase that figure by at least the twelve officers and thirteen soldiers paroled with it.[18]

Some of the difficulty in nailing down the true headquarters strength—or even the strengths of the individual cells that comprised the complete headquarters—arises from the arcane system the Confederacy used for strength accounting. At various times during the war the Army of Northern Virginia reported the headquarters as comprising fourteen officers and no enlisted men. At other times, the Army of Northern Virginia headquarters battalion was listed as having from nine to twelve officers and 114 to 228 enlisted soldiers. One authority suggests that the 1st Virginia Battalion, the army provost guard for the last two years of the war, which habitually reported an unusually large number of officers for a battalion of five companies, may have been a convenient reporting device for accounting for excess staff officers.[19] Whatever the accounting technique, one must conclude that Lee's staff was small only in the number of troops who lived and worked at the primary headquarters site. The true strength of the Army of Northern Virginia headquarters fell somewhere between the low figure of 14 general staff officers habitually reported and a high figure of 695 officers and men obtained by using the greatest numbers reported and including the provost guard, signal detachment, and army artillery headquarters.

Determining the size of the subordinate headquarters of the Army of Northern Virginia presents equal problems. An abstract of field returns from November 20, 1862, reported Longstreet's staff as thirteen officers (the same day Jackson reported only one staff officer, a figure that throws doubt on his accounting procedures). Less than a month later Longstreet reported thirteen general staff officers present for duty, but an additional fifteen officers listed as "staff" appear directly below them. Twenty-two officers, excluding the commander, received paroles from Longstreet's First Corps headquarters, although the summary in the *Official Records* only reflects sixteen. None of the above reports shows any enlisted soldiers or civilians working at headquarters, although there were certainly several dozen. Longstreet's corps artillery headquarters at Appomattox had three enlisted men, the quartermaster four, the ordnance trains twenty-six, and the medical director two; in addition, three headquarters couriers turned themselves in separately. Jackson's staff generally mirrored Longstreet's in reporting about thirteen staff officers, but the corps commissary alone had two officers, four civilian employees, and a permanent courier not included in that figure. At Appomattox, Second Corps headquarters paroled 27 or 28 officers (including the commander and provost guard) and 115 to 119 enlisted men exclusive of its ordnance train. Eighty-five of the enlisted men were from the provost guard, but the headquarters, hospital, and trains combined to list eleven couriers (one underage), four telegraph operators, a clerk and two orderlies of the military court, six hospital stewards and attendants, five teamsters, a wagon master, a quartermaster sergeant with the ambulance train, and a blacksmith. The Second Corps artillery headquarters paroled eight officers and twenty-two enlisted men. The Third Corps staff paroled twenty-two officers with First Corps, thirteen enlisted men and sixteen slaves from the ordnance train, twenty-four enlisted men from the quartermaster, and five couriers. The *Official Records* summary shows twenty-eight officers and 119 enlisted men. Cavalry headquarters strength is easier to estimate than the infantry corps. Jeb Stuart, who was criticized for his large retinue, averaged fourteen staff officers from January to July 1862, although the number crept up to twenty by

October of that year. Those figures compare quite favorably with counterpart infantry staffs. From October 1861 until Stuart's death at Yellow Tavern (May 11, 1864), forty-eight officers and about two hundred troopers served at least some time on his staff. One cavalry staff officer remarked, "With the couriers and all the departments connected with the Cavalry Corps headquarters, our encampment was a large one, numbering over one hundred persons and about two hundred animals." Another soldier estimated that twenty staff officers and couriers actually accompanied Stuart on the battlefield.[20]

Division and brigade headquarters varied radically in how large a staff they reported. On the same November 1862 return cited above, Lafayette McLaws's division showed thirty-five staff officers present for duty, while John B. Hood reported sixteen. Major General Charles W. Field's staff and couriers on one battlefield in 1864 totaled nine men. Brigade headquarters strengths are even more difficult to pin down. The forward element at the command post was fairly small, but the brigade trains absorbed significant numbers of men. One infantry brigade train fielded a force of about fifty to defend itself against Union cavalry at Williamsport after Gettysburg. The parole of twenty-two soldiers—clerks, wagon masters, forage masters, carpenters, teamsters, and blacksmiths—from the quartermaster's detachment of a single cavalry brigade and its regiments gives some indication of size. Besides soldiers, the cavalry brigade had eight hired civilians still employed by its quartermaster at Appomattox—a sixty-year-old guard, a free black blacksmith, four free black teamsters, and two slave teamsters.[21] Of these enlisted and civilian quartermaster employees, the clerks, wagon masters, and forage masters probably did at least some logistics planning and coordination (staff functions), while the rest were workers—part of the headquarters but not necessarily part of the staff.

In any case, there was a long tail behind the Army of Northern Virginia, some of it staff. However, the assertion that staffs were not large enough to perform their required duties in battle may still be correct. With much of the headquarters strength absorbed in the trains, the number of staff officers on a battlefield was often quite small. Alexander remembered the combined staffs of P. G. T. Beauregard and Joseph E. Johnston on the field at First Manassas (July 21, 1861) as "some 30 or 40 in all," enough to control a battle even depending on messengers as the only means of communication. However, describing a meeting between himself and Generals Jackson and Longstreet on the Antietam battlefield on September 17, 1862, Major General John G. Walker, a division commander, wrote, "By this time, with staff-officers, couriers, etc. we were a mounted group of some ten or a dozen persons." At the point in the battle Walker described, many staff officers and couriers were already off on missions; nevertheless, seven to nine men (subtracting three commanders) is a very small group for the combined staffs of two corps and a division to have immediately available in the heat of battle. Contemporaries frequently remarked about seeing Lee alone on battlefields, and many stories survive about the commanding general borrowing officers to carry messages at critical moments when his staff was totally committed. The same was true of subordinate headquarters. At the close of the second day's attack at Gettysburg, Longstreet was alone and had to ask a member of Lafayette McLaws's staff to inform General Lee of the failure of the attack.[22] A. P. Hill used the expedient of borrowing underemployed artillery staff officers to supplement his headquarters. "General Hill is in the habit of using me as a staff officer," J. H. Chamberlayne, an artillery battalion assistant adjutant general, wrote home, "that is he tells me to do this or that, anything that comes to hand, I have no specific duty as a member of his staff, and am not really on it; but being aid or adjutant of Col. Walker who is on Gen. Hill's staff, why, as long as our quarters are with the General he uses my services, specially in the absence of his regular staff. In time of battle particularly he keeps me very busy."[23] Lee might have preferred to move about alone, and using available officers as Hill did was efficient, but being forced to borrow officers to perform essential duties meant that staffs were too small.

In general, however, size was not the major problem of the staff of the Army of Northern Virginia. Division headquarters and above seem to have commonly had a hundred or more officers and soldiers engaged in various staff and support tasks. How commanders used those assets—especially in battle—and the training and efficiency of the staffs were much more significant problems than numbers. The Confederacy gave its army structure in law and provided for staffs to support commanders at all levels. If the staff organization they adopted was not perfect—either too large or too small, incomplete or ill defined—the rebellious states still managed to keep armies in the field and fight effectively throughout a long war.

12

Chapter 2

THE GENERAL STAFF IN THE ARMY OF NORTHERN VIRGINIA

Chief of Staff, Adjutant General, and Inspector General

The officers of the general staff were at the heart of the headquarters of the Army of Northern Virginia. They managed the day-to-day operations of the army's most important functions. Understanding their general duties and the problems they faced is essential to an appreciation of the army's staff system.

CHIEF OF STAFF

If there was a position on the staff about which contemporaries disagreed most as to both function and authority, it was the chief of staff. The title cropped up formally and informally at all levels of command in the Army of Northern Virginia (and its precursor organizations) from the earliest days of the war. At First Manassas, Major General P. G. T. Beauregard referred to Colonel Thomas Jordan as his chief of staff. In June 1862, Army of Northern Virginia general orders announced Lieutenant Colonel Robert H. Chilton as "the chief of staff of the commanding general." During the peninsula campaign, some observers called Major Robert L. Dabney, an assistant adjutant general, Jackson's chief of staff, although it is not clear whether he used the title. Major A. S. "Sandie" Pendleton was Jackson's chief of staff after Dabney and continued to serve in that position for Richard B. Ewell and Jubal Early. Ewell commended Pendleton, using the title chief of staff, in his Gettysburg after-action report. Colonel G. Moxley Sorrel definitely considered himself James Longstreet's chief of staff before being promoted and given a brigade command. J. E. B. Stuart commended "Lieutenant-Colonel [Luke T.] Brien, First Virginia Cavalry, my Chief of Staff," for efficiency and gallantry during the Battle of Williamsburg (May 5, 1862), and Heros Von Borcke, a Prussian volunteer who had a distinguished career with the Rebel cavalry, later claimed to fill the same position for Stuart. A division commander in his report on Gettysburg cited his chief of staff for bravery. In general orders issued upon assuming command of the Department of North Carolina in September 1863, Major General George E. Pickett announced Major Charles Pickett as his chief of staff. Instructional manuals mention the position in passing as an assumed duty of the adjutant, without further explanation. Technically, however, there was no provision in either law or regulation for a chief of staff until June 1864, and then it was only for the army and not its subordinate commands.[1]

Contemporary usage of the term varied according to the source from a title for the senior staff officer of the Adjutant and Inspector General Department at headquarters to the primary administrator of the unit to something akin to a deputy commander. There was never any thought, however, of the staff working for the chief of staff rather than for the commander, as modern staff doctrine dictates. The intent of Congress when it finally established the position was clearly that the chief of staff should be the head administrator of the army. The initial law, vetoed for other reasons, used the term explicitly, while the final version retained the description of the function without using the title. General Beauregard seems to have had that meaning in mind when he said of Colonel Jordan, "I found my chief-of-staff sunken upon the papers that covered his table, asleep in sheer exhaustion from the overstraining and almost slumberless labor of the last days and nights." That Beauregard called Jordan his chief of staff in one reference, referred to him as "my efficient and zealous assistant adjutant general" later in the same report, and left him at headquarters during First Manassas supports the same definition of the chief of staff's function.[2]

It is not clear what Robert E. Lee meant when he announced Lieutenant Colonel Chilton as his chief of staff in June 1862. Chilton probably got the title because Lee intended him to be the chief administrative officer. This interpretation gains credence from the last sentence of the October 1862 general order appointing Chilton as inspector general of the Army of Northern Virginia: "All communications heretofore addressed to him as assistant adjutant-general will hereafter be directed to Capt. A. P. Mason, assistant adjutant-general." A year and a half later, though, after Chilton's promotion to brigadier general, subordinates again addressed letters to him as "Chief of Staff, Army of Northern Virginia," which reinforces the idea of the chief both as the ranking Adjutant and Inspector General Department's corps officer in the headquarters and as the senior administrator. While arguing that Chilton did not really perform the duties of chief of staff, Sorrel said, "But Lee really had no such chief about him. The officer practically nearest its duties was his extremely efficient adjutant general W. H. Taylor." Sorrel seems to assume the chief of staff was the officer responsible for administration. By his own admission, Walter Taylor was the "indoor man" who handled the mountains of paperwork that flowed through the Army of Northern Virginia headquarters.[3]

However, there are also indications that the chief of staff had other distinct duties. Taylor thought the chief of staff had a definable set of responsibilities and that Chilton did not perform most of them. Taylor had mixed emotions about Chilton's potential departure from army headquarters and the probable loss of some of Taylor's responsibilities to a more proactive chief of staff. Unfortunately, Taylor did not describe the duties he believed Chilton should have been doing. Others indicated they expected a chief of staff to function as a staff coordinator, trainer, and even as a deputy commander. Henry Kyd Douglas criticized Stonewall Jackson's chief of staff thus: "And as for training a staff to its duties, he knew nothing about it."[4] Heros Von Borcke said, "The position of a senior staff-officer in the Confederate army was a very important and responsible one, and General Stuart had given me instructions, in his absence, to issue any necessary commands in his name." He expounded further, "I was informed by General Stuart that he was to start the next day on an extended military expedition, and that much as he regretted being constrained to leave me behind, it was yet necessary that I should remain, to fill his place in his absence, to act for him in emergency, and to keep up frequent communications with General Lee."[5]

A. P. Hill operated the same way with his chief of staff, Lieutenant Colonel William H. Palmer, habitually leaving him at headquarters to handle matters in Hill's absence. Sorrel, who seemed to use the title in one way when he talked about Lee's staff, used it differently when he referred to his own position in Longstreet's headquarters:

> With the growth of Longstreet's command my duties had become doubly important, and with weighty responsibilities. The General left much to me, both in camp and on the field. As chief of staff it was my part to respond to calls for instructions and to anticipate them. The General was kept fully advised after the fact; but action had to be swift and sure, without having to hunt him up on a different part of the field.

The change of movement of a brigade or division in battle certainly carried a grave responsibility, but it has often to be faced by the chief of staff if the general happens to be out of reach. Nearly two years of war on a grand scale had given me experience and confidence, and Longstreet was always generous with good support when things were done apparently for the best.[6]

D. H. Hill, while discussing Jackson's first chief of staff, Robert L. Dabney thought it natural that the general picked a Presbyterian minister and "clothe[d] him with the power of carrying out [Jackson's] mysterious orders when he was temporarily absent."[7]

Lee wanted a chief of staff who was free from administrative office work so he could supervise the activities of the army. He recommended to Jefferson Davis, "I would reduce [a commanding general's] aids & give to his chief of staff & Inspr Genl assistants, or they will never be able to properly attend to their outdoor & indoor work, which from the condition of our army, as before stated is very heavy." Lee expected his staff "to teach others their duty, see to the observation of orders, & to the regularity & precision of all movements."[8] The chief of staff would presumably be a major actor in such endeavors.

At least some contemporaries, however, thought the chief of staff was an essentially honorary title for the officer responsible for the mundane operations necessary to support a large headquarters, much like a modern headquarters commandant, who oversees the organization, movement, sustainment, and internal arrangement of the headquarters while serving as the commander of the enlisted soldiers serving on or supporting the staff. William Blackford, an engineer on Jeb Stuart's staff, criticized Von Borcke for misusing the title.

> [Von Borcke] got General Stuart to place the body of couriers detailed at headquarters, some forty or fifty men, under his command and to give him the title of Chief of Staff in consequence. We could not conceive why he was so tenacious of this trifling matter until his book appeared after the war in which he calls himself Chief of Staff of the Cavalry of the Army of Northern Virginia. This position, Chief of Staff, in European armies is second in importance to that only of the General himself. In our army there is no corresponding position, the Chief of Staff in this case being only the officer who managed the domestic affairs of the military family at headquarters.[9]

Despite contemporary disagreement, some positive conclusions about the position of the chief of staff are possible. First, the position came from tradition and usage rather than law or regulation. Second, although Lee formally appointed one chief of staff, the position was generally informal. Next, the chief of staff was invariably the senior officer of the adjutant and inspector general corps in the headquarters—none of the other general staff ever claimed the title. Finally, the duties, power, and prestige of anyone claiming the title were entirely dependent on the situation and on his relations with the commanding general.

ASSISTANT ADJUTANT GENERAL

In the field the principal representatives of the Adjutant and Inspector General Department bore the title of assistant adjutant general in higher headquarters and adjutant in the regiments. By tradition, there was only one adjutant general, who ran the department in Richmond unless the president took direct command of the army; thus, officers of his department in the field were necessarily assistants regardless of grade, position, or responsibility. In 1864 Congress authorized each field army and corps two assistant adjutants general with rank of colonel, while divisions got two lieutenant colonels and brigades two majors. However, the situation in the Army of Northern Virginia never reflected that organization. The War Department acted before Congress did to establish authorizations for field headquarters, and the department was more liberal than its legislative masters. General orders published in April 1864 authorized two colonels, two lieutenant colonels, and two majors from the department for each army headquarters. The intent was that these six officers would serve in two three-man teams to perform respectively the adjutant and inspection functions of the department. The same order gave corps headquarters two lieutenant colonels and two majors from the adjutant and inspector general corps—again, to split the adjutant and inspector duties. Two majors were authorized for a division; each brigade got a single captain.[10]

Assistant adjutants general (AAGs, as the title was habitually abbreviated) were the general-purpose officers on a field staff. Army regulations did not contain a specific section on the duties of the adjutant general, as they did for some staff positions. Other sources available to the assistant adjutant general told him he was responsible to the commander for the flow of paperwork in the army and should maintain the headquarters logs and records. He also published all orders in the name of the commander and was the regular channel through which subordinate commanders corresponded with the commanding general. The AAG's primary specified staff functions fell in the area of administration, personnel management, and strength accounting; however, any function not specifically enumerated for another staff member usually fell to the AAG by default. The scope of an assistant adjutant general's duties can be roughly determined by examining the functions performed in Richmond, since field AAGs provided most of the input to the department. A partial list of the Adjutant and Inspector General Department's functions includes keeping general files and records; receiving, opening, recording, and distributing mail; issuing and recording all general and special orders; administering personnel actions, including leaves, absences, transfers, details, discharges, and resignations; managing the appointment, promotion, and assignment of officers and settling questions of rank; monitoring unit muster rolls, strength accounts, and officer elections; handling all matters dealing with courts-martial and administrative examining boards; supplying stationery, office furniture, blank forms, and printing; preparing papers for the adjutant general's signature or endorsement; responding to letters received by the department; and maintaining internal records like an "endorsement book" to record correspondence returned with endorsement of which no copy was retained.[11] The assistant adjutants general at various levels in the Army of Northern Virginia performed these functions as discrete actions for their units, by forwarding information, correspondence, and recommendations to the department, or by carrying out departmental decisions and policies. Besides the above duties, AAGs did whatever the commander wanted and acted as much like a modern-day operations officer as any staff member in the Civil War.

Paperwork was the heart of an adjutant general's existence, and the Army of Northern Virginia generated plenty of paperwork to keep him busy. Sandie Pendleton griped about the incessant toil and trouble of an AAG's life: "Publish a General Order to be ready to march at dawn, give Mr. Thinginbob a pass, send pickets on the Luray road to watch the enemy, etc." Major Frank Paxton wrote home during his time on Jackson's staff, "Whilst the army has been apparently idle, I have been unusually busy during the last week. Everybody seems to be making application for something, and my office is crowded with business." Paxton returned to the theme in his next letter, "The last week was one of quiet and stagnation like the week before. . . . Yet I have been kept so busy that the time passed fast enough. I have general charge of the orders and correspondence, which has given me full employment."[12] Walter Taylor remembered, "To one not experienced in such matters, no just conception can be formed of the voluminous character of official papers that find their way to army headquarters whenever a halt is called in active operations and an opportunity is offered the men to present in writing their petitions and grievances. Sometimes it would seem as if every man in the army had some matter to submit for the consideration of the commanding general."[13] Taylor's was not a postwar exaggeration. He wrote a friend in 1864 to decline a wedding invitation: "My dear Lucien pardon my egotism if I dwell for an instant on the duties of my position that you may see how utterly impossible it is for me to be absent from my post—This military dept. now embraces all of Virginia & N. Carolina all the troops in the two states report to *Gen. Lee*—I am his only adjutant—This is enough to give you a faint idea of what rests on my shoulders, & the amount of labor which daily claims my attention—I cannot be absent even for one day—My health (?) & comfort require a short respite from office work, & I have long desired a short leave but in these active times, it is truly impossible for me to be away."[14] Not only could Taylor not take leave, he could not even get out regularly for exercise. When he left the office for any extended period during the day, the paperwork so overwhelmed him on his return that he quickly gave up trying.[15]

Typical of the correspondence that tied Taylor down might be an artillery sergeant who (with his commander) wrote the secretary of war three times in two weeks in an attempt to get a commission. Multiplied by the number of men in the army with similar requests, such persistence would create a substantial flow of paper. Surprisingly, paper traveled fairly quickly through the Army of Northern Virginia staff system. A typical request from a company for a routine action, like having a soldier examined by a medical board, moved from the company to army headquarters in four days, despite the requirement that such a request receive endorsements from the regimental surgeon, regimental commander, brigade commander, division commander, and corps chief of staff before being approved by the army assistant adjutant general.[16]

Besides correspondence from the ranks, there were other administrative chores that added to the crush of paperwork. Most of these tasks were imposed from above. For example, Congress enacted a bill requiring the secretary of war to maintain and have available for public inspection records of the names of all slaves in the employment of officers or soldiers and the names and residences of the slaves' owners.[17] Collecting, forwarding, and updating that information (which was of little or no military use) must have been a trial for the beleaguered assistant adjutants general.

When temporarily relieved of the burden of administration, AAGs were often at a loss for something to do. One of Stonewall Jackson's AAGs wrote to his mother, "Now there is nothing to do. Frank Paxton having charge of the office-work, I have been reading Carlyle's 'Cromwell.'" Another AAG wrote home, "I brought on with me Herschel's Astronomy, and whenever I convict myself of having clearly nothing to do I betake myself to the study of a little mixed mathematics. This always effects a cure, it either interests me, or suggests something else to do as a means of escape."[18] However, lack of work was uncommon. Robert E. Lee interrupted a letter to his daughter, "I wish you were here with me today. You would have to sit by this little stove, look out at the rain, & keep yourself dry. But here comes in all their wet, the Adjutant Generals with the papers. I must stop & go to work. See how kind God is, we have plenty to do in good weather & bad."[19] Lee did not always consider paperwork a blessing, and his staff diligently screened the papers he saw personally to reduce them to an absolute minimum. Despite the screening, the editors of Lee's wartime papers estimate that six thousand total items survive from Lee's correspondence.[20]

Even at the regimental level, the paperwork was burdensome. By regulation a Confederate regiment was supposed to maintain a compilation, indexed by date, of all general orders received; a regimental order book (indexed); a letter book of all the commander's official correspondence, also indexed; an indexed file of all letters received; and a descriptive book with the personnel records of the regiment supported by monthly returns—also, of course, indexed. Some regimental sergeants complained that buying paper to keep up with the various reports cost half their pay.[21]

Most of the routine paperwork dealt with personnel actions affecting individual soldiers. There were incessant requests to have somebody (usually a relative) assigned to a unit or to be reassigned to the cavalry, artillery, quartermaster, or whatever corps struck the requesting soldier's fancy. It did not help that the adjutant general's department in Richmond dabbled in individual personnel actions. Lee complained in an unusually blunt letter to Secretary of War G. W. Randolph that the adjutant general's department was reassigning or detailing Army of Northern Virginia troops without his knowledge. Recent special orders had transferred privates in the Army of Northern Virginia to different regiments, while two went to the Signal Corps, which Lee considered large enough. Twenty-three privates had been detailed to commissary, ordnance, medical, or "special duty not named." Lee asked the secretary to inform him if current policy relieved him of the responsibility of reviewing such transfers. The very next day, Lee fired off another letter to Randolph complaining about a new special order that directed the reassignment of two privates out of the Army of Northern Virginia and granted a captain a thirty-day leave without Lee's knowledge. "I regard the subject as one of immediate importance to the efficiency of the army," wrote the general.[22]

Although vexing, problems caused by meddling from Richmond always paled in comparison to the individual personnel actions generated in the field. The most pressing personnel actions changed over time. Early in the war, reenlistment and methods for granting reenlistment leaves without reducing the army to impotence were hot topics. In the middle years, when the strength of the army became a problem and the leadership withheld authority to approve routine actions like furloughs and leaves at increasingly higher levels, the stream of paper flowing through headquarters became a torrent. As the war wound down, desertion took center stage as the critical personnel issue. Reporting and monitoring that misconduct must have been a full-time job for AAGs by 1865, when the Army of Northern Virginia lost as many as 1,094 soldiers to desertion in a single ten-day period, and a letter from General Lee on the subject included 21 enclosures, subenclosures, and endorsements.[23]

But the assistant adjutants general could not concentrate exclusively on the major personnel issues. The Army of Northern Virginia was subject to the quirks of procedure and paperwork that arise naturally in large bureaucracies and frequently cause problems for both individuals and personnel managers. When the 1st Engineer Regiment formed in 1863, the Corps of Engineers assigned Captain Robert Stiles, who held an engineer appointment but was serving as an artillery officer in Henry C. Cabell's battalion, to duty with the regiment. Colonel T. M. R. Talcott, the engineer regimental commander, repeatedly reported Stiles absent; Cabell replied that he could not release Stiles from his current assignment. The commanders conducted a running paper skirmish through adjutant general channels until the matter finally reached the department in Richmond, where it proved too thorny an issue to resolve and lingered until Stiles was promoted in the artillery. As another example, in 1863 when the Army of Northern Virginia ordered all men not on a unit muster roll enlisted, Sandie Pendleton, Second Corps AAG, went to conscript Jed Hotchkiss. Hotchkiss, Stonewall Jackson's longtime topographical engineer, had never received a commission and thus was not on a muster roll. (On what authority he was getting paid is an interesting question that should have given the responsible quartermaster nightmares.) Jackson was sympathetic but characteristically unbending in following orders, and Hotchkiss had to go to Lee personally to be exempted from conscription.[24] Such minor personal problems are only amusing at a distance. To the AAGs who had to handle them, these matters would have been a bother and a diversion from more important work.

If the issue at stake was significant, the distraction from other work could be enormous. Jackson's arrest of A. P. Hill at the beginning of the Antietam campaign ignited such an issue. When Hill's anger abated enough for him to write, he began a letter-writing offensive to clear his reputation. The two generals declared an informal truce so Hill could lead his division at Harper's Ferry, Antietam, and Shepherdstown, but Hill resumed his paper offensive with a vengeance during the winter lull that followed. He had his staff "preserve every scrap of paper received from Corps Hd. Qrs. to guard myself against any new eruption of this slumbering volcano [Jackson]." In turn, Jackson had most of his staff conducting interviews and writing letters to gather evidence and support for his charges against Hill. Lee and his staff had to consider and respond to the tempest.[25] Only Jackson's death put a halt to the extremely disruptive exchange.

Even if not so obviously significant, some personnel actions were just too hard to accomplish. For example, in the fall of 1862 Congress authorized the award of medals for conspicuous courage in battle to one private or noncommissioned officer in every company. After a battle each company was to vote at its next muster to decide who should receive the award. The company commander would then forward the name through channels to the president. This admirable program was too much for the administrative system to handle; the Confederacy could not even obtain suitable medals for the award. It took a year to devise a scheme to recognize valor in battle. The adjutant general's office announced the creation of the roll of honor to be published in general orders, read to the troops in formation, and preserved on file in Richmond. Even this simplified plan was difficult to administer. In August and December 1864 the department was still retroactively publishing partial rolls of honor for the peninsula campaign, which had taken place more than two years earlier.[26]

Besides individual personnel actions common to all soldiers, the AAG administered a separate system of officer management that had its own arcane set of rules, often foisted off on the field armies for implementation. Consider the difficulty of identifying and correcting dual commission problems raised by the following general order: "All general staff officers who hold appointments as such in the C[onfederate] S[tates] Army, and who have received, or may hereafter receive, appointments in the line of the Provisional Army of the Confederate States, will immediately signify to this office their preference for one or the other of these appointments, as both cannot be held by the same officer."[27]

Although supposedly centralized, the officer-management system frequently got out of control. A combination of sloppy record keeping in Richmond and the habit of reassigning officers in the field without notifying the department negated any hope of effectively managing officers. In September 1864 the adjutant general took drastic action to regain control by issuing a general order requiring all general staff officers to report "with the least delay practicable" their rank, staff corps, position, present duty assignment, and assignment authority plus any future change of assignment. Failure to do so would result in immediate discharge from the service.[28] Technical questions about subjects like the source of officer appointments or problems related to managing the system were rare, however, compared to recommendations for promotion and assignment—the primary actions in the officer-management arena.

Promotions were especially sensitive in an age when officers considered their date of rank and consequent seniority extremely significant. In the Army of Northern Virginia the question of a candidate's home state complicated promotions. Non-Virginians complained that promotions went disproportionately to Virginians—a charge about which Lee was sensitive. Also, as the program to brigade together regiments from the same state progressed, appointing brigadier generals from the appropriate state became an issue. Moxley Sorrel won promotion to brigadier because Lieutenant General A. P. Hill was concerned about the condition of a Georgia brigade, and Sorrel, the chief of staff of another corps, was the best-qualified Georgian available. To complicate matters, Civil War leaders had favorites and protégés and made no bones about advancing them. After returning with his corps from assignment with the Army of Tennessee, Longstreet tried several schemes to get a favorite, Brigadier General Micah Jenkins, promoted to command John B. Hood's division. (Hood had been severely wounded at Chickamauga [September 19–20, 1863] and command of his division was unresolved.) Jefferson Davis appointed Major General Charles Field instead. Longstreet's numerous attempts to shuffle Field aside to make room for Jenkins were thwarted, and Longstreet was eventually reprimanded for the tone of his letters. Even when favoritism or matters like an officer's home state was not an issue, what might be considered obvious recommendations for promotion were still not easy. Lee was usually straightforward about such matters, but when he recommended Longstreet and Jackson for promotion to lieutenant general he also gave strong support for promoting A. P. Hill and E. K. Smith. Simultaneously, the commanding general declined to recommend promotions to major general to replace the officers being promoted on the theory that President Davis had enough information to make those decisions. One would think that Davis would be better able to make promotions to corps command than division command—Lee certainly did a few months later when he made recommendations for promotion and command down to specific brigades in his proposal to reorganize the army after Jackson's death.[29] In fact, Lee and Davis frequently corresponded on general officer promotions to every grade.

Generally, recommendations for promotion were individual matters based on the need to fill vacancies. Sometimes, however, commanders elected to make mass recommendations. For example, Stuart felt compelled to append a letter recommending several officers for promotion or appointment to his report on the celebrated ride around George B. McClellan's army in June 1862. At other times, reorganization within the army resulted in multiple simultaneous promotions. An obvious illustration is the reorganization of the Army of Northern Virginia from two corps into three after Chancellorsville (May 1–4, 1863); however, the series of artillery reorganizations as that branch tried to modernize its command structure is perhaps a better example. When Congress decided to appoint field-grade artillery officers in proportion to the number of guns in a unit, Secretary of War Judah P. Benjamin required the Army of Northern Virginia to report its number of artillery pieces and provide a rank-ordered list of artillery officers so the president could do justice with promotions. General William Pendleton invariably included recommendations for promotion with the various schemes for reorganizing the artillery he periodically submitted to Lee.[30] The evaluations that went into such recommendations could sometimes be quite brutal. Colonel Stapleton Crutchfield, Second Corps chief of artillery, wrote in an evaluation of one of his subordinates for promotion to battalion command,

> He is an excellent artillerist, a good shot, and very fond of the scientific part of the service . . . but not good at managing men, hard on his horses, and not at all apt to require the captains of batteries under him to take good care of their horses. He is rather indifferent to what he regards as the drudgery of the service, and while the qualifications he does possess will render him a very valuable field officer of artillery, it will not be in the sphere of the constant commandant of a battalion.[31]

In any case, promotions generated paperwork for the AAG. The papers associated with the recommendation for promotion of one artillery lieutenant to captain and his assignment to battery command began with a letter from the battalion commander to the secretary of war. The letter had positive endorsements from the corps artillery headquarters and the army chief of artillery. Accompanying the request was a letter of recommendation from the officer's current commander with endorsements, a letter of recommendation from A. P. Hill (his corps commander) with endorsements, and the letter of resignation of the current battery commander with battalion, corps, and army artillery endorsements. Lee did not like the packet and had Walter Taylor return it with some questions. William Pendleton resubmitted the packet, providing answers to Lee's questions and enclosing a letter of waiver of claim to promotion (with endorsements) from one of the battery officers and a statement that the other had failed an examining board. Lee forwarded the packet to Richmond with an endorsement recommending approval. The gears of bureaucracy did not grind fast enough for Pendleton, who sent a follow-up letter asking to rush the appointment. Taylor forwarded the letter to Richmond for Lee. While waiting for the expected approval, Army of Northern Virginia headquarters cut a special order assigning the officer to (and placing him in temporary command of) his prospective battery.[32] All that paperwork was required for one insignificant promotion from lieutenant to captain, and this litany does not even include the administrative actions to process the associated resignation and the report of the examining board.

Examining boards were another AAG function. Besides promoting officers, and much more directly the AAG's responsibility, officer management involved eliminating unfit officers. Age, infirmities, wounds, and miscarriages of the election system used to select most junior officers resulted in many officers unfit for their duties or excess to the army's needs. Congress established a system to deal with this problem. Commanding generals could appoint examining boards to determine the fitness of officers. Boards submitted their findings through channels to the president, who could either retire the officers honorably or drop them from the rolls. The need was pressing, and examining boards became routine. An artillery commander recommending promotion of an officer from another unit to command a battery justified his failure to select the new commander from within the battery by saying that the battery officers were "inexperienced and unfit for the position." He closed his recommendation with the offhand comment, "Of course the Officers of the Crenshaw Battery above mentioned; viz., 2nd Lieut. A. B. Johnston & 2nd Lieut. Thos. Ellett, must go before the examining board." More than a year later, another promotion recommendation for the same officer (who was captured and interned before he could receive the first promotion) contained the following information: "Of the two officers in the company, one waives his claim to promotion, and the other fails to pass a satisfactory examination."[33]

To support the boards and provide evidence, regimental commanders were supposed to compile monthly tabular reports on their officers, "in which shall be stated the number of days each officer has been absent from his command, with or without authority, or on sick leave; the number of times each officer has been observed to have been absent from his command when on march or in action; when and where each officer has been observed to have performed signal acts of service; when and where negligent in the performance of duty and inattentive to the security and economy of public property."[34] Besides providing the blank forms and administering the nightmare of paperwork resulting from such monthly reports, the assistant adjutants general appointed and oversaw the activities of the examining boards.

Like other managerial activities in the Confederacy, the examining boards soon became a source of irritation as paperwork clogged the system and results fell short of expectation. Eventually, Lee had to write to Adjutant General Samuel Cooper and Secretary of War Seddon to complain that it took six months from the time board results left his headquarters to get them back approved—a delay that effectively negated the usefulness of the only tool he had to eliminate incompetent or unfit officers. Davis recognized the administrative burden but insisted that Lee take steps to assign permanently disabled officers to the Invalid Corps and appoint temporary replacements for captive and wounded officers even as the armies faced off for the slaughter at Cold Harbor (June 3, 1864).[35]

It is not clear how much commanders consulted their AAGs on officer-management matters; however, commanders sought advice at least occasionally. Lee called in Sorrel and asked his opinion about who should succeed Longstreet when the latter was wounded in the Wilderness (May 5–6, 1864). Lee valued Sorrel's opinion because of his long service with and intimate knowledge of the corps. The promotion eventually went to Richard H. Anderson, the man Sorrel recommended, although it is impossible to make a direct connection between the decision and the recommendation. Similarly, Captain Alexander C. Haskell, the AAG and chief of staff of Brigadier General Samuel McGowan's South Carolina brigade, worried about who would assume command when McGowan was wounded. Haskell told A. P. Hill and Lee that the brigade had no confidence in the senior regimental commander and recommended Colonel Abner M. Perrin instead. "They heard me separately and asked some questions and I went back to camp," noted Haskell. Perrin got the promotion. Regardless of how much influence the staff had, all the associated paperwork flowed through adjutant general channels. Besides standard promotion paperwork, letters from disgruntled officers required response. An aide of Lee's remembered, "Written complaints of officers as to injustice done them in regard to promotion he would sometimes turn over to an aide-de-camp, with the old-fashioned phrase, 'Suage him, Colonel, suage him'; meaning thereby that a kind letter should be written in reply."[36] Combined with the myriad matters about enlisted soldiers, personnel management comprised a significant portion of the assistant adjutant general's work.

Unit strength accounting, not one of the Confederate Army's fortes, was another AAG responsibility. Regulations required regimental commanders to submit monthly strength reports and an annual roll-up (with reasons for changes) on special forms through channels to the adjutant general in Richmond. After every battle, units theoretically reported the number of friendly killed, wounded, and missing in action along with enemy prisoners of war and property captured. Individual deaths, both battle and nonbattle, generated reports, inventories of personal effects, and final settlements of pay and clothing accounts. All these reports should have provided a comprehensive accounting of unit strengths. Sadly, although reliable enough in the aggregate, Army of Northern Virginia strength figures do not give an accurate picture at the microscopic level of individuals and small units unless supporting company muster rolls survive. Regulations dictated special reporting procedures to account for some enlisted personnel, like band members and staff noncommissioned officers, only in the aggregate regimental strength figures and not with a specific company; however, such techniques provided for only a small fraction of the men serving away from their units.[37]

The Confederacy used a system of detailing soldiers from line companies to do support tasks instead of reassigning them to specialized support units or headquarters companies with separate strength authorizations. In modern terms, there were no headquarters, transportation, or quartermaster units with tables of organization and equipment to account for support personnel. Thus, a soldier might be on an infantry company muster roll and shown present (or absent) for duty on the regimental strength report for his parent regiment, while he actually worked somewhere in the regimental, division, corps, or army headquarters or trains—and the numbers in question were not trivial. Very early in the war, when he was still commanding a brigade, Longstreet asked for bakers from outside his unit since "the details from my own brigade are so heavy that I do not wish to order it from my own." One brigade that disbanded in 1864 "numbered at the time of its dismemberment 700 present for duty, and 600 absent on special details." The 13th South Carolina Volunteers listed fifty soldiers detailed as teamsters, nurses, provost guards, couriers, blacksmiths, ambulance drivers, pioneers, commissary sergeants, ordnance sergeants, and conscription enforcers. The detailed soldiers were as close as the regimental trains and as far afield as South Carolina. Nineteen of these soldiers were medically disabled; the rest were able-bodied.[38] Details of that size not only make calculating the effective combat strength of Confederate units difficult but also disguise the size of organizations supporting the frontline regiments. Modern experience suggests that the practice of detailing soldiers without a strict method of accounting for them also invariably leads to excessive growth of headquarters.

But detailed soldiers were only part of the problem. At army headquarters it was difficult to even estimate effective unit strength. Lee wrote to Seddon that he was missing 11,610 soldiers from three divisions that had submitted reports in response to an inquiry about absentees. The best Lee could do to categorize those men was, "Some of these are prisoners, some deserters, others at home permanently disabled, and others properly detailed. Many of them, however, are absent at the hospitals, either as patients or nurses, ward-masters, clerks, etc.; many more detailed as disabled men in conscript camps and Government workshops."[39] To portray the magnitude of this problem in the lower-level units, four regiments for which figures survive of Brigadier General George H. Steuart's brigade in the Gettysburg campaign reported 3,215 men on their rolls and only 1,672 (52 percent) present.[40] If subordinate commands did not annotate their reports or use the proper format, the army staff was forced to estimate whether absentees fell in categories as divergent as detailed (properly or improperly), sick, on leave, prisoner, or deserter. The difference in terms of managing unit strength was significant.

Accounting for battle casualties in the Army of Northern Virginia was as mystifying as strength reporting. The standard categories of killed, wounded, and missing seem to be distinct and self-explanatory, but placing casualties in those categories after battle apparently was not. Problems arose mainly in the category of wounded. Differences in extent of wounds allowed significant latitude for interpretation. An example from a battery commander after the Battle of Brandy Station (June 9, 1863) illustrates the difficulty. "Of the 36 men that I took into the engagement, but 6 came out safely; and of the 30, 21 are either killed, wounded or missing, and scarcely one of them is there but will carry the honorable mark or the sabre or bullet to his grave."[41] One suspects that the nine men who were not killed, wounded, or missing but who also did not "come out safely" were wounded lightly enough that they did not require hospitalization and thus were not included in the formal figure for that category. If so, the battery commander was accounting for his men exactly as prescribed by orders. Frustrated by the tendency of commanders to report every minor wound as an indication that the unit was hotly engaged and performed with valor, Lee told his subordinates in a general order:

> The Practice which prevails in the army of including in the list of casualties those cases of slight injuries which do not incapacitate the recipient for

duty, is calculated to mislead our friends and encourage our enemies by giving false impressions as to the extent of our losses. The Loss sustained by a brigade or regiment is by no means an indication of the magnitude of the service performed or peril encountered, as experience shows that those who attack most rapidly, vigorously, and effectually generally suffer least. It is, therefore, ordered that in future the reports of the wounded shall only include those whose injuries in the opinion of the medical officers, render them unfit for duties.[42]

Despite, or perhaps because of, the potential inaccuracies, unit strength reports occasionally raised eyebrows. Lieutenant Colonel Sandie Pendleton, Second Corps chief of staff and AAG, wrote to Major General John Breckinridge in 1864, "Your last 'field return' shows a falling off of 2,462 in the number of men reported present for duty." Breckinridge scrawled a note to his AAG on Pendleton's letter, "See if the officer requires written statements and have full reports this evening from the whole command." The adjutants general of Breckinridge's division probably got little sleep that night. Some of the inaccuracies apparently escaped notice at the time. A. P. Hill's biographer points out that Hill's divisional casualty figures for Antietam do not match the sum of his brigades' reports. The killed-in-action figure is only off by one, but the brigades reported 304 wounded instead of Hill's 282 and reported six missing that he omitted completely.[43]

However, inaccuracies and questions about figures were not the biggest strength-reporting headache for assistant adjutants general. Easily the biggest problem was getting the reports submitted at all. Lee had to remind commanders of the requirement to submit strength reports as early as May 1861, when he was still commanding the Virginia state forces. In October of that year the adjutant general issued detailed procedures to supplement regulations, including the entire spectrum of monthly strength reports, annual returns, returns of deceased soldiers, and postbattle personnel reports. Reminders about the importance of strength reports had to be issued in general orders in June and September 1862, with the September order originating from the War Department in Richmond.[44] In that same month, Colonel Chilton found it necessary to write to the two corps commanders, "As half a quire of foolscap paper will last one year for a morning report, containing, as it does, thirty-four lines, and it is the labor of half an hour to rule the columns of a morning report for one month, the morning report will be made every morning to the regimental or battalion commander and sent through brigade to division commanders."[45] However, the problem never went away. In December 1863 Cooper wrote to Seddon in an attempt to explain why he could not tell Congress how many substitutes were serving with the army. The adjutant general complained that he would have to search muster rolls for years past, and "these rolls have not been received with any degree of regularity, notwithstanding they are required by the Army Regulations to be forwarded every two months." Cooper speculated that the failure to submit required reports was due to neglect, sudden moves, and enemy action.[46] Whatever the cause, irregular submission combined with inaccuracies and arcane procedures to make strength accounting in the Army of Northern Virginia an AAG's nightmare.

Besides personnel and unit-strength management, the AAG handled various other administrative actions. Supervision of the military postal system was often one of them, although that duty was never officially assigned by law or regulation and was often handled by other officers (especially the quartermaster) or ignored completely depending on the units, circumstances, and individuals involved. The Army of Northern Virginia had an informal method of delivering the mail. Letters, both official and personal, traveled to and from the army by military courier, private individuals who happened to be going in the right direction, and the Confederate Postal Service. Friends and acquaintances traveling to and from the army who might carry letters were, of course, a hit-or-miss proposition; couriers and the postal system carried most of the mail.

The Army of Northern Virginia, especially when operating near Richmond, established regular courier routes to the capital. Lee told his wife to send anything she had for him to his quartermaster's office in Richmond, since "my couriers always go there & start from there. In fact that is their abiding place in Richmond." At other times he took advantage of the Adjutant and Inspector General Department's regular courier to retrieve clothing stored in the capital with his son, Colonel G. W. Custis Lee, an aide to Jefferson Davis. Walter Taylor's fiancée implied that her house was a regular stop on the army headquarters courier route, even referring to "my courier, the one who brought me my mail every day from headquarters." Occasionally during the war, couriers reached the army faster than telegrams. Permanent courier lines organized on the pony express model connected distant commanders. In the spring of 1862 Stonewall Jackson fussed about the arrangement of his courier lines to Ewell and Joe Johnston.[47] But no amount of fussing could stretch courier lines to cover all the necessary bases.

If a courier was not convenient, the Confederate Postal Service ran routes to the army. Soldiers could send official mail without a stamp, thereby obliging the recipient to pay the postage. The law also allowed a soldier's personal mail to be forwarded without charge from the old post office if he had been lawfully reassigned or moved; otherwise, regular postage was paid. Civilian and detailed military postal clerks sorted the mail at established post offices and forwarded it by a variety of means to the field. Some units had official or semiofficial postmasters who picked up and delivered mail. One soldier wrote home, "The postmaster for the Brigade has just informed me that he is going back with a mail in a few minutes, & I write hurriedly to tell you I am well." When the army settled down, such delivery could become routine. "I expect a regular mail line will now be established to Winchester & I hope to be able to send you a letter often." Even as far away as Carlisle, Pennsylvania, a soldier could write home that mail "comes regularly once a week, our mail carrier going to Winchester after letters written to the Brig., Division & Corps as found at the top of this page and it will reach me surely as ever." Occasionally, individuals made special arrangements through private parties for mail service. An inspection of the depot at Danville, Virginia, cited surgeon Fauntleroy for improperly contracting with a civilian for mail service, presumably for the hospital. However, as a rule, experience with the postal service was probably unsatisfactory. A discouraged Brigadier General Dorsey Pender wrote to his wife, "Honey, I do not expect you will get this so I will close and write again soon. Our mailman has been robbing the mail and throwing the letters away." Another brigadier, Paul J. Semmes, wrote home, "The army has no mail arrangements yet."[48] The diary of a chaplain who frequently delivered his regiment's mail contains the entry

> Postoffice clerks offended. Some time before I found a large amount of printed matter at the Post Office for my regiment, which the clerks had neglected to send us from day to day. I wrote to the Postmaster and asked him to stir up his clerks. I presume he stirred them up. Some of the handsome young men were of the right age to be soldiers. They had been detailed as Army postal clerks. My note to the Chief gave them some fear of being sent to the ranks. They looked at me in anger and asked me to tell them when I had anything to complain of. I am glad to say I never found occasion to complain.[49]

A South Carolina surgeon had a similar analysis of postal clerks but recommended a more aggressive solution: "The mails seem to be greatly deranged again, for I have not heard one word from you in two weeks. These clerks in the postoffices are the contemptible imps of cowardice who seek all the soft and safe places. They should be placed in the ranks and made to fight, and their places given to young ladies who are refugees from within the enemy's lines and who would be glad to secure such employment."[50] Walter Taylor thought the army postmaster deliberately delayed his personal mail a day or two as part of a bureaucratic battle to get more soldiers detailed to the postal section. Sending and receiving mail to distant states like Texas was virtually impossible late in the war, but even in 1861 the combination of distance, inefficiency, and changing unit locations made military mail unreliable. Thomas J. Goree complained constantly about writing home and not receiving any response. When the young Texan finally got a letter that had been a month reaching him, he asked the folks back home for forgiveness, adding, "I now take it all back and shall put all the blame on the mails, since I find that you write." Even Robert E. Lee had to intervene at least once with the Postmaster General, John H. Reagan, to recommend techniques to solve the problem of inefficient mail delivery when the trains had to stop five miles short of the Fredericksburg station during the winter of 1862.[51] The mail system of the Army of Northern Virginia was loosely organized and supervised. What successes it achieved and the failures it suffered should properly fall on the shoulders of the army's AAGs.

Assistant adjutants general also oversaw the administration of the criminal-justice system (although judge advocates conducted the court proceedings; see chapter 5). Supervising the criminal-justice system involved selecting members for courts-martial, appointing them in orders, processing the resulting paperwork, and executing sentences. McHenry Howard, an assistant inspector general acting as AAG in the temporary absence of the incumbent, recalled receiving one evening a package of "bulky courtmartial proceedings" containing the approved sentences of ten prisoners convicted of desertion. In the morning, Howard donned his full dress uniform and took a chaplain with him to inform the prisoners of their fate. That afternoon, he formed the division in a hollow square to observe the execution of all ten deserters.[52] Supervising the actual execution may have fallen to Howard in his normal role as an inspector instead of his role as acting adjutant, but the duty was obviously the responsibility of a field staff officer from the Adjutant and Inspector General Department.

Another administrative duty of the AAG was supplying all the blank forms that fed the paperwork ogre that was administration in the Army of Northern Virginia. There were required forms for hundreds of reports, and all of the forms had to come from somewhere. Regulations even promised a warrant of rank for every noncommissioned officer, signed by the regimental commander and adjutant, on a blank form provided through adjutant general channels. The Richmond bureaucracy worried about getting its reports on proper forms and reminded the field to submit "timely requisitions" for blanks. Closely associated with the function of providing blank forms was the requirement to print orders, proclamations, and other material for mass distribution. Regulations authorized department and division commanders to print orders. The Army of Northern Virginia had a military printing press early in the war. Porter Alexander remembered that "Gen. Beauregard had the poem ["Maryland, My Maryland"] printed on our headqrs. press (which printed all orders) & distributed to all who wanted." Some printing was also contracted to commercial establishments. The printed product ranged from letterhead stationary to general orders to preprinted special forms for frequent actions like passes and furloughs. The adjutant general's department even resorted to the expedient of informing the field, "Hereafter all orders from this office published in the Richmond Enquirer will be considered by the Army as official." The volume of printing (and the resulting paperwork) could be quite heavy. Lee mentioned in a letter to Jackson that he had received all three hundred copies of general court-martial proceedings from Second Corps, but he was only supposed to receive half of them.[53]

Finally, AAGs did some functions we associate with the operations officers on a modern staff. The extent of such activity should not be overemphasized and was very much influenced by the personalities of both commander and staff officer, but these responsibilities lay with AAGs and nobody else. Jed Hotchkiss, Jackson's topographical engineer, gave an illustration of an AAG conducting planning and coordination. "General Ewell came down and Major Sorrel of Longstreet's Staff and with Gen. Rodes they planned the route of General Rodes and the movement of the Second Corps." As the Army of Northern Virginia uncoiled for the Battle of the Wilderness, Moxley Sorrel issued what we would call today a warning order to the corps while his commander was busy writing to Lee. Then Sorrel recommended routes of march for the subordinate units, secured Longstreet's approval of his scheme, and followed the warning order with more detailed movement instructions. That sequence of actions is very close to what we expect of a modern operations officer. A. C. Haskell told about a series of tactical suggestions he made to Henry Heth (who was temporarily commanding his own and the brigade of which Haskell was AAG) at Chancellorsville. Heth accepted the recommendations, which fit the spirit if not the exact letter of his orders from the division commander, even to the point of reversing orders he had already issued.[54] Such recommendations from staff officers on the battlefield were common and probably represent their biggest and most normal contribution as operations officers. Elsewhere, however, Haskell implied he had a more significant operational role. While complaining to his mother about wanting to command "instead of always acting in another's name," he explained, "I am with a General now (General Abner Perrin) who makes my position as pleasant as its nature permits. On the battlefield, as we were a few days ago, I could have nothing to complain of; he taxed me to the best of my judgment and powers of command, and gave me in everything a full share. But when all this is over and we come down to the petty office drudgery and clerkship, I get out of temper and patience."[55] Thus, Haskell thought that other than acting for someone else, his battlefield duties were close to command— an implication that he had significant operational input. In that vein, it is also interesting that Ewell took Sandie Pendleton for an all-day inspection trip along the corps lines as soon as Pendleton returned from a long wedding-and-honeymoon furlough. Only after the inspection did Pendleton return to the office. Ewell obviously thought his assistant adjutant general and chief of staff needed immediate familiarity with the tactical situation, which would have been unnecessary (or of lesser importance) if his duties were completely administrative. In a less substantive vein, AAGs for some units kept official diaries analogous to modern operations logs.[56] Though commanders generally served as their own operations officers during the Civil War, trusted assistant adjutants general did perform some modern operations planning and coordination duties. They always prepared written orders when used and supervised execution.

INSPECTOR GENERAL

Officers from the same pool as the AAGs did the second half of the Adjutant and Inspector General Department's function—inspection. The Confederacy's decision to combine those staff functions under one department and allow officers to rotate freely between positions was not universally acclaimed. One critic believed the arrangement unintentionally slighted the inspector's function. According to him, a separate inspector general could better coordinate his field officers so "the duties of the latter would be directed and made uniform, efficient, and productive of substantial results. . . . The Inspector General would have perfect knowledge of the personnel of his department, could instruct them as to their many important and ill-defined duties, of which, by the way, general officers have meager and very inadequate conception."[57] Conversely, Jefferson Davis presented several reasons to retain the joint Adjutant and Inspector General Department. First, European armies did not separate the functions; second, an officer whose only duty was conducting inspections would be underemployed both in war and peace; third, an officer who had served as an adjutant would be more familiar with regulations and thus better able to inspect; and finally, a permanent inspector who did a good job ran the risk of alienating his fellow offi-

34

cers, while one who did inspections "from time to time" deserved respect for excellence in the "temporary discharge of an unpleasant duty."[58] Despite the arguments on both sides, the department in Richmond remained unified, and its officers in the field rotated freely between adjutant and inspector duties, blurring the distinction in practice if not in theory.

Legally only allocated by 1864 on the basis of one assistant inspector general with rank of major per brigade, officers bearing that title were common in all headquarters both before and after that date. The general order that served as the true authorization for field staffs, although it made no distinction between the functions of assistant adjutants general and inspectors general, allocated enough officers for each army to have a three-man team of inspectors headed by a colonel plus a separate medical inspector, for each corps to have a two-man team and a medical inspector, and for each division to have a major (the medical inspection function became an additional duty of the chief surgeon). Brigades had no separate inspector of any kind; in fact, Army of Northern Virginia general orders had specifically revoked the legal authorization for a brigade inspector even earlier. Cavalry divisions and brigades seem to have received an exemption to the army order and later received authorization for an additional adjutant and inspector general corps officer, who was probably intended as an inspector. Whatever the intent, cavalry brigades began reappointing assistant inspectors general a week after relieving them in response to the original order. As early as January 1863, without higher authority, the Army of Northern Virginia artillery assigned a captain and a first lieutenant as inspectors of artillery for its subordinate corps.[59]

Since inspectors came from the same staff corps as adjutants and authorization documents usually made no distinction between them, there was room for confusion. The tendency to use adjutant and inspector general corps officers interchangeably only exacerbated the problem. As mentioned earlier, Assistant Inspector General McHenry Howard sat in as assistant adjutant general when the incumbent was temporarily absent. Officers frequently used the title assistant adjutant general almost like a rank, even when serving as inspectors. Colonel R. H. Chilton, appointed inspector general of the Army of Northern Virginia in October 1862, signed a letter forwarding inspection reports in November 1862 as assistant adjutant general. Longstreet appointed an inspector using the following words: "Capt. Osmun Latrobe, assistant adjutant-general is announced as assistant inspector-general of this command."[60] If separating officers of the adjutant and inspector general corps by function was occasionally difficult, discriminating between the functions was not. Inspectors had two major duties: they conducted inspections to determine the state of readiness of the army, and they enforced regulations and discipline.

More than any other officer, the staff officers designated inspectors—often with a specific specialty, like inspector of artillery, ordnance inspector, or inspector of cavalry—were the eyes and ears of the commanders. The inspectors' primary tool for fulfilling this role was the formal inspection. Regulations gave inspectors very broad powers and outlined an almost limitless scope for their inspections:

> Inspection reports will show the discipline of the troops; their instruction in all military exercises and duties; the state of their arms, clothing, equipment, and accoutrements of all kinds; of their kitchens and messes; . . . of the stables and horses; . . . the zeal and ability of the officers in command of troops; the capacity of the officers conducting the administrative and staff services; the fidelity and economy of their disbursements; the condition of all public property . . . and any information whatsoever, concerning the service in any manner or particular that may merit notice, or aid to correct defects or introduce improvements.[61]

Regulations also specified what to inspect, how to inspect it, and which officers from the unit should accompany the inspector during each phase of the inspection.[62]

In a circular issued in 1864, the Adjutant and Inspector General Department expanded the description of an inspector's duties found in regulations. The circular directed the inspector to army regulations for an explanation of the procedure for conducting a muster and in-ranks inspection of the troops and their individual equipment. It then enumerated a detailed list of other areas for inspection.

> The inspection under arms completed, examine the police of camp, quarters, hospitals, and guard-houses; the number of prisoners in the latter, and the nature of the charges against each; the messing arrangements, and the character and quantity of the rations issued. If troops inspected are artillery or cavalry, see the guns and caissons are properly parked, ammunition chests full and properly packed, and the ammunition dry and serviceable; that harness and horse equipments are properly cleansed, greased, and placed on racks raised from the ground; the number, character, and condition of the guns, caissons, and horses, and that the latter are properly groomed and fed and never used except for public service; the number of stables and their location, which should be upon dry, sloping ground and well protected from the northern winds. The same examination should be extended to all army transportation. . . . The company and brigade records should be next examined with reference to the strength,

present and absent, reporting by name all officers and numerically all enlisted men improperly absent from inspection or their commands. . . . Learn whether the orders issued from the War Department and the different headquarters of the army are duly promulgated, understood, and observed throughout the command.[63]

If that were not enough, the circular also directed verification of the number of rations issued against the number of troops present; an inspection of ordnance returns; an examination of the medical, commissary, quartermaster, and ordnance equipment, records, money, and accounts; plus a check to see that no able-bodied men were detailed to support functions.[64]

Commanders supplemented the instructions to their inspectors to emphasize their own particular concerns. For example, besides standard items, Brigadier General Pendleton ordered his artillery inspectors to report on topics ranging from "the supply of forage, its source, and prospect in future" to "the attention to, or violation of, rights of citizens." Pendleton also required his inspectors to examine all horses the subordinate batteries condemned as unfit for further service and determine what caused the horses' poor condition. Stuart ordered his brigade inspectors to aggressively inspect to ensure that directions to reduce tents and transportation were obeyed.[65]

A general order issued in the spring of 1864 directed all field army inspectors to submit monthly inspection reports (on the proper form supplied by the department). The reports would include all inspection results from brigade-sized and larger units with an indication of any changes since the last report. The same general order required brigade assistant inspectors general to formally inspect their units three times a month, division inspectors to check every subordinate unit twice a month, and corps inspectors once a month. The order required inspectors at army headquarters to check as many units as possible every month. "To avoid harassing the troops by too frequent inspections," all subordinate inspectors would accompany senior inspectors when they visited units and count it as one of their required inspections.[66] The troops did not escape harassment, though—there was still the inevitable inspection before the inspection. One regimental officer wrote to his wife, "Well I am through with muster Rolls for tonight and find my duties increased. I am the only Captain on duty here now. We have but five and two are sick and two under arrest, and tomorrow the General comes to inspect our forces here. I shall be busy I tell you. We have been having an inspection this evening preparatory to tomorrow and a very troublesome and tedious business it is."[67]

Army of Northern Virginia inspectors took their instructions seriously. Reports by regiment detail strength; type and condition of arms on hand, including the number of men missing weapons; the state of clothing and the number of shoeless men; the condition of regimental camps and their cleanliness; and an overall evaluation of discipline. Inspectors did not pull punches. A report on Hood's division included a rating for each artillery battery and a rank-ordered list of the batteries in terms of efficiency. Statements like "horses showing neglect, axles of pieces and harness requiring grease" were common. But inspectors also offered useful recommendations and passed on tips. The same report contains the suggestion, "leather equipments, however, hard and stiff requiring Captain Reilly's system to soften and supple them, the use of neats-foot oil, which he obtains from cattle-feet thrown aside at the commissary pens." Matters of greater significance than techniques of softening leather also cropped up in inspection reports. "After an official inspection of the whole command in March or April, 1863," said Howard, "I had deemed it a serious duty to make it a part of my report that the sallow complexions and general appearance of the men indicated that they were insufficiently fed, and to urge that the ration should be increased."[68] Such inspections provided commanders a useful snapshot of the readiness of their commands.

Besides standard inspections, commanders dispatched their inspectors general on special missions. In October 1862 Lee sent an inspector to investigate a complaint by D. H. Hill that transportation for his division was inadequate. The inspector's findings must not have made Hill happy—the inspection concluded that Hill's headquarters had twice the authorized number of wagons (although three of his small wagons only carried the equivalent of two four-horse wagons), the brigades and regiments had all their authorized wagons, and the ordnance, commissary, and forage trains had sufficient transport. In his letter forwarding the inspecting results, Lee offered his assessment: "I think that with care and attention they will furnish comfortable transportation for his division"— not the kind of statement a division commander wants to see from his army commander. Braxton Bragg, while commanding in North Carolina under Lee's supervision, dispatched inspectors to collect data about "many detached men serving in various capacities, mostly fancy duty." Special inspections were occasionally sweeping and ominous in scope. In March 1864 the War Department borrowed Brigadier General William N. Pendleton and dispatched him to the Army of Tennessee to conduct a special inspection of that army's artillery. If results were poor, Pendleton was available as an immediate replacement for the chief of artillery. In the end, Pendleton found the Army of Tennessee's artillery in fairly good shape (except for the efficiency of some senior officers) and returned to the Army of Northern Virginia. Conversely, special inspections might be mundane. General orders in 1864 directed inspectors together with quartermasters and landowners to inspect privately owned bivouac sites upon occupation and departure of troops to provide a basis for settling claims for damages.[69]

Inspection results remained in military channels as confidential documents. When Congress in 1862 requested a copy of a recent inspection report on the condition of the troops in the Valley District, Jefferson Davis declined to release the report, in part because of confidentiality requirements. "The usual and generally necessary practice is to consider inspection reports as confidential. It would frequently happen that the publication of such reports would needlessly wound the feelings of officers and would promote discord and heartburnings among the troops."[70]

The intent of inspections was to evaluate the state of readiness of a unit and assess its discipline and compliance with regulations. The assistant inspector general's second role was a variation on the same theme— he served as the commander's enforcer. Lee said, "The greatest difficulty I find is in causing orders and regns [regulations] to be obeyed. This rises not from a spirit of disobedience but from ignorance. We therefore have need of a corps of officers to teach others their duty, see to the observation of orders, & to the regularity & precision of all movements." Lee was describing the enforcer function of the assistant inspector general. Six months earlier, he explained that function even more clearly: "If, in addition, a proper inspector-general, with sufficient rank and standing, with assistants, could be appointed to see to the execution of orders, and to fix responsibility of acts, great benefits and savings to the service would be secured."[71] The inspectors of the Army of Northern Virginia accepted their role as specially appointed enforcers of discipline. Captain Howard noted after observing men tearing down fence rails for their campfires, "As assistant inspector-general, for so General [George H.] Steuart had announced me, it was my duty to take particular notice of such violations of orders and breaches of discipline, and I rode among the men peremptorily ordering them to take the rails back, which they did, but with much grumbling and show of angry dissatisfaction."[72]

Later in the war Howard mellowed, but he still commented on an incident when hungry soldiers took potshots at migrating geese. "And I was much scandalized, being an inspector and concerned about breaches of discipline, by much popping of guns at them. But the temptation was very great." Captain Howard was not alone in seeing enforcing discipline as the assistant inspector general's special role. Captain William J. Seymour, AAG for Hays's brigade, commented, "Our men got quantities of liquor here [Waynesboro], and I had great trouble in keeping them in ranks. Inspector General Chew, being taken sick, had to stop on the way and I had to discharge his duties, as well as those of Adjutant Genl. during the remainder of the march to Gettysburg." Seymour eventually hit on the idea of making the most obstreperous drunks ride on top of the cooking pots in the brigade wagon until the rough ride had them begging to walk.[73]

Individual transgressions were not the only target of enforcement. Unit failures also evoked staff oversight. During the Second Manassas campaign, Jackson, disillusioned by repeated failures of A. P. Hill's division to move promptly at the specified hour, dispatched staff officers to stay with each of Hill's brigades to ensure compliance with march orders. During the Antietam campaign, one of Jackson's inspectors relieved a popular regimental commander on the spot when he caught soldiers from the regiment taking apples from an orchard against specific orders. In a slightly less aggressive mode, Longstreet sometimes had his staff officers stay with George Pickett "to make sure he did not go astray." As the Army of Northern Virginia retreated from Richmond in April 1865 and command began to break down, Captain Howard observed a snarl of artillery and trains blocking the road with no obvious effort being made to untangle the mess. "Never, I thought, was the necessity of a well organized corps of inspectors, with high rank and well defined authority, so apparent as in this retreat."[74]

The enforcer role extended onto the battlefield. The assistant inspector general served as the commander's direct link to the provost marshal and provost guard for supervising the important function of preventing straggling, looting, and the natural tendency of soldiers to drift to the rear, especially when escorting wounded comrades. A circular of instructions for inspectors told those staff officers, "Preparatory to battle inspectors will locate their provost guard at eligible points for arresting all stragglers." Commanders commended inspectors for rendering "signal service by preventing all straggling and plundering" and cited their inspectors and provost marshals in the same sentence of official reports. Inspectors reported the number of prisoners taken to their commanders. A young volunteer at Gettysburg found himself working for a division assistant inspector general supervising the evacuation of wounded and prisoners.[75]

When crisis loomed, Lee was not hesitant to remind his commanders about the usefulness of their inspectors. As the Battle of Cold Harbor approached, Colonel Taylor wrote the command, "I am directed by General Lee to say that he wishes you to get every available man in the ranks by tomorrow. Gather all the stragglers and men absent without proper authority. Send to the field hospitals and have every man capable of performing the duties of a soldier returned to his command. Send back your inspectors with instructions to see that the wishes of the general commanding are carried out."[76]

Related to the role of enforcer was the supervision of executions ordered by the courts. While the judge advocate and assistant adjutant general handled the legal paperwork, the assistant inspector general supervised firing squads. While working to gain a stay of execution for a man in his brigade, Howard commented, "I met Major E. [Edwin] L. Moore of Major General [Edward] Johnson's staff—being in fact the assistant inspector-general of the division and having special charge of such matters—and I represented to him that the execution could not well be carried out while we were practically in battle array."[77] Fortunately, this aspect of an inspector's duty occupied a negligible portion of his time and attention.

Besides inspections and enforcement, other miscellaneous duties fell to the assistant inspector general. Early in the war, inspectors were constantly busy certifying militia and volunteer units for national service. Henry Kyd Douglas, as an assistant inspector general for Jackson in early 1862, commented, "A week passed during which I was kept busy with Maj. [William S. H.] Baylor, organizing and apportioning recruits and militia." Other miscellaneous duties included inspecting pickets, collecting captured enemy equipment, and paroling prisoners.[78]

Regardless of other duties, the assistant inspector general's main responsibility was always to serve as the staff eyes and ears of the commander. Through formal inspections and special emphasis on enforcing discipline, he identified problems and taught members of the chain of command their duties.

Chapter 3

THE GENERAL STAFF IN THE ARMY OF NORTHERN VIRGINIA

Quartermaster, Commissary, and Medical Director

CHIEFS OF QUARTERMASTER AND COMMISSARY

We now shift to the primary logistics staff officers of the Army of Northern Virginia. Although the field representatives of the quartermaster and commissary departments had distinctly different responsibilities, law and regulation generally treated them as a class. They used similar procedures to accomplish their missions and frequently collocated (at least in the same town) their depots and trains. They faced the same problems and had to share the most important resources to solve those problems. Recognizing the possibility for confusion, we shall consider them together to avoid duplication.

The quartermaster had perhaps the most specifically described duties of any officer of the general staff. In broad outline, he was to provide "quarters and transportation of the army; storage and transportation for all military supplies; army clothing; camp and garrison equipage; cavalry and artillery horses; fuel; forage; straw and stationery."[1] Combined with the provisions of law assigning paymaster duties to the corps, that list virtually defined a quartermaster's job. Of course, regulations—especially plagiarized regulations—do not necessarily mirror reality. For example, early in the war the Ordnance Bureau provided certain quartermaster items, like knapsacks, and since each cavalry trooper supplied his own mount, the regulatory requirement to provide cavalry horses was never a major responsibility of the Confederate quartermaster. Conversely, the short description above does not touch on many duties of the quartermaster, like paying all the miscellaneous expenses of the army (per diem, postage, burial expenses, and so forth), procuring all building materials and tools, and myriad other incidentals.

The chief commissary of subsistence quite simply procured and issued food. He also handled such necessities as soap and candles and luxuries like tobacco. In principle, the Confederate Subsistence Bureau tried to centralize purchase of foodstuffs by government contract or direct purchase and provide rations to the armies from central district or state depots. When that system worked, the field commissary officer's duties were the receipt, accounting, storage, breakdown, and issue of rations received. There were regulatory provisions for direct local purchase by commissary officers as a backup to the primary issue system. Later in the war, when the ration situation became critical, Congress authorized impressment of food in emergencies.[2] Unfortunately, the ideal centralized procurement system never worked perfectly, and field officers devoted considerable effort to acquiring foodstuffs, frequently exercising their direct purchase and occasionally their impressment options.

Early laws authorized quartermasters and commissaries only for the regiments and brigades. Field armies worked around the need for those staff officers at higher headquarters, depots, and hospitals by forcing one regimental officer to do the duty of both quartermaster and commissary so the second authorization could be used elsewhere. Congress solved part of the problem by authorizing quartermasters for depots and hospitals. Nevertheless, in late 1863 Secretary of War J. A. Seddon complained that units in the field still had to fill army, corps, and division quartermaster and commissary positions by posting officers from brigades, declaring the brigade position vacant, and requesting a replacement. This had become a recognized practice, but the adjutant general's department "in the absence of express law, felt an embarrassment in either making such appointments [to division, corps, or army staffs] or in giving to the officers assigned rank appropriate to their superior position and more extended duties." Not until 1864 did Congress finally rectify this problem. The matured Confederate staff organization for armies in the field as embodied in the 1864 legislation provided chiefs of quartermaster and chiefs of commissary at the rank of colonel for army headquarters, a lieutenant colonel from each department at corps, and majors at division. The functions then skipped directly to the regiments.[3]

Quartermaster and commissary officers, along with others who handled funds and property, had to "previous to their entering on the duties of their respective offices, give good and sufficient bonds to the Confederate States fully to account for all moneys and public property which they may receive." By late 1863 a "good and sufficient" bond equated to $20,000–$30,000 Confederate. Perhaps because of the size of the bond, quartermasters seem to have neglected this provision. The adjutant general felt compelled to threaten to drop from the rolls all officers who had failed to secure the required bond, although the order announcing that dire threat contained an escape clause permitting commanders to grant unbonded quartermasters leaves of absence to secure a bond unless prior failure to do so resulted from negligence.[4]

Whether bonded or not, quartermasters and commissaries had considerable regulatory help in performing their duties and accounting for the property and funds in their care. Article 40 of army regulations contained eight pages of procedures directed at quartermasters for accounting for public funds and property. The regulations then went on to explain in detail when, how, and on what forms to make reports and gave samples of sixty-four separate report formats for quartermasters. A special publication of extracts of regulations and reports essential for quartermasters ran 123 pages. Like quartermasters, commissary officers had plenty of guidance. Regulations described the process for obtaining commissary supplies, established the individual ration, detailed issue and accounting procedures, and provided policy for feeding special categories of soldiers like officers, recruiters, and extra duty men. To control the process, the regulations contained thirty-six pages of forms. There was also regulatory guidance on such topics as substituting desiccated vegetables for beans or rice; estimating the weight of beef on the hoof; reconciling the estimated and butchered weights of meat; returning all barrels and boxes through channels; accounting for waste due to evaporation and leakage or theft; and issuing "anti-scorbutics" (fresh vegetables, pickled onions, sauerkraut, molasses, or vinegar) on the finding of a surgeon. However, the extensive regulatory provisions for both departments were not necessarily effective. They contained all the traditional procedures for controlling supplies and funds but were frequently violated through ignorance, lack of training, or inefficiency. To show the size of this problem, in the spring of 1864 more than nine hundred Confederate quartermasters, many responsible for accounts as large as $1 million, had not turned in the required reports on their accounts for even the first two quarters of 1862.[5]

Quartermasters and commissaries in the Army of Northern Virginia worked under two special handicaps that were distinct from those rising naturally from the logistic situation of the Confederacy. First, the logistics bureaucracy with which they dealt managed to develop very quickly into a labyrinthine tangle of offices, agents, depots, and bureaus that must have been confusing, at the very least, to even an experienced officer. An authority on Confederate logistics gives the following example of the quartermaster organization in Georgia in 1863 as typical of the complex nature of the logistics bureaucracy. There were ten depots and shops scattered around the state that worked directly for the department in Richmond; a superintendent of railroad transportation with headquarters in Augusta and agents in five other cities; tax-in-kind officers with depots for collecting and storing goods in eight towns; a Field Transportation Division with headquarters in Augusta and inspectors at three other locations as well as with the Army of Tennessee; an inspector of slave transport in Macon; supervisors of animal purchase in four cities; a horse infirmary in Oconee; a wagon shop director in Augusta; and a grain purchaser and forage depot supervisor for the Army of Northern Virginia in Augusta and Albany, respectively.[6] And the bureaucracy spread beyond the upper echelons of the organization. Until late in the war, when manpower shortages forced consolidation of functions and elimination of redundant staffs, layers of useless functionaries stood between the soldier and his source of food and supplies. A division commissary chief in 1862 noted:

> General [David R.] Jones ordered me to assume charge of the [division] commissariat though there was nothing for me to do. But he was devoted to red tape, and to give my position the appearance of having something to do he required all brigade commanders to come to me to get their orders for everything. I had consequently to receipt to the Chief Commissary of the army for the supplies of some 12,000 men. In a very short time I was charged with hundreds of thousands of dollars of provisions of all kinds, though I never saw any of them excepting perhaps when I met a drove of cattle or wagon-train loads of flour and groceries. . . . The brigade commissaries resented greatly having to ride several miles every day to get orders from me for their supplies.[7]

Commissary officers even dealt with separate bureaus at separate depots to obtain cattle and hogs.[8] Such bureaucratic layering and sprawl, complicated by a tendency to centralize decision-making in Richmond, could only serve to hinder efficient logistic activity.

The second handicap under which quartermaster and commissary officers labored was a cultural bias. In a sense, they were not looked on as truly military or as part of the team. After the war a division staff officer who had no difficulty remembering the names of individual couriers could not recall the name of his division commissary officer. A private wrote about his potential for promotion as a quartermaster, "I wd [would] have to be attached to a staff or be in a department, with military rank perhaps but civil duty."[9] It was a small step from performing civilian duties to being a civilian masquerading as an officer—a common view of the logistics staff. Worse, as a group, quartermasters and commissaries were considered cowardly profiteers who exploited their safe positions in the rear to line their pockets at public expense. Although the author of the following statement was in the Army of Tennessee, his brothers in Virginia probably shared his sentiment: "The organization of [the quartermaster] department was defective in consequence of the appointment of incompetent officers and assistants. Men who were afraid to expose their hides to the enemy's bullets obtained through favoritism lucrative positions in the department of subsistence, hence the disastrous consequences."[10] Even charitably, line and other staff officers viewed positions in the logistic branches as cushy duty. Thomas Goree, James Longstreet's aide, wrote to his brother, a quartermaster sergeant in Missouri, "You have never explained to me how it was that you were taken prisoner at Pleasant Hill [April 9, 1864]. You belong to the Q. M. Dept. and I did not know that *it* was ever in danger except from raiding parties who go round to the rear." Goree advised his brother not to seek temporary duty away from the army and instead "retain your present *comfortable* position" in "comparatively a safe place."[11]

Nor was such sentiment confined to troops in the line. During debate in the House of Representatives about the bill to authorize quartermaster and commissary officers for division, corps, and army staffs, Henry S. Foote, a powerful congressman from Tennessee, "made a furious attack upon the bill. The bill proposed to advance a set of jackanapes by the title of quartermasters and commissaries to the rank of Colonel, Lieutenant Colonel, and Major—men who had never placed their lives in danger on the field, or rendered one single act of service in the military department; gobbling sons of plunder, robbers and scoundrels, he would strip them of all rank. They were unworthy of even a third lieutenancy. He would degrade them to their proper level."[12] Congressman Foote had earlier called quartermasters "agents of Mammon" and complained that after the war the Confederacy would be awash in men calling themselves "colonel this and major that" who had never fought but had spent the war as quartermasters and commissaries. Not one to sugarcoat his feelings, Congressman Foote personalized his sentiments by calling Commissary General Lucius B. Northrop "a curse to his country" and making such slurs as "he had injured the country more than the enemy," "he looks more like a vegetarian than any man [I] ever saw," and "Northrop should be dragged from his position. Such a man as Northrop would bring disgrace upon any government."[13] In the main, such sentiments were not directed at officers in the field armies but at those in the rear areas and specifically at Colonel Northrop (whose personality won him few friends); however, one gets the impression from contemporary reports that field officers were excused from persecution due to perceived lack of opportunity rather than to higher dedication or moral standing. For example, consider this report of a speech in the House by Congressman George N. Lester of Georgia defending field logistics specialists: "He did not think that the quartermasters and commissaries on duty with the army in the field, as a general rule, were obnoxious to the charges and complaints of fraud and peculation which it was the purpose of this bill to remedy. These men who are constantly on duty in the field seldom have an opportunity to make money or perpetrate fraud, even if they were disposed to do so."[14]

Soldiers in the field did not appreciate their logistics specialists, even when the latter acted aggressively to solve perceived problems. One veteran writing an immediate postwar history of his brigade noted that upon return to their winter quarters after Chancellorsville, the brigade discovered that some unnamed quartermaster had shipped off their gear.

> It seemed that during our absence, there had arisen a great panic somewhere in the quartermaster's department of the army. Perhaps Stoneman's famous raid to Richmond, perhaps rumors of danger approaching from down the river, had occasioned it. I do not know which; nor do I know when the order originated, to pack up as much baggage as the wagons would carry and abandon the rest. But I do know that the guards were ordered away from the camps, that what could be conveniently transported on the wagons was removed to Guinea's Station, that tents were burned, and that all private baggage was left to take care of itself . . . but we felt rather poorly rewarded for a week of exposure, labor and danger, to find our tents gone, the ground they had occupied wet and muddy, all our property gone, and more than all, nobody to blame.[15]

Provocateurs in Congress conducted a four-year campaign against corruption in the quartermaster and commissary departments. They proposed such techniques as a scheme to require all logistics officers to provide a list of their personal economic holdings before the war and a current inventory of the same, coupled with provisions for confiscating any "overplus" property. Another proposal would have required district attorneys to investigate every quartermaster, commissary, and disbursing officer in the army for potential past, present, or future fraud. There was even a congressional investigation of whether the commissary had supplied troops in the field "unsound and rotten tobacco."[16] Such punitive legislation and investigations never passed or produced serious repercussions, but their proposal and serious debate illustrates the bias against logistics officers prevalent in the Confederacy.

Of course, neither arcane bureaucracy nor the cultural bias against lo-gisticians was nearly as responsible for hindering the efficient supply of the Army of Northern Virginia as the Confederacy's legendary lack of in-dustrial capacity and transportation. As early as the autumn of 1861 the logistics departments essentially gave up actively trying to supply the trans-Mississippi, which was simply too remote and too strategically in-significant to justify the expenditure of resources. Distance and signifi-cance, however, were never problems for the Army of Northern Virginia, always the premier army with the highest priority operating close to the capital in the principal theater of war. That army's primary logistic prob-lem was the inability to obtain or transport needed supplies. The Con-federacy attacked these problems in several ways.

The principal means of supplying the field armies was through cen-tralized purchasing and distribution. The quartermaster general estab-lished districts with local agents who had exclusive control of purchasing and contracting in their areas. Agents collected goods at depots for issue to field quartermasters upon approved requisitions through channels. Later, the department established government-run factories to produce critical items such as shoes and clothing. Theoretically, a depot agent who could not fill a requisition could call on the resources of another depot. When the centralized purchasing and depot system was firmly es-tablished, the government officially discouraged efforts by the armies to help themselves by obtaining goods locally, although the prohibition was never completely effective and major categories of supply (like forage) were always exempt. By the spring of 1863 Quartermaster General Abraham Myers succeeded in wresting from field commanders any con-trol they might have exercised over the depots as military department commanders, declaring local purchase an emergency procedure only, prohibiting competition among purchasing agents and field quartermas-ters for critical items like harness and hides, and requiring all requisitions to be processed through Richmond for approval before being filled at the depots. That same spring, Commissary General Northrop reorganized his department to establish centralized control, much like the quarter-master general.[17]

Richmond and Staunton served as the main depots for the Army of Northern Virginia, with others established at various times at Manassas, Winchester, Culpeper Courthouse, Danville, Lynchburg, Gordonsville, and other sites. Depots became logistic hubs for all types of goods and services besides quartermaster and commissary supplies. The army quar-termasters ran convoys of wagons to and from the depots, hauling for-ward needed supplies, food, ammunition, and troops. E. Porter Alexander noted that even after Antietam (September 17, 1862), when the Army of Northern Virginia was operating a hundred miles from its base at Staunton, the roads were good, and food, clothing, and ammunition arrived steadily to bring the units back to normal—the major limiting factor being the number of available wagons.[18] In late 1864, when Jubal Early was operating in the Shenandoah Valley of Virginia, Brigadier General Clement A. Evans wrote home, "Staunton is a busy depot now. Here all the wounded & sick are brought to be distributed elsewhere. Here the Advance Stores are collected & sent to the Army, as well as Quartermaster & some commissary stores. And here they send all returning soldiers in bodies of one to two hundred to be armed and sent down the Valley."[19] Under the proper conditions, the depots supplied all the needs of the army. Unfortunately, the conditions were seldom favorable. The commander of the Staunton depot, H. B. Davidson, complained during the Gettysburg campaign that he had no soldiers but Lee's orders required at least five hundred troops to accompany supply convoys headed for the army, while "every day we get letters from the army telling us to push forward the ammunition."[20] In such circumstances the Army of Northern Virginia had to resort to other means to fill its needs.

One of the most obvious, lucrative, and consistently exploited sources of supply for Confederate soldiers in Virginia was the Union army. Despite assertions that an excess of ardor at the beginning of the war inhibited the effective pillaging of overrun federal camps, the Rebels systematically looted their enemies and scavenged battlefields on both a personal and organizational basis from the first Battle of Manassas to the end of the war. A preliminary and incomplete list of captured goods taken from the Manassas battlefield is incredible. It enumerated a wide variety of weapons and ammunition; horses, saddles, bridles, and other tack; wagons, artillery battery wagons, ambulances, and traveling forges; medical gear; engineers' and carpenters' tools; cooking utensils; clothing, blankets, tents, trunks, and carpetbags; and miscellaneous items like coffee mills, barrels, coils of rope, and handcuffs. Alexander claimed that Stonewall Jackson's train of captured goods from the May–June 1862 Shenandoah Valley campaign was a double line of wagons stretching seven miles along the road from Winchester.[21] Many a Confederate went into battle dressed in Yankee blue or sporting a rain slicker liberated from the enemy. The story of Robert E. Lee on the Antietam battlefield asking his staff to identify the flag of A. P. Hill's approaching blue-clad troops to determine if they were friend or foe is indicative of the reliance of the Army of Northern Virginia on its opponent for uniforms. Troops were bitter when major Union depots fell into their hands and the supply services did not exploit them fully. Twenty years after the fact, a

South Carolina lieutenant colonel told a veterans' gathering about the capture of the Union depot at Manassas during the Second Manassas campaign, "Now, had we had an active, efficient, and well organized quartermaster staff, why could not all these supplies of clothing and shoes have been distributed amongst us? No enemy was pressing us from early morning for the rest of the day, and the details, which were ordered in the afternoon, too late for the purpose, might have effectually distributed the much-needed shoes to our bare-footed men."[22] Perhaps if the unit had been less concerned with grabbing champagne, whiskey, lobster salad, sardines, corned beef, candy, cakes, nuts, fruit, and pickles when they looted the trains in the Manassas siding, they might have solved their clothing problem despite quartermaster inefficiency. And reliance on captured Union sources of supply was not limited to the early days of the war, when victories were more plentiful. In the discouraging days around Petersburg, Brigadier General James H. Lane wrote, "Many of the Yankees in their flight in the recent fight cut the straps of their knapsacks and let them drop as they heeled it back. The battle-field was a rich one, and my brigade bears me out in the assertion, as they have a great many sugar-loaf hats, blue overcoats, oil-cloths, shelter-tents, etc., etc."[23]

On occasions when the Army of Northern Virginia operated on Union soil, it expanded its propensity to live off the enemy to include the civilian population. Lee issued and strictly enforced orders about individual looting, and the army (conveniently overlooking flagrant violations) prided itself on its excellent behavior in enemy territory. However, Lee made equally vigorous provisions for collecting supplies in a large-scale, organized way. A cynic would say this was little less than official looting limited more by the inability to gather and transport all the spoils than by chivalrous concern for the citizens of Maryland and Pennsylvania. There is a reason the chapter detailing the Confederate advance into Pennsylvania in Edward Coddington's classic study *The Gettysburg Campaign* is titled "The Confederates Plunder Pennsylvania." Even a small expedition like Stuart's Chambersburg Raid (October 1862) detailed one-third of its manpower "to visit all houses and seize horses . . . [and] took the corn right from the field, having no trouble about a Qr. Master buying forage."[24] The Pennsylvania campaign of 1863 and Jubal Early's operations in 1864 offer the best examples, since the Maryland campaign of 1862 was brief and restrained by political considerations.

On its march to Gettysburg in 1863, the Army of Northern Virginia both exploited the Union army and levied and aggressively collected "contributions"—payable in cash or goods—from the Northern towns through which it passed. Richard Ewell's corps, in the lead, had considerable success in collecting supplies. At Winchester and Martinsburg they captured twenty-eight artillery pieces, three hundred loaded wagons, an equal number of horses, six thousand bushels of grain, and considerable quantities of quartermaster and commissary stores. One of Ewell's divisions remained three days at Williamsport, where it scoured the surrounding countryside, getting five thousand pounds of leather, thirty-five kegs of gunpowder, and two to three thousand head of cattle, among other things. At Chambersburg, Ewell requisitioned enormous amounts of clothing, harness, horseshoes, leather, grain, bread, salt, flour, potatoes, coffee, and sugar; the citizens could not fill the entire order, but he got most of it.[25] Of his activities in York, Pennsylvania, in 1863, Early wrote, "I then made requisition upon the authorities for 2,000 pairs of shoes, 1,000 hats, 1,000 pairs of socks, $100,000 in money, and three day's rations of all kinds. Subsequently between 1,200 and 1,500 pairs of shoes, the hats, socks, and rations were furnished, but only $28,600 in money was furnished . . . the mayor and other authorities protesting their ability to get any more money, as it had all been run off previously, and I was satisfied they made an honest effort to raise the amount called for."[26] One remarkably frank participant said of the Pennsylvania invasion, "Of course, it goes without saying, that the quartermasters, especially of artillery battalions, were, confessedly and of malice aforethought, horse thieves. It was, perhaps, adding insult to injury to offer to pay for the horses, as we did, in Confederate money; yet occasionally the owners took it, as 'better than nothing'—how better it would be difficult to say."[27] Another officer describing Pennsylvania to his family noted the "huge barn[s], out of which our Quartermasters draw unlimited supplies of all kinds of grain etc. Of course we are not annoyed by settling bills." An artilleryman on that campaign barged into a church service and held the congregation at gunpoint while his gunners outside secured the churchgoers' horses. He then issued receipts for payment by the Confederate government after the war. Those particular horses and their abductors fell into the hands of Union cavalry before they could rejoin the Rebel column, but most Pennsylvanians who "contributed" to Lee's army were not so lucky.[28]

Early's orders during his 1864 campaign in the valley are instructive both as to procedure and intent in such operations: "You will have secured for the use of the entire army such public stores as may have been left by the enemy. All shoes in the private stores will be secured in like manner. You will seize all other goods in the stores of Martinsburg [West Virginia], and place them in charge of a responsible and competent quartermaster to be confiscated for the benefit of the Government;

and take the most efficient measures to prevent plundering or private appropriation of these goods or any other captures."[29]

Besides directly seizing goods, Early's troops also levied requisitions, contributions, and taxes payable in cash on the municipalities they occupied. They extorted $20,000 from Hagerstown (July 6), $5,000 from Middletown (July 8), and $200,000 from Frederick (July 9). The Hagerstown figure might have been a mistake by a subordinate who dropped a zero, and the authorities in Middletown negotiated their contribution down to $1,500, but all three towns paid the requested levies. The city of Hancock avoided paying $30,000 only because of the propitious arrival of federal troops before the money could be collected. These were significant figures at a time when a Springfield musket cost about fifteen dollars to manufacture. It took the city fathers of Frederick eighty-seven years to pay back the five bankers who underwrote their contribution to the Confederacy.[30] Unfortunately for the Army of Northern Virginia, even in the halcyon days when it seemed to master any Union army it faced, Yankee sources never supplied enough booty to fill the needs of either quartermaster or commissary.

As a last resort, the Army of Northern Virginia impressed goods from its own citizens, although the law required payment of fair compensation in such cases. The quartermaster general published detailed procedures for impressing supplies as early as November 1861. At the turn of the new year, the Army of Northern Virginia directed quartermaster and commissary officers, with the approval of their respective chiefs, to impress supplies if owners refused to sell or asked exorbitant prices.[31] One cavalry staff officer thought the practice became more than a last resort for horse soldiers. He wrote, "Our Cavalry Service has got to be *odious*. Continually in the rear of our Army we have to subsist by plundering and stealing and many a home has been made desolate by the approach of Stuart's Cavalry. The standing order is *impress* everything that may fall into the Enemy's hands—and thus we March with the wailing of women and children constantly singing in our ears."[32]

Congress stepped in to regulate impressment through legislation in early 1863. A year later, general orders implementing new legislation tightened procedures further by requiring a written offer to buy the goods before impressing them and granting owners resort to the opinion of two disinterested local residents if they and the impressing officer disagreed on compensation. Of course, citizens could rarely be expected to agree with their government or its agents on the value of their possessions. The War Department tried to head off disputes over compensation by publishing authorized price lists for various items. Official prices were invariably under the fair market value of the produce, and inflation outdated most price lists before they could be published. To complicate matters for the Army of Northern Virginia, Lee had a personal aversion to the technique. To get around both the stigma and restrictive procedures of impressment, on at least one occasion the general represented what was essentially an indirect impressment as a request to "borrow" corn for fodder.[33] Such was Lee's reputation that this ploy and subsequent pleas for contributions of food and fodder were generally well received and produced remarkable results. But prestigious commanders and powerful tools do not ensure plentiful supplies—it also takes efficient staff work.

The quartermaster and commissary officers in the Army of Northern Virginia suffered from the same deficiencies as staff officers. They were untrained for their positions and overwhelmed by day-to-day crises. The result was a stumbling attempt to gain control of the requisition and issue process and an almost total failure to accurately estimate future needs or to communicate those needs to the logistics system. It was not until relatively late in the war that the army quartermaster stopped simply forwarding regimental requests to Richmond and began consolidating requisitions. Before May 1862, regimental and brigade requisitions went directly to the depots without even passing through the army headquarters to get the commanding general's approval. In December of that year the War Department finally had to prohibit field quartermasters from visiting Richmond to obtain supplies and insist that they forward requisitions only. The Army of Northern Virginia quartermaster staff never completely solved the problem of deciding what the subordinate units needed, what was on hand at various locations in the army, and what they should requisition from Richmond. Lee raised a ruckus about shoes and blankets in the fall of 1862 but was unable to tell the War Department exactly how many of those items his army lacked. The quartermaster general stopped shipping shirts and underwear to the Army of Northern Virginia in the spring of 1864 based on the incorrect estimate of an assistant quartermaster in Lee's headquarters that they had enough. As late as 1865 the quartermaster did not have a system in place to identify shortages of common clothing items. When Robert E. Lee's wife, Mary, forwarded a sack of socks and gloves to the army, her husband wrote back, "Before distribution [Major Janney of the quartermaster] has to see in what brigades the men are in most need. This takes some time in the beginning, but goes on rapidly when commenced."[34] Nor was there a comprehensive method of accounting for captured equipment. Regulations required reports, and some were submitted in great detail; however, even the best were not definitive. Major John A. Harmon, Jackson's quartermaster chief, reported a long list of captured items in a combined report covering two quarters of 1862. He listed everything from 14,061 pounds of horseshoes to bundles of telegraph wire to quires of paper and envelopes to shoes and tents. There was even detailed accounting for twelve packs of playing cards, seven pairs of suspenders, and pairs of ladies (two), misses (two), and children's (three) shoes. But Harmon had to close his report with a telling comment: "In addition to the above, which is a list of the captured property that came into my possession, a considerable amount came into the hands of the various quartermasters of the command, which, it is supposed, they have reported to Richmond. A large amount of the property captured, however, was not turned into the quartermaster's department at all, the order to turn over such property not having been fully carried out, especially in the cavalry."[35]

Even if they knew what they needed, the field logistics officers never mastered the bureaucratic requisition process. They sometimes appear to have assumed that their department heads would divine the army's requirements by telepathy. When the adjutant of Harry Hays's Louisiana brigade wrote his congressman about the lack of shoes, clothing, and blankets, Quartermaster General Myers immediately dispatched an agent with one thousand pairs of shoes and new uniforms for the brigade. Myers had previously informed the secretary of war, J. A. Seddon, that he had filled all requisitions, and as the secretary noted, "The fault must then be in the Army." In another case, Lee complained about lack of shoes, and within two days the quartermaster dispatched 8,153 pairs to the Army of Northern Virginia (not counting four hundred pairs a week going regularly to Jackson's corps). Those shoes were not conjured out of thin air. They should have been available through normal issue channels had they been properly requested. As late as 1865, troops in the Army of Northern Virginia needed shoes while the quartermaster had an abundance on hand, needing only requisitions to forward them.[36] The instances of both the quartermaster and commissary general learning of shortages in the Army of Northern Virginia only when Lee wrote to the president or secretary of war are simply too numerous to be isolated cases. Often, the official reply to Lee's high-level inquiries was that the requested material was on hand in depots, but nobody had asked for it.

Lack of coordination also plagued the logistics staffs, both in Richmond and in the field. The Quartermaster Department controlled Confederate railroad transport (as much as anybody controlled it), but coordination or prioritization of shipments did not occur without the intervention of high-level officials. Food sat at railroad depots awaiting shipment while soldiers went hungry. Badly needed freight cars reached their destinations and sat, more useful to shortsighted field quartermasters as temporary warehouses than as carriers of goods. Uncoordinated distribution in the field meant some units missed rations for days at a time, while others ate regularly. A staff officer recognized the coordination problem when he wrote home, "At New Kent Ct. House I saw our commissary officer draw 20 bushels of corn to parch for his men!—had nothing else—But this was bad management. The Government had provisions in abundance but they were not in reach."[37] Neither quartermaster officers nor commissary officers could pry wagons and troops from the army to collect food and forage from the fields, where it eventually rotted since the farmers could not harvest or transport it to market. Agents from the Quartermaster Department competed with quartermasters from the army to buy leather and other goods, thus artificially inflating prices and ensuring that nobody's needs were satisfied. The commissary establishment in Richmond had absolutely no idea how much food the Army of Northern Virginia purchased or gathered on its own, and the quartermaster general could not even guess how many uniforms the states supplied their regiments. Lack of simple coordination between the staffs in the capital and the field doomed the logistics effort to be at best inefficient and at worst a disaster. Actuality tended toward the latter.

The quartermaster and commissary systems of the Army of Northern Virginia were not complete failures, however. The logistics officers did some things well, especially as the war progressed and they learned their jobs. For example, given proper warning, they positioned supplies in advance to support maneuvers. Lieutenant Colonel James L. Corley, the army chief quartermaster, stockpiled a thousand bushels of corn at Madison Courthouse in November 1862 to refill Jackson's forage wagons as his corps moved toward Fredericksburg. At the end of the same year the quartermaster and commissary jointly positioned five thousand bushels of corn and five thousand rations of hard bread at Culpeper Courthouse to support J. E. B. Stuart's Christmas raid. Commissary officers surveyed nearby regions to estimate supplies available and pinpoint critical facilities like mills where buying or impressing supplies would be easiest. Major Wells J. Hawks, the Second Corps Chief of Commissary, surveyed several counties in the spring of 1863 and sent the Army of Northern Virginia commissary officer a long list of mills with their estimated capacity and distance from the nearest town. He even estimated (Hawks claimed conservatively) that there were two hundred thousand bushels of wheat in Jefferson County and one hundred thousand bushels in Charles Town, West Virginia, above the needs of the local civilians. As another example of logistics planning, in preparation for the opening of the 1863 campaign season, the Army of Northern Virginia quartermaster issued instructions for marking and collecting, transporting to Richmond, and storing in government warehouses all unnecessary public and private property. On a smaller scale, logistics officers habitually preceded units on administrative movements to arrange quarters and rations.[38]

Besides doing some planning and forward thinking, Rebel quartermasters and commissaries, especially at the lower echelons, were excellent scroungers and innovators. In the winter of 1863–64 at least one brigade constructed its own warehouse and collected bacon from the local farmers as tax in kind (an operation reserved by law for specially appointed agents). The brigade commander considered this a precaution against the failure of normal rations-issuing channels. He also felt compelled to establish his own forage depot fifty miles from his brigade camp to collect forage and tend the brigade's horses.[39] And, of course, without strict enforcement of discipline the soldiers took care of themselves. A shocked surgeon commented during the movement to Second Manassas,

> Whenever we stop for twenty-four hours every corn field and orchard within two or three miles is completely stripped. The troops not only rob the fields, but they go to the houses and insist on being fed, until they eat up everything about a man's premises which can be eaten. Most of them pay for what they get at the houses, and are charged exorbitant prices, but a hungry soldier will give all he has for something to eat, and will then steal when hunger again harasses him.[40]

The observation could have been made about any of the Army of Northern Virginia's campaigns and applied equally to its adversaries. One Confederate commander felt obliged to show the superiority of his troops by quoting a Union newspaper in his report on the Antietam campaign (when the Army of the Potomac was on friendly soil): "The well-fed, well-clothed Union soldiers laid waste everything before them, plundering houses, hen-roosts, and hog-pens, showing an utter want of discipline."[41]

To this point we have discussed the quartermaster and commissary jointly; however, the two departments were not alike in every aspect. Besides their common problems and procedures, they faced peculiar difficulties and devised unique solutions based on the nature of their work. We will now address some of those issues individually.

CLOTHING, SHOES, AND CAMP EQUIPMENT

After experimenting with other systems, the Confederate authorities committed themselves at the end of 1862 to clothe their soldiers by direct government issue. Authorizations were based on a three-year cycle with the largest issue the first year, but Johnny Reb could theoretically expect at least one coat, one hat, two pairs of trousers, three sets of flannel underwear, and four pairs of shoes and socks a year. He was also due one overcoat and two blankets during the three-year period. Because of their duties, mounted troops got a stable frock and engineer and ordnance soldiers received an annual issue of a set of overalls. Company commanders issued new uniforms twice a year—in special cases, more often—and accounted for individual uniforms on company records. In early 1864, responsibility for issuing and accounting for individual clothing moved from the company commander to the quartermaster.[42] At least that was the plan.

Ready-made clothing did not exist in the South at the beginning of the war. The Quartermaster Department resorted to buying bulk cloth and using volunteer or contracted women to sew uniforms—a system that failed miserably by the end of 1861. Government-owned and operated factories were the solution, and the department cranked them up all over the South. The new factories, however, did not prevent a major clothing crisis in the Army of Northern Virginia in the fall and winter of 1862–63. As discussed in the previous section, the field quartermasters deserved a large share of the blame for this situation, but even after continuous shipments throughout the winter, inspection reports still showed barefoot and ill-clothed troops. Labor was part of the problem, especially in the case of shoes. Congress authorized and Lee grudgingly sent men with experience as cobblers to serve at quartermaster shoe factories. When finally operating at capacity, government factories supplied a prodigious amount of clothing. From July 1864 to January 1865 the Army of Northern Virginia received 104,199 jackets, 140,578 pairs of pants, 157,727 cotton shirts, 167,872 pairs of shoes, and equivalent numbers of hats, underwear, socks, and other items from the quartermaster. However, such production did not prevent the recurrence of shortages of clothing and shoes. The spring of 1864 saw a crisis in underwear, and since no factories in the Confederacy could manufacture blankets, they remained scarce throughout the war. Nevertheless, shoes continued to be the major problem—the troops simply wore them out faster than the South could manufacture them. As one Confederate put it, "My clothing wear out very fast in the Army."[43]

Quartermasters attempted several other schemes to clothe the troops. At the national level, the government imported uniforms, boots, and the machinery to manufacture them through the blockade. Staff officers rushed to the army quartermaster's office when a shipment of "common English boots of yellow leather" arrived, but imports never filled the need. Some states, especially North and South Carolina and Georgia, shipped large amounts of uniforms and shoes to their soldiers. For example, between July 1864 and January 1865, Georgia issued more than twenty-five thousand complete uniforms and 37,657 pairs of shoes to its soldiers (although it is impossible to determine how many went to the Army of Northern Virginia). That system satisfied one North Carolina brigade commander, but relying on home-state supply did not help units from more distant or occupied regions like Texas and Louisiana. Individuals sent friends and family members in the army food and clothing as best they could, and relief societies and charitable organizations pitched in to help. For example, private citizens of Charleston sent 1,500 pairs of shoes to a South Carolina brigade in Longstreet's corps in 1864. Even Mary Lee organized friends and relatives to knit for her husband's army, an effort that produced socks by the score when thousands were required.[44] The most efficient expedient, however, was local manufacture of items like shoes that the army could produce itself.

As early as the fall of 1862 Longstreet encouraged his soldiers to use hides of slaughtered cattle as temporary shoes. During the winter of 1863–64 his corps made a hundred sets of moccasins a day from the same material, but untanned hides proved very unsatisfactory as shoe leather. In January 1864 Lee began a lengthy correspondence with the Quartermaster Department about his shoe problem. Lieutenant Colonel Corley, Lee's quartermaster, thought the army could make one-third to one-half of the shoes it needed if the department would supply the necessary leather. Brigadier General Alexander R. Lawton, the quartermaster general, replied that although the sample shoes Lee sent with his letter compared favorably with those the government factories produced, he opposed making shoes in the field. Lawton promised to fill requisitions for leather to repair shoes but not to make them. The Quartermaster Department was making five hundred pairs a day, which should suffice. Lee obviously did not accept the quartermaster general's answer and soon dispatched two of his assistant quartermasters to the Shenandoah Valley to buy leather.[45] Despite the absence of official support and a lack of leather, the Army of Northern Virginia was soon in the shoemaking business. They started by doing repairs: said James H. Lane, a brigade commander, "My shoe-shop is now in operation, but as the government will not allow us to exchange hides for leather, and is unable to furnish leather in any quantity, we will confine ourselves to cobblers' work altogether. I do not expect there was ever seen another such lot of old shoes as that sent up this morning to be half-soled and patched. To see them all arranged in the shops by regiment and labeled with the owners' names elicited many hearty laughs."[46] The Army of Northern Virginia did not confine itself to repair work for long, though. Lane's men soon "commenced making shoes and continued it with great success until the close of the war." He sent shoemakers home to get their tools, recycled uppers, and got leather for soles from North Carolina.[47] Such expedients helped but did not solve the supply problem.

PAY

Paying the army was a major headache for the quartermaster corps. Troops would go for months without pay and then receive such big sums that they had no safe way to send the money home. Government fiscal policy and lack of cash were always the main problem, but bureaucratic inefficiency did not help. An impression of quartermasters as underemployed, acquired in the small peacetime regular U.S. Army, contributed to the inefficiency. The law establishing the Confederate general staff assigned the paymaster function to the Quartermaster Department rather than forming a separate administrative department. Regulations envisioned paying the troops at least every other month with funds forwarded to the field by the quartermaster general. There were provisions for deserters' pay, travel pay, pay to laundresses, audits, pay estimates, and myriad other financial minutia, as well as an ample number of forms and reports.[48]

It quickly became apparent that the size of the task and the administrative burden justified a separate bureaucracy. In August 1862 the Senate Military Affairs Committee reported out a bill to establish a Paymaster's Department. During debate, proponents argued "that on account of the press of business in the Quartermaster's department it was impossible to pay the troops regularly," while opponents suggested that there were "a number of officers in the Quartermaster's department who were idle and inefficient. If the troops remained unpaid it was because the Quartermasters did not perform their duties."[49] Jefferson Davis waded into the argument with decisive effect in a letter to Congress: "The organization of the Army of the Confederate States gives a paymaster to each regiment, by devolving the payment of troops on the regimental quartermaster, a system by which we avoid at the same time all danger from delay in payment by the absence of the proper officer, as well as the hazard of transporting large sums of money from camp to camp, as would be the case if a corps of officers were employed for the sole purpose of paying the troops."[50]

No Paymaster's Department was ever established, but the president and congressional opponents were shortsighted on the issue. Not everyone had the luxury of a brother who could visit for a week to help pay the troops, as one harried brigade quartermaster found necessary. The Army of Northern Virginia decided the workload justified dedicated officers, even if not from a formally authorized paymaster's corps. Officers within the headquarters were forced to deal exclusively with pay matters and became de facto paymasters. As early as April 1863 Captain A. Elhart was essentially the Second Corps paymaster, making the necessary estimates for submission to the department and disbursing pay when received. At the beginning of 1865 the adjutant general, Samuel Cooper, bowed to the inevitable and recognized conditions as they existed in the field. His office issued orders forbidding anyone except the chief quartermaster of an army from issuing orders to "quartermasters performing duty exclusively as paymasters"—a step that recognized the legitimacy of such positions. Parole lists include officers who reported their positions as paymasters rather than as assistant quartermasters on both the Army of Northern Virginia and Third Corps staffs as well as at least four divisions.[51] Dedicated paymasters did not solve the pay problems of the army, but they were an organizational step to address the issue.

TRANSPORTATION

Perhaps the biggest and most persistent problems of the quartermaster were associated with transportation. The impact of railroads on the Civil War has attracted much historical interest, but rail transportation was primarily the responsibility of the staff in Richmond, not the Army of Northern Virginia. The Confederate government debated the legality and efficiency of centralized control of railroads, Secretary of War Seddon asked permission to build and maintain the most important lines to give the military unrestricted access, the adjutant general and the quartermaster general, Samuel Cooper and Abraham Myers, squabbled over who should have staff supervision over railroads, and nobody was willing to stop civilian traffic and shipping to support the army. However, field staffs participated in such arguments only peripherally. There was no Confederate counterpart to Herman Haupt, who organized and ran the railroads efficiently for the Army of the Potomac. The primary responsibility of field quartermasters in the Army of Northern Virginia was to requisition trains, assemble troops and equipment, eliminate and store excess baggage, and prioritize loads. Soldiers might be required to cut fuel and pump water en route, but commanders were prohibited from interfering with rail transport except in extreme cases. In emergencies, Lee could only rely on telegrams to railroad superintendents asking that they repair their lines as quickly as possible and inform him when he could ship troops.[52] However, unlike their minor role with the railroads, field transportation was primarily a responsibility of quartermasters in the Army of Northern Virginia. The difficulty of providing wagons, horses and mules for trains and artillery (and to a lesser extent cavalry), and fodder for all the animals of the army constantly plagued the quartermasters. The problem started with the very basic subject of authorizations for transportation.

Predecessor organizations of the Army of Northern Virginia took the field overloaded with personal and unit baggage. Joe Johnston claimed, "This army had accumulated a supply of baggage like that of Xerxes' myriads."[53] Reflecting back with the benefit of four years of experience, Confederate staff officers recognized the problem.

> In connection with this process of training down to fighting weight, it occurs to me that the wagon train of the First Company, Richmond Howitzers, during the first nine months of the war was, I verily believe, quite as large as that of any infantry brigade in the army during the grand campaign of '64. Many of the private soldiers of the company had their trunks with them, and I remember part of the contents of one of them consisted of a dozen face and a smaller number of foot or bath towels.[54]

> When I look back at it in the light of subsequent experience, it would seem we were going upon a picnic instead of a march to war. We had two wagons for each company, besides private wagons owned by the officers of each making six in all. We learned before the war was over that besides the transportation of the quartermaster and commissary departments, one wagon for a brigade was enough.[55]

Officials did not long ignore such profligacy. General P. G. T. Beauregard ordered modest baggage reductions (one wagon per company and five for regimental headquarters) but simultaneously prodded Richmond for transport to relieve a perceived shortage. When the quartermaster general could not fill his requirements, Beauregard dispatched Colonel James L. Kemper, a Virginian familiar with the local area, to get two hundred good wagons. Kemper filled the order and might have gotten more, but Beauregard limited the number to avoid offending the Richmond bureaucracy. Apparently two hundred wagons did not satisfy the requirement, however. Beauregard was soon complaining that his brigades were "destitute of transportation," and he could not advance

61

without one hundred more wagons. Typically, the quartermaster general answered that he could send the wagons but had not heard of any shortages.[56]

Asking for wagons and having them available soon became an unheard-of luxury. By October 1862 Lee was strictly limiting wagon authorizations. Regiments got a wagon for every hundred men plus one each for the headquarters, medical supplies, and ordnance. Higher headquarters authorizations were slightly more liberal. About the same time, Lee ordered reductions in the army reserve ordnance train to fill almost one hundred shortages in division ordnance transport. Ambulances and medical supply wagons had to be protected from misuse by nonmedical personnel or they would not have been available for their primary purpose when needed. Six months later, the Army of Northern Virginia reduced transportation authorizations again. Officers' baggage and the various headquarters took the main reductions this time, and some authorizations (if not eliminated) changed from four-horse to two-horse wagons. An artillery battalion headquarters with two wagons was supposed to carry "cooking utensils, desks, papers, and tents of the field officers, assistant quartermaster, surgeon, and ordnance officers" in one and a hospital tent, medical equipment and supplies, and stretchers in the other. The same artillery battalion, assuming it consisted of four batteries, would have had fourteen total wagons—a reduction of about one-third that still left approximately 250 wagons for the army's artillery alone. Immediately after Gettysburg, the Army of Northern Virginia underwent a further reduction in authorized transportation. Regiments went to a wagon for every three hundred men, and the staffs suffered further cuts. Jed Hotchkiss, a topographical engineer, packed his gear and shipped it home since there was no space in the available wagons. Hotchkiss considered the reduction "a necessary thing, as our wagons, ambulances, and artillery extend over some fifty miles of road when on the march." Captain William W. Blackford, an engineer on Stuart's staff, did not think the reductions went far enough, and before war's end his assessment proved to be correct. In June 1864 Early reduced his corps' wagons in preparation for the Shenandoah Valley campaign to one per corps, division, and brigade headquarters and one for every five hundred men.[57] The intent was to move unencumbered by long trains, but the order also reflected the reality of a Confederate corps' field transportation.

The main transportation issue, though, was not excess baggage, authorizations, or availability of wagons—the crux of the problem was always horses. Major J. G. Paxton, the inspector of field transportation who was the head horse supplier for the Confederacy late in the war, estimated the average life expectancy of a horse with the artillery or transport service to be just seven and a half months. Mortality in the cavalry was even higher. Every fifteen months the Army of Northern Virginia needed seven thousand horses and fourteen thousand mules. By the summer of 1862, the loss of Missouri, Kentucky, western and middle Tennessee, and trans-Allegheny Virginia deprived the South of its best sources of quality horses. Prices of horseflesh skyrocketed with the retreat of Confederate forces into Mississippi. The horse situation ground inevitably downhill after that. Lee issued strict orders on treatment of horses. However, battle losses, hard service, poor rations, inadequate care, disease, and a tendency to work the beasts beyond the limits of rehabilitation scuttled even the best efforts of the commander.[58] Ancillary but extremely important issues, like the lack of horseshoes and traveling forges, only intensified the problem.

Subordinates innovated. In the summer of 1862, Brigadier General William N. Pendleton dispatched Major H. B. Richardson of his staff to establish depots near Winchester where sick and overworked horses could recover. A year later, the cavalry initiated a similar operation, the "camp of disabled horses," under the supervision of the division quartermaster. By the end of the war, the system of remount depots, called horse infirmaries, expanded until the Army of Northern Virginia shipped worn-out horses as far as Georgia and had four thousand cavalry horses convalescing in South Carolina alone. Cavalry operating in the Shenandoah Valley in 1864 had to send all but ten horses per regiment off to rest and graze. None of these expedients worked well enough to make a dent in the horse supply problem. Many horses arrived at the infirmaries so sick that they had to be put down immediately; others were too exhausted to ever completely recover. In the last fifteen months of the war, 6,875 horses and 2,885 mules arrived at Virginia horse infirmaries, while the infirmaries only returned 1,057 horses and 1,644 mules to the army. An astonishing 2,884 horses (42 percent) died during rehabilitation.[59]

The Army of Northern Virginia quartermasters became directly and personally involved with the horse supply problem. In an unusual move that short-circuited normal procurement channels, the army quartermaster, Lieutenant Colonel Corley, provided money and authorized the Second Corps artillery to send two men from each battalion to buy any horses they could find. However, the staff was not always so helpful. Days after making the above arrangements, Corley rebuffed a request from Brigadier General Pendleton for more horses. The quartermaster's records showed he had recently issued 273 horses to the Second Corps artillery, while returns of horses compared with guns on hand verified a need of only fifteen. Lieutenant Colonel Corley might have guessed the condition of the Second Corps' horses when its officers accepted several unfit horses the quartermaster had not planned to issue. Besides quibbling over requirements, the quartermasters used another standard technique to address shortages—they rationed scarce assets. Orders shuffled horses from less important units to keep units with a higher priority moving. Artillery batteries, major consumers of horses, were inactivated because of lack of animals. At the start of the Gettysburg campaign, the chief of engineers in Richmond, Colonel Jeremy F. Gilmer, reminded Lee that the horses for a pontoon bridge the general wanted had been used to fill requisitions from Longstreet's corps. The engineers could ship the bridge by rail, but Army of Northern Virginia teams would have to move it from the railroad depot. Internally, commanders also set priorities for remounts in their units. In the spring of 1863, Brigadier General Pendleton told the quartermaster to issue one-third of available horses to First Corps artillery units and two-thirds to the Second Corps. Quartermasters also initiated and backed schemes to increase the supply of horses. In February 1865, Major A. H. Cole wrote to Corley about the difficulty he was having buying horses because of the shortage of cash. Cole suggested that anything Corley could do to help would be appreciated, a transparent plea to get Lee's prestige behind Cole's horse-purchasing efforts. Lee forwarded Cole's letter to Seddon with a suggestion to use cotton and tobacco instead of cash to buy horses, an idea that probably originated with Lee's staff.[60]

The cavalry had special problems with horses. Confederate law assigned the individual trooper responsibility for providing his own mount. The government compensated cavalrymen whose horses were killed in action but made no provisions for broken-down or sick animals. A cavalryman whose horse died either replaced it himself at his own expense or served the rest of his tour in the infantry. The chronically slow reimbursement system (up to six months from death of a horse to payment) meant that even soldiers due compensation did not have cash to buy a new mount. There was soon a very sizable contingent of temporarily dismounted cavalrymen tagging along behind the cavalry corps and innumerable troopers wandering the South trying to find remounts. The problem was so severe that the Cavalry Corps preprinted special forms to ease the administrative burden of furloughing troopers to find remounts. Despite the lack of legal responsibility, the Quartermaster Department had to step in. Quartermaster General Myers sent agents to Texas in 1862 in an attempt to obtain horses for resale to dismounted cavalrymen. Expansion of the horse infirmary system to include cavalry mounts is another example of the quartermaster system trying to help individual troopers. The cavalry also took care of itself by appropriating for individual use captured horses that should have been turned over to the quartermaster as government property. In a typically cavalier statement about his actions during a skirmish at Bristoe Station before Second Manassas, Henry Kyd Douglas said, "At the invitation of the officer in command, Colonel Thomas T. Munford, I joined him, for I was in need of a fresh horse and another pistol. A charge was made upon the place, the federal guard of cavalry put to flight with a few prisoners, and I got a horse and a pair of pistols." Another time, Douglas replaced a large and ornery white mule he had been reduced to riding with a handsome black horse captured by some Louisiana troops.[61] Like every other aspect of supply, though, captures from the enemy were not frequent enough, abundant enough, or dependable enough to fill the need.

Compounding the shortage of horses was the periodic shortage of fodder—another quartermaster responsibility. The campaigns of 1862 that cleared federal forces from Virginia saved the grain crop and allowed the army to forage locally, but Lee's troops quickly consumed the supplies within easy reach. By the fall of 1862 Lieutenant Colonel Corley had officers surveying supplies of corn, hay, wheat, and pork in distant Virginia counties. Lee sent the results to the adjutant general so the Quartermaster and Commissary Departments could procure the needed supplies. To exploit the state's potential, the quartermaster general divided Virginia into four districts, each under an officer charged with purchasing and shipping forage. The results were not satisfactory. By early 1863 the quartermaster had to impress trains to haul fodder to the Army of Northern Virginia from eastern North Carolina. Lee's quartermaster had been promised rail delivery of ninety thousand pounds of forage daily—about half the army's requirement—but received barely thirty thousand pounds. Every pound shipped by rail had to be hauled seventy miles by wagon to reach the animals that consumed it. In February, General Pendleton ordered his quartermaster to survey the fodder situation along the Virginia Central Railroad and the James River Canal; to procure forage, grain, and hay; and to ship his purchases to the batteries by railroad and canal. March 1863 orders reduced the forage ration to eight pounds of corn and six pounds of hay a day—regulations stipulated a normal ration of fourteen pounds of hay and twelve pounds of grain.[62]

Lack of forage forced the army to disperse. Porter Alexander located his artillery battalion near Bowling Green, far from the main army. Pendleton, his superior, commented, "This is a long, long way, but as the grazing is, I believe, good, I will not insist on your moving. General Lee thinks it too far, as myself." Such arrangements not only subjected the army to increased risk in case of attack but were administratively inconvenient ("the examining board and court-martial are also both nullified by the distance") and wore out horses maintaining communications.[63] Only the arrival of spring grass alleviated the situation.

The forage shortage recurred the next winter. By fall of 1863 the Army of Northern Virginia had exhausted local fodder supplies and was depending completely on daily delivery of twenty boxcars or five thousand bushels of corn from as far away as Georgia. Railroad officials were reluctant to ship corn if there was any other cargo available, so the forage shortage quickly came to a crisis. Lee had to scatter his army again, especially the cavalry and artillery, to feed its animals—to say nothing of its soldiers. Pendleton again dispatched officers to scrounge fodder from distant locales. The absence of much of Longstreet's corps, sent west to operate with the Army of Tennessee, alleviated the problem somewhat and prevented total disaster, although Longstreet suffered his own logistics problems in Tennessee. Still, forage remained such a problem that in May 1864 the Confederate Senate examined the merits of reducing the amount of cavalry in service.[64] Again, spring—rather than efficient staff logistics work—solved the problem.

The winter of 1864–65 was another tough one for the animals of the Army of Northern Virginia. Forage came to the army around Richmond and Petersburg over tortuous and insecure rail and wagon lines. One gets some appreciation of the situation from a wounded Alexander, who while traveling south from Richmond on furlough caught a ride on a forty-wagon quartermaster wagon train. The road was so poor and the going so awful that Alexander finally dismounted and walked. Afoot and wounded, the artilleryman actually outpaced the wagon train. Lee's pleas for food and forage during this period have a familiar ring, and the situation was no better in detached elements. In February 1865 a desperate Early, operating in the Shenandoah Valley, resorted to granting soldiers furloughs if they would take horses home with them to graze. Early claimed this was his only means to save the animals from starvation.[65]

Between chronic shortages of wagons, horses, and forage, it is little wonder the Army of Northern Virginia struggled throughout its existence with field transportation. Of all the quartermaster failures, this was the most significant.

RATIONS

The aspect of Confederate commissary operations that was most damaging throughout the war was not lack of food or transportation—although both were critical—but personality. The commissary general, Colonel Lucius Bellinger Northrop, was an intelligent officer who understood the problems he faced, knew commissary operations, and generally devised workable solutions. His flaw was his personality. Northrop could not get along with anyone. Northrop was a West Point classmate of Jefferson Davis, who was his friend and sponsor in the Confederate hierarchy. Contemporaries considered Northrop an inefficient administrator whom Davis inexplicably supported long after the colonel had proved incompetent. Northrop started offending people early in the war by squabbling with Beauregard over the supply situation before First Manassas, purchasing policy, and assignment of commissary officers. The two continued fighting over the same issues after the war. Next, Northrop alienated Joseph E. Johnston by criticizing the loss of huge amounts of supplies caused by Johnston's precipitous withdrawal from Manassas in early 1862. That dispute also continued after the war.[66] In both cases, Northrop had excellent (or at least defensible) arguments; in neither was the loss of confidence of the commander in the field worth the debate.

Commissary General Northrop could not even get along with the gentlemanly Lee, although they did not publicly air their differences. Charles Venable, Lee's aide throughout the war, mentioned "some strong interviews and correspondence with the Commissary Department." The provocation in that particular case—a sandwich made of a sliver of meat between slabs of oak bark received from an anonymous soldier—was high. Still, it is difficult to imagine Lee, who seems to have avoided personal confrontation at almost all costs, conducting either strong interviews or correspondence with anyone he respected. Northrop himself gave a hint of the relationship between the two in a letter to Lee: "My last conversation with you respecting subsistence stores terminated by your stating substantially that responsibility in that direction did not rest on you." The commissary general then went on to lecture the army commander on the relationship between controlling territory and the ability to obtain foodstuffs. Such correspondence does not convey an impression of great rapport, and one wonders how it was received three weeks after Gettysburg. Lee reached the point that he would not even receive Northrop's emissaries. The commissary general sent Colonel James R. Crenshaw to see Lee about borrowing wagons and a cavalry escort to gather thirty to forty thousand bushels of badly needed wheat for the Army of Northern Virginia. Lee kept Crenshaw waiting for hours before finally declining to see him and sending him off to deal with the staff (who could not act without the Commander's approval). The animosity between Lee and Northrop rubbed off on the army staff. In March 1864, Walter Taylor listed two vital prerequisites to winning the war: one was the return of Longstreet's corps from Tennessee; the other was the immediate relief of Northrop.[67]

The friction between Northrop and Lee was not simply personal—they also disagreed on fundamental policy issues. The commissary general placed all Confederate armies on reduced meat rations in April 1862. Throughout the fall of that year, Lee ignored the reduction and issued the full meat allowance to compensate for lack of vegetables. He also ignored specific commissary instructions to extend the meat ration by using necks and shanks. Northrop was probably unaware of Lee's transgression, since the Army of Northern Virginia was drawing the additional meat from its immediate vicinity in the Shenandoah Valley. The issue surfaced in November when the army moved out of the valley. At Northrop's instigation, the secretary of war, George W. Randolph, directed Lee to comply with the official ration. Lee's appeal fell on deaf ears. In January 1863, transportation problems thwarted plans to supply meat from elsewhere in the Confederacy, and the Army of Northern Virginia faced starvation. Northrop ordered a draconian reduction in the ration of one-quarter pound of meat to be supplemented by increased issue of sugar. Lee complained and Northrop lectured, "the intervention of commanding officers with the ration is unauthorized and unadvisable for many reasons; but under existing circumstances it is mischievous . . . commanding generals . . . should not be permitted to issue any order respecting rations whatever." Although such an attitude could not have helped their personal relationship, it points more importantly to a basic disagreement on policy—and significantly, the issue was the line between command and staff authority. Surprisingly, Lee seems to have lost the fight. He could not even prevail on less significant issues. In the summer of 1864, Lee wrote to Davis trying to overturn a decision by Northrop that prohibited the general's staff from locally purchasing soap because the commissary general thought the price was too high.[68] Obviously, in this area of commissary policy, Northrop reigned supreme.

Another major policy dispute between Northrop and the commander of the Army of Northern Virginia was over the practice of impressing supplies from friendly civilians. Lee philosophically and morally disagreed with impressing; Northrop came to see it as the only way to feed the army efficiently. The issue first raised its head in early 1863 when Lieutenant Colonel Robert G. Cole, Lee's commissary chief, wanted to trade local farmers sugar for bacon. Lee supported the idea, but Northrop objected. He contended that the army should use the sugar and impress the bacon as well. In the fall of the same year, Lee and Northrop dragged Seddon into a full-fledged correspondence war over the legal, moral, and practical implications of impressing foodstuffs. Lee lost the legal argument but won the moral point, largely because he could simply refuse to take action; however, the issue was not dead. In January 1865, Seddon tactfully wrote to Lee, "I fear the extraordinary power reposed in commanding generals of impressing without limit will have to be resorted to by you." Lee countered, "There is nothing within reach of this army to be impressed, the country is swept clear. Our only reliance is on the railroads." Northrop, of course, disagreed. He suggested that Lee's prestige could get anything the army needed. Lee still refused to use impressment but did issue an appeal to the patriotism of local farmers, who quickly furnished the needed food.[69]

Colonel Northrop insisted on supplying the Confederate forces at Manassas in the first year of the war by central purchase and issue. By the fall of 1863, however, he changed his tune and disavowed any intent to supply "the army of General Lee with either flour or any other supplies from Richmond, so long as they could possibly be subsisted from the country in which they are operating." That statement perfectly characterized the mixture of local purchase, scrounging, and formal delivery that typified the hand-to-mouth existence of the Army of Northern Virginia. Even more than in the quartermaster arena, the commissary depended on the ingenuity of its officers to feed the troops. The army contracted with farmers and millers to purchase wheat and flour, sometimes hauling grain to the mills in army wagons and occasionally even threshing the crop. Commissary officers bought fields of standing corn and the fences surrounding them so the troops could roast corn over rail fires for their next day's ration. Throughout the war, the army served as its own butcher and meat packer. The enemy provided occasional supplements to the ration—especially treasured in that department were coffee, sugar, soap, and cigars. Early fed his troops in the Shenandoah Valley in 1864 by purchasing grain with funds extorted from Maryland towns. Stuart's cavalry corps provided its own meat for periods as long as eighteen months without any issues from the commissary. Some individual officers became almost legendary scroungers. Major Raphael J. Moses, Longstreet's chief of commissary, was such a person. Contemporaries wrote in mixed amusement and admiration of his technique of seizing mill records to identify how much flour local farmers produced, information that allowed Moses to efficiently ferret out hidden stores. The English observer Arthur Fremantle commented at length on Moses' activities during the Gettysburg campaign—his glee at finding a large stash of hats and his technique of using an axe to encourage shopkeepers to open their stores. Even modern historians compliment the major's "extraordinary efforts to move foodstuffs forward" during the Knoxville campaign, when Moses commandeered a train, formed a makeshift crew from an infantry regiment, and sent the train on its way to the front. Captain Francis Dawson claimed that Fremantle was wrong and it was Dawson who found the cache of hats; however, Major Moses' reputation was the result of an accumulation of incidents, not that one alone.[70]

But innovative and imaginative efforts could not stave off the food shortage forever. By 1864 both the Virginia countryside and the rail lines that supplemented what the army could glean from that previously rich region were worn out. The situation only got worse as the war dragged into 1865. The commissary officers tried every conceivable means to acquire food, finally resorting to buying it from the enemy. The Army of Northern Virginia actually got much of its food late in the war through enemy lines by trading with northern speculators. To feed the army, Lee and his staff actively encouraged such activity by arranging contracts and permits.[71]

The Confederacy and the Army of Northern Virginia faced enormous and perhaps insurmountable problems in the quartermaster and commissary arenas. The government tried to establish centralized systems to produce or procure supplies, with varying and generally decreasing degrees of success. The Army of Northern Virginia quartermaster and commissary staffs, however, did not exploit those systems effectively. The improvisations of local purchase, on-site manufacturing, scrounging from the enemy, and impressment did not meet the need. As a group, the quartermaster and commissary staffs of the Army of Northern Virginia were well intentioned, hardworking, and inefficient. It is indicative that Walter Taylor described John Harmon, the Second Corps quartermaster, as "the most efficient of his class I ever met" but went on to add that he "possesses peculiar attractions for me because of his childlike simplicity and gentleness of disposition."[72] Gentle, childlike logisticians were not what the Army of Northern Virginia needed.

MEDICAL DIRECTOR

The main providers of medical care in the Army of Northern Virginia were the surgeon and assistant surgeon assigned to each regiment. Staff support for those frontline doctors was the responsibility of the surgeon general and the Medical Department in Richmond. At army and corps headquarters the surgeon general's representative was called the medical director. He was tasked with "the general control of [the] medical officers and hospitals" of his unit. Until March 1863, such supervisory control included the various general hospitals located in the army's geographic region. Divisions had a chief surgeon, usually the senior medical officer of the division, who was relieved of regimental medical duties to oversee the operations of the other medical personnel in the division. A senior surgeon performed the same function for a brigade without relief from regimental duty. By 1864, medical officers theoretically had ranks in addition to their rating of surgeon or assistant surgeon (although they were seldom used), and a colonel was authorized for each army, a lieutenant colonel for each corps, and majors for division and brigade headquarters. Additionally, army, corps, and military department headquarters had medical purveyors, officers who purchased or requisitioned supplies—essentially medical quartermasters.[73]

Like other staff functions, the Confederates lifted the infrastructure of their medical system from the prewar U.S. Army. At first blush, there was plenty of administrative guidance. Eight pages of regulations (supplemented in 1863 by four and a half pages of addenda reflecting experience gained in the war) established procedures for the Medical Department, while tables of authorized medical equipment and supplies ran to fourteen pages. Twenty-six pages of forms, report formats, and certificates doubled the substantive sections of the regulations.[74] However, the medical structure envisioned by the regulations was not adequate for a large war with extensive casualties. This was particularly true above the regimental level, where systems for coordination of medical activities, evacuation of casualties, hospitalization, rehabilitation, and return to duty or medical discharge of patients were missing or inadequate. The surgeon general, Samuel P. Moore, ran an ad hoc operation using regulations, directives, and general orders to guide his subordinates until the spring of 1863, when a comprehensive system of handling sick and wounded finally emerged.

In its mature form, the Army of Northern Virginia's medical system identified sick soldiers at morning regimental sick call and evacuated wounded from the battlefield using litter teams and ambulances. In either case, patients who could not be treated on the spot were evacuated to brigade or division field hospitals, generally transient facilities housed in tents or temporarily occupied buildings. There, a triage system prioritized patients. If the wound required amputation, surgeons did the operation as close to the front lines as possible, usually in the brigade or division field hospital. Long-term treatment or hospitalization necessitated evacuation to a permanent hospital at a logistic depot or one of the general hospitals in Richmond. At the general hospital, a board of doctors examined patients twice a week to determine their condition. Soldiers expected to recover within thirty days remained at the hospital; more seriously wounded who were fit to travel received furloughs to convalesce at home. Boards recommended the discharge of permanently disabled soldiers. Upon recovery, wounded soldiers theoretically returned to their units, although many remained at the hospitals doing odd jobs or caring for other wounded.

The quality of medical support in Confederate armies has long been a subject of debate. Soldiers complained about incompetent doctors and worried about their chances of recovery. William Pendleton, suffering from jaundice, was much less critical than most when he remarked to his wife, "But I am beginning to have my doubts about being adequately attended to here. Randolph Page [surgeon to the artillery] is right far off and has a great deal to do, and it is not always practicable to get the most proper medicine." A private probably echoed the sentiment in the ranks when he wrote home, "I have a perfect dread of the hospitals." Few surgeons entered the army with any knowledge of military medicine, and frequent turnover meant the loss of what expertise they gained. Brigadier General James H. Lane listed six physicians who served as his brigade surgeon during the war, a turnover rate that illustrates the experience problem. Inexperience was compounded by a lack of understanding of the medical corps' relationship with other staff branches or the reason for following regulations. Although such charges may be overblown, they reflect the perception of the day. Congress worried constantly about the efficiency of the medical corps, and the president challenged the legislators' proposed solutions without disputing the existence of the problem. Jefferson Davis thought weeding out incompetent surgeons by examining boards was a better (and less expensive) way to increase efficiency than appointing an additional assistant surgeon to each regiment. The president won that skirmish. Regulations established a board of three officers to "scrutinize rigidly the moral habits, professional acquirements, and physical qualifications of the candidates, and report favorably, either for appointment or promotion, in no case admitting of a reasonable doubt." An assistant surgeon was eligible to appear before the board for promotion after five years of service. Refusing to appear or failing the board were cause for immediate dismissal from the army.[75] Such harsh measures reflect the extent of the perceived problem with medical care in the field.

Conversely, the doctors on the spot and their defenders thought they were providing the best possible care. After Chancellorsville, Surgeon Lafayette Guild, medical director of the Army of Northern Virginia, said of his subordinates, "As a body of professional gentlemen [they] compare favorably with any other similar organization upon this continent . . . Their conduct on many bloody battle fields has secured to them an enviable reputation, and has elicited praise from all who have witnessed their noble self sacrifice during and after a battle." Despite his protestations that "having been assigned suddenly and unexpectedly to the onerous and responsible duties of medical director of this large army, without instructions of any kind and without knowledge of the previous orders and assignments of medical officers of an army already engaged in action, my own position, of course, has been embarrassing," Guild's personal dedication and efficiency were unquestioned.[76] Similarly, the medical hierarchy in the corps headquarters generally received high marks. Typical of evaluations made long after the war is one of Surgeon Hunter H. McGuire, medical director of the Second Corps: "With his personal skill as an army surgeon and ability to advise and direct in the treatment and the operation of others, Dr. McGuire rapidly developed remarkable administrative ability. There was an extensive and immediate work of organization devolved upon him—appointments, instructions, supplies to be secured, medical and hospital trains to be arranged, hospitals to be established. All this work of immense importance was to be done in the midst of active campaigns, with the army in motion, and often in battle."[77]

But nobody claimed that the surgeons of the Army of Northern Virginia were great bureaucrats. They might be energetic and tackle difficult organizational and professional tasks efficiently, but they never earned a reputation for their paperwork. Field surgical reports and forms were difficult to maintain under the pressure of battlefield casualties. Faced with record keeping or tending patients, doctors treated patients. Sometimes, they simply ignored paperwork completely. Early in the war, the surgeons were not efficiently organized and probably did not realize they should submit reports. General orders had to direct brigade commanders to appoint brigade surgeons and immediately submit lists of sick and wounded. Guild made excuses and the U.S. surgeon general commented that records captured after the war were kept "with commendable exactness," but neither can hide a general lack of attention to administrative detail. In mid-August 1862, Guild forwarded a consolidated casualty list for the Seven Days' Battles, although the report omitted Longstreet's and Jackson's divisions, which had still not submitted their figures. Not until April 11, 1863, did complete returns for the Seven Days' Battles reach Richmond. Guild commented on this deficiency, "Previous to the engagements medical officers failed to supply themselves with the means necessary for keeping a list of casualties, and without a regularly systematized method of registration at the field infirmaries during and after a battle no great accuracy of records can ever be attained." The fluidity of battle made record keeping difficult, said the medical director, "even if [the surgeons] had been supplied with tabular field notes." Apparently, Guild was not able either to institute a "regularly systematized method" or to issue "tabular field notes," since within a month of this report his surgeons were again having difficulty reporting casualties after Antietam. Three weeks after that great bloodbath, Guild had to admit in a letter to Samuel Moore, the surgeon general, that casualty reports were coming in slowly but that he hoped to have a complete report soon. He did have the proper forms for his report, since the letter enclosed the duplicate receipt for the blank forms he received from the surgeon general. Conversely, shortly after Chancellorsville, Guild reported that the field hospitals contained 132 men too severely wounded to be moved to the railroad for transportation to Richmond.[78] His surgeons could accurately track patients on hand, even if they were less scrupulous about accounting for all those they treated.

Guild recognized the administrative deficiencies of his department. Like many of the army's medical difficulties, lack of sufficient personnel—in this case, on the staff—contributed to the problem. In January 1863 Guild submitted "a rough draft of orders or regulations" to promote efficiency by significantly increasing the size of the medical staff in the field. Guild warned Moore, the surgeon general, that Lee supported the plan and intended to carry it out in the Army of Northern Virginia even if the department rejected it for armywide use: "[General Lee] has instructed me to furnish him with the number and names of medical officers who are to constitute the members of the staff corps of the medical department of the Army of Northern Virginia. When this is accomplished, an additional number of about forty medical officers will be required, and I would respectfully request that the same number if available, be ordered to me with as little delay as possible."[79] Medical director Guild's proposed staff increase may have been a recognition of existing fact. Medical staffs had already grown beyond the single authorized medical director. In November 1862 Longstreet's medical staff consisted of three surgeons and an assistant surgeon, although Arthur Fremantle only remembered three doctors on the First Corps staff during the Gettysburg campaign. Other corps and division staffs had increased as well. Nevertheless, since Guild estimated he would need forty physicians to fill vacancies created as he moved people to the staff, his proposals must have been significant. The Army of Northern Virginia headquarters medical staff certainly increased over time. By war's end, ten doctors, including medical purveyors and inspectors, were serving under Guild. Richmond at least tacitly acquiesced to this staff increase, warning only that "assistant medical directors and assistant medical inspectors not being authorized, the titles will not be used."[80] There was no reason to issue such an order if abuses did not exist, but banning use of the title did not prohibit filling the position.

Guild's proposals to increase the medical personnel in the regiments—the doctors who directly treated patients—did not meet with the same success as his staff increases. Congress passed a bill supported by Guild and Lee that would have added a second assistant surgeon to each regiment, but President Davis vetoed the legislation as too expensive and unnecessary. Davis reminded Congress that the secretary of war already had authority to appoint as many assistant surgeons as the service needed, and the president had both authority and an appropriation of $50,000 to hire surgeons temporarily in emergencies. No additional medical personnel ever joined the regiments. A more successful program was the Reserve Surgical Corps. Under that scheme, medical directors could request augmentation before a battle from surgeons normally assigned to general hospitals. The system temporarily increased the staffs of field hospitals during periods of greatest need, although Guild complained that the reserve surgeons were always anxious to return to their usual hospitals.[81]

Another necessary medical function for which there was insufficient personnel was evacuating wounded from the field. Regulations authorized litters for regiments but no men specifically to carry them. The result was a flood of soldiers helping wounded friends to the rear after the first crash of musketry. Perhaps motivated more by a desire to keep the troops in ranks than concern for the wounded, leaders sought solutions. By early 1862 a technique emerged in Stonewall Jackson's division that was soon adopted throughout the army. Each company detailed two men to serve as litter bearers under the direction of the regimental surgeon—everybody else was told to stay in ranks. This system did not please Guild, who remarked, "The present impromptu ambulance system of this army requires radical changes, and it is to be hoped that the efforts now being made to improve the efficiency of this important branch of our service may be successful." Guild was apparently referring to congressional attempts to establish an Infirmary Corps or Ambulance Corps, a permanent unit of fifty field medics, litter bearers, and ambulance drivers per brigade. That initiative fell on hard times when Davis vetoed the bill as he had the bill to add surgeons to the regiments. Davis did not like the fact that the Infirmary Corps had no assigned surgeons, no provision for medical supervision, and no specified duties. Without a permanent organization to conduct field evacuation, the army continued the practice of detailing litter bearers. Fremantle described McLaws's division on the road in June 1863: "In rear of each regiment were from twenty to thirty negro slaves, and a certain number of unarmed men carrying stretchers and wearing in their hats the distinctive red badges of the ambulance corps."[82]

Besides litter bearers, the evacuation system of the Army of Northern Virginia depended on horse-drawn ambulances. These proved to be a source of almost perpetual concern. There was a constant lack of vehicles and horses. Guild consistently rated ambulances and horses among his most pressing problems. Part of the difficulty in an army starved for transportation was the understandable but shortsighted practice of pressing ambulances into other than medical service. An ambulance full of food or supplies at the beginning of a battle was lost for medical service. Regulations were clear that "ambulances are not to be used for any other than the specific purpose for which they are designed, viz: the transportation of the sick and wounded." In some cases this was an effective deterrent, and surgeons maintained control of their vehicles. For example, Brigadier General Paul Semmes, trying to get back to the army, mentioned that he had to get a surgeon's permission to throw his gear on a medical supply wagon. Abuses abounded, however, and the adjutant general had to issue general orders reminding the field that medical wagons were for medical purposes only. Although they were on the quartermaster's property book, they were under the exclusive control of the surgeons. General orders did not necessarily help when the chain of command did not consider ambulances top priority. Brigadier General Maxcy Gregg and his assistant adjutant general, Major Alexander C. Haskell, together replaced wounded or dead mounts on the Antietam battlefield by unharnessing an ambulance team. The officers kept the ambulance horses for three days until the army got back to Virginia.[83] Presumably, the ambulance that did not rate as high as command and staff mobility remained on the battlefield.

Even if commanders did not always support him, Dr. Guild did have some help in the ambulance area. He coordinated with the Richmond Ambulance Committee, a volunteer civilian organization, for direct support to the army. The volunteers of the committee participated effectively in almost every battle of the Army of Northern Virginia. They were on the peninsula in 1862 with thirty-seven ambulances, processed seven thousand casualties after Chancellorsville, and spent three weeks moving wounded in Winchester after Gettysburg. By war's end, the Army of Northern Virginia had informally established its own ambulance corps. Two officers in Lee's headquarters at Appomattox listed duty positions with the Reserve Ambulance Company, and twenty-nine enlisted men were paroled from the Army of Northern Virginia Ambulance Corps.[84] Guild seems to have rationalized his ambulance service despite the president's veto.

Besides the regimental surgeons, soldiers drawn from line units staffed the field hospitals of the Army of Northern Virginia. Stewards, noncommissioned officers who took care of medical stores and supervised the other enlisted men, coordinated the efforts of nurses, cooks, and laundresses. Each company provided one nurse and two cooks, while laundresses seem to have been mainly fixtures of the regulations and depot hospitals unless the army was in winter quarters. Theoretically a regiment had three fourteen-by-fifteen-foot hospital wall tents, a Sibley tent, and a common tent, although shortages of both tents and transportation reduced what was actually carried. Supplying adequate food to field hospitals was also a problem. At the end of 1863 the commissary general directed assignment of an assistant commissary officer to each division hospital during battle for the specific purpose of obtaining and issuing rations.[85] To guarantee compliance, he charged corps commissary officers with ensuring that the order was properly executed.

Initially, army medical directors also had responsibility for larger, permanent hospitals. When the Army of Northern Virginia established Winchester as a major logistics depot, Lee sent Guild there to supervise securing, manning, and organizing appropriate hospital facilities. Guild would get plenty of legal and regulatory guidance in his effort. The Confederate Congress began passing legislation on hospitals early and continued its work on that subject throughout the war. Unlike his vetoes of legislation affecting field medical operations, Davis signed the hospital bills. Just days after Dr. Guild was ordered to Winchester, the president signed into law a bill providing detailed instructions on hospital organization and administration. Gradually, however, hospital administration was withdrawn from the field. In October 1862, medical director Guild thanked Surgeon General Moore "for relieving me from the care and responsibility of hospitals left in the rear of the army." Later that same month the adjutant general, Samuel Cooper, told local commanders that they were still technically in charge of the hospitals in their area but should leave their operation to the hospital's senior surgeon except in extraordinary cases. In March 1863 the War Department completely removed general hospitals from the supervision of field armies and placed them under direct control of the surgeon general—in fact, general orders specifically directed field medical directors not to meddle with the general hospitals.[86]

The medical organization had two distinctive features that set it apart from other staff agencies: it operated its own supply and inspection systems. Other departments, like the Signal Corps and engineers, provided limited specialized supplies to their units in the field, but not as extensively as the medical department. The Confederate medical supply system handled large quantities of specialized items, as one might expect, but it also issued items (like candles and blankets) normally provided by the traditional logistics branches. Nationally, there was a network of medical purveyors to purchase and collect medicine and surgical equipment in depots. Field medical purveyors could then requisition supplies from those depots. Regulations stipulated that "medical and hospital supplies will be issued by Medical Purveyors, on requisition, (Form 5), in duplicate, approved by the medical director, and exhibiting the quantities on hand of articles wanted." For a nonbureaucratically oriented department, that provision might have been a nightmare. An uncooperative purveyor could reject a requisition because it was not on the proper form, not in duplicate, not approved by the medical director, did not show the quantity on hand, or did not match his estimate of what a unit needed. The absence of complaints about rejected requisitions shows a certain bureaucratic flexibility (or disregard) on the part of the purveyors. Alternatively, field armies could directly obtain medical supplies using their own medical purchasing agents. In the absence of a medical purchasing agent, regulations authorized quartermasters to buy medical goods. Despite the traditional image of Confederate armies as desperately short of medicine and medical equipment, direct medical purchases do not seem to have been as common as in either commissary or quartermaster operations. Four days after the Battle of Antietam, when demand for medical supplies must have been extraordinary, Lee wrote that a Medical Department purchasing agent had joined his army. The general commented, "Although there is not much for him to do at this time, I have thought it best to keep him with the medical purveyor of this army for the present." Conversely, only days after Lee penned that remark, Cooper, the adjutant general, issued orders requiring medical purveyors to impress all medical supplies in the hands of speculators, so the situation may have been worse than Lee realized.[87] Whatever the state of medical supplies, it is significant that the Confederate Medical Department, like both its contemporary and modern counterparts in the U.S. Army, ran its own supply operation.

The Medical Department also ran its own inspection program, which seems to have grown from the following regulatory requirement: "Medical Directors, Chief Surgeons of Divisions, and Senior Surgeons of Brigades will inspect the hospitals of their commands and see that the rules and regulations are enforced, and the duties of the Surgeons and Assistant Surgeons are properly performed." That responsibility was soon vested in specific individuals who conducted inspections as their primary duty, like assistant inspectors general, but worked for and reported to the medical director. Like their counterparts in the Adjutant and Inspector General Department, medical inspectors could find detailed instructions on conducting inspections in the regulations. Commanders appointed medical inspectors on orders and told them to "at once proceed to a rigid and thorough inspection of the medical department of this command." By the end of the war, there were two full-time medical inspectors working in the Army of Northern Virginia headquarters alone.[88]

Closely allied to the inspection function but the duty of all medical personnel, not just inspectors, was the medical corps responsibility for camp sanitation and the general unit health. Surgeons were expected to know the conditions in camp, learn about common local diseases and treatments, watch the soldiers' clothing needs, insist on cleanliness and personal hygiene, ensure water was pure, and make dietary recommendations. Sanitation was not a particular strength of Rebel soldiers or the Army of Northern Virginia, and disease racked the army during the first fall and winter of the war. The countryside around Manassas was malarial, and regiments from isolated rural regions suffered from common communicable diseases like measles when first exposed to them. Over time, vaccinations, developed natural immunity, and improved sanitary practices rigidly enforced by officers and doctors reduced those problems. Surgeons recommended substitutes for vegetables missing from the diet, and Lee ordered his troops into the fields in search of sassafras, wild onions, garlic, lamb's quarter, and poke sprouts—expedients he recognized could not be found locally in sufficient quantity to prevent the onset of scurvy. Nevertheless, the army remained reasonably healthy considering its poor diet. By February 1864 Guild could report, "The sanitary condition of this army is unprecedentedly good . . . at no preceding time has our army exhibited so much health and vigor."[89]

One final issue the medical director faced was the status of medical personnel captured while tending wounded. This was a thorny issue for both Rebel and Yankee armies. Doctors who faced internment as prisoners of war were not inclined to stay with their patients, while neither side trusted the other to properly care for its wounded. Dr. Hunter H. McGuire, Stonewall Jackson's medical director, convinced his commander during the valley campaign to initiate a program of releasing captured medical personnel. In May–June 1862, George B. McClellan and Lee agreed to treat captured medical personnel as noncombatants rather than as prisoners of war. The adjutants general of the opposing sides confirmed the deal struck in the field by issuing general orders releasing medical prisoners of war. The system continued with only temporary interruption throughout the war. Based on this recognized noncombatant status, Army of Northern Virginia commanders and surgeons unhesitatingly left medical personnel with wounded whose condition prevented evacuation in places as far removed from friendly soil as Pennsylvania.

When the opposing armies remained near battlefields, their medical directors arranged truces to recover wounded, exchanges of wounded, and passage of medical personnel and supplies through the lines. For example, after Chancellorsville, letters went from Army of Northern Virginia headquarters to forward divisions, certainly with the knowledge if not at the urging of Surgeon Guild, authorizing passage of Union doctors and medical supplies through the lines to tend Union wounded.[90]

In all, the medical system of the Army of Northern Virginia was fairly modern in concept and design. It was severely understaffed and lacked authorized medical units but managed to work around those deficiencies by the time-honored method of detailing troops from the ranks. The medical staff officers developed a workable if not perfect method of evacuating casualties to progressively more sophisticated facilities. They had administrative systems to account for casualties and provide medical supplies. If they lacked medicine, horses, and ambulances, they did the best they could with the material at hand. Any lack of medical staff planning probably reflected more the secrecy of the commanders than inadequacy of the staff.

Chapter 4

SPECIAL STAFF IN THE ARMY OF NORTHERN VIRGINIA

The general staff handled much of the staff work of the Army of Northern Virginia, but there were staff functions outside their purview. Theoretically, these were specialized activities, although it is difficult to explain why they were more specialized than medicine. Confederates called the men who performed specialized staff duties the chiefs of special services—we call them the special staff.

CHIEF OF ARTILLERY

The function of the chief of artillery in the Army of Northern Virginia changed over time. The position began as a vaguely defined title for the ranking artillery commander supporting a division or higher unit. He advised the commanding general on artillery issues but mainly busied himself with his own command. The history of artillery organization in the Army of Northern Virginia is a story of artillerymen progressively wresting control of the batteries from infantry commanders, consolidating them into battalions, decentralizing control of the battalions, and reducing the tactical and command duties of the army chief of artillery while increasing his staff responsibilities. The law creating the Confederate military establishment provided for a Corps of Artillery organized like a big regiment with a single colonel and a tiny staff of one adjutant and a sergeant major. That organization never percolated out of the realm of theory onto the field. With a few exceptions (like the Washington Artillery of New Orleans), the basic artillery unit at the beginning of the war was the battery—with no higher artillery headquarters. Every infantry brigade had an attached battery that took its orders from the brigade commander. The army chief of artillery kept excess batteries under his own control and provided general supervision to the batteries supporting infantry brigades. Contemporaries complained that this was an extremely inefficient organization both administratively and tactically. To compound the inefficiency, William N. Pendleton, the chief of artillery of the Army of Northern Virginia for the entire war, initially split command of the Artillery Reserve batteries between himself and Major James B. Walton—perhaps to appease Walton, since Pendleton was promoted over him.[1] To his credit, Pendleton recognized the deficiency or at least the inefficiency of having batteries attached to brigades with no senior artilleryman responsible for their employment or administration. "Our artillery, in common with a good many other things," Pendleton wrote to Robert E. Lee, "needs more system. For want of this I find myself perplexed and even distressed at the want of efficiency. With all diligence I cannot get such reports as are necessary to enable me to see what our strength really is and how it is applied, nor can I without such knowledge satisfy you on these points. Nothing is more certain than that I ought to have at all times and be ready to spread before you a bird's-eye view of the artillery force, with its actual distribution and capacity for diffused or concentrated action."[2]

The artilleryman submitted a draft general order to address the problem for his commander's consideration. Lee took Pendleton's suggestion and published orders defining the responsibilities of the division and army chiefs of artillery. Previous to the order, division chiefs of artillery "existed and acted only at the discretion of their division-commanders and were often charged with the additional duties of chief of ordnance." The Army of Northern Virginia now held the senior artilleryman in each division responsible for "all the batteries thereto attached, whether acting with brigades or held in reserve. A battery duly assigned to a brigade will, until properly relieved, report to and be controlled by the brigade commander. It must also; however, report to and be inspected by the division chief of artillery, as he may require."[3] Pendleton also wrote his own job description and had it blessed in the general order: "The army chief of artillery will have general charge of that branch of service and special direction of the general reserve. He will, under instructions from the commanding general, see that the batteries are kept in as efficient a condition as practicable, and so distributed as to promise the best results. To this end he will require from the several chiefs of artillery weekly returns, exhibiting the condition of each battery and where it is serving. He will also make to the commanding general a tri-monthly report of his entire charge."[4]

This general order and the reasoning behind it are significant in two respects. First, Pendleton justified his proposal to Lee in terms of a classic staff function—he could not gather or provide the commander the information necessary to make rational decisions about artillery employment. And second, the order formally established and specifically defined the duties of the chiefs of artillery. They were responsible for all the artillery supporting their division or army; however, theirs was a complex mix of responsibility with varying degrees of authority. Significantly, the order did not use the word command, since there was no simple organizational way to assign command above the battery. In fact, the order reinforced the brigade commander's control over assigned artillery. Division chiefs of artillery only had staff responsibility for reporting and inspecting the batteries serving with their subordinate brigades. That relationship was even more stark for the army chief of artillery. Pendleton was to monitor the condition and assignment of the artillery—staff functions. The order even directed specific reports to facilitate that process. Conversely, unassigned batteries fell directly under the chiefs of artillery. In the case of divisions, he was in charge of them; the army chief had "special direction" of the reserve batteries. Thus, the general order gave the chiefs of artillery mixed command and staff responsibility and authority.

Brigadier General Pendleton's failure to get any of his reserve guns into action at Malvern Hill (July 1, 1862) compared with Colonel Stapleton Crutchfield's ability to mass twenty-eight guns from two brigades at White Oak Swamp (June 30, 1862) convinced reformers like E. Porter Alexander of the need to reorganize the batteries into battalions.[5] It may also have convinced Alexander to quietly work to remove the artillery from Pendleton's tactical control. After the Seven Days' Battles, the Army of Northern Virginia began to take informal steps to consolidate artillery batteries into battalions. The easiest targets were the batteries in the army reserve, and they were the first formally organized into battalions. Because Pendleton split their command when he formed the general reserve, those batteries had been loosely grouped into two battalion-like organizations for some time. Formation of artillery battalions from the reserve batteries supporting the habitually associated divisions that would soon formally become corps took a more hesitant and uneven course. In either case, the initial formation of artillery battalions was awkward and ad hoc. Alexander commented,

> When first organized, the battalion suffered for the lack of field and staff-officers, owing to the fact that they were not organizations authorized by law, and consequently no appointments could be made for them. . . . The staff-officers for the battalions, and the Chiefs of Artillery, were provided generally by details from the batteries, which, though somewhat detrimental to the latter, operated well enough, except for quarter-master and

commissary duties, for which bonded officers of these departments are absolutely required. Supernumerary officers of these and the medical departments were, however, gradually collected, and the battalions being organized and supplied exactly as regiments, everything worked smoothly.[6]

Alexander thought the stopgap system of detailing officers from the batteries to the battalion staffs worked well, but it was less than an ideal solution. Staff positions were impossible to fill if doing so required action from Richmond. The Adjutant and Inspector General endorsement on a request to promote an artillery sergeant to lieutenant for assignment as a battalion assistant adjutant general shows the frustration:

> If Mr. Chamberlayne can refer the Secretary to any law authorizing the appts [appointments] of Adjts [Adjutants] to Battns [Battalions] he will be most happy to appoint him[. H]e has already recommended him to Govr Letcher for appt [appointment] in the State forces.
> The difficulty of appointing him in the Artillery Corps is that the number is limited and Va has more than her share.
> That [few] persons who have served in the Artillery have been appointed except in a few cases where Generals entitled to Ordnance Officers have nominated infantry officers for that post.[7]

The embryonic artillery battalions theoretically requisitioned their support through the army chief of artillery's staff but found that procedure cumbersome and inconvenient for securing quartermaster, commissary, and ordnance supplies. In the end, they obtained those categories of support directly from the army staff, as the infantry units did. There were problems with that system as well. Stapleton Crutchfield wrote to tell his AAG, who was on furlough in Richmond in January 1863, to stay a few days longer to try to track down ordnance supplies and to scrounge a complete set of general orders from the Adjutant and Inspector General's office. Crutchfield's comment about the general orders is telling: "I have *none* of them [general orders] and find I want them every day more or less. The Arty never before having been separated from Brigades they never were furnished me & now I can't well get along without them." Whatever their support relationship, command of artillery units still ran through the supported infantry commanders (except for the army reserve battalions). For example, in early October 1862 Major General Lafayette McLaws reported his supporting artillery battalion unfit for service. The report went through infantry channels, and Lee's staff directed McLaws to release the battalion while ordering Pendleton to take steps to refit the unit.[8]

The rigors of the Second Manassas and Antietam campaigns in the summer of 1862 forced another reorganization of the artillery of the Army of Northern Virginia. That major realignment offered an excellent opportunity to complete the modernization of the artillery structure; however, the combination and shuffling of batteries, guns, horses, equipment, and officers that occurred at Pendleton's urging in October 1862 happened within the framework of the prevailing structure. Existing battalions were treated as such, but Pendleton did not seize the opportunity to reorganize unattached batteries. The army artillery reserve and primary control of committed artillery stayed at brigade and division level. Lee even reminded his division commanders of their special responsibility for the condition of their artillery horses and charged them to work through the division chiefs of artillery to ensure that the artillery got adequate forage from the quartermaster. Although there were generally two battalions or their equivalent of reserve artillery in each corps (in addition to the army reserve), there was no real corps chief of artillery. That title, which may not have been common at the time, merely designated the senior artillery battalion commander in the corps.[9] Still, for existing battalions, the reorganization was significant. J. H. Chamberlayne, a battalion AAG who said before the reorganization that A. P. Hill used him as a staff officer because his battalion commander was a staff officer, suddenly found himself functioning as part of a real command.

> Since leaving Gordonville our quarters have always been with the General [A. P. Hill]; but within a few days past the batteries have been consolidated as a Corps altogether under [R. Lindsay] Walker's control, which arrangement gives me more to do as adjutant of artillery, but as our quarters are now with the Batteries I cease to be called on as one of the general staff [of A. P. Hill].
>
> You see, the Batteries before received orders from and camped near their Brigades, but now all camp together and receive orders but from Col. W[alker].[10]

The Battle of Fredericksburg (December 13, 1862) prodded the reorganization that finally officially severed the command relationship between batteries and brigades, formalized the artillery battalion organization, and clarified the position of corps chief of artillery. After consultation with his main subordinates, Pendleton recommended a new structure to Lee that included properly resourced staffs for artillery battalions—one to support each division and two in reserve under corps control. Pendleton offered his boss the following advice about the corps chief of artillery: "It is respectfully suggested that the officer to act as Chief of Artillery to the Corps might be most efficient in that capacity if relieved from the burden of a special command." Pendleton also assigned the battalions of the army reserve to corps and thus actually (if not formally) disbanded the reserve organization. "But, although our reserve under Pendleton had never found the opportunity to render much service, its being discontinued was due to our poverty of guns, not dissatisfaction with the system." Lee issued the necessary orders to effect the reorganization before the onset of the campaign season and tactfully solicited Jefferson Davis's opinion on the reorganization ex post facto. The general order implementing this reorganization promised the new battalions surgeons, ordnance officers, and quartermasters as soon as possible. About command and control it said, "All the battalions of each corps will be under the command of, and will report to, the chief of artillery for the corps. The whole in both corps will be superintended by, and report to, the general chief of artillery." Thus, the corps chiefs of artillery had command of the artillery battalions assigned to infantry corps, and the command relationships of battalions with their supported infantry divisions was theoretically broken. However, the position of division chief of artillery did not disappear. In fact, this position, even if technically relieved of authority, was useful as a subterfuge to place officers in command of artillery battalions before the War Department approved their promotions.[11]

The change in artillery relationships was not easy. Pendleton had to chide one of his better battalion commanders who apparently either resisted or did not understand the new command lines.

> I was surprised to find to-day that your battalion had not been removed. I thought you clearly understood the views which I expressed in our conversation a few days ago, as the direction also of the commanding general, viz, that there no longer exists a fixed relation between any infantry division and any one artillery battalion. To prevent the continuance of the idea of any such relationship, and to bring your battalion more into association with the others, so as to secure more through unity of administration in the artillery of the First Corps, and at the same time to get your horses into new pasturage, I wish you to secure a good camp back on Telegraph road. . . . Colonel James B. Walton, chief of artillery, First Corps, complains that he gets no returns from you, and cannot learn where you are. Please communicate with him at once. . . . Your report should come through him.[12]

Faced with a challenge over command of artillery during Pendleton's temporary absence, Lee backed away from completely severing the relationship between infantry divisions and their supporting artillery battalions. It would take time and practice to achieve that result.

The reorganization of the army into three corps after Chancellorsville triggered the final major structural reorganization of the artillery of the Army of Northern Virginia. The already reduced army artillery reserve was formally dissolved. Primary command and tactical control of artillery moved to the corps level both in fact and on paper. However, the implementing general order did not clearly delineate command responsibilities and might have produced serious misunderstandings. The order told the corps chiefs of artillery to report through artillery channels but also to keep their corps commanders informed and make reports required by them. It placed the corps artillery under the corps commander in battle but also permitted the army chief of artillery, using the commanding general's authority, to "command the artillery on any part of the line, and use it at such points as may be needed." Porter Alexander contended that despite the potential for confusion, Pendleton became "a staff-officer of the Commanding General's charged with the supervision of that rather peculiar branch of the service, and only giving orders through the corps commanders except in matters of mere routine and report."[13] The chief of artillery of the Army of Northern Virginia seems to have accepted and even welcomed this change. Pendleton noted: "Having assigned the reserve artillery battalions, I have no special charge, but superintend all the artillery, and direct in battle such portions as may most need my personal attention. This is a better arrangement, I think. My work will be much as it has been, but freer, as none of the petty details of one or two battalions will require my care."[14]

Overall, the final reorganization was effective without being a completely clean break with the past. The new structure relieved Pendleton of the business of command and tactics and left him free to concentrate on administrative and staff matters. That portion of the reorganization largely worked. Instead of maneuvering batteries and battalions, Pendleton spent the early part of the Gettysburg campaign at Culpeper organizing the artillery trains. When he finally joined Lee on the march, he described his duties as "attending near the Commanding-General to be ready for such service as might be required." A critical observer after the war thought Pendleton's new position was closer to that of an ordnance officer than to that of chief of artillery, since the corps artillery chiefs did the tactical management of that arm. However, Lee's senior artilleryman continued to function from time to time in the command chain and on the battlefield. The artillery general hustled batteries onto Herr Ridge during the first day's fight at Gettysburg and did not hesitate to order a corps chief of artillery to immediately send his caissons back for resupply a few days later. An acting chief of artillery during Pendleton's temporary absence in April 1864 ordered the Second Corps artillery to "grazing camps," a significant act that would deprive the corps of immediate artillery support. Even Alexander, who criticized Pendleton's tactical performance throughout the war, admitted that sometimes the army artillery chief had a better grasp of the overall tactical situation than a corps chief of artillery could have.[15]

The position of the corps chiefs of artillery did not develop exactly as intended in the final artillery reorganization scheme primarily because commanders did not implement its provisions evenly. The actual power of the chiefs of artillery varied from corps to corps. Longstreet's ranking artilleryman, Colonel James B. Walton, grew too old for active campaigning and his health was poor—besides, Walton never had Longstreet's total confidence. Longstreet kept the position of chief of artillery in First Corps largely titular while Colonel Walton was the senior artilleryman in the corps and assigned duties that might have been the chief of artillery's to others. Thus, for example, Alexander conducted the First Corps preparatory fires for Pickett's charge. Not until the spring of 1864, when Alexander won promotion to brigadier and assignment as First Corps chief of artillery, did the position acquire the power and responsibility it had possessed for almost a year in the other corps.[16] Even though the reorganization of the Army of Northern Virginia artillery after Chancellorsville was imperfectly implemented and thus did not immediately rectify all the ills of the previous system, it was a major step in rationalizing command and staff arrangements.

Pendleton was not satisfied with his success. In May 1864 he recommended another radical reorganization of the artillery. In a draft bill forwarded through channels for consideration by Congress, Pendleton proposed brigading artillery battalions and grouping large brigades into artillery divisions. Lee made substantive changes to Pendleton's proposal before forwarding it to the Secretary of War J. A. Seddon. Jefferson Davis, who disagreed with some of Pendleton's fundamental recommendations, waylaid the bill and substantially redrafted it.[17] Nothing, consequently, ever came of this attempt, which actually had more to do with increasing the promotion potential for artillery officers than with increasing organizational efficiency.

As artillerymen in the field slowly forced the reorganization of their branch, infantry brigades lost their assigned artillery and the staff functions that accompanied it. Simultaneously, the chief of artillery of the army increasingly became a true special staff officer, moving gradually away from direct command of batteries and battalions to purely staff supervision. Artillery organization evolved at different rates in the corps of the Army of Northern Virginia, with the cavalry and Longstreet's First Corps lagging behind their sister units in consolidating power in the chief of artillery. Nevertheless, by 1864 all three corps artillery units were organized and staffed very much like divisions. Infantrymen accepted the idea that the artillery could support without being under the direct command of the infantry divisions and brigades. The corps and division chiefs of artillery were still the commanders' primary artillery advisers, but they functioned both as commanders and staff officers. Brigadier General Armistead L. Long eventually even divided his Second Corps artillery into two "divisions"—a move probably intended to streamline command and control and free him to concentrate more on the staff aspects of administering the force.[18] Late in the war, the chief of artillery of the Army of Northern Virginia (by then almost exclusively a staff officer) and the corps chiefs of artillery had large staffs of their own.

Two special topics deserve mention in connection with the artillery. First is the status of the horse artillery assigned to the cavalry. As with other organizational innovations adopted by the Army of Northern Virginia, the cavalry was slow embracing artillery reforms. Batteries remained attached to cavalry brigades long after they had been withdrawn from infantry brigade control. The position of chief of artillery in the cavalry also lagged behind its counterpart in the infantry in acceptance and power and remained more a command than a staff position. Perhaps most remarkable, the horse artillery was never really under the absolute supervision of the army chief of artillery like the other units of his branch. Artillery reports frequently—almost habitually—omit the horse artillery. The gunners with the cavalry corps made decisions and implemented policies in contradiction to Pendleton's expressed desires. At one point, Lee had to step in personally to wrest captured field pieces from J. E. B. Stuart's gunners, who wanted to increase the size of their batteries. Lee and Pendleton both objected to expanding the horse artillery to six-gun batteries because of lack of horses, but Stuart's artillery chief, Major R. F. Beckham, effected the expansion anyway. Stuart approved, although his ambulances and ordnance wagons were so poorly horsed thereafter they were virtually useless.[19] Overall, the cavalry corps' artillery operated as a special case throughout the war.

A second special circumstance was the unique position of the artillery, especially early in the war, with respect to its equipment. Before the Confederate ordnance corps was fully operational, the Army of Northern Virginia chief of artillery served as his own purchasing agent. After First Manassas, Joseph E. Johnston sent Pendleton to Richmond to rustle up artillery equipment. Despite difficulties, Pendleton managed to obtain a substantial amount of gear. One observer actually believed Pendleton had been temporarily appointed chief of ordnance, and Johnston thought his chief of artillery was more valuable in the role of purchasing agent than with the command. He denied Pendleton's request to return to the army, and the commander asked instead that his artillery chief try his hand at recruiting artillerymen and cavalrymen. Fortunately, the need to keep the chief of artillery engaged on ordnance business quickly disappeared when the ordnance corps became fully organized and operational. The direct involvement with equipment issues did not end, however. Artillerymen debated the proper mix of smoothbore and rifled pieces and ordered manufacture of specialized items like mortars. And although providing for the efficient collection of captured enemy equipment was a priority throughout the army, no other branch went to the extreme of ordering special mounted teams to stand ready during battle to race forward and drag off captured guns, as rare as that event might have been in practice.[20]

CHIEF OF ORDNANCE

William Pendleton may have been pressed into duty at the outset of the war to procure artillery, but that function belonged to and was ably performed for the rest of the war by the Ordnance Bureau. Although technically organized as part of the artillery, the Ordnance Bureau operated independently both in Richmond and the field. The chief of ordnance on a field staff was a specially qualified artillery officer who had "the charge and direction of the depots of ordnance and ordnance stores for the supply of such army." Regulations required him to work with the chief of artillery and the ordnance officers in the organizations above him to "anticipate, if possible, and provide for all the wants of the army connected with his department." The ordnance department supplied and repaired all rifles, pistols, swords, and cannons and the ammunition they fired. In addition, caissons, artillery harness, traveling forges, repair parts and accoutrements for weapons, and specialized tools came through ordnance channels. Early in the war, the bureau even issued knapsacks, haversacks, and canteens—items properly furnished by the quartermaster. Regulations for ordnance officers touched on such topics as the organization of the national armories, procedures for handling unserviceable ordnance stores, prices for small arms, provisions for supplying ordnance to militia in national service, contracts, and accounts. However, a significant part of the ordnance regulations was a sixteen-page list of a bewildering assortment of ordnance equipment with type classifications and almost forty pages of forms and reports.[21]

The Confederacy realized from the start that it would need ordnance material to fight for independence. Laws passed in the spring of 1861 authorized the contracting, purchase, and manufacture of weapons and munitions and assigned the ordnance function to the artillery. The adjutant general quickly appointed an experienced ordnance officer from the U.S. Army, Josiah Gorgas, to head the Ordnance Bureau. Gorgas set out with determination to create an arms manufacturing and import industry in the South. Unfortunately, his initial efforts necessarily concentrated on the organization of his bureau at the national level and not on the deployed armies. For the first year of the war, the ordnance staff function in the field was ad hoc. There were few ordnance officers below division and corps headquarters, and the position was frequently an additional duty at all echelons. After First Manassas, Captain E. Porter Alexander picked up responsibility for ordnance activities in addition to his assignment as the army signal officer. Alexander found himself confronting a daunting task without any established system. He solved the problem by implementing the ordnance structure that would serve the Army of Northern Virginia throughout the war. Alexander had ordnance officers designated at all echelons down to brigade and ordnance sergeants appointed in the regiments. He issued blank inventory forms and demanded weekly reports so he could track the wide variety of weapons on hand by type and caliber to ensure that regiments received the proper ammunition. Alexander established an ordnance storehouse at the railroad station and organized brigade and division ordnance trains to move ammunition from the storehouse to the troops. He required subordinate units to estimate consumption and keep ammunition available in the trains for at least one battle. Alexander also formed an army reserve ordnance train to haul emergency supplies and recruited gunsmiths, blacksmiths, and other artisans to repair weapons from small arms to cannon.[22] By the time this energetic engineer turned signalman turned ordnance chief left the staff to become an artilleryman, he had put in place all the elements of the Army of Northern Virginia's ordnance structure.

General orders and legislation in April 1862 formally established the ordnance structure of field armies on the lines Alexander had already sketched. The relevant part of the legislation authorized every regiment to have an ordnance sergeant. Later regulations would require these non-commissioned officers to have eight years service (four as a sergeant) before appointment—a provision prudently suspended indefinitely, since no one could meet that qualification. General orders published simultaneously with this law required the appointment of full-time ordnance officers at every level from division up. Vacancies were to be filled immediately and names reported to Richmond. Commanders could not change their ordnance officers without prior approval received through the army chief of ordnance from the bureau in Richmond. Unit ordnance officers would be attached to the Ordnance Bureau and would report and requisition through ordnance channels. Although ordnance officers in the field served on the staffs of their respective commands, the general order required them to take their instructions from the bureau unless there was a direct conflict with the commander's orders. Instructions for field ordnance officers approved by the secretary of war came out less than a month later to supplement the general order that formalized the ordnance structure. Those instructions established reporting channels and requirements, directed ordnance officers to procure an ordnance wagon (separate from the reserve train wagons) for each regiment, explained the ordnance sergeants' duties, and published doctrine for ordnance operations during battle. On July 1, 1862, the war department issued orders amending the field ordnance structure to add a first lieutenant ordnance officer at each brigade headquarters. The Ordnance Bureau soon consolidated and expanded all these instructions in a special field manual for its officers. In the fall of 1862 Congress authorized appointment of additional ordnance officers and assignment of a lieutenant colonel to each army staff, a major to each corps staff, and captains and lieutenants to division and brigade staffs. A year later, the adjutant general authorized two assistants for the army chief of ordnance and one for each corps ordnance chief. These authorizations, of course, hardly reflected reality. In 1862, Alexander already had two officers running the reserve ordnance train, and William Allan had two primary officer assistants to help him run the Second Corps ordnance operation. When Lieutenant Francis W. Dawson joined Longstreet's ordnance staff in the summer of 1862, he became the fourth officer in the section. Appomattox paroles show seven ordnance officers with the staff of the Army of Northern Virginia. The final 1864 law to organize field staffs authorized an ordnance colonel, lieutenant colonel, major, and captain for units from army to brigade level, respectively.[23]

Ordnance officers, at least after the fall of 1862, had the distinction of being the only officers in the army who had to pass a test to gain appointment or promotion. Gorgas, the chief of the Ordnance Bureau, convinced Confederate authorities to require an examination for all ordnance officers because he wanted efficient officers in ordnance service and probably more importantly because he was trying to relieve himself of "much political contrivance" and "a thousand personal solicitations." General orders established an examining board, announced prerequisites and test subjects, and created testing procedures. One hundred of five hundred applicants for commissions showed up in Richmond to take the first test; between forty and fifty passed. The examining board then visited armies in the field and tested candidates already serving in the army.

The examination for a lieutenant's commission "embraced only an ordinary English education, with a full examination on the Ordnance Manual." Gorgas said captains had to pass a test that "involved a fair knowledge of a college course of mathematics, and none, I believe, passed this except the M.A.'s of the University of Virginia." Test questions ranged from figuring simple percentages and writing a twenty-line essay about the war to answering technical questions about the chemical composition of gunpowder and solving more complicated algebra, trigonometry, and mechanics problems. Because there were serving officers who might not have the education required to pass the test, each army commander could appoint one or two distinguished officers based on recommendations alone. Serving officers who were not completely exempted still got preferential treatment. Dawson, the assistant ordnance officer for Longstreet's corps, thought taking the exam for promotion was unfair. He protested directly (in person) to Secretary of War Seddon: "I explained to him that I had been too long in the field to know as much as a youngster who had just been graduated from college, and that if my promotion depended upon my familiarity with Conic Sections and the Calculus, I should probably remain a Lieutenant all my life." Seddon put an endorsement on Dawson's board paperwork instructing the board to take the lieutenant's objection into consideration when evaluating answers to theoretical questions. With such help (and having his friend Peyton Manning sitting as the president of the board), Dawson was able to answer many questions "I don't know" and still win promotion. However, understandable preferential treatment for proven serving officers occasionally became outright abuse of the system. McHenry Howard, a Marylander whom Brigadier General George H. Steuart appointed ordnance officer of the Maryland Line after Howard lost an aide job when his general was killed, remarked, "It had been published in General Orders that ordnance officers were to be appointed throughout the army after passing special examinations, but [Steuart] was confident of having this requirement dispensed with in my case and discouraged my suggestion that I ought to apply for such examination." More typical, however, is a comment by Frederick Colston, ordnance officer for Alexander's artillery battalion who won promotion and appointment as an assistant ordnance officer on the army staff. "In September 1864, after passing the examination of the Ordnance Board, I was commissioned Captain of Artillery on Ordnance Duty." In any case, lack of authorizations restricted ordnance appointments in the Army of Northern Virginia more often than lack of candidates who had passed the examination.[24]

The physical organization, control, movement, and operation of the ordnance trains consumed much of an ordnance staff officer's time. By the summer of 1862 the Army of Northern Virginia's ordnance train had mushroomed to between eighty and one hundred wagons—a major supervisory burden. Subordinate units had proportionately smaller but still substantial ordnance trains. For example, artillery battalions had about one ammunition wagon in the corps ordnance train for every three guns, or thirty to forty wagons full of artillery ammunition alone in each corps ordnance train. Besides ammunition wagons, ordnance trains had wagons full of tools, repair parts, and broken weapons as well as traveling forges and specialized equipment. Although the authorities in Richmond did not follow P. G. T. Beauregard's recommendation that the Army of Northern Virginia establish its own cartridge-manufacturing facility, they did see the practicality of repairing small arms in the field. Alexander, as the army chief of ordnance, established a weapons-repair capability in the army reserve ordnance trains, and in the spring of 1862 he was even converting flintlock muskets to percussion firing systems at a small facility in Gordonsville.[25] "There had been with the Second corps no field repair shop, or other means of repairing slight damages to arms," William Allan commented. "Soon after taking charge I obtained through Colonel Briscoe G. Baldwin [army Chief of Ordnance], from the field park of the army, four or five gunsmiths and a good harness maker, with a small equipment, including a large tent, and attached this to our corps reserve ordnance train. These men were worthy and excellent mechanics, and did a great deal of useful work. Several thousand stand of arms in the course of the campaign were rendered serviceable, which otherwise would have had to go to Richmond, and a good deal of artillery harness was repaired."[26] Allan even attempted to get lathes and bushings equipment from Richmond so he could make his own repair parts, a step that would have increased the size and complexity of the corps ordnance trains significantly.[27] Each added capability increased the number of wagons and people in the ordnance trains. All those vehicles, their drivers, and the ordnance sergeants and artisans accompanying them required organization, leadership, and supervision. Just running the day-to-day operation of the trains was enough to keep a chief of ordnance busy.

When distances were short and transportation available, the ordnance trains supported the army efficiently; however, when the army moved quickly, it often outdistanced its trains and stressed the ordnance system. Alexander reported no problems supplying ammunition during the relatively compact fighting of the Seven Days' Battles on the peninsula and even had time to dabble with a reconnaissance balloon. On the other hand, Lee's quick march north at the conclusion of the peninsula campaign left his trains stranded out of supporting distance near Richmond. Alexander commented, "I followed as rapidly as possible, but could not overtake the army until Chantilly. Then I replenished all expenditures, so the troops advanced into Maryland with everything full." Alexander kept his trains close to Lee's headquarters during the Maryland campaign, shuttling wagons back and forth from the main supply point at Staunton, until ordered south of the Potomac immediately before the climactic battle at Antietam.[28] Being close to the army made support easier, but proximity also had its disadvantages. Increased distance from supply points and railroads meant long hauls for wagons. The Second Corps ordnance officer, Lieutenant Colonel William Allan, gave a good description of the planning, coordination, and effort required to resupply ammunition at extreme distances. Supporting Jubal Early's 1864 valley campaign he noted, "Next morning (20th) [September 1864] a courier was sent from Strasburg to Staunton to have supplies shipped from Richmond to the latter place and a train of wagons was sent for it. These wagons had to travel seventy miles to Staunton. They obtained a relay of horses at Harrisonburg, got to Staunton early on the 21st of September, were loaded and started back for the army on the same day, and changing teams at Harrisonburg, the train was approaching the battlefield on the afternoon of the 22d when the disaster of Fisher's Hill was in progress."[29] Proximity to the army also increased the vulnerability of the ordnance trains, as the capture by Union cavalry escaping from Harper's Ferry of forty-five wagons from Longstreet's ordnance train during the Antietam campaign dramatically demonstrated. In another instance, Allan found his trains trapped by unfordable streams and threatened by cavalry. He was forced to spend a day unloading all the wagons, ferrying ammunition in a leaky rowboat, fording the empty wagons, drying out ammunition, reloading the wagons, and fleeing the cavalry before he was again able to support his corps. Longstreet's artillery ordnance train parked so close to the field at Gettysburg that incoming artillery fire forced it to relocate during the battle, causing confusion and preventing efficient resupply of ammunition during the preparatory fires for Pickett's charge.[30]

However, train management was simply a method of accomplishing other functions. The major duty of a chief of ordnance was supplying weapons and ammunition to his force. The running controversy over the proper number of cannons for the Army of Northern Virginia and whether to calculate that figure in terms of guns per man or guns per regiment seems to have been conducted by Lee, Pendleton, and Gorgas; however, field ordnance officers faced the problem of supplying ammunition for the guns on hand. Keeping up with demand was difficult when one gun could fire 160 rounds in a single, relatively small action, as a horse artillery piece did at Brandy Station. It was even harder in a major battle like Gettysburg (July 1–3, 1863), when a pair of guns fired two hundred rounds in two hours on the second day and a single gun fired three hundred rounds the following day. Those figures are extreme, but consumption was still enormous—one authority estimated the Army of Northern Virginia fired ninety thousand artillery rounds at Gettysburg, although that figure is almost twice what he estimated was available. Infantry ammunition expenditure was equally high, but it was never as high as anticipated and thus not as big a problem. Individuals and specific units might fire extraordinary amounts—one veteran said his company fired 128 rounds per man while serving as skirmishers at Cross Keys (June 8, 1862)—but overall consumption never met projections. The *Ordnance Manual* called for two hundred rounds per man split between what the soldier carried on his person and what was in the trains. Ordnance returns after First Manassas showed an expenditure of nineteen to twenty-six rounds per man, so the two hundred-round basic load was excessive. Gorgas calculated the infantry ammunition expenditure at Chancellorsville and Gettysburg (the highest he could find) as between twenty-five and thirty rounds per man and decided quite logically that a basic load of sixty rounds was sufficient if the field armies had proper procedures to reallocate ammunition among units. In the spring of 1863 the Ordnance Bureau issued instructions to cease the universal practice of issuing each man on the eve of battle twenty rounds over what he had in his cartridge box (i.e., sixty total rounds).[31] That practice led to waste, since ammunition in the soldiers' pockets was easy to lose or damage.

The Army of Northern Virginia had already recognized the problem of loss and spoilage—compounded by the practice of cutting up cartridge boxes to repair shoes, thus exposing all the ammunition to the elements—and instituted rigorous procedures to inspect and account for ammunition.

> To correct the evil, a system of reports was prepared, by which the exact condition of the ordnance in the hands of the men was obtained every two weeks, and the difference between the present and the preceding report had to be accounted for, even down to every round of ammunition. Orders were issued from army headquarters providing for the inspections on which these reports were to be based, and directing that all damage to ammunition, arms, and equipment, due to carelessness or neglect should be charged against the men or officers who were to blame.[32]

Ordnance officers could call for a brigade Board of Survey to decide liability in disputed cases. Once the brigade commander approved the board's findings, the ordnance officer could garnishee the soldier's wages to recoup the government's loss. Unfortunately, the army still had trouble keeping track of ammunition. In December 1864, when Lee dispatched Robert F. Hoke's division to Wilmington, North Carolina, the unit reported on arrival that it only had thirty rounds per man, and the local armory could only supply an additional ten rounds per man. Lee immediately dispatched 250,000 rounds, but he also fired off a letter to Braxton Bragg, then commanding in North Carolina, demanding that he investigate the situation. Colonel Briscoe Baldwin reported that Hoke's ordnance officers had personally supervised the loading of eighty rounds per man on the train carrying the last brigades, and an equivalent amount accompanied the first train. Lee wanted to know "what has become of the ammunition they set out with?"[33] The ammunition was probably somewhere in Wilmington, but there was an accountability problem if the responsible officers did not know where.

Stopping wastage, forecasting consumption, and accounting for ammunition and equipment all required reports and paperwork. As with the other staff sections, ordnance officers had trouble meeting the administrative demand. Reports were chronically late. The bureau in Richmond eventually issued stern orders in an attempt to pry from the army the required quarterly reports of ordnance stores on hand in the field: "Should any officer fail to render the return required on the 1st of January next, within twenty days thereafter, the brigadier-general commanding the brigade to which the officer is attached will cause charges for 'disobedience of orders,' or of 'neglect of duty,' as the case may require, to be made and forwarded without delay to the general commanding, for his action. The same action will be taken on every subsequent omission to render such returns."[34] There is no evidence such draconian procedures produced more than temporary results.

If keeping up with paperwork and other problems was not enough, people at all echelons of the army kept dreaming up ideas for new and unusual weapons and ammunition. Lee convinced the government to construct an iron-plated railroad gun for use during the peninsula campaign of 1862 and then twisted the secretary of the navy's, S. R. Mallory, arm to get sailors to man it. In a less eccentric vein, the army commander also had his staff write Colonel Gorgas to request five hundred carbines. The chief of artillery, William N. Pendleton, sought ordnance help through the Army of Northern Virginia chief of ordnance, Briscoe Baldwin, in developing "stink shells" to produce a choking or suffocating cloud on impact. Less came of this scheme than of Lee's railroad gun, although Colonel Gorgas promised to pursue the matter if ordered. Alexander lobbied for mortars and hand grenades and then complained when the powder for the mortars was not of sufficiently large grain to allow his gunners to count their charges by individual grain.[35] Fortunately, most of these efforts were on a small scale or came to little, so the chief of ordnance did not have to spend excessive time dealing with them.

With all the competing demands, an ordnance officer's daily routine could be quite diverse and hectic. Alexander's journal described the major events of a typical day, October 15, 1862. He received a telegram from the depot in Staunton requesting disposition instructions for the artillery located there to which he had to reply. He then telegraphed Gorgas in Richmond to increase a recent request for small arms by two thousand. Next, Alexander wired Staunton again asking how soon they would be ready to issue arms and at what daily rate. He then wrote to an artillery battery commander advising him to retain the three-inch navy Parrott guns he had and offering to requisition special ammunition for them. Another artillery battery then submitted a requisition for four artillery pieces. That request necessitated a policy decision on reequipping batteries that Alexander submitted to William Pendleton, who told Alexander to issue the pieces from other inefficient batteries, a decision Alexander implemented. He then wired Staunton a request to forward two hundred rounds of twenty-pound Parrott ammunition. The commander of the Staunton depot replied with the disturbing news that he had wagons on hand but nothing to ship. He asked Alexander to intercede with Gorgas since repeated requests from Staunton had produced no results. Alexander wired Gorgas before completing his duties for the day. The only typical activity that Alexander escaped that day was the arrival or dispatch of a wagon train (fifteen to twenty-five wagons or thirty thousand to fifty thousand pounds of cargo on average). Of course, unexpected events occasionally interrupted the routine. Two days later, Alexander noted, "Troops under arms in camp, and wagon trains loaded and harnessed up. Headquarters camp removed half a mile to a grove. Enemy in position in front of our pickets during the day but withdrew near sundown." The scare did not completely interrupt normal activity, however. Alexander still had to deal with the usual flow of paperwork and requests, plus the arrival of twenty wagons full of arms and accouterments.[36]

As much as any other department, the ordnance corps of the Army of Northern Virginia lived off captured enemy equipment. Regulations contained general guidance on appropriating enemy goods for Confederate service and the specific direction that "after an action, the officers on ordnance duty collect the munitions of war left on the field, and make a return of them to the General." This was not an esoteric regulatory provision as many were—it was a reality in the Rebel army. On the way to Gettysburg, First Corps staff officers told British observer Arthur Fremantle, "In every battle we fight we must capture as much ammunition as we use." Fremantle observed, "This necessity, however, does not seem to disturb them, as it has hitherto been their regular style of doing business." Obviously, faced with such a requirement, the ordnance officers needed an efficient system of recovering and reissuing captured enemy weapons and ammunition. Without such a system, the soldiers took matters into their own hands—troops on both sides of the Civil War felt free to swap rifles or commandeer any other equipment they fancied if they happened upon something they liked during battle. Both to ease the difficulty of supplying ammunition to units with mixed armament and to get better control of captured small arms, the government eventually issued orders prohibiting soldiers from appropriating rifles on the battlefield.[37] General orders, however, could never completely stop the practice. Even totally unchecked, though, the practice of direct replacement of weapons by individuals on the battlefield did not significantly reduce the number of weapons the Army of Northern Virginia captured.

The weapons picked up after First Manassas went to Richmond, where they equipped new units. An observer noted, "The Yankee muskets are distributed daily. There were 27 Captains at one time to day in the building where they are kept Selecting for their Companies; and this happens every day." The Seven Days' Battles further increased the booty to be issued, while an observer commented that after Cedar Mountain (August 9, 1862), Stonewall Jackson "occupied himself in gleaning the battle-field of arms." The Army of Northern Virginia could not gather much from the Antietam battlefield but had the spoils of Harper's Ferry in compensation. Porter Alexander, still the army chief of ordnance at the time, took every empty wagon he could find to Harper's Ferry, loaded immediately useful ammunition for return to the Antietam field, and shipped to Winchester the rest of the loot taken when the garrison surrendered. After Chancellorsville, an ordnance officer spent a week gathering abandoned small arms from the battlefield.[38] Policing that field was particularly difficult. Lieutenant Colonel Baldwin reported to Richmond,

> The field is so extensive—ranging from Fredericksburg, a distance of 10 miles, through dense woods and deep ravines—that it has been very difficult to collect the arms and almost impossible to estimate their number. I would say that there may be almost 20,000, of which 12,000 may be set

down as trophies. They have been collected and placed in prominent places on the roadside, and are being transported to the railroad depot as speedily as our limited transportation and broken-down condition of the animals will admit. I will have the field thoroughly gleaned.[39]

Even Gettysburg produced some captured material, and Gorgas estimated that the Confederate armies as late as 1864 netted fifteen thousand captured small arms after subtracting their own losses.[40]

Accounting for the constant influx and loss of weapons was as big a problem as accounting for personnel. Ordnance officers eventually instituted procedures for handling the weapons of wounded and furloughed soldiers, accounting for arms received and issued, and controlling captured weapons. Those policies were probably about as effective as other Army of Northern Virginia administrative accounting procedures. The department did manage to become bureaucratic very quickly, though. In June 1861 headquarters returned an energetic regimental commander's request for powder and caps so he could make his own cartridges (he already had lead). The endorsement (originally approved and then scratched out) returned the request for completion—it did not state the quantity of powder and caps on hand as required by recent special orders.[41]

Besides their standard duties, chiefs of ordnance, like most other staff officers, handled miscellaneous other jobs. For some reason, Allan assumed responsibility for marking and storing the knapsacks of his corps. He commented, "During the winter [1862–63] General Jackson requested me to have the knapsacks of the men marked in white paint. In the active campaigning of the preceding summer his men had been compelled to store their knapsacks, I think in Harrisonburg, and it was some months before they saw them again. As they had not been marked in any way, great confusion and loss resulted."[42] Allan went to Richmond personally to scrounge stencils and paint. Despite the effort, his program was not totally successful, since only one division chief of ordnance pursued the program with diligence, and marking the other division knapsacks was not completed before the 1863 campaign season opened. During the next winter, Lieutenant Colonel Baldwin, who followed Alexander as chief of ordnance of the Army of Northern Virginia, appealed to Allan for assistance in obtaining timber for gun carriages to fill a shortage in the Richmond factories. The resourceful ordnance officer found a stand of oak and gum, secured a large detail of soldiers, located a portable steam-powered saw mill, and ran the mill around the clock to harvest the timber. He then unloaded half of the Second Corps ordnance wagons so he could use the teams and running gear to haul the timber three to four miles to the railroad. Allan noted that the property owner whose lumber he harvested was understandably upset and protested through military channels to Richmond; however, the operation was completed and the timber spirited away before a reply arrived. The winter of 1864–65 found the Second Corps chief of ordnance setting up his own blacksmithing industry on a massive scale in an attempt to fill the need for horseshoes and nails. Allan established twenty forges in Waynesboro, Virginia, using locally scavenged equipment supplemented by some sent from Richmond. He then sent his trains under cavalry escort into disputed territory to get iron from Columbia Furnace. By spring, Allan's smithies produced twenty thousand pounds of horseshoes and nails; however, Philip H. Sheridan's cavalry captured most of that inventory before the Rebels could use it. Besides forging horseshoes, Allan decided to fill the demand for currycombs, a minor but important item, locally. He had his gunsmiths fabricate the necessary tools and went into the currycomb business. The ordnance trains of the Second Corps eventually manufactured 1,500 to 2,000 combs. Unfortunately, most of the currycombs (like the horseshoes and nails) fell into the hands of federal raiders. One division chief of ordnance in the fall of 1864 filled his empty ordnance wagons with coal requisitioned from residents of the valley—he did not note why he chose coal for ballast, only that he paid in federal dollars and was exceedingly polite so no one could object.[43]

Overall, whether performing their primary function or involved in secondary activities, the chiefs of ordnance in the Army of Northern Virginia achieved herculean results. Despite supply shortages and the lack of a mature arms industry in the South, the Army of Northern Virginia never suffered a critical munitions shortage.

CHIEF OF ENGINEERS

Regulations outlined the responsibilities of the Chief of Engineer as follows: "The duties of these corps usually relate to the construction of permanent and field fortifications; works for the attack and defence of places; for the passage of rivers; for the movements and operations of armies in the field; and such reconnoisances and surveys as may be required for these objectives, or for any other duty which may be assigned to them. By special direction of the President of the Confederate States, officers of engineers may be employed on any other duty whatsoever."[44]

Engineers were elite. Although there were engineer companies for specialized tasks like constructing pontoon bridges and eventually a regiment of combat engineers with each field army, engineering was primarily an officer function. Engineer officers were theoretically the best educated and trained in the army. The provision allowing them to perform nonengineering duties by special direction of the president was an 1863 modification of the regulations to nullify the sixty-third article of war, which specifically prohibited assigning engineers to "any duty beyond the line of their immediate profession," since their functions were "generally confined to the most elevated branch of military science." Perhaps because they dealt with such weighty subjects, or were assumed to know their duties, army regulations did not give engineers much detailed guidance. Three pages of text on the construction of permanent fortifications, a section on siege operations, and fifteen pages of report formats are the extent of their regulatory instructions. Regulations did include a section, probably written by an engineer, on the care of permanent fortifications. There, commanders learned that walking on any slope or dragging cannons across sidewalks was forbidden, while keeping the grass mowed, the wooden floors swept, and drawbridges cleaned and oiled was required. Above all, stated the regulations, "No alteration will be made in any fortification, or in any building whatever belonging to it, nor in any building or work of any kind . . . except under the superintendence of the Engineer Department, and by the authority of the Secretary of War."[45]

The adjutant general published more practical guidance on the duties of engineers in June 1863: "The senior officer of engineers serving with an army in the field will be responsible for the proper execution of all duties appertaining to his department; and the orders of the commanding general relating to the engineer service will be communicated through him, and he will recommend to the general commanding the assignments of junior officers of engineers to serve with corps, divisions, and brigades." That section described the duties of the chief of engineers of a field army. Later paragraphs of the same order outlined what the War Department expected engineers to do.

> The duties of officers of engineers serving with the armies of the Confederate States in the field, camp, or cantonment are as follows: To make reconnaissances and surveys of the section of the country occupied by our forces and as far as possible of the country held by the enemy, embracing all the information that can be obtained in reference to roads, bridges, fords, topographical and military features, the character and dimensions of the water courses, the practicability of constructing fixed and floating bridges, the extent of wooded and cleared lands, and the capacity of the country to supply the general wants of the army; to make detailed examinations and surveys of positions to be occupied for defensive purposes; to select the sites, and form plans, projects, and estimates for all military works, defensive or offensive, viz, field forts, batteries, rifle-pits, lines of

infantry cover, military trenches, parallels, saps, mines, and other works of attack or siege; also works for obstructing rivers and harbors; to prepare such maps and plans as will give a full knowledge of the ground and proposed works, and submit same to the commanding general for his information and consideration, and forward, through the proper channels, copies of all reports, memoirs, estimates, plans, drawings, and models relating to the duties above enumerated to the Engineer Bureau, at Richmond.[46]

Despite the incredible length and convoluted construction of that single sentence, the order exactly explained the duties of field engineers.

There was no specific allocation of engineers to unit staffs. The department assigned officers, and commanders allocated them internally as needed, limited only by the total number of engineers authorized by law. That technique, although reasonable in concept, caused problems early in the war when requirements far exceeded the number of qualified officers. Commanders besieged Richmond with requests for engineers. Congress responded to the shortage by granting authorization for one hundred additional engineer officers to serve during the war. Later, the problem became lack of engineer troops rather than officers. The initial meager establishment of companies of pontooners, sappers, miners, and bombardiers could not fill the field engineer need. In the spring of 1863 Congress authorized (and the field armies each began trying to form) a regiment of engineers based on a hundred-man company to support each infantry division. Theoretically, the recruits for these engineer companies were to come from the divisions they would support; however, commanders balked at releasing infantrymen from the line. For example, Jubal Early refused to provide manpower, made the engineer company commander his staff engineer, and sent the lieutenant back to the artillery where he had served before being appointed an engineer. The 1st Regiment of Engineers eventually formed in the Army of Northern Virginia by the expedient of selecting conscripts who possessed basic mechanical or trade skills from the training depots. Because of the difficulty of recruiting and equipping the engineer regiments, it was a year after their initial authorization before Secretary of War Seddon could report their complete organization and declare himself satisfied they would "prove eminently advantageous in facilitating the movement and providing the defences of our armies." As Seddon predicted, the engineer regiments proved to be a useful and necessary addition to the army.[47] One engineer regimental officer commented that there were "miners, sailors, carpenters, blacksmiths, masons, and almost every other trade among them," while the officers and noncommissioned officers were either professional civil engineers or well-educated men with special me-

chanical qualifications. He went on to describe the training and employment of the engineer companies: "We were armed and drilled as infantry, and in campaigns served as infantry unless there were military
bridges or other works to construct. In sieges we served as sappers and
miners. Two companies of the regiment were equipped as pontooners,
each being furnished with a train of boats mounted upon wagons made
for the purpose, and these companies were drilled in the art of taking up
and laying down these bridges across streams until they became experts
at it. The men of the other companies were instructed in the art of making gabions, sap-rollers, cheaux-de-frise, and other siege material."[48] By
war's end, besides ample engineer staff officers, the Army of Northern
Virginia had its engineer regiment of twelve companies serving mainly
with the divisions for which they were recruited.[49]

Unlike the chief of artillery, who was frequently both a commander
and staff officer, command of engineer troops was separate from the
staff function. Lee's chief of engineers coordinated all engineering activity in the Army of Northern Virginia and as the ranking engineer was responsible for all the engineer troops, but he did not directly command all
or part of his forces like the chief of artillery did for much of the war.
Also unlike the rest of the Army of Northern Virginia staff, which was
remarkably stable throughout the war, Lee had difficulty finding and
keeping a chief of engineers. This problem plagued the Army of Northern Virginia from its inception. Joseph Johnston was so frustrated in his
attempts that the bureau recommended he pull an infantry general for
temporary duty as his chief of engineers. Johnston did not take that advice and instead appointed the ranking engineer, Captain Powhatan
Robinson, as the chief.[50] Major Walter H. Stevens, technically the chief
of construction, filled the chief's role when Lee assumed command of the
army. Lieutenant Colonel Jeremy F. Gilmer, who later became the chief
of the Engineer Bureau in Richmond, was Lee's senior engineer later in
the summer of 1862. Lieutenant Colonel William P. Smith served a stint
as chief of engineers through the fall and winter of 1863–64, and Major
General Martin L. Smith served from April to July 1864, when he went
to the Army of Tennessee. The same Walter H. Stevens (now a colonel
and soon to be a brigadier) who had performed the duties previously
held the post from Smith's departure to the end of the war.

Lee lobbied constantly for a chief of engineers. In March 1863 he
complained to Gilmer, by then running the bureau in Richmond, that
Longstreet had requested an engineer to do mapping and reconnaissance
around Petersburg. Lee had two new engineer officers available and
would have sent one or both but did not know their qualifications. The
Army of Northern Virginia commander stated, "If I had an experienced

engineer officer capable of conducting the professional operations of that department in this army, young officers could be advantageously employed." A year later, faced with increasing engineer strength, Lee lobbied for an engineer general officer. In a letter to the bureau Lee requested a brigadier general to supervise Colonel Thomas M. R. Talcott's 1st Engineer Regiment, six separate engineer companies, and the various engineer staff officers. "This would make an appropriate command for a brigadier-general, who should be chief engineer of the army." The army commander even proposed three candidates for the position. Lee may have been making an uncharacteristic attempt to have a relative—his son, Custis, who was moving from duties as Davis's aide—assigned to his staff. However, a letter to Custis on the subject implied that although his son was the primary candidate, Lee wanted a chief of engineers even if Custis did not get the assignment. "It is necessary that the Corps of Engineers attached to this army be reorganized and strengthened," wrote Lee. "I also want a proper Chief. If you do not take the service now offered, and will accept that of Chief Engineer of this Army, I will apply for you. If you do not take it, I will apply for some one else."[51] If Lee really wanted his son, his request was too subtle: the bureau assigned Martin Smith. At least one officer, A. C. Haskell, thought Smith was an excellent choice and that Lee needed the help, writing home, "I had a long ride on the lines today with General [Cadmus M.] Wilcox and General Martin Luther Smith, a distinguished officer who has just arrived to go on duty as General Lee's Chief Engineer. He is a splendid looking soldier, and I think it will be a pleasure to be placed on a line of battle by a man with such talent and character as his face and bearing exhibit. I am really glad that General Lee has an Engineer, at last, upon whom he can devolve some of his most burdensome duties."[52]

For much of the war, four major activities dominated Confederate field engineering: reconnaissance, mapping, mobility operations (bridging and construction of temporary roads), and selection and construction of defensive positions and field fortifications. After mid-1864, when the fighting in the east stagnated in the trenches around Petersburg and Richmond, traditional siege and countersiege tasks eclipsed those of the more mobile years.

Nineteenth-century soldiers considered individual reconnaissance, especially terrain reconnaissance and the examination of enemy defensive positions, a unique engineering capability. Although all staff officers did reconnaissance, engineers were presumed to have a peculiar talent for that duty. The intensive study of topography and fortification that differentiated the education of qualified military engineers from their civilian peers gave them a skilled and critical eye for terrain and defensive positions. Such training was as useful in examining an enemy's position as in establishing one's own. William Blackford, Stuart's engineer, said, "As Engineer officer my duty, on the approach of a battle, was to reconnoitre the positions of the enemy and ascertain and report his movements." Stuart defined his engineer's duties more broadly but in the same vein. The cavalry commander complimented Blackford for being "always in advance, obtaining valuable information of the enemy's strength, movements and position, locating routes and making hurried but accurate topographical sketches. He is bold in reconnaissance, fearless in danger, and remarkably cool and correct in judgment."[53]

Engineer reconnaissance began before anticipated battles or campaigns to familiarize the commander with the terrain. As one example, Beauregard dispatched three engineer officers on an extensive reconnaissance of the Manassas area and westward before First Manassas. In another case, Lee, while contemplating Union options before Fredericksburg, dispatched Captain Conway R. Howard, one of his engineers, on a scouting mission. Howard reported, "In pursuance of your orders to that effect, I have finished an examination of the Rappahannock River with reference to positions suitable for forcing a passage from the north side, and have the honor to report." Blackford conducted a similar reconnaissance of a different section of the Rappahannock about the same time.[54]

Engineer reconnaissance was often critical to developing plans of battle. Henry Kyd Douglas claimed that before Chancellorsville "Major Jed Hotchkiss, Jackson's topographical engineer, had been sent out in the night to ascertain whether there was not a feasible route around the right flank of the enemy. His report with a map satisfied General Lee that it was practicable."[55] Early gave an even more detailed account of how engineer reconnaissance, again conducted by Hotchkiss, influenced tactical planning. Immediately before the Battle of Cedar Creek (October 19, 1864), Hotchkiss returned after dark from a scouting mission, reported Early,

and he gave me a sketch of the enemy's position and camps. He informed me that the enemy's left flank, which rested near Cedar Creek, a short distance above its mouth, was lightly picketed, and that there was but a small cavalry picket on the North Fork of the Shenandoah, below the mouth of the creek, and he stated that, from the information he had received, he thought it was practicable to move a column of infantry between the base of the mountain and the river, to a ford below the mouth of the creek. He also informed me that the main body of the enemy's cavalry was on his right flank on the Back Road to Winchester. The sketch made by Captain Hotchkiss, which proved to be correct, designated the roads in the enemy's rear, and the house of a Mr. Cooley as a favorable point for forming an attacking column, after it crossed the river, in order to move against the enemy and strike him on the Valley Pike in rear of his works. Upon this information, I determined to attack the enemy by moving over the ground designated by Captain Hotchkiss.[56]

Most prebattle reconnaissance, of course, did not have as much influence on tactical planning. Hotchkiss's account of an incident in an earlier campaign is perhaps more representative: "There Generals Ewell, Johnson and Early discussed the plan of capturing Winchester and Martinsburg. I was at the conference and made some suggestions as to routes, etc. which were afterwards adopted." It is also possible that Hotchkiss as an individual had inordinate influence. Douglas Southall Freeman intimated that Hotchkiss's reconnaissance skills and innate sense of terrain were key components of Stonewall Jackson's success. While discussing Jackson's less than stellar performance during the Seven Days' Battles, Freeman noted that Hotchkiss was mapping the Shenandoah Valley at the time, and "with Hotchkiss away, Jackson was not blinded, but his vision was dimmed."[57]

Whatever the degree or source of its influence on tactical planning, engineer reconnaissance did not cease when bullets started flying. Battlefield staff operations will be discussed in chapter 10, but engineers continued scouting throughout combat. Their scouting prowess also contributed to postbattle activities, especially retreats, when they had time and safer conditions under which to conduct their missions than in a pursuit. For example, Blackford related the orders he received when Stuart returned from a meeting with Lee after Antietam: "[He] told me to proceed at once and examine the Potomac River in our rear above the regular ford near Shepherdstown, and find, if possible, a ford by which cavalry could cross, and that I must do this without making inquiries among citizens; that if such a crossing could be found, to place some men at it and station a line of men at intervals of a couple of hundred yards along the route leading to the place so that I could guide a column of cavalry to it in the dark without fail, and that I must report to him by sundown."[58]

Mapmaking was closely related to reconnaissance and often a product of that activity. The antebellum South was poorly mapped—there was no great demand for maps and thus no need to produce them. The best prewar map of Virginia was a nine-sheet rendering on a scale of five miles to the inch first published in 1827 and reissued with corrections in 1859. The same map was also available after 1859 on a single sheet at a scale of ten miles to the inch. The war provided a terrific stimulus to mapmaking. Both the Union and Confederate armies quickly set about mapping the areas in which they operated or planned to operate. There was no specific provision for drawing, reproducing, or supplying maps in the organization of the Confederate War Department—that function fell naturally to the engineers. Although early in the war some map reproduction occurred directly in the Engineer Bureau offices, the Army of Northern Virginia deserves credit for establishing the Confederacy's Map Bureau. In June 1862 Walter H. Stevens, Lee's chief engineer, sent Captain Albert H. Campbell, one of his assistants, to Richmond to establish a map-reproduction facility for the army. Campbell's operation grew, began supporting requests from outside the Army of Northern Virginia, and eventually became the government Map Bureau. By the end of 1862 the Map Bureau was producing lithographed maps of the general theaters of war and a variety of 1:40,000– and 1:80,000–scale county maps. They even pioneered some early use of photography for map reproduction. Jackson's chief of engineers, James K. Boswell, who visited the bureau in 1863, was pleasantly surprised to find "very good maps of various counties in the state." He took some back with him.[59]

Although significant, the Map Bureau could not come close to filling the cartographic demand, especially the need for detailed local maps that facilitated military operations. Maps remained scarce in the Army of Northern Virginia throughout the war. Frederick M. Colston, an ordnance officer setting off on a mission in March 1865, remarked, "Before leaving, Colonel Baldwin had given me the map used at headquarters, and which was issued only to corps commanders and heads of departments."[60] Since supplying maps from a central facility could not fill the need, field engineers had to take up the slack.

All engineer officers did some mapping and pitched in to copy maps when the need was critical, but the topographical task quickly developed into a specialty. The Army of Northern Virginia and its corps headquarters established more or less formal topographical engineering sections. Hotchkiss, Jackson's topographer and one of the premier Confederate mapmakers, and others spent most of their time gathering data and drawing or making copies of maps. Hotchkiss's journal is littered with entries like "Worked at Map and reconnoitering, as usual." Topographical engineers rode over and actually surveyed (if time and assets permitted) terrain, sketching as they went. An engineer conducting such a survey usually took one or two couriers or assistants along; they would ride off to nearby farmhouses to ask the name of local landmarks while the topographer sketched. If mapmakers could not get access to the terrain, they bought or borrowed existing maps and talked to anyone who knew the area in question. Once the topographical engineer gathered the data for his map, he spent days combining sketches and other bits of information and rescaling the drawing. Other qualified engineers or clerks checked and verified all work. If the map included troop positions or movements (such as maps drawn to accompany after-action reports), the commanding general approved the draft before final processing. The topography section spent days copying and coloring the resulting map by hand—one small square at a time—and adjusting the scale if necessary as they went to produce a single copy of the finished map. The product could be reproduced in limited numbers by hand if needed immediately; otherwise, it went into the section's map file, where it served as a reference and formed the basis for other maps. Using that method in January 1863, Hotchkiss took thirteen days to gather the information, produce the draft, and gain Jackson's approval for a relatively simple map of the frontline trace. Confederate engineers stayed on the Manassas battlefield a full month surveying and preparing maps of the first battle there. Hotchkiss's survey alone for the Chancellorsville report map took a week and required the assistance of a detail of several soldiers. Considering the effort involved, it is a wonder that Jackson told Hotchkiss, "Do not be afraid of making too many."[61]

As the war progressed, map libraries grew in the various headquarters, and engineers, by consulting their own files or borrowing from other topographers, had increasingly reliable sources of data from which to construct their maps. Time spent sketching the ground thus decreased; however, gathering data even by borrowing from existing files still consumed effort. Hotchkiss consulted Blackford's map library to obtain information for his after-action report map of Fredericksburg, a process that took most of a day. (Hotchkiss socialized while Blackford's clerks copied the map he wanted.) In another instance, Hotchkiss borrowed maps from Lee's engineer, and his whole section spent the next day and a half copying what they needed so they could return the originals. Despite the time and energy required to make even a simple map, the engineers of the Army of Northern Virginia turned them out in respectable quantity. Hotchkiss reported producing 101 different maps in 1864 alone, not including sketches and copies.[62]

Such a labor-intensive method of producing maps resulted in increasing allocation of manpower to the effort. Blackford got two assistants in the winter of 1862–63, and with their assignment could begin a map library. He later hired a civilian assistant or clerk at ninety dollars a month to copy maps. By midwar, Hotchkiss was running a small section comprising himself and as many as three clerks and draftsmen. Hauling around such an operation with its associated drafting tables, equipment, and map libraries strained limited transportation assets. It is thus not surprising that as the war dragged on Hotchkiss and his mapping section spent more and more time operating from a fixed base in Staunton. Hotchkiss passed most of the winter of 1864–65 living at home, while his men worked at an office he rented.[63]

Obviously, not every circumstance demanded a formal map, and most immediate tactical situations could not wait for the engineers to grind through the tedious process of mapmaking. The solution was the battle-field sketch. Few Rebel engineers were as bold (or stupid) as the Yankee topographer who set up his drafting table in front of the Yorktown (April 5–May 3, 1862) works and began sketching—he was killed by an artillery round fired by a Confederate gunner who did not like his insolence—but sketching could be done in a less ostentatious and much safer manner.[64] Hotchkiss claimed that Jackson "was quick in comprehending topographical features. I made it a point, nevertheless, to be always ready to give him a graphic representation of any particular point of the region where operations were going on, making a rapid sketch of the topography in his presence, and using different colored pencils for greater clearness in the definition of different surface features."[65] Elsewhere, Hotchkiss described the process for a specific instance. His journal entry for May 8, 1862, the date of the Battle of McDowell during the valley campaign, reads: "Having reached the summit [of Bull-Pasture Mountain] I took Gen. Jackson out to the right of the gap to the end of a rocky spur overlooking Bull-Pasture Valley and showed him the enemy in position near McDowell. At the same time, he looking on, I made him a map of McDowell and vicinity, showing the enemy's position, as in full view below us."[66]

Mobility and countermobility operations were also major engineer functions. The report of an artillery officer during the Cold Harbor campaign describes a typical mobility operation. "Under Colonel [Henry C.] Cabell's instructions and with the aid of the division pioneer corps, I opened roads through the woods for the more rapid and convenient transmission of artillery ammunition, and put up two or three little bridges across ravines with the same view." Bridge building and destruction were commonplace and were certainly not the exclusive province of the engineers. E. Porter Alexander, at the time the army's chief of ordnance, and his assistant spent a night on a raft under a stone arch bridge over Bull Run mining holes and placing five hundred–pound charges to drop the span. That was typical of engineer officer duty; however, engineer officers usually had their own or detailed infantry troops along to do the dirty work under the bridges. Hotchkiss took a cavalry escort (which he claimed was drunk on applejack) with him when he set out to burn two bridges in the spring of 1862, and Blackford did the same when he destroyed the railroad bridge at Catlett's Station. On the construction side, Hotchkiss once proposed constructing temporary bridges based on wagon beds, a suggestion Jackson accepted, detailing an engineer with impressed slave labor to execute it.[67]

Delineating and preparing field defensive positions was a final major engineer task. One of Lee's first acts after assuming command of the Army of Northern Virginia was to dispatch his engineers to examine its disposition, rearrange the positions as necessary, and oversee the work of construction parties reinforcing the defense. Orders to Major Walter Smith told him to find and establish a defensive line—not necessarily continuous but strengthened as necessary at critical points—and gave authority to requisition troops and tools for construction. Smith reported the next day with his plan, which Lee approved while taking the opportunity to give the young engineer specific instructions about spades, shovels, and picks and about how to deal with the York River Railroad. Engineers could become high-handed about their responsibilities for designing defensive positions. Porter Alexander said the engineers who laid out the positions on Missionary Ridge ignored the wishes of commanders on the ground (except one brigade commander who convinced the engineer to allow him to position his own line) and constructed that fatally flawed defensive position according to their own design or instructions from on high. Conversely, commanders often overrode or ignored good engineering advice. Boswell, Jackson's chief of engineers, commented in his diary, "Spent the day [January 5, 1863] on Genl. [D. H.] Hill's line, who interferes as usual and insists on acting as [his own] engineer. I am disgusted and will let him take his own way." Boswell also thought Brigadier General Robert E. Rodes ignored sound engineer advice, writing: "Spent the day building a battery for Genl. Rodes on the river. He wishes me to build breastworks eight feet high along the river bank. I think it perfectly useless; talked with Genl. Jackson about it; he agrees with me, but says that Genl. Rodes can put up such works as he thinks best." Sometimes when commanders and engineers disagreed about emplacements, the engineers persisted and proved to be right. Alexander related a story about laying out the gun pits on Marye's Heights at Fredericksburg with Captain Samuel Johnston, one of Lee's engineers. Alexander convinced Johnston to position the pits further forward than originally intended. Alexander had to "take the cussin" with Johnston when Lee inspected the lines, but the positions proved their worth in the battle that followed.[68]

General orders prescribed the system for laying out and marking defensive positions, and in at least some cases engineers of the Army of Northern Virginia followed those instructions precisely. Blackford described selecting, occupying, and constructing the trench line at Cold Harbor in 1864 as follows:

> The work had to be done at night, of course, as it was in close proximity to the enemy. During the day the ground was thoroughly examined with our glasses, and as soon as it was dark enough, a long cord was stretched all along the front, and on this cord at intervals of a few feet white bits of cotton cloth were tied to render the position of the cord visible. Picked men held the cord in their hands at intervals of fifteen or twenty feet, and about one hundred feet in distance from each other were placed Engineer officers. Each officer was directed to advance his part of the line a certain number of paces, these directions having been previously ascertained by daylight either by estimation or triangulation. The cord was thus carried forward silently, the men crouching low to avoid the incessant skirmish fire of the enemy. After the line officers had reached their assigned distances, by pacing, the line was then carefully inspected, and advanced or retired as deemed judicious. After this was done, the fact was reported to the infantry commanders, and the work details bearing picks and shovels as well as their arms moved silently forward until they struck the stretched cord, with the little white fluttering tags, held up by the men of our [engineer] regiment a couple of feet above the ground. Along the cord the infantry line was formed and went to work with a will getting themselves covered before daylight revealed their position to the enemy. As soon as the infantry line was formed, the cord was taken away and rolled up for use elsewhere.[69]

In terms of the siege and countersiege operations that dominated engineer work around Richmond and Petersburg during the final phase of the war, the great French engineer of two hundred years earlier, Sebastien le Prestre de Vauban, would have been comfortable with the activities of his counterparts in the Army of Northern Virginia. They constructed extensive earthwork fortifications using slave labor so lavishly that it was expedient to preprint and mass produce labor vouchers. Besides building fortifications, Confederate engineers also undertook more active defensive measures. For example, they aggressively countermined in areas where the enemy was likely to try to dig under the entrenchments. That countermining effort failed to detect the federal mine that produced the Crater (July 30, 1864); nevertheless, it was well organized. An engineer captain, Hugh Thomas Douglas, was charged with directing countermining. He wrote formal instructions on construction of countermine galleries—length, depth, grade, drainage, and so forth.—and procedures for listening and reporting evidence of Union mining. He also issued detailed instructions on organizing countermining teams and set up two fifteen-man daily shifts per mine.[70] It is fair to conclude that

Army of Northern Virginia engineers practiced the traditional siegecraft of their day.

Engineers, of course, did various miscellaneous tasks not directly associated with their primary duties. The Army of Northern Virginia's 1st Engineer Regiment served a temporary stint as prison guards in Richmond in 1864. Later that year, Hotchkiss sent one of his assistant topographers to lead a party charged with repairing telegraph lines near Harrisonburg. Generally, though, the engineers concentrated on engineering tasks. Although the irascible Early declared, "The main use I had for a pioneer corps was to bury dead Yankees and horses," most commanders found their engineers to be useful and necessary additions to the staff and army.[71]

THE SIGNAL CORPS

The Confederate Congress established the Signal Corps in April 1862 with an authorized strength of ten officers and ten sergeants. The legislators let the secretary of war decide whether this embryonic agency should serve under the Adjutant and Inspector General Department or the Corps of Engineers, a decision ultimately made in favor of the former. At the bureau level in Richmond, the Signal Corps managed the Confederate signal and cipher systems, manufactured or procured signal and cipher equipment, and ran a strategic intelligence operation that smuggled information, newspapers, packages, letters, and people into and out of enemy territory. In the field armies, they operated semaphore systems, provided cipher support, did limited signals interception and decoding, and provided tactical and operational intelligence.[72]

The primary mission of the Signal Corps was to pass messages using the rudimentary semaphore system developed by the U.S. Army in the immediate prewar years. The signal officer's job was to position small parties of signalmen, armed with flags for use during the day and lanterns during the night, on terrain that offered visibility between stations. Properly sited on favorable terrain, the system could transmit messages rapidly—certainly faster than a courier could travel on horseback. For example, one signal officer claimed his line could send messages fifteen miles through six stations in twenty minutes. At a time when the limits of the fixed telegraph network made it impractical for anything but strategic communications and Southern armies, lacking the materials for extensive use of field telegraphy, depended on mounted couriers to transmit most of their communications, the Signal Corps' semaphore system was potentially invaluable. By the time Confederate commanders recognized this fact, however, signalmen had already proven their worth in the field. Captain E. Porter Alexander had participated in experiments with signaling before resigning from the U.S. Army. He organized, trained, and equipped a small signal detachment for General Beauregard's force and provided invaluable tactical intelligence during the first Battle of Manassas.[73]

The performance of Porter Alexander's signal detachment during and after First Manassas provided ample evidence for any skeptics. Sent from Richmond to give Beauregard's forces in Northern Virginia the benefit of his limited signal expertise, Alexander organized a small communications unit by convincing Longstreet and David R. Jones each to detail ten to twelve intelligent privates for signal duty. Using equipment he had procured or fabricated in Richmond, Alexander trained his men, conducted reconnaissances, selected positions, and established signal stations to support the army's deployment along Bull Run. From the vantage point of the station on Wilcoxen Hill during the battle, Alexander spotted the Union flanking movement against the Confederate left. He signaled the brigade commander on the threatened flank, "Look out for your left. You are flanked," and dispatched couriers to Beauregard with the same warning. After the battle, Alexander established signal stations to link forward outposts to the main army lurking outside Washington and to support Rebel agents inside the city. For his efforts, Alexander received glowing mention in Beauregard's official report of the battle, and Adjutant General Samuel Cooper offered him the position of head of the Confederate signal service. Unwilling to leave the army in the field, Alexander turned down the offer to head the Signal Corps, but the performance of his ad hoc organization had made its mark.[74] There was suddenly a great demand for signal detachments.

Unfortunately, the Confederate Signal Corps did not expand rapidly enough to fill the perceived need. In April 1862 Jackson wrote to Longstreet from his position in the Shenandoah Valley asking to borrow a man "who understands Alexander's system of signals." Apparently receiving no assistance from Longstreet, Jackson turned a few days later to Lee: "Please send me part of Alexander's signal corps, if you can spare it; if not, please send me the system of signals, so that I may have persons instructed. The enemy's signals give him a great advantage over me." Lee responded promptly, "Two signal-men have been ordered to you. They can readily instruct as many as you may require." This expedient solved Jackson's immediate problem, but the technique of home-growing signalmen eventually became an issue. Theoretically, the size of the Signal Corps tripled in September 1862 to a total authorization of sixty-one officers and men, but as with the initial authorization, the legal expansion lagged considerably behind events in the field. One authority estimates that 1,500 men served as Confederate signalmen during the war. Eventually, the Confederacy had a regular Signal Corps and a two-company-sized independent signal system operating along the James River from Norfolk to Petersburg. One signal officer and as many signal sergeants or detailed men as were necessary served with each army, corps, and division headquarters. In January 1863 Adjutant General Cooper felt compelled to publish a general order prohibiting anyone except properly appointed signal officers from performing signal duties and promising to assign a qualified officer to any general who needed one.[75]

The flat, wooded terrain of the peninsula limited the effectiveness of the semaphore system, and its early sponsor, Alexander, abandoned his signal duties to concentrate on a career as an artilleryman—a track he had been pursuing for some time in his position as both ordnance and signal officer for the army. However, when the fighting returned to the more favorable terrain of Northern Virginia, the Signal Corps again began to contribute directly to the campaigns. Captain Joseph L. Bartlett reported that on the field at Second Manassas (August 29–30, 1862) he operated from Lee's headquarters on the Warrenton Pike, sending and receiving messages the two miles to Jackson's position. When Lee moved, Bartlett displaced his signal station to support the new head-quarters location. In the subsequent Antietam campaign, signal stations with the Confederate units on Loudon Heights and Maryland Heights were the main reason Jackson could coordinate the encirclement of Harper's Ferry. The Signal Corps, through the station with McLaws's division on Maryland Heights, also provided Jackson contact with Lee to supplement the stream of couriers between the two commanders. Some unmentioned staff officer, probably Captain Bartlett, Jackson's signal officer, obviously organized and coordinated this complex communications effort. After the retreat from Maryland, Lee made efforts to extend the signal line through Thornton's Gap so he could remain in contact with Jackson's forces and rued the deficiency in signalmen that hindered the task.[76]

The mountains that separated the Shenandoah Valley from the rest of Virginia were an obstacle to other forms of communications, but they provided the Signal Corps exactly the type of terrain needed for its work. Jackson got good service from his signalmen there, and Early did the same during his 1864 valley campaign. While camped at Fisher's Hill, Early established (and later fought several sharp skirmishes to maintain) a signal station on Three Top Mountain, a spur of Massanutten Mountain near Strasburg, from which he could establish communications with Richard H. Anderson's forces in the Luray Valley.[77]

As with any communications network, there were occasional abuses of the Confederate signal system. Not all the message traffic was strictly official. Major General Stephen D. Ramseur, commanding a division, got a message before the Battle of Cedar Creek: "Wigwagged from station to station down the Valley from Staunton, it read simply, 'The crisis is over and all is well.'" This cryptic message announced the birth of his daughter.[78] Doubtless, other such messages passed between signal stations during the war.

Besides passing official and unofficial messages, the Signal Corps served an important function, perhaps more valued at the time than its contribution in the field of communications, as an intelligence-collection asset. The vital staff function of collecting and evaluating intelligence will be examined in detail in chapter 10, but some discussion of the Signal Corps' role in that effort is appropriate here. Located by necessity on high ground that commanded views of the surrounding terrain and provided with powerful telescopes to see flags on distant peaks, a signal station was also perfectly situated and equipped to observe enemy activity. Both armies exploited this capability and used some signal stations exclusively in that role rather than for passing message traffic.[79] From their lofty peaks, signalmen gathered tactical and operational intelligence, but their contribution to strategic intelligence came from the unlikely function of the corps as the Confederate spymasters.

The practice of using the Signal Corps to handle spies and strategic intelligence began very early in the war and stemmed from two separate conditions: the lack of a formal intelligence agency and the problem of communicating with agents on enemy soil. The Signal Corps offered a potential solution to the communications problem, and there was no competing staff department to assume the function of handling agents, so the entire field of strategic intelligence fell to the Signal Corps by default. Major William Norris, chief of the Signal Corps, established and operated a system of spies and agents in the North known as the Secret Line that was controlled by the Signal Corps' Secret Service Bureau from the back room of Norris's offices in Richmond. Norris's methods impressed British observer Arthur Fremantle, although Lee viewed some reports of Union troop strength he received from Richmond skeptically. However, Lee did not have to rely exclusively on Major Norris's clandestine operations for strategic intelligence—the general ran his own signal officers across the Potomac to report on enemy troop movements. The practice of using signal officers as agents and agent handlers was well established in the Army of Northern Virginia. Alexander recruited agents and devised communications methods for agents already in place while he was Joe Johnston's signal officer. Alexander's memoirs outline the complex scheme he conceived to pass instructions and receive messages from an agent on Capitol Hill. Alexander called one operative in his net "an instructed signal observer" and praised another for passing in and out of enemy lines for several months. Later, Lee kept a permanent observation post in position to overlook the Potomac and maintained a line of signal stations from that post to the telegraph station at Fredericksburg so he could keep abreast of federal shipping and troop movements. During the early stages of the Gettysburg campaign, Lee directed A. P. Hill to order a signal officer on the Potomac "to discover what is doing on the Potomac and at Aquia."[80] Such activity by its signalmen, along with other sources, kept the Army of Northern Virginia apprised of the theater strategic situation.

At the operational level, in modern terminology the arena below strategy where military commanders craft campaigns from battles to achieve their objectives, as distinct from the tactical maneuvers on the battlefield, the Signal Corps also contributed to the intelligence available to the Army of Northern Virginia. General Lee based some of his maneuver decisions during the Second Manassas campaign on information from the signal station on Clark's Mountain. During the Gettysburg campaign, Major General Alfred Pleasanton, the Union cavalry commander, complained that "the gaps in the Blue Ridge are guarded, and from their signal stations they can see every man we bring against them." In September 1863, Brigadier General William Pendleton wrote his wife that the signal stations were reporting significant Union troop movements, and the Army of Northern Virginia was preparing to move to counter. Signalmen on Clark's Mountain detected and reported by flag to Richard Ewell's nearby headquarters for relay to Lee the initial Union movements that opened the Wilderness campaign. Lee's subordinate commanders also exploited operational intelligence from signal stations and even planned their campaigns to avoid revealing their movements to federal stations. While detached to the Army of Tennessee outside Chattanooga, Longstreet used his signalmen to observe the town of Bridgeport and operate a signal line from their observation post to his headquarters. However, he said that the fact that "General Bragg denied all reports sent him of the enemy from my signal party" negated the value of the information thus gained. When returning from the Chambersburg raid in October 1862, Stuart assumed that the federal signal station on Sugar Loaf Mountain would observe his march and used a deceptive route to cause the pursuing Union forces to concentrate in the wrong place.[81] Such examples show the utility of information obtained by the Signal Corps in planning and executing campaigns.

At least one authority believes that the Confederate Signal Corps' primary contribution as an information gatherer for the Army of Northern Virginia was at the operational level; however, it also provided tactical intelligence when the terrain suited. The most obvious example is First Manassas, where signalmen "maintained their position in the maintenance of their duties—the transmission of signal messages of the enemy's movements—for several hours under fire." But First Manassas was not the only battlefield on which Rebel "flag floppers," as they were derisively called by their comrades in arms, contributed. As one example, after the Maryland campaign of 1862, Stuart cited his signal officer, Captain Richard E. Frayser, for rendering "important services to the Commanding General from a mountain overlooking the enemy on the Antietam." At Fredericksburg just before the famous battle, Longstreet established a signal line to keep the forward divisions in "rapid communication" with his pickets—a tactical use of signal if ever there was one.[82]

When the terrain or situation did not offer the long-range vision the Signal Corps needed for either communications or intelligence gathering, its members became couriers, scouts, or agents. It is instructive that in the dense vegetation on the Chancellorsville battlefield a signal sergeant, William E. Cunliffe, was killed by the same friendly volley that brought down Stonewall Jackson, who slumped from his saddle and was caught by his signal officer, Captain Robert E. Wilbourn.[83] Those signalmen were certainly accompanying Jackson on his reconnaissance in their secondary roles as courier and staff officer, respectively.

Because of their value in both the communications and intelligence collection arenas, signal stations became high-value targets. There were a series of sharp skirmishes in the opening phase of the Antietam campaign over the signal station on Sugar Loaf Mountain. Stuart attacked the federal station on Fairview Mountain early in the Chambersburg raid in October 1862 to better his chances of conducting the raid undetected. The Rebel cavalry commander also lost his nephew and signal officer, Captain J. Hardeman Stuart, during Second Manassas when the signalman, unhorsed while leading an abortive raid on the U.S. signal station at View Tree, decided to join Longstreet's ranks as an infantryman. General Early fought a series of sharp skirmishes over his signal station on Three Top Mountain—losing and regaining the position several times before eventually sending a force of a hundred infantrymen to settle the issue.[84]

Besides the vulnerability of their mountaintop stations to attack, another major problem with the wigwag signal system used by the Signal Corps was its susceptibility to interception. A signalman standing on a mountaintop could be seen as easily by the enemy as by the station for which his message was intended. It did not take long to discover that couriers and telegraph lines were equally vulnerable. Authorities decided they had to encode messages, especially those sent by flag or telegraph. Of course, codes were not a new innovation. Although not initially used for signaling, cipher systems sprang up in the Army of Northern Virginia almost simultaneously with the outbreak of hostilities. In October 1861 Secretary of War Judah P. Benjamin sent Major General Joseph Johnston, commanding the Confederate Army of the Potomac—the army later renamed the Army of Northern Virginia—a letter forwarding a coded note in the belief that "Colonel [Thomas] Jordan has a key which will decipher it."[85] Jordan, who was still serving as Beauregard's AAG and chief of staff, responded, "The note in cipher was addressed to me— that is, to Thomas John Rayford, a name I adopted before leaving Washington, for purposes of cipher correspondence with Mrs. [Rose O'Neal] Greenhow, by whom the note was probably written. . . . The cipher I arranged last April. Being my first attempt, and hastily devised, it may be deciphered by an expert, as I found after use of it for some time."[86] Jordan went on to inform the secretary that he had devised another, presumably better, cipher system for use by Mrs. Greenhow but had not delivered it before her arrest. The situation was out of control if individuals in the field were inventing and using private codes so that messages received in Richmond had to be sent to the field for decoding. The solution was for the Confederacy to adopt a standardized cipher system. The design and control of that system fell to the Signal Corps.

Although the bureau in Richmond designed the cipher system, implementation and training necessarily fell to signal staff officers in the field. To aid them in this task, the Signal Bureau published and distributed a confidential training pamphlet. The basis of the cipher system was a key word or phrase and a simple matrix of letters. To encode a message, one simply wrote the key phrase repeatedly, wrote the message below it, and entered the matrix using the letter of the key word along the top and the corresponding letter of the message down the side to find the coded letter at the intersection of line and column. Signalmen were taught the system and entrusted with the key word, which changed periodically to avoid compromise. After training their men, division signal staff officers were required to also instruct the adjutant of every regiment in their division about the signal system. The same general order urged all general officers to have their aides and assistant adjutants general trained as well. Since there was little reason for those staff officers to learn the wig-wag system, the intent of the order was likely to facilitate cipher training, although it is unclear what coded messages regimental adjutants needed to send. Walter Taylor claimed that he personally encrypted and decoded all the telegraphic correspondence between General Lee and President Davis. He even complained about being forced to decode non-critical messages.[87] Taylor, an assistant adjutant general, not a signal officer, must have learned the code system from the army signal officer.

The Confederacy's cipher system produced mixed results. There was occasional confusion, as when Lee's headquarters had to telegraph to Davis's aide, "The President's telegram cannot be deciphered. Has the key word been changed lately?" Such confusion was compounded when operators made mistakes in transmitting messages. Also, a large and apparently effective cottage industry dedicated to cryptography sprang up on both sides of the Mason-Dixon line concurrent with the introduction of ciphers. The Yankees read Rebel codes with disturbing ease. For example, a Union signal station intercepted and deciphered the message announcing the initial Union moves in the Wilderness campaign mentioned above. However, breaking codes was not one sided. In August 1864, Lee sent Early a copy of "the enemy's signal alphabet as deciphered by some of our signal corps here."[88] Lee felt compelled to have his aide warn Early, "We read [the enemy's] messages with facility, and the general thinks it may be of service to you, but advises that care be taken to conceal the fact of our knowledge of the alphabet. The enemy also reads our messages and the general suggests that your signal men be put on their guard to prevent the enemy obtaining information by that means."[89] General Early must have taken the warning seriously, since for the benefit of eavesdropping Union signalmen he began sending deceptive messages implying that Longstreet's corps was rushing to his aid. Finally, as Lee's message shows, the Army of Northern Virginia considered its ability to read enemy messages an important secret. Signal officers occasionally risked compromising that secret by disclosing intercepted material to unauthorized people. Before Chancellorsville, Lee learned that information from an intercepted message only he was supposed to have seen was being discussed in Brigadier General James H. Lane's brigade of A. P. Hill's division. Lee had Jackson trace the leak and at least temporarily relieved the offending signal officer, Captain R. H. T. Smith.[90] That incident got intertwined with the Jackson-Hill squabble, and Lee eventually backed off relieving the signal officer, but the episode demonstrated one of the vulnerabilities of the infant cipher and interception system.

Although not a direct responsibility of the signal officer, the telegraph also deserves mention. When the location of the Army of Northern Virginia headquarters was convenient to a telegraph line, electronic transmission became a primary means of communication for messages suitable for that media. The postmaster general supervised the Confederacy's telegraph system, and the operators at normal stations were civilians. Standing orders required army commanders who wanted to change stations or operators to request such changes through the postmaster general. In practice, telegraph support was usually obtained by communicating through military channels or directly with the superintendent of the local telegraph company. For example, in May 1864, when General Lee set up the Army of Northern Virginia headquarters at Atlee, he requested an operator from the superintendent of the South Telegraph Company through military, not postmaster general, channels. Frequently, the best way to get access to the telegraph was to establish a special military station or line. When the army established lines for its own purposes, the law required it to pay the civilian operators at the rate prescribed by the postmaster general for operators under his control.[91]

However, not all telegraph operators with the army were civilians. General Beauregard had field telegraph lines strung from his headquarters to the different outposts that kept watch on Washington, D.C., after First Manassas. During the Petersburg siege, tactical telegraph lines ran at least to some of the division headquarters. It is reasonable to assume that the operators for such lines were soldiers. Heros Von Borcke claimed, "General Stuart was always accompanied by his own telegraph operator, who had no difficulty in connecting his portable instrument at any point on the wires, and could thus read off and reply to messages *in transitu*." To add credence to Von Borcke's claim, Stuart added a memorandum to his Gettysburg report praising "my field telegraph operator (J. Thompson Quarles)," and a student of Stuart's staff found records of Private Thompson J. Quarles, "chief of field telegraph," and a man named Sheppard, who also served as Stuart's telegraph operator. Having a chief of field telegraph implies there was someone for the chief to supervise, so Lee's cavalry commander may have kept a small group of telegraphers close at hand. The parole of ten "Confederate States military telegraph operators connected with the Army of Northern Virginia" would suggest that Lee kept a substantial group of telegraphers himself, although it is difficult to determine if they were soldiers or civilian operators who habitually supported the army.[92] For purposes of this study, the importance of the telegraph and how it served the Army of Northern Virginia is simply that someone—certainly a staff officer, either the signal officer or assistant adjutant general—had to control and coordinate the activities of the telegraph operators supporting the army.

The signal officer, chief of ordnance, chief of artillery, and chief of engineers comprised what we would call today the special staff of the army. Together, the general and special staff could perform the major functions associated with supporting an army logistically and administratively and providing necessary combat support; however, some essential staff functions did not fall within the areas of expertise of the officers discussed so far. The personal staff of the general performed those functions.

Chapter 5

PERSONAL STAFF IN THE
ARMY OF NORTHERN VIRGINIA

AIDES-DE-CAMP

Although a formally authorized member of the staff, the duties of an aide-de-camp were surprisingly poorly defined. Outside of the provision that "General Officers appoint their own Aides-de-Camp," the regulations contained no description of an aide's responsibilities or duties. This omission was probably intentional, since traditionally aides are the most personal of staff officers, and even today their duties are always what generals decide they should be. Customarily, aides took care of the personal needs of their generals, delivered messages, and performed whatever other duties might be required. The Confederacy eventually settled on an authorization of two aides per general officer with ranks varying according to the rank of the general.[1]

Aides may not have had formally prescribed duties, but it is possible to determine what contemporaries believed to be their proper function. Since there were servants, cooks, and orderlies aplenty at headquarters to care for a general's personal needs, his aides' only real use was as a messenger during battle. P. G. T. Beauregard seems to have vested the transmission of orders exclusively with aides. His report on First Manassas implies that he considered E. Porter Alexander to have essentially changed duties in midbattle when the latter began carrying messages: "Capt. E. P. Alexander, C. S. Engineers, gave me seasonable and material assistance early in the day with his system of signals. . . . Later, Captain Alexander acted as my aide-de-camp in the transmission of orders and in observation of the enemy." D. H. Hill seemed to make a similar distinction in a letter to his wife: "I wrote Joseph [Hill] yesterday letting him [know] that I would give him the posn of Military Secretary. . . . He would have about four hours writing daily and would be my Aid in battle."[2] In a letter about staff organization to the chairman of the Senate Committee on Military Affairs, Robert E. Lee commented, "In the field all the members of the staff departments can perform the duties of aides. Off the field the aides have less duty than officers of the staff departments. . . . It is better, I think, to give more strength to the adjutant and inspector generals' department and to diminish the aides."[3] Lee apparently based his assessment on observation of his own aides. According to Walter Taylor, the commanding general's aides did almost no work around the headquarters. Taylor felt he had to impose on friendship and on Charles Venable's good nature to get the aide to help with paperwork at all (although Venable pitched in when Taylor was absent). Taylor expressed the perceived difference between aides and assistant adjutants general when he wrote, "I am afraid I am sometimes envious or selfish when I see these good fellows [the aides] without a care and with not enough to do to annoy or hurt them, but I cannot grumble *now*, this being one of the bad effects of my promotion [to lieutenant colonel in the adjutant general corps], heretofore being a gentlemanly A. D. C. I could quarrel to my heart's content, as I was required to perform duties not legitimately mine—now I must grin & endure it." Not until 1865 did Lee recognize the maldistribution of work in his staff and have Taylor delegate some of the paperwork to the aides.[4]

Lee's were not the only aides who performed their primary function in battle and were underemployed at other times. Thomas Goree, James Longstreet's aide throughout the war, commented, "The most of the other generals permit their staffs to remain idle except in a fight, but Genl. Longstreet tries to keep his in employment. One he has to act as quartermaster for the brigade, another as commissary, another as provost marshal, and myself as ordnance officer. Mine is about the easiest position of all."[5] Goree was not precise with his use of terms, but it is evident that Longstreet was having his aides assist the general staff and special staff or fill vacancies to keep them busy while they waited for the next battle.

The performance of the staff, and thus also aides, in battle will be discussed in chapter 10. To explain why this breed of staff officer existed, it is sufficient here to quote General Richard B. Ewell: "I send my aide because it is impossible to write or forsee every point that arises."[6] Unlike a courier, who delivered written messages, an aide was expected to be familiar with the situation and his commander's intent and to be able to answer questions and clear up confusion.

Despite their rather innocuous duties, or perhaps because of them, aides-de-camp caused no end of debate and political turmoil. The Confederate military and government squabbled endlessly about the proper number and rank of aides for a general. The practice of appointing aides based solely on the desires of the general they would serve led naturally to abuses. Braxton Bragg wrote of "a system of favoritism and nepotism"; Senator Edward Sparrow explained to his colleagues during debate on a bill to restrict aides to the rank of captain or lower that generals appointed their friends as aides and "there was objection to confer[ing] upon men thus chosen such high rank as was now provided by law."[7] Jefferson Davis explained to the Senate that he was defying the law and giving newly appointed aides no higher rank than lieutenants because "it has been the practice, because of their personal and confidential relations to their chief, to appoint upon his nomination. To this there seems to be no paramount objection, while the rank of such officers is of the subaltern grade; but if they have high rank, for many and obvious considerations, their selection cannot be controlled by the personal preferences of the general with whom they are to serve." The president told both houses nearly a year earlier in a veto message, "The number and rank of aides-de-camp allowed by the bill are believed to be greatly in excess of those allowed by other governments and quite unsuited to the nature of ours. They would rather impede than improve the service. They would encourage love of ostentation and feed fondness for vain display, which should rather be discouraged than fostered."[8]

Despite the president's hearty disapproval, there was an easy way around both Davis and Congress for any general fond of surrounding himself with numerous aides. The practice of accepting volunteers on the staff was a simple means of securing aides in excess of the official authorization. Gentlemen, frequently politically powerful men who wanted to serve without the long-term commitment of enlistment, might volunteer to act as an aide to a general without pay or official status. They were usually given honorary rank roughly equivalent to their social position to facilitate dealing in a military environment. Volunteer aides were most common in the early days of the rebellion, when there was still a sense of glamour and excitement and no draft with which to contend, but the practice continued in isolated instances until relatively late in the war. A resolution to ban the use of volunteer aides was introduced in the Confederate Congress in August 1862 but never emerged from committee.[9]

Politicians were favorites as volunteer aides. General Beauregard had James Chesnut and William Porcher Miles, both South Carolina politicians with the honorary rank of colonel, with him at Manassas. Chesnut, perhaps more famous today for his diarist wife, Mary, had been a state congressman and senator on and off from 1840 to 1858, when he was appointed to a vacant U.S. Senate seat. He was a delegate to the South

Carolina Secession Convention and congressman in the Confederate Provisional Congress. After First Manassas, he served as aide to the president and commander of troops in South Carolina. Miles had served as mayor of Charleston, U.S. congressman, delegate to the secession convention, and on the Military Affairs Committee in the Confederate Provisional Congress. From 1862 to 1865 he returned to Congress as the chairman of the Military Affairs Committee: "Miles was P. G. T. Beauregard's major spokesman in Richmond." Besides these politicians, Beauregard had Alexander R. Chisolm, his regular aide, who served as a volunteer captain until formally appointed as a lieutenant in 1862. A contemporary observer, William M. Owen, who was as impressed by the buckets of mint juleps served at headquarters as the officers and seems to have mixed Joe Johnston's and Beauregard's staffs, commented that Johnston "also had a number of volunteer aides, all men of distinction. Ex-Governor James Chesnut, William Porcher Miles, Col. John S. Preston, and ex-Governor [John L.] Manning, a most charming gentleman." Alexander R. Boteler, an influential congressman from Winchester, Virginia, served as a colonel and volunteer aide to Stonewall Jackson when Congress was in recess. After Jackson's death, Boteler assumed a similar position as a volunteer aide to Jeb Stuart.[10]

Such politically powerful staff members were useful beyond their immediate duties on the battlefield. Beauregard's letter giving Alexander instructions about lobbying for additional artillery for the army included the suggestion, "Colonels Preston, Miles, and Chesnut may be able to help you." Beauregard also used his volunteer aides directly. While involved in a squabble with the Commissary and Quartermaster Departments, the general used Miles to get his grievances aired in Congress. His disclaimer to President Davis that the letter Colonel Miles read on the floor "was written only for the purpose of expediting matters" rings hollow. Beauregard also used his relationship with Miles to monitor the deliberations of the congressional committee on flags and to push his own idea about the design of the Confederate battle flag.[11]

Like Miles for Beauregard, Boteler served both Jackson and Stuart as a conduit to Congress, bypassing the formal chain of command. Jackson corresponded frankly with his volunteer aide when Boteler was sitting in Congress, telling the congressman, "As you are a member of my Staff, I write to you more freely than I would have further known." Only a fool would think correspondence from Jackson would remain totally confidential in Richmond, and Jackson was no fool. In fact, Boteler routinely passed correspondence he received from Jackson to the secretary of war, J. P. Benjamin. In at least one instance, Jackson went to Boteler in a direct attempt to urge Congress to adopt a policy that Jackson had discussed with Lee without getting a satisfactory answer.[12] While serving Stuart, Boteler passed a letter from a cavalry brigade commander to the secretary of war with the ingenuous caveat, "The letter was intended solely for my own information, and if by transmitting it to the Department I transgress any rule of the service or conventional propriety, I feel assured that a sufficient apology both to Colonel [John R.] Chambliss [Jr.] and yourself will be found in my anxious wish to promote the good of the service."[13] Both Chambliss and Boteler knew the War Department's strict regulations prohibiting correspondence with Richmond except through proper channels. To be fair to Boteler, he was not a simple political hack. When in the field, he performed a variety of tasks well for General Jackson. For example, in June 1862, while he and Jackson were traveling to Richmond at the beginning of the Seven Days' campaign, Boteler took dictation and fired off telegrams to headquarters on subjects from the movement of brigades to requisitions for battle flags.[14] On several battlefields, he carried messages gallantly, like any other aide.

Political volunteers could be useful for other purposes as well, especially in dealing with the border states. Jackson took Colonel S. Bassett French, a Marylander from Virginia governor John Letcher's office, with him as a volunteer aide on the 1862 invasion of Maryland. Judging from the failure of Maryland to rise when the Army of Northern Virginia marched onto its soil, French's political influence must not have been quite what Jackson hoped. In 1863, Jubal Early, commanding one of the leading divisions in the initial stages of Lee's second invasion of the north, had Mr. Lake, "a citizen of Maryland, who had been sent through the lines the day before our arrival," as a volunteer aide.[15] Lake may have had political connections, although in 1863 there was little hope of Maryland rising, and he may have been attached mainly as a guide.

However, all volunteer aides were not politicians. Occasionally, a wandering officer assigned elsewhere volunteered for temporary duty on the staff. Major John Tyler, who had been an aide to Major General Sterling Price in Arkansas and intended to return there, sent Price a report on the Army of Northern Virginia that included the information that he had "been riding with the staff of General Lee and so passed through the battles of the Wilderness, of Spotsylvania Court-House, and of those since fought here on the line of the Chickahominy." Especially early in the war, when the administrative system of officer appointments was sluggish at best, volunteering as an aide was often the only way to begin service on the staff. To cite examples from just one corps, G. Moxley Sorrel started his illustrious career as a volunteer aide to Longstreet; Goree did the same and waited until January 1862 for his regular appointment; Frank Terry and Thomas Lubbock, two Texans who traveled with Longstreet and Goree, stayed with the general for a time as volunteer aides before returning to their home state to fight; and both Thomas Walton and John Fairfax, long-serving staff officers, began their careers on Longstreet's staff as volunteers. As late as the Gettysburg campaign, reports still mention volunteer aides on Longstreet's staff. The individual in that instance, Captain Stephen Winthrop, went on to be regularly commissioned and serve as a staff officer with the artillery and in Lee's headquarters. And even in July 1864 the army assigned Captain T. G. Peacocke of the British army to George Pickett's staff as a volunteer aide-de-camp with "all the benefits of the law in regards to rations and forage to officers in the field."[16]

Besides politicians and officers awaiting regular appointments, the volunteer aides also included individuals who can only be classified as true volunteers. Perhaps most famous of these was Captain W. D. Farley, volunteer aide to Stuart from the beginning of the war until his death at Brandy Station in June 1863. A comrade said of Farley, "Promotions and commissions had been frequently offered him by the General, but he refused them all, preferring to be bound to no particular line of duty, but to fight, to use the American phrase 'on his own book.'" Less known and operating for only brief periods were individuals like a twelve-year-old boy named Randolph who delivered messages between Stuart and Jackson on the Antietam battlefield. John M. Daniel, a reporter for the *Richmond Examiner* who served briefly as a volunteer on A. P. Hill's staff during the Seven Days' Battles until slightly wounded at Gaines's Mill (June 27–28, 1862), may have been another such an individual, or he may have been a newspaperman looking for a story who got more than he bargained for.[17]

Of course, not all volunteer aides worked well, and getting rid of them was difficult because of their volunteer status. A Confederate officer wrote home about such a case, "A Very good thing happened here yesterday. In consequence of a Gen. Order from Lee, Division commanders all appointed enrolling officers to enroll all citizens following the Army as sutlers, volunteers etc. etc. Lewis Randolph, Signal Officer in the Division was the man selected by [Brigadier General Robert E.] Rodes, and he made an effort to catch Yancy, who had been hanging about Brigade Hd. Qrs. for some months in the capacity of volunteer aide, but he was on the lookout and escaped to Richmond. . . . The joke is so much relished in the Brigade in consequence of the utter worthlessness of the boy, that I could not help mentioning it."[18]

Overall, aides and volunteer aides were a motley crew that drew excessive political flack, but nobody ever suggested that the army should do without them.

JUDGE ADVOCATE GENERAL

Although the articles of war and army regulations laid out procedures for courts-martial, listed as offenses everything from use of profanity to treason, and prescribed harsh maximum punishments (for example, death for sounding a false alarm or giving away the watchword), there was initially no judge advocate assigned to field armies. The first posting of lawyers to field staffs was in October 1862, when Congress established standing military courts for each corps to relieve the pressure of forming courts-martial with line officers. In 1864 Secretary of War Seddon proposed adding a lieutenant colonel judge advocate to the staff of each army to evaluate in the field those cases that automatically required review. Congress never sanctioned that proposal in law, but the Army of Northern Virginia enacted it in practice. Henry E. Young, a major and assistant adjutant general on Lee's staff from at least July 1863, was addressed in correspondence as the judge advocate general of the Army of Northern Virginia. Major Young's duty position as listed on the Appomattox parole was also judge advocate general of the Army of Northern Virginia.[19] The staff judge advocate busied himself primarily with the administration and conduct of courts-martial and the military court system.

As distinct from the traditional courts-martial, the Confederate military court system was a response to the tremendous straggling that plagued the Army of Northern Virginia in the Maryland campaign of 1862. Searching for a way to improve discipline, Lee proposed the appointment of permanent courts for each corps. Lee hoped thereby to impose "Prompt and certain punishment of offenses . . . and it was impossible to accomplish this objective by convening courts-martial in the midst of active operations." The administration in Richmond supported its premier commander, and Jefferson Davis recommended the scheme to Congress in September 1862. Congress acted quickly to establish the courts, and in late December 1862 the adjutant general published orders announcing appointments. Composed of three judges chosen from outside the army, each military court had a captain who served as a permanent judge advocate, a clerk, and another captain called the provost marshal who performed as a bailiff. The courts had broad jurisdiction (although they could not try general officers) and were permanently in session. In May 1863 Congress extended the military court system to the military departments, and three acts in February 1864 added a court for cavalry divisions, clarified jurisdiction and provisions for review of proceedings when two or more corps were together under control of an army, and authorized temporary appointment of field officers to the courts if a regular member had a conflict of interests in a particular case. To reduce abuses and facilitate assigning healthy men to the ranks, Congress revoked in January 1864 the right of each court to appoint its own clerk and provost.[20]

Initial response to the military courts was favorable. Porter Alexander commented, "We now had in operation what I think was an improved system for court martials. Instead of detailing a lot of officers away from their duties to comprise a court, three military judges were appointed for each corps, & they comprised a permanent court—two making a quorum." Captain Charles M. Blackford, the judge advocate for Longstreet's First Corps court, wrote to his wife that his court would open on February 2, 1863, and had a large number of cases waiting, twenty or so of them capital cases. By July though, he reported, "The court is working very smoothly now and we are cleaning up all the business of the corps and emptying the guardhouses in every division, which is an infinite relief to the army."[21]

A permanent judge advocate of a military court had duties similar to his temporarily detailed counterpart on a court-martial, the main difference being the assistance available from the clerk and provost. The judge advocate made all the physical arrangements for the trial—secured an appropriate building from the quartermaster, arranged for fuel, and so forth. He served as the court's law officer and also conducted the government's prosecution. He rewrote improperly drafted charges and furnished the accused a copy, reading the charges to illiterate soldiers. He summoned witnesses for both prosecution and defense and took necessary depositions. He prepared a brief if he felt it beneficial. Notwithstanding his prosecutorial function, the judge advocate gave the defendant advice if asked and protected the accused's rights during trial. He arraigned the prisoner and accepted his plea, swore in witnesses, recorded findings and sentences, and forwarded the required paperwork to the approval authority after the trial. The courts seem to have physically rotated from division to division through their corps, living at division headquarters, holding sessions in a convenient building, and dealing with all of one division's cases before going to the next. For example, Captain Blackford was with Pickett's division on the march to Gettysburg and at the headquarters of John B. Hood's division after the battle.[22]

The military court system, however, was not able to keep up with the caseload in the Army of Northern Virginia for long and soon produced its own bureaucratic nightmare that critics found as oppressive as the courts-martial it was intended to replace. In March 1865 Alexander, responding to a circular requesting suggestions on how to prevent desertion, recommended the opposite approach from the centralized military courts. He advocated jurisdiction for desertion cases be given to regimental courts to avoid the inconsistent sentences and technical burden of the corps court system. Alexander complained that once a prisoner was charged and his plea accepted, the charge could not be changed and the courts could not find defendants guilty of lesser offenses (like disobedience of an order instead of desertion) than those charged. Lee, the initial advocate of the military courts, complained that the required complex review procedures converted "military courts practically into courts-marshal and sacrifices the chief benefits that were anticipated from the former." The administrative burden of reviewing all the cases was excessive at best and was impossible to manage if the army were engaged in active campaigning. Given a choice between courts-martial and military courts, with his role the same in either case, Lee said he would select courts-martial and avoid the added burden of transporting and feeding the military courts. Secretary of War Seddon, apparently unwilling to eliminate the military courts completely, sought to alleviate Lee's administrative burden by giving him qualified staff help. Seddon recommended to Congress that a colonel judge advocate be added to each army staff "to review in the first instance all sentences of the military courts, courts martial and examining boards." At the same time, while formalizing the field staff organization, the adjutant general specified that at each army headquarters "one assistant to the senior assistant adjutant and inspector general, selected with a view to his special qualifications for the duty, will be charged with the examination of court-martial records."[23] Appointment of a judge advocate on the army staff may have relieved Lee's administrative burden, but it could not clear the backlog of cases on the docket.

The innovation of military courts supplemented rather than displaced the traditional system of courts-martial. As one example of the continued prevalence of courts-martial, Clement A. Evans served for up to a month at a time as a member of courts-martial in May–June 1863, January 1864, and November 1864. In March 1863, A. P. Hill and Dorsey Pender sat together on a court. Pender commented, "It's going to be a tedious job indeed." At the time of his January 1864 court-martial stint, Evans claimed that there were twelve courts like the one on which he served sitting simultaneously in the Army of Northern Virginia. Since each court could try four cases in the six hours the commander required it to meet daily (although complicated cases took much longer), Evans estimated an average of two convictions a day per court: "This makes six hundred convicts for one month from this army."[24] Evans's estimate, added to the cases tried by the corps military courts, gives a hint of the extent of the administrative problem about which Lee complained.

Whether apportioned by military courts or courts-martial, justice in the Army of Northern Virginia was a peculiar blend of traditional legalism, harsh expediency, and occasional clemency operating inside a system that mixed the impersonality of bureaucracy with the fickleness of individual egos. As an example of legal technicalities, Stonewall Jackson got embroiled with Adjutant General Samuel Cooper in a controversy over whether the new corps courts were required to take the oath prescribed in the articles of war. The adjutant general returned several cases from Second Corps because they did not contain evidence that the court had taken the oath. Jackson replied that the omission was intentional. He believed the military courts differed from regular courts-martial and requested a ruling from the attorney general. The matter remained at a stalemate until the attorney general, Thomas H. Watts, finally ruled in Jackson's favor almost a year later.[25]

Expediency manifested itself in a rush to justice that saw suspects executed on the spot or subjected to drumhead courts-martial that produced similar results with a minimum of formality. Moxley Sorrel commented about an incident during the Second Manassas campaign, "It was in these operations that a spy was taken. He had murdered one of our cavalry couriers, and was caught almost red-handed, and with papers on him compromising enough to hang a dozen spies. Nevertheless we gave him a trial. I convened a drum-head court martial of three brigadiers and they sentenced him to be hanged immediately."[26] On March 28, 1865, when the South was considering raising regiments of slaves, Longstreet decided to recommend soldiers who apprehended deserters for commissions in the proposed black regiments. On March 30, Longstreet forwarded to army headquarters his first four recommendations for promotion of privates (from three different regiments) to officer positions in black regiments. The deserters whose apprehension gained their captors this reward had already been tried and convicted and would be executed the next day.[27] If the initial letter left Longstreet's headquarters early in the morning and the second late at night, it still took less than seventy-two hours to inform the corps of the new policy; catch, try, convict, and sentence several deserters; and report the results up the chain of command from regiment to army level.

But the system could also be forgiving. In June 1863, Longstreet granted clemency to all officers and soldiers in his corps under arrest or serving sentences for noncapital offenses. Two months later, Lee granted armywide amnesty for deserters and men absent without leave or serving sentences for those offenses. In 1864 Lee remitted the sentences of several convicted deserters based on youth or good conduct and returned them to the ranks. He considered granting clemency to other offenders but thought that doing so would undermine discipline. "The escape of one criminal encourages others to hope for like impunity," commented the army commander.[28]

The Rebel personality at work within the bureaucracy was most evident when officers were charged with crimes. Several staff officers told anecdotes about getting gussied up in sword belt and sash to arrest whatever general had most recently displeased their boss. Legends abound of Army of Northern Virginia general officers marching under arrest at the rear of their units, only to be released (usually by Lee personally) at the onset of battle to lead their men to glory. Longstreet got into a protracted squabble with Brigadier General Evander McIvor Law in December 1863 over the latter's attempt to resign. Law reached Richmond with his resignation, where he was convinced to burn the letter and return to the army. Longstreet then arrested him for stealing his own letter and conduct prejudicial to good order. Jefferson Davis intervened to overturn the charges; however, Longstreet defied the president and rearrested Law. The situation was not resolved until Law was wounded and transferred to the cavalry, outside Longstreet's command. In the legal fireworks between Jackson and A. P. Hill (see chapter 2), Hill used Henry Kyd Douglas as an intermediary and advocate to gain temporary release from arrest to lead his division into battle. Individual quirks and egos operated at lower levels as well. Porter Alexander, serving as president of a court-martial in the winter of 1862–63, presided over the case of a deserter from his own artillery battalion—a desertion Alexander took as a personal affront. He had been instrumental in apprehending the man "and then I considered him mine to shoot, after certain tedious formalities." Alexander's court found the man guilty, of course, although he escaped from jail before the sentence of death could be confirmed and executed. Usually, though, court members did not have a personal interest in a case; occasionally, they did not have any interest at all. While sitting on a court-martial in January 1864, Evans made entries in his journal and wrote letters to his wife, although he assured her, "I will try to keep one ear open to the testimony."[29]

Outside the courtroom, especially if the army were on the move and the court could not meet, the judge advocates became a staff resource. The civilian judges got a break, but an extra staff officer was always welcome. The First Corps judge advocate Charles Blackford noted, "We have just finished one of the most terrible marches in history. I was detailed to staff duty and marched with the army although the rest of the court went by train." Before Charles Blackford's court was fully organized and ready to open, Brigadier General Robert H. Chilton put the judge advocate to work at Army of Northern Virginia headquarters. During the invasion of Pennsylvania, a bored Blackford admitted to his wife, "On the march I have little to do; nothing indeed but act as an aide and carry messages along the column, which is not laborious." But unemployed lawyers did not simply carry messages. On one occasion, Blackford guided a column on a night march, and another time he conducted a reconnaissance of the Little River from Edgewood to its mouth.[30] Although not trained as an engineer, Blackford probably qualified for the latter duty based on two years' experience as a cavalry company commander.

Whether serving as typical staff officers or in their role as the legal specialists of the command, judge advocates performed valuable services for their commanders.

CHAPLAINS

Any mid-nineteenth-century army could be expected to have chaplains, and the Army of Northern Virginia was no exception. Strangely, however, for a nation with an army that became famous for its deeply religious leaders and periodic spiritual revivals, the Confederacy made scant provision for military chaplains. The second article of war warned, "It is earnestly recommended to all officers and soldiers diligently to attend divine services" and imposed severe penalties for those who "behave[d] indecently or irreverently at any place of divine worship." There were also special provisions for chaplains' rations and specific punishments for chaplains who went absent without leave. However, that was about the extent of the attention paid the military clergy. The initial law that organized the army did not even mention chaplains. Jefferson Davis had to prod Congress: "I also call your attention to an omission in the law organizing the Army, in relation to military chaplains, and recommend that provision be made for their appointment." The resulting law implied that chaplains were officers but did not assign rank or even prescribe a uniform for the military clergymen it authorized. Having no rank or uniform may have been a blessing in disguise. Chaplains generally did not want to appear too military, although some means of identification was necessary to ease the problem of moving about and dealing with the army. The chaplains of Second and Third Corps of the Army of Northern Virginia eventually adopted a gold bullion C and half olive wreath on a two-and-a-half-inch black background as their badge of rank and position. Of more significance, however, than problems of rank or uniform was the lack of a chaplain's department in Richmond to coordinate or sponsor military ministry (although Senator Louis Wigfall of Texas sarcastically "moved that The Chief of the Ecclesiastic Department have the rank title and pay of a Brigadier General" during debate on increasing the rank of some department heads).[31] No central authority coordinated the chaplains' efforts or even provided a description of their duties. Everyone assumed chaplains would preach, but when, where, how often, and to whom was left entirely to the individual.

To complicate matters, the Confederate Congress contained influential members who were opposed to military chaplains or at least to paying for their services. Within three weeks of passing the initial authorization for chaplains in the army, Congress acted to reduce their pay to a paltry fifty dollars per month based on the theory that someone who preached once a week should not receive the same pay as someone who worked every day. That rate of pay remained in effect until April 1862, when chaplains got a raise to eighty dollars a month, still not enough to meet their needs. Until January 1864 chaplains received a private's rations instead of being allowed to purchase food from the commissary like other officers, and it was not until the same date that the government consented to provide forage for their horses. During the debate about providing forage, Congressman William Russell Smith of Alabama opined that "chaplains were mere drones, who ought to be in the army with a musket on their shoulders." He pointed out that the Confederacy was having enough difficulty feeding its army without increasing the problem by feeding chaplains and their horses. The pay and compensation issue was significant. Home churches wanted preachers in the pulpit, not in the field with the army. After months without a pastor, William Pendleton's congregation in Lexington, Virginia, asked him to either resign as pastor or return to civilian life and minister to them. When Pendleton stayed with the army, the church found another pastor and told Mrs. Pendleton she would have to move out of the rectory. Pendleton, with a brigadier's salary, could afford to rent the rectory from the incoming pastor; however, most chaplains would have faced unacceptable personal hardships in similar circumstances.[32]

Even to draw what little support he deserved a chaplain needed a formal commission, a notoriously slow bureaucratic process that sometimes took more than a year.[33] The words of Randolph McKim, a staff officer who resigned his commission to study for the ministry and then returned to the Army of Northern Virginia intending to be the chaplain of Major R. Preston Chew's artillery battalion, illustrate the chaplains' frustration: "But I was to be disappointed. I learned on investigation that formal application for my appointment as chaplain of the battalion had never been made, and Major Chew informed me that until I received the appointment I could not draw rations or forage. He proceeded at once to make the formal application to the Department, but, pending its action, I had no *status* in the army, and was obliged with great chagrin to leave camp and await my commission as chaplain."[34] McKim never got the appointment with Chew's battalion, since the law did not authorize chaplains for artillery battalions. Several months after beginning his effort to secure a chaplaincy, McKim finally got a commission as chaplain of the 2d Virginia Cavalry and rejoined the army.

Low pay and poor governmental support were major impediments to recruiting chaplains. The only potential solutions lay outside official channels. Many southern churches supported ministries to the army, and some units supplemented the pay of their chaplains with voluntary contributions from the troops. One brigade got pledges of fifty dollars per month from each company to support a brigade chaplain. An astute observer noted that those pledges would amount to an annual salary of $55,000, but he unfortunately did not record the preacher's response to such a generous offer. The North Carolina Presbytery decided in May 1862 that $1,000 a year was necessary to supplement a chaplain's government pay. In 1863 the Presbyterian Executive Committee provided supplementary pay for twenty chaplains with the Army of Northern Virginia. Even $1,000 to supplement his military pay did not completely compensate a good preacher for the loss of potential civilian earnings. D. H. Hill wrote to his wife about one chaplain, Reverend Sprunt, "He was offered a salary of three thousand a year to preach at Wilmington but declined in order to serve as a Chaplain on six hundred salary. There are still some disinterested men in this world."[35] Hill calculated the chaplain's pay on the outdated scale of fifty dollars a month and did not mention any supplement he might have received, but Hill was still right that Reverend Sprunt took a significant pay reduction to serve in the army.

Out of patriotism, spiritual zeal, or a belief that clergy should not be in the pay of the state, some ministers served as volunteers, called missionaries in the religious context. Many missionaries served short stints with the army, but evidence of large numbers of long-term volunteer chaplains is skimpy. Chaplain John W. Jones wrote at the time, "I say *chaplains,* for I know of but *two* missionaries now present in the whole army [of Northern Virginia]. Those good brethren who resolved at the Georgia Baptist Convention that governmental chaplaincies were wrong, and they would do the work of army evangelization as voluntary missionaries, must all have gone to General Hood's army. I have seen none of them here." Despite volunteers and support from home churches, recruiting and retaining qualified chaplains for the army was a constant problem throughout the war. At times half the regiments in some corps were without their authorized ministers.[36]

The law never authorized staff chaplains, posting them exclusively to regiments. However, many higher headquarters devised some arrangement to coordinate religious matters (usually by assigning a regimental chaplain double duty), and the most religiously aggressive established what were essentially unofficial headquarters or staff chaplains. Lee did not have a permanent chaplain on the Army of Northern Virginia staff, although many prominent clergymen assigned to or visiting the army preached at headquarters. Likewise, Longstreet's First Corps seems to have done without a permanent staff chaplain. Conversely, Jackson's Second Corps had Rev. B. T. Lacy as unofficial corps chaplain, although one contemporary, Rev. J. William Jones, pointed out that calling him corps chaplain was incorrect "for there was no such rank; and indeed, Confederate chaplains had no military rank whatever, but were all on the same footing of equality as simply preachers and spiritual leaders of their commands." Regardless of the technicality, Jackson had Lacy commissioned as a chaplain, provided him a horse, let him share the general's room, and kept him at corps headquarters without a specific regimental assignment. A. S. "Sandie" Pendleton, Jackson's AAG and chief of staff, noted that Lacy "has stirred up the chaplains a great deal and infused some of his own energy into them, and is doing a good work." In 1864 Jones was in fact the corps chaplain of Third Corps, even if he denied the existence of such a position. The divisions in the various corps made similar arrangements, although a division chaplain's responsibilities were almost always additional to his regimental duties. For example, Rev. A. C. Hopkins served as a division chaplain in Second Corps, and although he retained the title of chaplain of the 2d Virginia and filled that role, he also called himself the chaplain of Gordon's Division and functioned as such.[37]

Chaplains, whether serving with the staff or line, performed a basic set of duties with emphasis on specific tasks varying according to the whims, beliefs, talents, and personality of the individual chaplain. They universally conducted Sunday services and evening prayer meetings. They conducted baptisms and administered the sacraments according to the rites of their denomination. They visited the sick, buried the dead when the situation permitted, comforted the sorrowful, and offered private counseling on religious and personal matters. They used volunteer labor to build chapels when the army went into winter quarters. Depending on funds and the availability of materials, most conducted aggressive campaigns to distribute Bibles, prayer books, religious tracts, and pamphlets. In general, chaplains tried to keep religion in the soldiers' lives. Some also taught reading and writing, and many wrote to the families of killed or wounded soldiers, the most diligent attempting to notify the kinfolk of Union soldiers whose bodies they could identify. At least one chaplain Alexander D. Betts, wrote an annual letter to the home church of each of his military parishioners with news of their soldiers and requests for prayers. As that industrious clergyman noted, "This was expensive and laborious work." Another, Nicholas Davis, worked diligently at building and furnishing regimental and brigade hospitals and wrote letters to the *Richmond Whig* begging for donations of shoes and socks to clothe his destitute military parishioners, a plea that produced favorable results. Chaplain Betts went so far as to borrow a quartermaster's wagon and driver to exhume the body of a recently killed officer to ship it home to North Carolina. Rev. Hopkins devoted time to soliciting and publishing writings from other chaplains on topics like "Profane Swearing" and "Christ our Substitute." As a cavalry chaplain Randolph McKim formed a branch of the Young Men's Christian Association in his regiment and conducted occasional meetings of that group. That same minister also formed and rehearsed a choir to sing at services. A Catholic priest, James Sheeran, devoted himself more directly to the good order and discipline of his regiment. He berated stragglers, confronted commissary officers who issued short rations to men in the guardhouse, and even forced the resignation of a captain the soldiers thought cowardly.[38]

Either by common consent or out of necessity, staff chaplains spent most of their time ministering to headquarters personnel and subordinate units without a chaplain. Of the chaplains mentioned above, Rev. Lacy preached at Army of Northern Virginia and Second Corps headquarters and "in the more destitute [for chaplains] commands of the corps." In his annual report to the Virginia Baptist Sunday School and Publications Board, which had appointed him "Missionary-chaplain to A. P. Hill's Corps," Rev. Jones described his duties much like Rev. Lacy's: "I have confined myself chiefly to those regiments and brigades most destitute of ministerial labor." A. C. Hopkins directed his ministerial efforts primarily toward a brigade of his division that had no chaplains assigned, toward prisoners in the stockade, and toward an engineer unit that was not authorized a chaplain. He also conducted nightly "family worship" for the staff in the division headquarters. A visiting missionary to Rodes's division established a daily rotation system of preaching so he could work his way through the five brigades of the division, which was extremely short of chaplains.[39] But if all they did was preach at the headquarters and to units without a chaplain, calling these ministers staff officers would be inaccurate. The other part of being a corps, division, or brigade chaplain was the requirement to coordinate religious activities within their commands—a staff function. This was a much more difficult proposition than preaching and one most chaplains performed with only mediocre success.

Chaplains might technically be soldiers, but most owed their primary allegiance to their churches. Few of the normal military means of exerting control were effective with them. Military clergymen invariably had horses, which gave them great freedom of movement and made controlling them difficult. They did not necessarily eat or sleep with their regiments. Chaplains spent long periods away from their units, visiting hospitals or doing other things of less obvious direct connection to their duties. Three-month furloughs spent in Richmond and elsewhere were not uncommon, especially during the harsh winter months. Passes to move unhindered (and thus uncontrolled) around the army were also not uncommon. One chaplain had a pass from his corps commander (obtained through the corps chaplain). The priest, James Sheeran, who was the chaplain of the 14th Louisiana, bearded Robert E. Lee in his den and emerged with universal passes for the three chaplains in his brigade good for the duration of the war and signed by Lee himself. No picket or provost marshal would challenge such authority. If a pass did not suffice, chaplains were not averse to simply taking off on their own authority—a serious offense if committed by a common soldier. One chaplain missed the Chancellorsville battle because he was en route back from a visit home, where he had purportedly gone to buy a horse and only incidentally to attend the birth of a child, an activity for which a requested furlough had been disapproved. An overworked Father Sheeran, on his own authority, "resolved to retire to Richmond and rest for a few days."[40]

In general, Confederate chaplains were individualists of the first order with their own ideas (religious and otherwise) of whose validity they were absolutely convinced. A story about Chaplain James B. Sheeran gives some indication of the attitude of chaplains about their place in military society.

Going to [Sheeran's] tent one day, General Jackson sternly rebuked the priest for disobeying his orders and reproached him with doing what he would not tolerate in any officer of his command. (The offense was apparently one of interference with military administration.) "Father Sheeran," said the General, "you ask more favors and take more privileges than any officer in the army." "General Jackson," said Fr. Sheeran, "I want you to understand that as a priest of God I outrank every officer in your command. I even outrank you, and when it is a question of duty I shall go wherever called." The General looked with undisguised astonishment on the bold priest and without replying left his tent.[41]

Although making guest preaching appearances at other units was common, one Second Corps North Carolina chaplain refused to let Rev. Lacy conduct services for his regiment based on the conviction that he did not need help being the chaplain of his own regiment. The combination of believing themselves above the military and strong convictions on minor matters like guest preachers made instituting significant policy initiatives extremely difficult. Left on their own, chaplains did not even congregate together socially, as one might expect. Rev. A. C. Hopkins noted, "One thing that struck me; there seemed to be no affiliation among chaplains. It was more than three months after my attachment to the brigade before I met one of its chaplains." Father Sheeran joined his regiment before First Manassas but did not meet Rev. Lacy, his corps chaplain, until August 1863.[42] Given those conditions and the lack of any legal or regulatory guidance on what a military chaplain ought to do, it was imperative that the senior chaplains devise some means to coordinate the activities of their peers.

The coordination technique eventually adopted by part of the Army of Northern Virginia was the Chaplains' Association. Initially organized by Rev. Lacy in 1863 as a Second Corps enterprise, the association quickly became a joint Second and Third Corps venture when the army reorganized after Stonewall Jackson's death. The association met frequently—ideally weekly—when the activity of the army permitted. Meetings often lasted all day, were recorded in written minutes, and dealt with a variety of issues important to chaplains. Rev. Lacy did not conduct the association meetings personally, a wise and perhaps inevitable choice given the absence of military rank and the unofficial nature of his position as corps chaplain. Instead, the chairmanship of the association rotated from meeting to meeting. Besides conducting the meeting, the chairman had the honor of delivering a sermon to the assembled clergymen. Occasionally, guest speakers appeared. Brigadier General William Pendleton, a prominent and very active minister as well as Lee's chief of artillery, noted in a letter to his wife about the first meeting he attended, "I was asked to address them and did so to good purpose, I trust. By unanimous resolution, I was asked to preach to them on the conditions of their work at such time and place as I might designate. I readily consented, and will do it, the Lord being my helper, as soon as I can." Besides Pendleton, other Army of Northern Virginia leaders lent legitimacy and support to the Chaplains' Association by attending meetings. Lee attended several meetings "and manifested the liveliest interest in the proceedings." Jackson attended meetings and discussed the association and how to improve its effectiveness with chaplains from his corps. Old soldiers even recalled Jeb Stuart, who was very religious, as an interested and active participant at Chaplains' Association meetings. Others remembered the dashing cavalry man as a "deeply interested listener" at the chaplains' meetings in the same thought with the more familiar image of him "amid the sweets of social intercourse."[43]

Quite naturally, part of every Chaplains' Association meeting was devoted to religious activities. Besides the chairman's sermon, there were discussions of theological topics like the importance of the sacrament of the Lord's Supper. But meetings were not simply theological seminars—they also addressed subjects of a military nature. Chaplains gave reports on the state of religion in their regiments. They discussed the shortage of chaplains in the army and devised plans to solve that vexing problem. Association members agreed to do "missionary work" in adjacent regiments without chaplains, and the group resolved to send an address to the "Church at home" to outline the spiritual needs of the army. That resolution resulted in a long letter written by Rev. Lacy to the churches of the Confederacy describing the need for chaplains, explaining the nature of their work, pleading for support, inviting church leaders to visit the army, and encouraging any means to help support military religious activities. The association identified the lack of chaplains assigned to hospitals as a problem and arranged to provide interim voluntary support while petitioning to find permanent chaplains. The association coordinated activities for periodic presidentially declared days of fasting and discussed techniques of ministry. For example, one meeting minutes noted, "Then followed a lengthy and interesting conversation about the chaplain's private work in his regiment, by conversation, etc." The association sent delegates—significantly Lacy and Jones, the corps chaplains—to Lee to urge better observance of the Sabbath in the army. The chaplains used meetings to air gripes: "Here the subject of some further provision for the chaplain's efficiency was discussed, e.g., his need of a tent for study, prayer-meetings, private conversations with inquirers, etc., and of forage for a horse." And the association got into thorny issues like the proper location and duties of a chaplain in battle: "Much conversation was had on this topic. Many chaplains stated what had been their habit." The association was not able to reach consensus on that issue, although they did agree it was wrong for a chaplain to take up a musket and join the fight. The best advice the chaplains could offer was that "no absolute rule can be laid down. A chaplain shall be wherever duty calls him, irrespective of danger."[44]

141

Such meetings were good for the chaplains' morale. One participant, Alexander Davis Betts, noted in his diary, "Good meeting. All day with them. Such meetings warm the heart and encourage us."[45] But morale was not the main intent. The Third Corps chaplain, John William Jones, purportedly using Stonewall Jackson's words, perhaps best summarized the reason for the Chaplains' Association thus: "Our chaplains, at least in the same military organization encamped in the same neighborhood, should have their meetings, and through God's blessing devise successful plans for spiritual conquests. All the other departments of the army have system, and such system exists in any other department of the service that no one of its officers can neglect his duties without diminishing the efficiency of his branch of service."[46] The Chaplains' Association provided a system for coordinating the efforts of military ministers. Unfortunately, the association seems to have been a Protestant-only organization. Father Sheeran only mentioned a meeting once, and then only to say he knew nothing about it when Lieutenant General Ewell asked what Sheeran thought of one of the association's pronouncements. Ewell even referred to the association, in Sheeran's recollection, as "the Council of Protestant Chaplains."[47]

Chaplains received good command support, at least from the higher echelons of the Army of Northern Virginia. Lee issued orders suspending military duties except for inspections on Sundays so that soldiers could attend services and reiterated the order when abuses cropped up. Commanders at all levels worked to recruit chaplains, some even complaining that their superiors favored preachers of their own denomination. Jackson made special efforts to fill chaplain vacancies, but Second Corps was still short half the required number in March 1863. The one area where commanders, following War Department policy, would not bend in the matter of recruiting was commissioning as chaplains preachers who had enlisted in the ranks. Conversely, soldiers who were also clergymen continued to minister on the side. General Pendleton claimed that one Sunday "hardly anybody in the State preached to more people than it was my privilege to do." Pendleton, however, may not have been as effective as he thought. Walter Taylor noted about the artillery commander, "I am not as averse to hearing the General as others but am always sorry to see him officiate because I know how the soldiers will talk about him." Pendleton may have had his critics, but he was only one of many soldier/clerics. Major Robert L. Dabney, Jackson's chief of staff until he resigned for reasons of health and a former professor at the Union Theological Seminary, preached whenever he had a chance—on at least one occasion to one brigade in the morning and to another in the afternoon. Dabney Ball, another officer/minister, rose from the position of chaplain of the 1st Virginia Cavalry to be Stuart's chief of staff. Even laymen pitched in when they saw a need. Jed Hotchkiss, the Second Corps topographical engineer, who was not a clergyman but invariably recorded where he attended church and the subject of the sermon, made one diary entry: "Sunday, April 9th [1863]. I got my pocket full of tracts and Testaments and went down the river to see my old pupil, Sam. J. Foner, who is in the guard house of the 10th Va. Regt. on charges of desertion to the enemy." Lieutenant McKim, who would eventually resign his commission to become a chaplain, was so religiously active while serving as an aide-de-camp that he was often mistaken for a chaplain.[48]

All in all, using techniques like the Chaplains' Association, missionary ministers, and ordained officers of the line, the staff chaplains of the Army of Northern Virginia provided religious support to the army as best they could.

PROVOST MARSHAL

Early in the war, the Confederate armies in the field found the need for military police. Although no separate provost marshal corps was ever established, army regulations provided, "When necessary, the General-in-chief or General of Division may appoint a provost marshal to take charge of prisoners with a suitable guard, or other police force." Provost marshals, appointed either temporarily or permanently, controlled stragglers, apprehended deserters and other criminals, guarded stockades, and performed law enforcement in cities and towns (both friendly and liberated) near the army or under martial law. Although the Army of Tennessee appointed a provost marshal general and assistants at various headquarters, the provost function was never formalized in the Army of Northern Virginia in a unique duty position on the staff.[49]

However, commanders often specially appointed officers as provost marshals for liberated towns or in critical situations. For example, general orders issued during the Antietam campaign, when straggling was especially bad, and repeated on the day of the battle appointed Brigadier General Lewis Armistead as the army provost marshal and charged him with preventing straggling, correcting "irregularities against good order and military discipline, and prevent[ing] depredations upon the community." Normally, the commander of the provost guard filled the role of provost marshal under the supervision of the assistant inspector general, who served as his principal staff point of contact. A series of orders established permanent provost guards at brigade, division, corps, and army levels and later expanded the system to include the cavalry corps. The troops designated for provost service were supposed "to be selected from the most reliable and efficient, and to remain upon the duty unless relieved from inefficiency or other cause," although some soldiers served temporarily with the provost guard simply because they were sick and could not march with their units.[50] Staff officers did not consider an assignment as provost marshal an appealing additional duty: Theodore Stanford Garnett wrote, "I was assigned as Aid-de-Camp, but was also made to perform the duties of Provost Marshal of the Division, whenever such disagreeable service was required. After serving with Gen. [W. H. F.] Lee as actively as I could all day through many long marches, skirmishes and battles, it was no pleasant duty to have to take charge at night of large numbers of prisoners and march many miles to deliver them over to Major [D. B.] Bridgeford, the Provost Marshal of the Army."[51]

From June 1863 to the end of the war, the provost guard for the Army of Northern Virginia was the 1st Virginia Battalion (the Irish Battalion). Its commander, Major Bridgford, was effectively the provost marshal of the Army of Northern Virginia. Although he signed some official reports as commander of the provost guard, he signed paroles as the army provost marshal. At the end of the war, Bridgford had an assistant provost marshal, four clerks, and two office orderlies in the provost marshal's office as distinct from the provost guard. Captain O. C. Henderson listed his duty on the parole roster as "Com'd'g 1st Va. Batt.," so Bridgford apparently had distanced himself from his command duties to concentrate on being the provost marshal. Bridgford and the 1st Virginia Battalion had their first exposure to provost duty in June 1861, when they performed the duty for General Jackson. After December 12, 1862, they served continuously until June 1863 as provost marshals for Second Corps, with Bridgford being the corps' chief provost marshal, thereafter becoming the army provost guard. The 1st North Carolina Battalion, commanded by Major R. W. Wharton, was detached from Robert F. Hoke's brigade of Early's division to assume Second Corps provost functions when the 1st Virginia Battalion changed duties. The 5th Alabama Battalion, after suffering significant casualties and losing its colors in Pickett's charge at Gettysburg, served as the Third Corps provost guard for the rest of the war. Longstreet's corps also probably had a permanent provost guard, although it has not been specifically identified. Lieutenant Colonel Robert P. Blount signed himself "Provost-Marshal, First Corps, Army of Northern Virginia" in a letter forwarding information he learned while a prisoner of war awaiting parole, so he probably considered it a permanent assignment. Identifying Colonel Blount or placing him with a unit is not easy. A Lieutenant Colonel Blount (whose first name is not given) served as a volunteer aide-de-camp to Longstreet in

October 1862, and a Lieutenant Colonel Robert P. Blount commanded the 9th Alabama Infantry Battalion (also called the 5th Alabama Infantry Battalion). However, this battalion was probably not the same 5th Alabama Battalion that was the Third Corps provost guard, since the former battalion served in the Army of Mississippi and fought only at Shiloh (April 6–7, 1862) before being reorganized.[52] Blount may have been serving temporarily as Longstreet's provost marshal while actually a volunteer aide-de-camp, or he may have commanded an unidentified First Corps provost guard unit.

Typical provost duties with a field army on either side during the Civil War included suppression of marauding, prevention of straggling, guarding and escorting prisoners of war, regulating military and civilian movement in the immediate vicinity of the army, and execution of courts-martial sentences involving imprisonment or capital punishment. The provosts in the Army of Northern Virginia would have had additional specialized duties like impressment of slave labor. Operation of the passport system to control civilian movement, a major provost marshal function in the Confederacy, fell largely to militia provost detachments in the major cities, rear areas, military departments, and on the railroads rather than to the provost guard of a deployed army. Army of Northern Virginia provosts also did not have to concern themselves with enforcing conscription or apprehending deserters (other than immediately as they tried to desert). In extremis, the provost guard served as infantry. For example, at the end of the first day in the Wilderness, a hard-pressed A. P. Hill relieved his provost guard, the 5th Alabama Battalion, from guarding prisoners and flung them at the federals in a desperate counterattack.[53]

Provost marshals exercised quite a bit of power and considerable discretion in the conduct of their duties. They were to detain civilians entering the lines, verify their purpose, turn away any whose reason for visiting the army the provost did not like, and obtain for those with legitimate business a pass signed by a division commander. During marches, they determined, with the assistance of an attached medical officer, whether stragglers should be arrested or were sick and would be allowed to ride in ambulances at the rear of the column. In battle, the provost marshals arrested or turned back men found behind the lines without proper passes, with the decision on whether to arrest or turn back left to the discretion of the provost. That difference could be significant, since those arrested were turned over "to the first major-general whose command was going into the fight, to place them in [the] front and most exposed portion of the command." The number of men thus arrested and escorted back to the front could be significant. The Second

145

Corps provost marshal reported arresting and returning to the fight 320 men on December 13, 1862, during the Battle of Fredericksburg, and another 206 the following day, numbers he considered "comparatively few in consideration of the size of the army" but larger than the number of prisoners of war he processed in the same period. The provost marshal had the authority to shoot on the spot men who refused to go forward or drifted to the rear a second time after once being returned to the front.[54]

By far, the biggest headache for Army of Northern Virginia provost marshals was prisoners, both Rebel and Yankee. The number of court cases prosecuted by the army kept unit guardhouses bursting at the seams. Prisoners of war were the special, although not exclusive, province of the provost. Capturing units located the provost guard as quickly as possible to rid themselves of their prisoners. During the Battle of Fredericksburg, Major Bridgford, still the Second Corps provost marshal at the time, reported receiving and shipping to Richmond 324 prisoners of war. Longstreet estimated that he turned over five thousand prisoners to the army provost guard during the Seven Days' Battles. From September 29 to October 1, 1864, Bridgford, by then the Army of Northern Virginia provost, processed 1,663 prisoners from relatively limited fighting at New Market Heights (September 28–30, 1864) during the Petersburg campaign. During the Bristoe Station campaign (October 1863), Major G. M. Ryals, the cavalry provost, reported processing 1,370 prisoners, and there are hundreds of such cases. The significance of such figures for a study of military staffs is the planning and coordination required to collect, guard, feed, and transport such large numbers of prisoners. Even the expedient of immediately paroling prisoners on the field, which eliminated the problem of guarding, transporting, and feeding them, had its own penalties. John H. Worsham, a soldier detailed to parole approximately seven hundred wounded Yankees captured in the Frederick, Maryland, hospital in September 1862 explained the problem: "I tell you it was a job, as I had to write every word of the paroles for those men in duplicate, one for the prisoner and one for us." It took him all night and most of the next morning to complete the task.[55] Whether they paroled or evacuated prisoners, the provost marshals had to be well integrated with the rest of the staff to accomplish their mission.

Chapter 6

STAFF SELECTION AND TRAINING

Whatever their duties, the Army of Northern Virginia had to recruit and train staff officers. This was not always the deliberate, rational process of picking the best officer from a pool of qualified candidates or of receiving a suitable officer through the normal replacement channels of modern staff systems. Selection and training of staff officers were areas in which the Confederacy clung to the ancient roots of traditional custom rather than displaying the competing tendency toward modernity.

STAFF SELECTION

Some staff positions required specially qualified officers. The examination required of ordnance officers has already been discussed, and surgeons, of course, had to have medical degrees. Similarly, artillerymen needed technical gunnery skills, especially since they often served both as commanders and as staff officers. Chaplains had to be ordained ministers, although recruiting letters from the Chaplains' Association stressed that they could not be just ordinary ministers but had to be effective gospel preachers who were willing and physically able to endure the hardships of their posts.[1] Quartermaster and commissary officers were supposed to be affluent enough to post bond. However, beyond such basic prerequisites there were no standardized selection criteria for staff officers, especially for aides-de-camp and members of the adjutant and inspector general corps. This led to abuses, especially early in the war as the Confederacy scrambled to form an army.

Contemporaries complained about nepotism, favoritism, and lack of qualification on Confederate staffs. Braxton Bragg, even as late as 1864, explained that staffs were "the mere creation of the general. Our present inefficiency is due almost entirely to this cause. A system of favoritism and nepotism has been the natural result." Earlier, S. W. Melton, of the adjutant general's office, commented, "Again men receive staff appointments simply because a vacancy exists, and the general with whom they are to serve asks for them, thus according everything to an authority which, let me repeat, is often not earnest, but much oftener swayed by personal partialities and considerations of policy and too often nepotism."[2] Secretary of War J. A. Seddon included the following in 1864 his report to Congress:

> The staff, affording to the quick intelligence of the general his perceptive and administrative faculties, should be constituted of the best material, have the highest attainable experience and qualifications, and be animated by strong incentives to activity and improvement. Unfortunately, in our army, it has not enjoyed the repute, nor perhaps, in consequence, commanded the merits desirable for its efficiency. From unavoidable circumstances, probably, the staff had been too much the object of favoritism, through recommendations on behalf of personal friends, or the refuge of supernumeraries and those by non-election or otherwise thrown out of the line of regular service. They have come to be considered in some measure as attaches to the persons and fortunes of their respective generals, rather than as officers selected for peculiar qualifications and assigned to special duties.[3]

Officers in the field saw it the same way. While still a private, J. Hamilton Chamberlayne wrote home with a mixture of resentment and pride,

> If I had claims on any of the Genls I would like best of all to be a staff officer; but I have not the claims. Wm Taliaferro, you say, expressed all manner of things to you; he is or soon will be a Brig. Genl., bid him appoint me his aide, or adjutant Genl. or brigade inspector, & see how many good reasons he will have for declining. You can ask him through Sue, if you choose, for you could do it without sense of obligation, but as for me "I'll none of it." If Wm T. because of his friendship for you chooses to ask me to his staff, I'll go & do the duties, but I cannot solicit, unless I am forced to do it. He would have merely to ask it of the Dept. & twould be done; but I cannot ask it, tho' may be you can.[4]

Nepotism in staff selection led directly to the perception (or fact) of favoritism and was thus a source of friction on the staff. An illustrative example is Richard Ewell's headquarters when he commanded Second Corps. Ewell had his stepson, Major Campbell Brown, on the staff. Around a campfire one night, an aide allegedly complained, "Old Ewell told me he never exposed Campbell but once and then was so miserable until he came back he did not know what to do; 'If anything had happened to him, I could never have looked at his mother again, sir.' " The

148

aide added before walking away, "Hang him, he never thinks of my mother, I suppose, for he pops me around, no matter how hot the fire is."[5]

Robert E. Lee recognized and lamented the problems of nepotism. He wrote to Jefferson Davis about staff reforms, "If you can then fill these positions with proper officers, not relatives & friends of the Commds [commanders]—who however agriable their Compy [company] are not always the most useful you might hope to have the finest army in the world." About bringing their son, Robert E. Lee Jr., onto his staff, the senior Lee wrote to his wife, "In reference to Rob, his company would be a great pleasure & comfort to me & he would be extremely useful to me in various ways. I have written to him to that effect. But I am opposed to officers surrounding themselves with their sons & relatives. It is wrong in principle & in that case the selection for offices would be made from private & social reasons, rather than for the public good. . . . there is the same objection to his going with Fitz Lee. He has Lees & relatives enough around him. I should prefer Rob's being in the line, in an independent position, where he could rise by his own merit, & not through the recommendation of his relatives."[6]

Despite such high-level disapproval of the practice, ties of kinship and friendship remained primary selection criteria for Army of Northern Virginia staff officers. The practice of appointing friends and relatives was widespread and applied to all sections of the staff and all echelons of command. Only extensive genealogical research beyond the scope of this work could definitively catalog the extent of family ties in the various Army of Northern Virginia headquarters, but a few randomly discovered examples suffice to illustrate the scope of the practice. As mentioned, Ewell had Brown as his aide-de-camp and assistant adjutant general. Brown was the son of Ewell's widowed cousin, Lizinka Campbell Brown, whom Ewell had courted before her first marriage, to whom he became engaged during the winter of 1861–62, and whom he married while recuperating from the amputation of his leg after Groveton (August 28, 1862). Thomas J. "Stonewall" Jackson and D. H. Hill had married sisters, and each took one of their wives' brothers as an aide (Joseph G. Morrison for Jackson and Randolph H. Morrison for Hill). Hill even complained that he was unjustly maligned for not taking both brothers when Joseph Morrison initially was not happy working for Jackson. At the start of the Gettysburg campaign, Jubal Early asked his brother, Captain Samuel H. Early, to join his staff and to bring along the latter's son, John C. Early, as a courier. John, just past his fifteenth birthday, apparently did not meet his uncle's expectations and returned home after the campaign. Richard Channing Price, Jeb Stuart's AAG, was a cousin of the cavalry commander and later brought his brother Thomas Randolph Price Jr. onto the staff as well. Stuart's signal officer was his nephew, Captain J. Hardeman Stuart, and his ordnance officer was another cousin, Captain John Esten Cooke. Major General William "Extra Billy" Smith had his son, Lieutenant Frederick Waugh Smith, as an aide. A. P. Hill's brother, Baptist, was his commissary officer; his nephew, Francis T. Hill, was an aide; and his brother-in-law, Richard C. Morgan, served as his assistant adjutant general. Henry Heth's brother, Captain Stockton Heth, was his AAG. William Pendleton had a nephew, Captain John Page, as his quartermaster and replaced him upon his promotion with another nephew, Captain John Meade. Heth's assistant adjutant general, Dudley D. Pendleton, was yet another nephew, and Pendleton's son, Sandie, filled that position briefly before moving to Jackson's staff. Pendleton's medical director, Dr. I. Randolph Page, may have been a relation through his wife, whose maiden name was Page. Richard H. Anderson's brother was killed at Williamsburg while serving as a volunteer aide to the general. Stephen D. Ramseur picked a cousin, Caleb Richmond, as his adjutant when he formed the 49th North Carolina Volunteers. Ramseur took Captain Richmond with him as an aide when he moved from regiment to brigade and eventually to division command. Ramseur had corresponded regularly with Caleb's older sister, Ellen, while a cadet at West Point and married her during the war, so Caleb became Ramseur's brother-in-law as well as his cousin. Dorsey Pender had his brother, David, as his commissary officer and asked his wife if she could convince her older brother to join his staff. John B. Gordon had his brother, Eugene, as an aide. William Barksdale had Captain John A. Barksdale as his assistant adjutant general and Lieutenant Harris Barksdale as an aide. Clement A. Evans schemed for several months to get his nephew, John Graham, who was approaching conscription age, assigned to his staff so he could keep the youngster safe. Brigadier General James H. Lane wrote about his aide, "My boy brother, J. Rooker Lane . . . at my request and on account of his youth, General Lee ordered him to report to me for duty." When E. Porter Alexander made brigadier, his aide was Willie Mason, his wife's youngest brother. Even Robert E. Lee, despite his disapproval of the practice, was not immune to temptation. He reluctantly decided against having his youngest son on his staff but asked George Washington Custis Lee, his oldest son, to accept assignment as chief of engineers, submitting his son's name as one of three candidates for that position.[7] That Custis Lee went elsewhere was a result of his father's refusal to make a blunt request, not his theoretical objection to nepotism.

The practice of hiring relatives for the staff was not limited to the general officers. Staff officers also worked to have relatives assigned with them. Captain Charles Blackford, the judge advocate, convinced his military court to hire his brother, Lancelot Blackford, as the court recorder, a position that Blackford assumed would be easier duty than service in the line and one that paid $120 a month as well. G. Moxley Sorrel, James Longstreet's chief of staff, worked with his older brother, a doctor in the surgeon general's office in Richmond, to get their younger brother, A. Claxton Sorrel, promoted from private to lieutenant in a Georgia regiment. Moxley then secured his younger brother an appointment as aide to Brigadier General Richard B. Garnett and later promotion to captain and assignment as assistant inspector general for Brigadier General John Bratton. Jackson's chief of commissary, Major Wells J. Hawks, kept his young son with him as a special courier. Thomas J. Goree used his influence as Longstreet's aide to get his youngest brother assigned as a courier at the headquarters of one of the divisions in Longstreet's corps.[8]

Beyond outright nepotism, there was the common practice of hiring old friends or acquaintances or their relatives. Lee knew Robert H. Chilton, his chief of staff and inspector general, well from the old army. William Pendleton had George W. Peterkin, son of an old friend, promoted from private to lieutenant to be his aide. Long after the war, Peterkin admitted that Brigadier General Pendleton granted him a closer relationship than his official position demanded based largely on the general's long friendship with his father. Pendleton even got his own job because of prewar connections. He had known both Joe Johnston and Jeff Davis at West Point, and the president based his appointment of Pendleton as chief of artillery largely on remembering him from cadet days. It probably did not hurt Pendleton when Lee took command of the Army of Northern Virginia that the artilleryman had also known his new commander at West Point. Early in the war, William Pendleton moved his son, Sandie, from his own staff to that of his friend and one-time tentmate, Jackson, who had known the younger Pendleton in Lexington, Virginia. Besides having Sandie Pendleton on his staff, Jackson asked for Lieutenant Colonel Stapleton Crutchfield as his chief of artillery. Crutchfield had been a cadet at the Virginia Military Institute (VMI), ranking first in the class of 1855, when Jackson was a professor there and later joined Jackson on the institute's faculty as an assistant professor of mathematics. "Their relations were based on mutual confidence in one another." Jackson's VMI connections also supplied his first assistant adjutant general, Lieutenant Colonel J. T. L. Preston, a co-founder of VMI and a fellow professor with Jackson before the war. Dorsey Pender wrote home that he had "the husband of Minnie Lord," someone his wife obviously knew, as his quartermaster. Lieutenant John W. Mallet said, "I was in the summer of 1862 serving most pleasantly as aide-de-camp on the staff of General Rodes, whom I had known well before the war." Sometimes the connection was more tenuous. Henry Kyd Douglas, serving at the time on Jubal Early's staff, discovered that a young courier was the son of Captain Randolph Ridgeley, a hero of Palo Alto, Resaca de la Palma, and Monterrey. Early had known Captain Ridgeley during the Mexican War and immediately commissioned the young Ridgeley and took him as an aide.[9]

However, a few caveats are in order to avoid leaving the impression that Confederate staffs were simply havens for friends and relatives. First, the socially prominent families of the South, especially those within a state, were likely to know each other and intermarry. They were also the main pool from which the Confederacy, for social and educational reasons, drew its officers. In such circumstances, commanders knew or were related to many qualified candidates for staff positions. In the scramble to organize an army from scratch it was natural to turn to known quantities. The case of Longstreet, who did not have local relatives or ties in Virginia, is instructive. Longstreet met the Texan who would serve as his aide, Goree, on the boat while traveling from Texas to Virginia to receive his assignment. He thought Goree was intelligent and clever and kept him as his aide throughout the war. Goree, with no political connections, had trouble getting his permanent commission (and thus his pay), and Longstreet had to intervene with the Texas senate delegation and the adjutant general to secure the appointment. One aide was not enough to fill even a brigade staff, so Longstreet scrounged around for help. Two other Texans who had been traveling with Goree stayed for a while as volunteers, but Longstreet had to ask Colonel Thomas Jordan, P. G. T. Beauregard's chief of staff, for staff officers. Jordan sent Longstreet a Georgian named Moxley Sorrel. Sorrel had failed to get a commission in Richmond and arrived at army headquarters with only a letter of introduction from his father, who had known Jordan briefly years before in Savannah. Jordan put the young Sorrel off for three days before finally dispatching him with three lines of introduction to Longstreet. It was a propitious move by the harassed Jordan—Sorrel and Longstreet hit it off. The young Georgian proved to be an excellent officer and stayed on Longstreet's staff, rising quickly to become the chief of staff, until promoted to brigade command.[10]

The point is not that Longstreet found good staff officers without resorting to kin or longtime acquaintants. It is that others who had nearby friends, relatives, or people whose reputations they knew made rational choices when they accepted them as staff officers, arguably more rational than Longstreet's method, which was after all mostly a matter of luck. Is not Lee's example of accepting Chilton, a friend whose qualifications he knew well, as his chief of staff (although he did not ask for him specifically) more sensible than Longstreet's method of building his staff by taking unknown quantities? Conversely, when Longstreet, generally a good judge of talent, picked people based on family reputation or ties, he occasionally got burned. Captain Macon Thompson from Mississippi, son of Jacob Thompson, who had been James Buchanan's secretary of the interior, was an unfortunate example. Sorrel commented about Captain Thompson, who served briefly as Longstreet's aide, "He was an extraordinary looking person. Nature had been unkind." Thompson's jaws were locked shut—he had some teeth removed so he could eat and drink. Sorrel's comment summed up this unfortunate young man's career—he "was not subject to military duty and soon returned to his home." That was not an isolated case. Dorsey Pender thought A. P. Hill was relieved when his inefficient brother-in-law, Major Richard C. Morgan, finally left the staff to join his famous brother, John Hunt Morgan, in Kentucky. D. H. Hill eventually had to ask his wife's brother, Lieutenant Randolph H. Morrison Jr., to resign his commission as an aide when poor health kept Morrison out of several battles, his primary responsibility.[11]

A second caveat is that friends, relatives, and acquaintances always were a minority on the staffs of the Army of Northern Virginia. Staff members who were not prewar friends or family members always outnumbered the examples of patronage. Also, the practice was not a Southern monopoly but was common on both sides of the Mason-Dixon line. U. S. Grant's staff was largely a crew from Galena, Illinois, by way of the 21st Illinois. They were completely inexperienced, but Grant knew them from his time working in his father's shop. However, it is unlikely Army of Northern Virginia commanders kept small staffs of nonprofessional acquaintances because they liked to micromanage their units, as John Keegan claims Grant did.[12] And finally, being a relative or friend did not necessarily mean that a staff officer was inefficient. Considering the almost universal lack of prior experience of the potential candidates, a son, nephew, or old friend might as easily prove to be as useful a staff officer as a stranger. Most of the previously cited examples of relatives and friends served admirably.

Staff officers got their positions for a variety of reasons—friendship and blood relation being only one consideration. Those reasons and the qualities considered in the selection process varied considerably. Jackson made room on his staff when Major E. Frank Paxton lost a reelection bid in the 27th Virginia Infantry Regiment. Jackson kept Paxton on the staff until he could promote the major to brigadier and put him in command of the Stonewall Brigade. Upon getting promoted to general, Moxley Sorrel picked his longtime courier sergeant, Spencer, who had proven himself often, as his aide. Jeb Stuart made a young private, Richard E. Frayser, who gave invaluable service as a guide on the ride around Mc-Clellan (June 12–15, 1862), a Signal Corps captain. Jed Hotchkiss got his appointment as Jackson's topographical engineer after submitting letters of recommendation and performing satisfactorily on an informal reconnaissance and mapping test. Some reasons even seem quixotic. Randolph McKim got his place on George H. Steuart's staff because he had been a good soldier and was the first to reenlist for the war, surely a unique reenlistment bonus, and Jackson only hired people who liked to get up early in the morning.[13]

Courage topped the list of personal qualities commanders sought in staff officers. When contemporaries commented on staff attributes, they inevitably mentioned bravery. Some men won appointment to the staff specifically because of bravery. William Blackford's financial and social status (he was prosperous, owned many slaves, and was married to ex-Virginia Governor Wyndham Robertson's daughter) probably impressed Stuart. However, what won Blackford appointment on the cavalryman's staff was returning under fire in the face of a pursuing enemy to retrieve a pistol lost while jumping his horse over a fence. Longstreet reportedly offered chaplain James Sinclair of the 5th North Carolina a position on his staff for leading his regiment in several charges at First Manassas. Private H. E. Peyton "stuck so tight and so gallantly to Beauregard" at Manassas that he made staff captain. Other qualities that rated high were efficiency, industriousness, affability, morals, and even looks. Some assessments from the time give the flavor of what commanders sought in their staff officers: "Possessing courage, good judgment, affability, and industrious business habits, he has proven to be most valuable in his official position." "Lieutenant [Oscar] Lane was a handsome, brave, chivalrous, dashing young officer. His humor, fine manners and generous impulses made him universally popular. He was the life of our headquarters, where he was beloved by everyone." Stuart "liked his staff to present a handsome, soldierly appearance, and liked a handsome man as much almost as he did a handsome woman." "Lieutenant Eugene Gordon, brother of Brig. Genl. Gordon . . . about nineteen years old, unexceptionable in morals, courteous in demeanor, brave in action, ambitious withal—suits the position which he temporarily holds, and discharges its duties admirably." "In the discharge of all office work, he was remarkably accurate, prompt and efficient; and on the field, quick, cool, bold and dashing—just the officer to inspire troops with confidence. . . . He too, was a very intelligent, highly educated, noble-hearted, Christian gentleman." "I have known him for a long time—He is honest, capable, and a devout Christian." Even good penmanship counted for something.[14]

The staff members had to be brave and efficient, but, equally significant, they had to get along together. Confederates frequently referred to their staffs as military families: "He will mess with me & constitute one of my military family like the others." Lee called his staff "my young family." The comments above about being courteous, gentlemanly, and quick witted strike directly at this trait. Sorrel described members of Longstreet's staff as "the most pious of churchmen and . . . a born bon vivant," or "much older than most of us, but 'bon comrade,' and [with] an exhaustless fund of incidents and anecdotes, which he told inimitably." Confederates even complained that regimental commanders emphasized affability over other qualifications when selecting their chaplains: "In nine out of ten cases, these officers prefer a good *companion* to a good *minister*."[15]

But companionability was important. It was one reason a commander might favor a socially adaptable friend or relative over a stranger. The staff had to live and work together efficiently twenty-four hours a day. Disruptive personalities could do tremendous damage. Normally, people who did not fit in either quit or were quickly reassigned. At least one officer left Brigadier General William Mahone's mess when the general's disappointment at not being promoted soured relations with his staff. Longstreet's most recent biographer thinks the general only kept the fiery Thomas Walton, who had an incredible temper and was difficult to live with, on his staff as a favor to a relative, L. Q. C. Lamar, who had been Walton's professor at the University of Mississippi. However, even Walton was affable when not aroused, and Longstreet's staff learned how to live with his tantrums. The author of a recent work on Stuart's staff thinks that the general worked hard to pick men with a combination of talent and personality that allowed them to live and work together harmoniously.[16] Contemporaries recognized that quality in Stuart as well. William Blackford commented, "Quick and warmhearted in his feelings, [Stuart] was liable to form sudden fancies for those who courted his good will, and in this way he put on his staff sometimes men who were not at all suitable; but though influenced by feelings, no one was quicker than General Stuart in detecting inefficiency, or want of courage and coolness in danger, or any departure from the course of a thorough gentleman, and no one was quicker in getting rid of the man who did not meet the requirements of his standards."[17] It is significant that Blackford mentioned not being a thorough gentleman as a disqualifier for service on the cavalry staff.

A final minor segment of the staff gained appointment based on service in foreign armies. A handful of men, mainly adventurers or soldiers of fortune, threw their lot in with the Confederacy. They naturally gravitated to staffs, since the Confederacy, although perhaps overly impressed by these foreign soldiers and enthralled by their eccentricities, did not often put them in the line. An Englishman, Lieutenant Colonel George St. Ledger Grenfell, who had made a reputation with John Morgan, rode for a while with Stuart's staff until he behaved shamefully in battle and left precipitously.[18] A more famous and more successful representative of this breed of foreign adventurer was Heros Von Borcke. Sorrel recorded his impression of the Prussian volunteer's arrival at the Army of Northern Virginia during the Battle of Seven Pines (May 31–June 1, 1862): "Here we saw for the first time the German Von Borcke, who, attached later to Stuart's cavalry, made some reputation. He had just arrived and could not speak a word of English; was splendidly mounted on a powerful sorrel and rode well. He was an ambulating arsenal."[19] Despite the plethora of side arms the Prussian carried, the usefulness of a staff officer who did not speak English is questionable. Von Borcke apparently learned the language quickly, although Stuart teased him constantly about his accent and broken English, since he performed valuable service for the cavalry commander until being gravely wounded.

Whatever their country of origin or reason for selection, no staff officer was worth much unless he knew his duties. The selection process did not and really could not take that into consideration.

STAFF TRAINING

One constant theme of both contemporaries and later observers has been the lack of training of Confederate staff officers. That should not have been a surprise. Few Confederate staff officers had any military experience. An analysis of the prewar occupations of fifty officers who served on Stuart's staff found students, lawyers, farmers, businessmen, teachers, doctors, clergymen, and a writer, but only three army officers or resigned West Point cadets. Ulysses Grant thought the Confederacy had an initial advantage because, since they did not have a regular army, all their experienced officers went to state units and thus were spread evenly across the army. Porter Alexander thought staff work was better in the Army of Northern Virginia than the western armies because the Virginia army attracted more former U.S. regulars.[20] However, the impact of soldiers from the old army on staffs was minimal even in the

Army of Northern Virginia. Most of the former officers of the U.S. Army who joined the Confederate cause served in the line—artillery and engineer officers being an exception. Even high-ranking prewar staff officers like Joseph E. Johnston, who was the quartermaster general of the U.S. Army when he resigned, served in the line rather than the staff.

There were some ex-regulars on staffs in the Army of Northern Virginia, though. Thomas Jordan, Beauregard's chief of staff, was old army with experience both in the Seminole War and in the Mexican War. When he resigned his commission to join the Confederate army, he was a quartermaster, and he spent most of the war as a staff officer. However, Jordan's time in the Army of Northern Virginia was limited. He primarily served under the two Johnstons, Beauregard, and Bragg in the West and in South Carolina. William L. Cabell, who served as quartermaster for Beauregard and Joseph Johnston, was an ex-regular quartermaster, but he also transferred to the western armies early in the war. Robert Chilton, Lee's chief of staff, had U.S. Army experience both in the line and as a paymaster. Henry Heth, a West Pointer with typical western prewar service, acted briefly as the quartermaster for Virginia but quickly left that post to move to the line. John M. Jones, who served as an assistant adjutant general for John B. Magruder, Ewell, and Early before moving to brigade command at the outset of the Gettysburg campaign, had experience in the West and Utah and taught tactics at West Point for seven years before resigning to join the South. Despite those cases, most of the officers with prewar staff experience gravitated to the departments in Richmond. Samuel Cooper, Josiah Gorgas, and Jeremy F. Gilmer, the adjutant general, chief of the ordnance bureau, and chief of engineers respectively, are good examples. Sorrel's comment about his own training is probably representative of the vast majority of Army of Northern Virginia staff officers: "I had no military training except some drill and tactics at school." Some officers even considered declining staff positions because of lack of qualifications until they realized they knew as much as anyone else.[21] The consequence of this inexperience in the field, especially early in the war, was improvisation. A quartermaster sergeant remembered,

> We did not have a single copy of the Army regulations in our office and if an officer had come to me with a requisition I should have thought he was putting on airs and wanted taking down. [Major John A. Harmon] bought everything he could lay his hands on and turned it over to the needy commands arriving daily, depending upon his office force to keep him straight, we trying by a sort of military double entry [bookkeeping system] to do so. How lamentably we failed, I suppose only the collapse of the cause pre-

vented being seen and known. The Major did not confine himself to Q. M. supplies, but bought and issued commissaries as well, made and fitted up caissons and did anything that no one else did and that meant pretty much all. In fact we did not know where the line was that divided the different fields and had no guide but our own crude ideas of the varied wants of the troops daily coming in with nothing.[22]

Results thus varied according to the energy, intelligence, initiative, and efficiency of the staff officers improvising the system.

The Confederacy (and the Union for that matter) had no school system to train staff officers. The curricula of West Point and the Virginia Military Institute, both famous for supplying Rebel officers, did not emphasize staff work. Staff training was necessarily on the job. However, even the best on-the-job program could not solve the problem of inadequate staff training, which lingered throughout the war. Beauregard mentioned "the rawness and inadequacy of our staff organization" at Manassas in 1861. During the battles on the peninsula in 1862, Henry Kyd Douglas said that Jackson's chief of staff, Major Robert L. Dabney, was "an excellent officer in camp, [but] was not equal to this occasion in the field. With no previous training, he had not been in the army more than three months and had no experience to fit him for the demands of his position. While he did his duty faithfully, he could not be of any service to the General in such an emergency; and as for training a staff to its duties, he knew nothing about it."[23]

While suggesting a different point of attack for July 3, 1863, at Gettysburg, Alexander commented, "That this was not realized at the time is doubtless partly due to the scarcity of trained staff and reconnoitering officers." One would think that by Gettysburg the Army of Northern Virginia staffs would have completed their apprenticeships and learned their duties in the hard school of practical experience. Alexander's comments may be an example of postwar exoneration of Lee (by then being actively canonized in the South), but inadequately trained staffs still seem to have been a problem. In 1864 no less an authority than Jefferson Davis commented on the years of formal schooling and experience European armies gave their staff officers and bemoaned that "we are forced to make experimental appointments of officers unprepared by any previous training, and who can acquire only in actual service that experience which must serve in place of well-grounded instruction."[24] However, the Confederacy did not rely entirely on on-the-job training, as the president implied. Although there were no formal schools for staff officers, Confederate leaders made efforts to distribute training literature to fill the educational gaps.

MANUALS AND PUBLICATIONS

There was plenty of published material for the ambitious staff officer to study as he learned his duties. As mentioned earlier, Confederate army regulations came out early and were republished regularly throughout the war. They contained at least minimal guidance for every staff officer, if only on the paperwork aspects of his job. If the Confederate regulations did not satisfy the need, some states published their own manuals. The difference between state and Confederate regulations was mainly in form rather than in substance. There were also several privately published manuals to instruct the novice on his duties. The most famous of these were William J. Hardee's *Rifle and Infantry Tactics* and William Gilham's *Manual of Instruction for the Volunteers and Militia of the Confederate States,* both of which were also in circulation in their prewar federal versions. In the preface of his manual, Gilham gave its purpose as "simply to aid the inexperienced so far as to enable them to become familiar with such principles and practical details of the military service as are absolutely essential to those who would be competent officers, whether in the line or in the staff."[25] In addition to drill and tactical doctrine for line officers, such manuals contained procedures, required reports, and sample forms of particular interest to staff officers.

The Confederacy also published several manuals on technical subjects. The quartermaster general extracted and published separately the regulations pertinent to officers of his corps in a special volume titled *Regulations for the Army of the Confederate States for the Quartermaster's Department Including the Pay Branch Thereof.* W. LeRoy Brown, an ex-ordnance officer, reported, "By direction of General J. Gorgas, the Chief of Ordnance, I prepared a Field Ordnance Manual by abridging the old United States Manual and adapting it to our service when necessary. This was published and distributed in the army." The ordnance manual gave the novice officer everything he needed to know: technical definitions, nomenclature, methods to designate ordnance pieces, common ordnance materials, spiking and unspiking procedures for cannons, maintenance tips, descriptions of projectiles, lists of all the parts of a gun carriage and harness, assembly and disassembly instructions for small arms, instructions for making gunpowder and cartridges, and even tips like "sabres are *curved* and swords are *straight.*" Ordnance officers had to study the manual—it served as the basis for the ordnance entrance examination. As another example, the Signal Corps published a classified manual for signalmen in 1862 and internal circulars throughout the war. These publications were good enough that the head of the corps searched for copies after the war to take with him to Chile, where he planned to establish a signal operation. When homegrown manuals were not available, Johnny Reb did not hesitate to use Union material. Captain James K. Boswell, Jackson's chief engineer, mentioned getting a copy of "Mahan's Permanent and Field Fortifications" from the bureau office in Richmond. Although the title does not match exactly, he probably referred to Dennis Hart Mahan's *A Treatise on Field Fortifications: Containing Instructions on the Methods of Laying out, Constructing, Defending, and Attacking Intrenchments: With the General Outlines Also of the Arrangement, the Attack, and Defence of Permanent Fortifications*. This was a standard work published originally in 1836 and in a revised and enlarged third edition by 1856. It was reprinted in New York in both 1861 and 1862. Alternatively, Boswell may have meant Mahan's *Summary of the Course of Permanent Fortifications and the Attack and Defence of Permanent Works for the Use of the Cadets of the U.S. Military Academy,* which had been in publication since 1850 and was reprinted in Richmond in 1863. Either book would have represented the most current Union military engineering doctrine available. As late as March 1865, the Corps of Engineers was still placing orders to smuggle U.S. Engineer Corps manuals south.[26]

Doctors and lawyers faced special problems. Medicine and law differed substantially in the military from civilian life. Special publications for those disciplines soon appeared. On duty with Longstreet outside Chattanooga in 1863, Charles Blackford wrote a pamphlet "for the use of our corps in all matters connected with courts-martial and breaches of military law." He said, "General Longstreet has sent it to Macon to be published. He ordered eight hundred copies to be printed for the use of the corps." Blackford's work eventually came into general use in the army. Charles Henry Lee, from the legal section of the adjutant and inspector general's office, published *Judge Advocate's Vade Mecum,* in its second edition by 1864, which gave detailed descriptions of all aspects of courts-martial.[27] Lee emphasized for his readers the legal and procedural differences between civil and military law.

The medical community tried to educate its members with a series of books, pamphlets, and journals. A short booklet on gunshot wounds that would have been helpful to the novice appeared in 1861. Julian John Chisolm's *A Manual of Military Surgery for the Use of Surgeons in the Confederate States Army* also appeared in 1861 and went into a second publication a year later. This detailed, three hundred–page manual with plates and drawings as well as an appendix of Medical Department regulations should have been a big help to surgeons in the field. Two other significant works on surgery were available by 1863: Edward Warren's *An Epitome of Practical Surgery for Field and Hospital* and Felix Formento Jr.'s *Notes and Observations on Army Surgery*. Warren's manual in particular was a huge collection of a variety of techniques, including amputation, resection, treating broken bones, and the use of chloroform. Additionally, as drugs became scarce, the surgeon general, Samuel P. Moore, issued first a pamphlet and later a book on using native plants for medical purposes. The book bore the imposing title *Resources of the Southern Fields and Forests, Medical, Economical, and Agricultural: Being Also a Medical Botany of the Confederate States with Practical Information on the Useful Properties of Trees, Plants, and Shrubs.* By 1864 Moore had also initiated the *Confederate States Medical and Surgical Journal,* which published articles by surgeons in the field on a wide range of medical topics, summaries of cases, hospital reports, and translations of articles from foreign journals. The February 1864 issue contained an article titled "The Medical Department of the Confederate States Army—Its Relations to the Other Branches of the Service, and the Duties of Its Officers." That article, had it been expanded in subsequent issues as promised, could have provided useful instruction on the staff, how it functioned, and the surgeon's nonmedical duties. Despite critics, who thought that Confederate doctors labored at a disadvantage for lack of a medical and surgical history of the Confederate States and a medical museum, the available medical literature was at least adequate by the standards of the day.[28]

Officers of both line and staff read and used these manuals. William Blackford, who became Stuart's chief engineer, said when he was raising a cavalry company early in the war, "I procured a copy of Hardee's tactics and studied it intently." The story of Brigadier General William "Extra Billy" Smith sitting under his umbrella reading commands to his drilling troops from the manual so intently he marched them into a fence may be apocryphal, but it is both common and instructive. Kyd Douglas reported a confrontation with Stonewall Jackson over guard instructions. When Douglas took refuge in the provisions of Gilham's manual, Jackson "admitted Gilham's authority, but had a copy of [Jackson's] order given me." During the winter of 1862–63, Douglas, then an assistant inspector general for the Stonewall Brigade, read the old army regulations, Egbert L. Viele's *Handbook for Active Service,* Charles Lee's *Judge Advocate's Vade Mecum,* "and other military books." An anonymous quartermaster annotated and cross-referenced his copy of the quartermaster regulations with notes to himself, updated transportation rates, and editorial comments when he thought the regulations did not reflect congressional intent. J. H. Chamberlayne, an artillery battalion assistant adjutant general, wrote to a friend, "Please upon good opportunity send me a vol. of good military science not elementary particularly, if you have such a one, illustrated by sketches of Nap's [Napoleon's] or Fredk's [Frederick the Great's] campaigns with maps." As late as 1865, after four years as an engineer and during the siege of Petersburg, William Blackford studied "a course of fortification, and read several books on other military subjects." Even Robert Dabney, about whose qualifications Douglas complained so vehemently, must have learned some contemporary military theory. He defined and used such Jominian terms as *strategy, tactics, strategic point, base of operations, line of operations,* and *line of communication* in the biography of Jackson he wrote during the war.[29]

In all, what is probably most remarkable about selection and training of the staffs of the Army of Northern Virginia is how well they did despite lack of prior experience and training. In Sorrel's words, "The staff had to be made up for the most part of alert young men, some of them in their teens, and it is remarkable that they were so readily found and so well performed their duties."[30]

Chapter 7

STAFF AUTHORITY AND RELATIONS WITH THE COMMANDER

FORMAL AUTHORITY

Modern doctrine teaches that a staff's authority comes from the commander it serves. A commander is totally responsible for and completely in charge of his unit. What authority he chooses to delegate to his staff to help him execute that responsibility is entirely up to him. Normally, commanders elect to vest a certain amount of authority in their staffs—the degree of authority usually varying inversely with the significance of the activity. Regardless of the activity or the amount of delegated authority they possess, staff officers always work in the name of their commander. The Army of Northern Virginia followed exactly the same principles. Colonel Walter H. Taylor, Robert E. Lee's AAG, explained the Civil War concept of staff theory: "The theory is that [the commander] is served by an officer who speaks by his authority and in his name, who is supposed to be so well informed as to his chief's views, and purposes, and so familiar with army regulations, as to be able to lay down definite principles and lines of action for guidance in determining all matters of army detail that would meet his approval, and to make all decisions of the questions presented to conform to these established principles."[1]

If anything, the Army of Northern Virginia was more formal about delineating staff authority than the modern U.S. Army. Custom dictated that staff officers be announced in general orders. Such orders, essentially duty appointment orders, usually ended in a phrase or sentence that described the broad scope of the officer's authority. A typical example is, "LTC B. G. Baldwin is announced as chief of ordnance of the Army of Northern Virginia and will be obeyed and respected accordingly." General orders announcing everyone from volunteer aides-de-camp to surgeons ended with the same phrase, "will be obeyed and respected accordingly." That was obviously a pro forma statement, but appointment orders at all command levels throughout the war included it. Even general orders appointing officers who were commanders in their own right (and thus had their own legal authority) to staff positions contained the stock phrase. Consider this order from First Corps: "Col. J. B. Walton, of the Battalion Washington Artillery, having reported for duty with his command, is announced as chief of artillery. He will be obeyed and respected accordingly."[2] The phrase was the commander's way of formally telling the command that the new staff officer had his stamp of approval and of granting him the customary authority of a staff position.

Early in the war, commanders thought it necessary to be more specific when appointing their staffs to avoid confusion about routine staff authority. P. G. T. Beauregard published a general order days before the first Battle of Manassas bluntly stating the authority of his staff. The order read, "The following are announced as the general and personal staff of the general commanding, and any written or verbal orders conveyed through them, or either of them, will be obeyed." Then followed a list of assistant adjutants general, aides-de-camp, volunteer aides, the chief of engineers and an assistant, the chiefs of quartermaster, commissary, artillery, and ordnance, and the medical director. At least one officer thought this general order was significant. E. Porter Alexander wrote later about ordering Colonel E. B. C. Cash's 8th South Carolina Regiment to cease firing at U.S. Congressman Alfred Ely, who was watching the battle. Alexander, an unknown staff captain, apparently expected Cash to ignore him and thought Beauregard's order gave him credence. He wrote, "I spoke authoritatively, for Beauregard had published an order that all officers of his staff spoke with his authority, & Cash recognized it & made no kick." Henry Kyd Douglas thought the absence of such legitimatizing orders a hindrance. At the beginning of the Shenandoah Valley campaign, Douglas was a lieutenant detailed to help Thomas J. "Stonewall" Jackson's assistant inspector general but was not yet formally appointed in general orders. While carrying instructions to Richard Ewell, Douglas encountered the command of Brigadier General Richard Taylor, which was preparing to move in the opposite direction from what Jackson's orders would require. Douglas thought the best he could do under the circumstances was suggest that Taylor wait until he heard from Ewell before moving. Fortunately, Taylor accepted the suggestion, Douglas found Ewell, and no harm was done.[3] A recognized staff officer, duly appointed in general orders, would have unhesitatingly ordered Taylor to hold his position and await orders.

Occasionally even later in the war, general orders spelled out staff authority in detail. When Robert Chilton moved from assistant adjutant general to inspector general of the army, the appointment orders read in part, "Brig. Genl. R. H. Chilton, having been assigned to duty as inspector general of this army, is announced accordingly, and commanding officers will accord to him all facilities in performance of his duties under the requirements of Paragraph 459, Article XXXV, of Confederate Army Regulations." As late as 1864 staff officers sometimes needed proof of their authority. Frederick M. Colston, an assistant ordnance officer, noted, "I was provided a special headquarters order, which permitted me to go in and about the army at all times, and call on all officers, etc., to give me any aid required."[4]

However, staff officers normally did not need special orders to exercise their authority. Commanders intended the enjoinder to obey and respect staff members in the initial appointing order to convey appropriate authority, especially in routine matters. Particularly when dealing with counterpart staff officers, the expectation was that staffs would function semi-independently, wielding the commander's delegated authority without bothering him with unnecessary detail. Using that theory, staff officers carved out their spheres of influence and decided what the commander needed to know. Sometimes they virtually ran their units. Taylor said in May 1864, "The General [Lee] has been somewhat indisposed and could attend to nothing except what was absolutely necessary for him to know and act upon." He wrote later, "The indisposition of General Lee here alluded to was more serious than was generally supposed." The power to decide what the commander needs to know and when he must become involved is tremendous. Taylor implied that in the case of Lee's illness the staff essentially ran the army, and no one noticed the difference. That was definitely the case when Lee was away and temporarily left the army in command of the next senior officer. "Usually, decisions not of the first magnitude were made by the staff and reported to the acting commander."[5]

Although generally practiced in the Army of Northern Virginia, not everyone accepted the theory that staffs could issue orders within their sphere of competence. An opposing school of thought insisted that all orders should flow directly from commander to commander. Lee faced this issue squarely. A. P. Hill complained about orders issued to his division through ordnance channels: "I conceive that the unity of my command is entirely destroyed, if my superiors can give orders direct to my staff and my knowledge of those orders made entirely dependant upon the will of the staff officer." Hill even ordered his signal officer to disregard staff orders to send three operators on a support mission—and then immediately ordered the operators dispatched in compliance with the same order sent to him through command channels.[6] Lee's response to Hill's advocacy of the exclusive use of command chain for communicating instructions is instructive.

Your letter of March 11, 1863, was forwarded to the Adjutant and Inspector General, Richmond, with the following remarks, a copy of which was sent you at the time:

Headquarters March 20, 1863.

Respectfully submitted to the Adjutant and Inspector General for decision.

My desire is to have the question decided correctly for the information of all.

My opinion is, that my chiefs of staff, in executing general orders in relation to this army can properly give directions to their subordinates in each corps relating to their several departments without my sending the order directly to the corps commander, and so down. It is the duty of the corps staff officers, on receiving these directions, to apprise the corps commander; so of the division staff officers.

If any objection to the execution exists, the commanders should apprise their principals, and, if necessary, suspend the execution till sustained. Otherwise I shall have to give all directions, and the corps and division commanders, etc., have to attend to all the staff operations, which, in the field, in time of action, etc., may be the cause of delay and loss, and at least half of the advantage of the general staff impaired.

The question was submitted to the honorable Secretary of War, whose decision is indorsed on the paper as follows:

April 24, 1863

The opinion of General Lee approved.
By order of the Secretary of War:
J. A. Campbell
Assistant Secretary of War

I request, therefore, that all orders from the chiefs of staff departments may be considered as emanating directly from me and executed accordingly.[7]

However, even such unambiguous and direct guidance on staff authority did not solve the problem for all circumstances or all times. Presuming the staff acted improperly, without the commander's knowledge, or without authority was always a convenient way to duck or ignore an unpopular order. For example, Lee had to write to Jackson in response to a complaint by D. H. Hill about a reduction in the transportation allocation, "This allowance was fixed by my order, and not by the chief quartermaster, as General Hill supposes."[8]

Some commanders ignored staff authority in more serious circumstances. Frequently, such incidents occurred on the battlefield, where staff officers met commanders in the latter's primary domain. The result was often a flat refusal to obey unless the order came through command channels. One witness wrote about such an incident during the Battle of Chancellorsville:

> A staff officer rode up and directed by command of General Stuart (who had assumed command after General Jackson was wounded), the officer commanding this brigade [the brigade his unit was supporting] to advance and charge the enemy, General Ramseur and myself being on the plank-road and hearing the order given. This brigade commander declined to move forward his command except by order of his division commander. General Ramseur then said to this staff officer, "Give me the order and I will charge." I remonstrated with him, saying as we had done the fighting of the two previous days, let this brigade move forward and we would support them. General Ramseur said no, repeated his offer to advance, when this [staff] officer said, "Then you make the charge, General Ramseur."[9]

Brigadier General Jerome B. Robertson, at Bean's Station, Tennessee (December 16, 1863), after Knoxville, received verbal orders to attack. He ranted and raved about lack of food and shoes and refused to advance without written orders. By the time the issue was resolved, the fighting had ended.[10]

A commander might also ignore a staffer by choosing which of conflicting orders to obey. During the Battle of the Wilderness, Lee sent Henry McClellan of Stuart's staff to order the lead division of James Longstreet's corps to march immediately to relieve A. P. Hill's exhausted troops on the Orange Plank Road. The division commander, Charles Field, demurred, although he began preparations for an early departure. During the night, Longstreet sent Field orders to move at one o'clock. Field told the waiting McClellan, "I prefer to obey General Longstreet's order."[11] Neither Field nor McClellan checked with Longstreet to clarify the conflicting orders. Field simply chose the order he liked best and consequently arrived on the battlefield too late to prevent the collapse of Hill's line.

At times, officers refused to acknowledge the authority of a staff officer based on firmer justification. Typically, such incidents involved staff officers trying to give orders to someone from another command, an act that clearly overstepped their authority. Randolph McKim, an aide-de-camp to George Steuart, tried to order two Louisiana regiments from another brigade to support a battery at Stephenson's Depot (June 15, 1863). "The Louisianians readily responded, but their commanding officer, 'thinking it best not to expose himself,' declined to accept orders from me, which of course he had a perfect right to do. Whether he ought to have refused my appeal is another question."[12] Sometimes, though, officers took observing technicalities to extremes. In such an instance during the Chancellorsville campaign, officers from A. P. Hill's ordnance trains were trying to get help defending their wagons during a skirmish near Catharine Furnace. A brigade ordnance officer recalled,

> At this moment Captain [Robert C.] Stanard, A. P. Hill's ordnance officer, rode toward me, calling me, and told me that some infantry refused to "go in" for him, but said that they would accept orders from me. I found Captain Moore, another Captain (whose name I have forgotten, I am sorry to say), and twenty-eight or thirty men, who had been left on picket in the morning with orders to follow the brigade as soon as relieved. Captain Moore said that my orders [as brigade ordnance officer] would relieve him, in the eyes of General [James J.] Archer, for not obeying instructions to follow the brigade without delay, and went in at once and drove the enemy's skirmishers, relieving the train of all annoyance.[13]

Archer's brigade was part of Hill's division. Captain Moore should have accepted orders from a member of his division staff as readily as he accepted those of his brigade ordnance officer. In another case, after the Battle of Winchester (May 25, 1862), Jackson sent A. S. "Sandie" Pendleton to order Brigadier General Steuart's cavalry to initiate a pursuit. Pendleton found the cavalry dismounted and grazing its horses several miles from the battlefield. Colonel Thomas S. Flournoy of the 6th Virginia Cavalry refused to obey Pendleton because Steuart had told the unit to wait there. Pendleton found Steuart, who insisted that he was under Ewell's command and any orders must come from that general. Pendleton told Steuart to obey the orders and he would inform Ewell. Instead, Steuart followed Pendleton in his quest for Ewell. When finally located, Ewell was surprised that Steuart had not taken the order. He ratified the instructions, and Steuart initiated a tardy pursuit.[14] The command relationship between Jackson and Ewell was confusing at the beginning of the Shenandoah Valley campaign, but at the time in question Pendleton certainly had authority to give Steuart orders in Jackson's name.

Fortunately, such incidents were rare in the Army of Northern Virginia. Most commanders accepted the authority of staff officers to issue orders in the commanders' names. In routine instances, obedience was normal. Most cases of questioning staff authority occurred when the officer stepped out of staff areas into the traditional tactical preserve of the commander.

Sometimes the staff officers of the Army of Northern Virginia practiced *auftragstaktik*. That Germanic concept, recently rediscovered by the U.S. Army, teaches that an officer must always understand and act to fulfill the commander's intent regardless of orders. If the situation changes so that previous orders no longer seem appropriate, an officer should ask for a change in orders. However, if time or circumstances do not permit formally changing orders, the officer must act on his own initiative to accomplish the commander's intent—in other words, he must actively disobey orders if he believes that following them will not result in what the commander wants. An officer who fails by not exercising initiative is as culpable as one who fails by disobeying orders. G. Moxley Sorrel gave a good example from the Battle of Chickamauga: "While [George H.] Thomas was heavily reinforcing his right, a column of fours was seen marching across Gen. A[lexander] P. Stewart's front. If attacked, its destruction was certain. I pointed this out to General Stewart, his position being admirable for the purpose. His answer was that he was there by orders and could not move until he got others. I explained that I was chief of staff to Longstreet and felt myself competent to give such an order as coming from my chief, and that this was customary in our Virginia service. General Stewart, however, courteously insisted that he could not accept them unless assured the order came direct from Longstreet."[15] The most Brigadier General Stewart would do was prepare to attack while Sorrel looked for his boss. When informed of the situation, Longstreet supported his chief of staff in what Sorrel called "thunderous tones." The attack went in successfully. The story, which Sorrel used to show the difference between the Army of Northern Virginia and the Army of Tennessee, makes it clear that both Longstreet and Sorrel expected that, faced with unforeseen circumstances or opportunities, a staff officer would make decisions in accord with the commander's intent and had the necessary authority to execute those decisions without consulting the commander.

Longstreet and Sorrel had an unusual degree of mutual trust and confidence, but examples like the one above are not limited to them. Kyd Douglas related an incident that occurred during Jackson's valley campaign. "General Jackson had gone off to direct [Colonel W. T.] Poague in person. Seeing the apparent intention of the Federal cavalry, I directed the officer commanding about one hundred infantry . . . to take these men to a stone fence along the road and prevent if possible the advance of the enemy." Brigadier General Clement A. Evans wrote about being wounded at Monocracy (July 9, 1864), "At this junction [Lieutenant E.

C.] Gordon acted on my general instructions to do in my absence what he thought I would do if present and riding along the line inspired the brave fellows afresh so that they charged again." Heros Von Borcke told of being left behind at headquarters when the cavalry went on a raid so he could make decisions, act in any emergency, and keep up correspondence with army headquarters in Jeb Stuart's absence. Joseph Johnston, on hearing of fighting at Ball's Bluff (October 21, 1861) "ordered [Colonel Horace] Randal to go there as quickly as possible, giving him authority to direct almost as he saw fit in his, General Johnston's, name." Major Thomas Walton and Lieutenant Francis Dawson of Longstreet's staff urged Lafayette McLaws to initiate an advance on Chattanooga immediately following the success at Chickamauga. McLaws thought such a move would produce excessive casualties without assured results; nevertheless, he recognized the staff officers' authority to order the advance: "[McLaws] said, however," wrote Dawson, "that he would make the advance if we gave him an imperative order in General Longstreet's name to do so." Walton and Dawson did not give the order and regretted it later when they discussed the matter with Longstreet.[16]

Another time that staff officers had an opportunity to exercise authority was during the temporary absence of the commander. When a commander went on leave or was gone on business for any significant period, an acting commander assumed his duties. At lower levels the acting commander usually moved up and actually assumed command of the unit. However, that was not the case when Lee left his headquarters. Lee frequently went to Richmond for consultation and conferences. In his absence, the staff arranged for the senior corps commander to assume command, but the acting commander seldom left his corps headquarters. Instead, the army staff continued to conduct routine business based on its staff authority and kept both Lee and the acting commander informed of important issues. Taylor's description of two such incidents is instructive:

Since the General left, my work seems to have increased. . . . To add to my embarrassment the enemy's troops in the Valley have, since General Lee's departure, become exceedingly active, and between the many reports from the scouts and the exaggerated & stampeding telegraphic dispatches I receive, I sometimes am in doubt whether I am on my head or heels. . . . All yesterday, last night and this morning, I have been harassed by these miserable telegrams. I Don't believe half of their contents and yet it is a terrible responsibility to assume, to disregard them. I desire to keep Genl Lee fully informed of what really occurs and is important for him to know, and yet he so dislikes to be unnecessarily annoyed by false and exaggerated reports, that I hesitate to be the medium of conveying uncertain statements. Then I must keep Generals Stuart and Ewell thoroughly posted & although it is such a trial "playing commanding general," that I have concluded never to accept that position, when the Government awakes to a sense of my merit to tender it beseechingly to me. All jesting aside, I only hope the General will get back before I forget some serious matter or make any unfortunate blunder. . . . I think seriously of ordering an advance on [George Gordon] Meade, or rather [Alfred] Pleasanton, as by the latest accounts he has superseded Meade. You know they say "when the cat's away, the mice will play," and in the General's absence it is quite ludicrous to see the airs we small fry assume. I claim to be in command of the army and we have many jokes amongst ourselves on that point. Of course we never trifle on these serious subjects outside our *family* gathering, but here we feel privileged to do whatever we choose.[17]

Taylor might joke about ordering an advance, but he clearly was exercising significant power in sorting through the various reports and deciding what Lee, Stuart, and Ewell needed to know. The joke about being in command was funny because, despite the obvious absurdity of the claim, it was close to the truth. A second example from Taylor shows just how true it was: "Gen'l Ewell who is supposed to be in command doesn't relieve me at all, nor does my friend [Robert] Chilton who terms himself 'Chief of Staff.' Neither has volunteered one single suggestion or in any way divided the responsibility. As for Genl Ewell he is 15 miles away and though I have kept him regularly & constantly informed of the enemy's movements yesterday and today I am yet to hear the first word from him." Taylor had clear indications of federal raids. Ewell was no help. The young assistant adjutant general asked Chilton for assistance but claimed that the chief of staff had no grasp of the situation. Taylor thought somebody had to do something, so he essentially assumed command. As he later told his fiancée, "I plucked up the necessary courage and on my own responsibility issued the orders for such movements as in my opinion the emergency required." Taylor was relieved when Lee returned and "had no fault to find."[18] That is a dramatic example of a staff officer exercising authority—authority he technically did not possess. Fortunately for Taylor, he made the right moves.

Staff officers, however, did not always make the right decisions when they exercised authority. When Longstreet was about to pursue the retreating federals at First Manassas, an unsubstantiated report arrived that the enemy was moving against the Confederate right flank.

I denounced the report as absurd, claimed to know a retreat, such as before me, and ordered that the batteries open fire, when Major [William H. C.] Whiting, of General Johnston's staff rising in his stirrups, said—

"In the name of General Johnston, I order that the batteries shall not open."

I inquired, "Did General Johnston send you to communicate that order?"

Whiting replied, "No; but I take responsibility to give it."

I claimed the privilege of responsibility under the circumstances, and when in the act of renewing the order to fire, General [Milledge L.] Bonham rode up to my side and asked that the batteries should not open. As the ranking officer present, this settled the question.[19]

During the Chancellorsville battle, Colonel Chilton arrived at Fredericksburg with verbal orders from Lee for Jubal Early and William Pendleton to withdraw and reinforce the main army at Chancellorsville. Both generals objected but obeyed reluctantly when Chilton insisted that Lee thought the move necessary. A note arrived later in the day saying that it was not Lee's intent to withdraw the forces at Fredericksburg if the commanders on the spot thought they could hold their position. Chilton misunderstood his commander's intent in that instance and almost caused a disaster. In a less serious example, Sorrel had to write a note to a subordinate unit saying, "I am directed to countermand the verbal orders that Major Stone, commanding, received from me but a few minutes since. Lieutenant-General Longstreet directs that you report without delay with your command to Lieutenant-General Jackson, commanding Second Army Corps, at present in the Valley." Sorrel also had to approach McLaws to ask if he could reoccupy ground from which the chief of staff had ordered McLaws to pull back after Pickett's charge. McLaws could not, but there was no harm done. Sandie Pendleton and Early exchanged heated words when Early learned that his assistant adjutant general and chief of staff had authorized the paymaster to pay the troops with greenbacks during the 1864 Washington raid. During the retreat to Appomattox, Colonel Charles Marshall of Lee's staff peremptorily ordered Major General William Mahone's division to move. Mahone thought the subsequent straggling was "entirely due to the improper interference" of Marshall and wrote to Lee that if the colonel overstepped his bounds again, the army commander would be short a staff officer.[20] Fortunately, staffs as a rule seem to have exercised their authority judiciously, and mistakes were few.

In a highly personal organization like a Civil War staff, the authority delegated was a function of the relationship between commanders and individual staff officers. Thus, understanding how commanders and staffs interacted, both personally and organizationally, is a significant issue.

PERSONAL RELATIONS WITH THE COMMANDER

In keeping with the analogy that a staff was like a military family, personal relations were generally amicable. Stories abound of good times and high jinks at headquarters, and rare indeed is the Army of Northern Virginia commander about whom some amusing, humorous, thoughtful, kind, or sympathetic anecdote does not exist. Such evidence supports the idea that the general climate in the headquarters was good; however, a good general climate does not necessarily transfer directly to individual cases.

Interpersonal relations were subject to the personalities involved. For example, while one finds few warm personal stories about Jackson, they abound about Lee. Douglas, who served on Jackson's staff and unabashedly admired the general, admitted that Jackson "had a hardness in exacting performance of military duty which had the flavor of deliberate cruelty"; on joining Jackson's command, Dorsey Pender noticed that the old-timers did not even ask their commander questions or guess at his plans. But Hunter McGuire, Jackson's medical director, who was as close to the general as anyone except Sandie Pendleton, looked back after thirty-four years and remember several incidents when Jackson was kind to troops. McGuire even remembered a keen sense of humor and a hearty laugh, although an early staff member called Jackson "grave as a signpost" with an occasional "laugh so awkward that it is manifest he never laughed enough to know how." However, few of the staff would have agreed with the surgeon's assertion that "Indeed, as I look back on the two years that I was daily, indeed hourly, with him, his gentleness as a man, his great kindness, his tenderness to those in trouble or affliction—the tenderness indeed of a woman—impress me more than his wonderful prowess as a great warrior." They certainly did not think it either funny or a sign of great character when Jackson ordered his servant to pour out the morning coffee and pack up the mess before anyone ate to punish the staff for waking late.[21] Even G. F. R. Henderson, a prominent Jackson biographer and a blatant admirer who found many amusing anecdotes about his subject, admitted,

> But if the soldiers loved Jackson for his simplicity, and respected him for his honesty, beyond and above was the sense of his strength and power, of his indomitable will, of the inflexibility of his justice and the unmeasurable resources of his vigorous intellect. It is curious even after the long lapse of years to hear his veterans speak of their commander. Laughter mingles with tears; each has some droll anecdote to relate, each some instance of thoughtful sympathy or kindly deed; but it is still plain to be seen how they

173

feared his displeasure, how hard they found his discipline, how conscious they were of their own mental inferiority.[22]

Conversely, the Lee legend, in its semiofficial compilation by the faculty of Washington College and Mary Lee, runs five hundred pages, including chapters with titles like "Duty, the Key-Note of His Life," "Modest Humility, Simplicity, and Gentleness," "His Spirit of Self-Denial for the Good of Others," and "His Love for His Soldiers and Their Enthusiastic Devotion to Him." Even Jackson's staff's personal anecdotes of the war were often about Lee. For example, Captain James P. Smith, one of Jackson's AAGs, told two stories about being teased by the army commander during the Chancellorsville campaign, and both involved waking Lee. In the first, Jackson sent Smith to inform Lee that Joseph Hooker was crossing the Rappahannock. Lee was asleep, but Charles Venable of his staff suggested that Smith should wake him. When roused, Lee reportedly said, "Well, I thought I heard firing, and was beginning to think it was time some of you young fellows were coming to tell me what it was about." Later during the battle, Smith returned from a mission to find both Jackson and Lee asleep under trees. He woke Lee to make his report. The army commander wrapped an arm around the captain, thanked him for the information, and began kidding him: "Seeing immediately that he was jesting and disposed to rally me, as he often did young officers, I broke away from the hold he had on me which he tried to retain, and as he laughed heartily through the stillness of the night, I went off to make a bed."[23]

The paucity of such anecdotes about Jackson and many other commanders reflects both the postwar fascination with Lee that encouraged recording such incidents and legitimate differences in personality and command style. Without a significant amount of evidence, it is impossible to draw conclusions about the relations between a commander and an individual staff officer, to say nothing of expanding that analysis to the staff in general. Interpersonal relations would have been different for each commander–staff officer pair and likely changed over time. Fortunately, such detail is not necessary to understand the staffs of the Army of Northern Virginia. A few general observations suffice.

By modern standards, nineteenth-century officers were very formal. For example, Lee, despite evidence of teasing, always addressed even his closest and most intimate staff officers by their ranks instead of their first names. One persistent legend of the Army of Northern Virginia is that Henry Heth was the only man in the army whom Lee called by his first name. That was a common practice. A. P. Hill, known as a very sociable fellow, did not use first names and maintained a polite distance from subordinates to preserve discipline. Of all his staff officers, Jackson reputedly only called Sandie Pendleton by his first name. While complaining about the lack of family news, D. H. Hill wrote, "Genl Jackson's notes are strictly official." It is interesting that not only did Jackson limit his correspondence with his brother-in-law to business, but D. H. Hill called Jackson "Genl" even in a private letter to his wife. A brigade assistant adjutant general commented about a departing commander, "[Brigadier General Abner M.] Perrin feels for me what, now that he is about to leave us, he has taken pains to express, a high esteem and regard."[24] It is significant but typical that Perrin waited until he was leaving to show such sentiment. There was also a pervasive norm of gentlemanly behavior among the southern aristocracy that comprised the Confederacy's officer corps. Combined, these characteristics would have produced a standard of proper but courteous interpersonal relations. More significant than how individual officers interacted are general attitudes that affected the entire relationship and traits that might have disrupted the harmony of the headquarters.

One general attitude evident in the Army of Northern Virginia was that staffs consciously tried to take care of their commanders. Major John W. Fairfax's special duty was to look out for Longstreet's welfare. Fairfax ran the general's mess, supplied liquor, and even saw to laundering Longstreet's clothes. However, not every general had a single officer dedicated to his care and feeding—normally, that was a task the staff shared. Kyd Douglas commented about the valley campaign, "for on that campaign each staff officer made it his special care to administer to [Jackson's] comfort and protect his health in every way possible." Jed Hotchkiss noted that he bought Jackson a new hat while purchasing one for himself. Henry McClellan told about tending an exhausted Jeb Stuart during the retreat from Gettysburg: "Knowing that he had eaten nothing within twenty-four hours, and that food was even more necessary for him than sleep, I took him by the arm and compelled him to his place at the table." Some of the attitude about caring for commanders reflected the perceived duty of the staff, especially the personal staff. When Brigadier General Steuart was wounded at Cross Keys, McKim, his aide, commented, "It was then my duty, as of his personal staff, to procure an ambulance and carry him off the field, and after that to find quarters for him in some safe place within the lines."[25] The tendency of the staff to look out for the general's welfare was thus a reflection of concern and respect but was also an absolute duty requirement.

Oddly, the staff did not expect its boss to reciprocate such consideration. When commanders were considerate, staff officers noted it, usually as an extraordinary event proving the humanity of their general. Mc-

Clellan provided a good illustration of that attitude. During the march to Yellow Tavern, he was on a mission while the rest of the staff slept at a rest halt. McClellan had just lain down when it was time to resume the march. Asked by his staff members if they should wake McClellan, Stuart replied, "No . . . he has been watching while we were asleep. Leave a courier with him, and tell him to come on when his nap is out." McClellan considered such concern for his welfare uncommon. He commented, "I gratefully accepted this unusual and unlooked-for interposition in my behalf."[26] If commanders treated them honestly and equally, staff officers could accept formality and treat consideration as an unusual reward. Relations did not suffer from that one-sided practice.

But, as in any family, all was not perpetual harmony in the Army of Northern Virginia staffs. The generals had their foibles, and staff officers had to tolerate them. Especially when preoccupied in thought, Longstreet would often mount and ride off without notifying his staff. Of course, he always expected his staff to follow. More disruptive to his staff was his moodiness when ill or disturbed. His aide, Thomas J. Goree, felt compelled to comment on this characteristic in a letter home: "At home with his staff, he is some days very sociable and agreeable, then again for a few days he will confine himself mostly to his room, or tent, without having much to say to anyone, and is as grim as you please, though, when this is the case he is either not very well or something has not gone to suit him. When anything has gone wrong he does not say much, but merely looks grim. We all know now how to take him, and do not talk much to him without we find out he is in a talkative mood."[27] Pender admitted to occasionally chewing out even old friends and good staff officers who got on his nerves, writing to his wife, "I am getting so that I cannot bear Maj. [Joseph A.] Englehard, he is so presumptuous but I will take some good opportunity to set him down, which will, I think, improve him. I gave Dr. Holt a raking last night and now one for the A.A.G. will I think set things right for awhile." Jackson's penchant for secrecy is legendary, but it often caused his staff tremendous consternation. In early December 1862, the staff believed that Jackson's corps would spend the winter in the Shenandoah Valley. They selected a vacant house and a delegation of staff officers approached Jackson about getting furniture for the proposed headquarters. A disingenuous Jackson told them to wait until the next day to decide what they needed. The next day arrived and Jackson put the corps in motion toward Fredericksburg.[28] In another instance, during the move to the peninsula in 1862, Jackson took off early one morning without telling his staff where he was bound. Douglas related,

General Jackson had disappeared and some of [the staff] reported to General Ewell for duty. He said with a grim humor that he was only commanding a division, marching under orders, but he didn't know where, and that at that time he had more staff than he had any use for. He expressed a suspicion that Jackson was in the vicinity of Richmond. So we went off, a staff in pursuit of a general, and took things easy while we could. . . .

About noon the next day we detected the General as he stepped from the cars at Mechum's River. . . . He had no instructions to give and did not trouble to ask the whereabouts of anybody. He had his trunk put on the train, remained about fifteen minutes, and . . . departed and gave us no sign.

Douglas's tone, even years later, shows how frustrating it must have been to work for an extremely secretive commander. Douglas said that Jackson never asked his subordinates for advice, and it was seldom offered.[29] With such a style and personality, it is amazing how dedicated and loyal his staff was.

Even the normally affable Lee occasionally got peeved and expressed in his own way a temper. Porter Alexander related a story about getting up at 1:30 in the morning so he would be ready to leave camp at 2:00 with Lee and the rest of the staff. Charles Venable, one of Lee's aides, rushed over to explain that the general was already waiting on the road. Lee insisted that the departure time was 1:00; all the staff had heard 2:00. The general, of course, was right. Lee grew increasingly irritated as the staff slowly assembled. When the unfortunate Venable, who was scheduled to act as guide, did not hear the commander's order to move, Lee sent a courier forward to take the lead. Alexander said that Lee spoke to Venable only formally and on business matters for a week or two after that. Taylor, a Lee idolizer, did not mention such a petty, vindictive streak in his commander, but he did admit that Lee was not always in a particularly pleasant mood. When annoyed, the army commander "manifested his ill-humor by a little nervous twist or jerk of the neck and head, peculiar to himself, accompanied by some harshness of manner." Confronting Lee in such a mood one day, Taylor got annoyed himself: "I petulantly threw the paper down at my side and gave evident signs of anger. Then, in a perfectly calm and measured tone of voice, he said, 'Colonel Taylor, when I lose my temper, don't you let it make you angry.'" That was not the only incident between the two. About another instance, Taylor said, "The General and I lost temper with each other yesterday, and of course, I was afterwards disgusted at my allowing myself to be placed in a position where I appear to such disadvantage. I couldn't help however; he is so unreasonable and provoking at times. I might serve under him for ten years to come and couldn't *love* him at the end of that period." Taylor had other complaints about his boss as well. The young AAG was extremely sensitive and needed frequent praise, but Lee dispensed that commodity sparingly. Taylor wrote,

> I do have to work pretty hard, but for this I care not. I am only too happy to know that I am of some use. I never worked so hard to please any one, and with so little effect as with General Lee. He is so *unappreciative.* Everybody else makes flattering speeches, but I want to satisfy *him.* They all say he appreciates my efforts, but I don't believe it; you know how silly & sensitive I am? Mary Lou says I am too exacting on my superiors—may be so? Whereas Joe Johnston and Beauregard and others have ten, twenty, & thirty Ajt. Generals, this army has only one and I assure you at times I can hardly stand up under the pressure of work. Now I don't care a great deal for rank, but I do want to hear that I please *my general.* When every body else on the staff goes on leave of absences and I cannot, I am not satisfied to have *others* say 'tis because my presence here is necessary. I want *him* to tell me, then I'll be satisfied.

Conversely, it took only minor acts, like the gift of a peach or an inquiry about his health, to pacify the fiery assistant adjutant general. The two had a strange love-hate relationship about which Taylor said, "Mrs. Lee (the old lady) is very sweet and attractive. I feel I could love her. I *don't think* I could entertain the same for the Gen'l." But shortly thereafter he wrote, "But I mustn't claim too much for our Chief. I fear I am already too proud of him and this army."[30]

Taylor was not the only staff officer put off by the commanding general. When Sandie Pendleton asked an innocent question while delivering the Second Corps report to Lee after the second day at Gettysburg, Lee responded so coldly that Pendleton remarked, "I never felt so small in my life. I lost no time bowing myself out and riding away, firmly resolving never to hazard any inquiry or conjecture to General Lee again." The army commander's habit of quizzing, teasing, and being overly solicitous of junior officers could be positively annoying. Francis Dawson, Longstreet's assistant ordnance officer, felt so uncomfortable around Lee that he did not even like eating at the army headquarters mess.[31]

Besides having foibles, commanders sometimes dragged their staff officers into their controversies. Sorrel signed a letter from Longstreet to a Richmond newspaper protesting the paper's coverage of the action at Frayser's Farm (June 30, 1862). The report flagrantly exaggerated A. P. Hill's role at the expense of both veracity and the other combatants. Because of the letter, Hill asked to be relieved of command under Longstreet, who recommended that Lee approve the request. Hill refused to comply with routine orders from Sorrel and indicated that he would no longer accept correspondence signed by the chief of staff. Longstreet and Hill exchanged letters, and then Longstreet sent Sorrel to arrest Hill. The incident became so serious that Hill challenged Longstreet to a duel. Eventually, Hill and his division quietly moved to Jackson's corps, where he immediately clashed with his new commander. Sorrel said that the transfer resolved the incident. However, relations between Hill and Longstreet remained on a strictly professional basis from then on, and even years later Sorrel worried about taking a brigade in Hill's corps. (Hill's friendly reception surprised him.)[32]

Relations among staff officers also varied. Some had difficulty fitting in or making friends with their compatriots. For example, Captain Dawson decided that Longstreet was "reserved" and most of his staff "positively disagreeable." Sorrel was "bad tempered and inclined to be overbearing"; Fairfax was "clownish and silly"; and Walton as "always supercilious." Dawson, a British citizen who had signed on as a seaman on a Confederate vessel to get to America and then found his way to Longstreet's staff, had a political argument with Walton about the place of foreigners in the postwar Confederacy. Their dispute would have resulted in a duel had Walton not been persuaded to apologize in writing. Dawson eventually found another posting on Fitzhugh Lee's staff, where he was very happy. Of Fitz Lee's cavalry staff, Dawson said, "There was no bickering, no jealousy, no antagonism. We lived together as though we were near relatives, and I have the fondest and truest affection for every one of them." However, staffs were large enough so that most people could make some friends. Even if Captain Dawson was unhappy on Longstreet's staff, he at least tolerated Osmund Latrobe and called Peyton Manning "exceedingly kind and considerate." Dawson's case was certainly not unique. Taylor claimed that Venable was "the only congenial spirit I have" on Robert E. Lee's staff and could be quite acerbic in his denunciation of Chilton. However, at other times Taylor referred to Chilton as a friend, said the other man had been "exceedingly friendly," hoped that Chilton received confirmation as a brigadier, and admitted they got along well (if only because Chilton did not interfere with Taylor's work).[33] Others also found themselves in less than ideal circumstances. Poor relations with the other members of the staff did not impair Taylor's or Dawson's efficiency, as was probably also true in other cases. The critical link was the one that tied staff officers to their commanders.

Despite the disruptive potential of differences in personalities and leadership styles, an incredibly close bond usually developed between commanders and their staffs. Alexander Haskell characterized his relation with Brigadier General Maxcy Gregg as being "the chosen friend of my chosen General." Haskell's daughter remembered annual family trips long after the war to lay a wreath at Gregg's grave. Even as a little girl she recognized her father's grief for his first brigade commander. Dawson claimed that he and Richard Anderson became close friends during the latter's tenure as acting First Corps commander. Such emotional attachment applied to less sociable commanders as well. Sandie Pendleton fainted when told of Stonewall Jackson's wounding. An obscure assistant quartermaster on Stuart's staff thought about the cavalryman's death, "to us who have been intimately associated with him—to me in particular—his loss is irreparable for in him, I have lost my best friend in the army." A successful and respected commander won intense loyalty that shared privation, triumph, and even occasional defeat could only strengthened. Conversely, in rare instances, a commander could sour his staff, especially if he failed on the battlefield. Sandie Pendleton was initially enthusiastic about Ewell as a corps commander; nevertheless, in November 1863 Pendleton wrote home, "But this disaster will require us not to trust again to the tender mercies of our superannuated chieftain worn out as he is by the prostration incident, in a man of his age, upon the amputation [of a leg], and doting so foolishly upon his unattractive spouse."[34] Such cases are rare, however, and Pendleton's bond with Jackson is more representative of the norm than his eventual lack of support for Ewell.

It is fair to assume that despite foibles and personality differences, most staff officers felt comfortable enough in their relations with their commanders to discuss issues, state opinions, make suggestions, and question orders. Taylor claimed that with Lee, "Our conversation, especially at table, was free from restraint, unreserved as between equals, and often of a bright and jocular vein." A typical assessment at other headquarters might be that of division assistant adjutant general D. L. Cross: "My present position is a very pleasant one, plenty of work and responsibility, but I find Gen. [Robert F.] Hoke to be a good man & a first rate soldier. I have not had a better place during the war than the one I now hold." When he finally found a commander and staff he liked, Dawson described the strong personal bond tempered by formal military protocol that was probably typical of the entire Army of Northern Virginia. "By General [Fitzhugh] Lee we were always treated as if we were his kinsmen, but, intimate and affectionate as our intercourse was, no one of us could ever forget the respect due to his rank." It is a little hard, therefore, to imagine Army of Northern Virginia staffs as John Keegan portrayed Grant's—like "a sort of barbershop meeting, where those with a place round the spittoon were as free to air their views as they were to spit tobacco juice."[35] Jeb Stuart and his staff around their nightly campfires may have approached that degree of informality, while individual pairs (like Longstreet and Sorrel) may have shared the implied mutual trust, confidence, and respect; however, relations on most Army of Northern Virginia staffs were outwardly more formal and restrained.

The best way to summarize personal relations between the commanders and staffs of the Army of Northern Virginia is to quote a qualified contemporary. Arthur Fremantle, a British observer, said, "Having lived at the headquarters of all the principal Confederate Generals, I am able to affirm that the relations between their staffs and themselves, and the way the duty is carried on, is very similar to what it is in the British army."[36] Fremantle thought commander-staff relations in the Confederate army were fairly normal. Living in close proximity under stressful conditions for four years naturally produced tension, but any impairment of efficiency from that source was only temporary. Other factors were more potentially disruptive to staff effectiveness than poor relations with the boss. One such area was the formal affiliation of the staff with the commander.

ORGANIZATIONAL RELATIONS WITH THE COMMANDER

Personal staff officers, especially aides-de-camp but also those unauthorized positions (like chaplains) on higher staffs, owed their appointments directly and personally to their general. Regulations authorized aides for generals, not for units. Aides thus served as long as their general did, got promoted when he did, and were suddenly unemployed and without rank if their sponsor was killed or captured. For example, a staff officer, Samuel Tupper, wrote home, "Our Genl. ([G. W.] Smith) has now command of this division I am consequently a grade higher in rank with increased duties." Another aide, McHenry Howard, commented about the death of his general, however, "At the conclusion of the burial service, being now without rank or place in the army—for my commission as first lieutenant and aide-de-camp was vacated by the death of General [Charles S.] Winder—I mounted my horse and rode over to our kind friends the Terrells whom we had left the two eventful days before." Lieutenant Theodore S. Garnett, Stuart's aide, found himself in exactly the same predicament when the cavalry commander fell at Yellow Tavern. Only fortunate happenstance and good connections in Richmond landed the unemployed aide on W. H. F. "Rooney" Lee's staff instead of in the cavalry company to which he originally enlisted. McKim suffered similar displacement when the general for whom he was an aide, Steuart, was wounded. McKim got Steuart to a hospital: "As a member of the personal staff of Gen. Geo. H. Steuart it was now my duty to be in attendance on him in the hospital until he should have recovered from his wounds, or until he assigned me to some other duty." Steuart's wound did not heal quickly, and he went to Savannah on a three-month medical furlough, and McKim said, "This threw me out of active service, and some time in December, 1862, I went to Staunton and arranged to remain there until such time as General Steuart should be able to take the field."[37]

The rules governing a general's personal staff applied in practice to other staff officers as well. The law authorizing field army staffs expressed the authorization in terms that implied assignment to the general personally rather than to the unit: "That to a lieutenant general commanding a *corps d'armee* shall be allowed, to be appointed by the President, with the advice and consent of the Senate." Whether based on that interpretation or simply tradition, there was a common belief that all members of the staff were assigned personally to their general and could expect to share his fortune. For example, Dawson was anxious to accompany Richard H. Anderson when he left temporary command of First Corps to assume his own corps command. Anderson offered Dawson a position as his ordnance officer but subsequently withdrew the offer. Anderson thought that he owed the job and promotion to his former division ordnance officer, a view the disappointed Dawson accepted. When generals changed jobs, they took their staffs with them, displacing any existing staff. For example, when Lee superseded Joseph E. Johnston in command of the Army of Northern Virginia, the new leader brought his entire staff with him. Since Lee did not have a full field staff, he retained Johnston's quartermaster, commissary, medical, and ordnance chiefs, but the rest of existing staff was suddenly redundant. All but one displaced member of the wounded Johnston's staff followed their leader into convalescence. The single holdover staff officer left Lee to rejoin Johnston when the latter retook the field. After Chancellorsville, Jackson's staff was apprehensive that A. P. Hill, who was expected to elevate his division staff when given corps command, might be appointed to take their fallen leader's place. The recent unfortunate dispute between Jackson and Hill probably caused a large part of their apprehension, but they also lobbied for a new commander who would not arrive complete with staff. Jackson's old staff was relieved when Ewell, who lacked staff at the time, got the nod for command of the Second Corps. Even then, Ewell brought with him an assistant adjutant general who had to be accommodated on the staff. Stuart's staff was not so fortunate when that general fell. The Cavalry Corps was not immediately reconstituted, and a staff officer, Philip H. Powers, noted, "Our military family is broken up and scattered." At other times, even late in the war when the practice was officially forbidden, the bureaucracy sanctioned staffs moving with their general. Although not a case that affected the Army of Northern Virginia, the adjutant general issued orders in March 1863 that "Brig. Gen. C. J. Polignac and staff will proceed without delay to Alexandria, La., and report to Lieut. Gen. E. Kirby Smith, commanding, etc., for assignment to duty." In 1864 the Army of Northern Virginia issued instructions that "Maj. Gen. J. A. Early, with his staff, will proceed to Staunton and resume command of the Valley District." An example of an earlier reassignment instruction said that Brigadier General Beverly H. Robertson "is authorized to take with him his assistant adjutant general, Capt. W. K. Martin, and aide; the other officers will remain on duty with the brigade." Even favorite clerks occasionally moved with their commanders, although that situation was exceptional and required special clearance.[38]

The theory of personal connection to a general caused tremendous mischief. A staff officer who lost his general had to rely on whatever connections he might have to find another posting. A contemporary commentator, Samuel W. Melton, deplored "the rule which throws out of commission an officer who happens, by accident entirely beyond his control, to lose his position; a rule which is utterly destructive of the esprit and efficiency of the staff."[39] Jefferson Davis vetoed a staff reorganization bill in part because "there will also be embarrassment in their tenure of office and assignment to duty, as when a general officer dies or is relieved from his command there remains no duties to be performed by the staff which has been authorized for him especially. However valuable or meritorious the officers may be, they are displaced by the staff chosen by the successor in command. Nothing remains but to deprive them of their commissions, without fault of their own, or to keep them in service as supernumeraries, and thus add to the number of officers already in excess of the wants of the Army." In the same letter, Davis commented on other evils of the system:

> If, otherwise, each staff officer becomes dependent upon the particular commander with whom he is serving, no means of comparison exists between the relative merits of the officers. Each looks for promotion to the favor of his general, and raises in grade, not by his own relative merit, but by the patronage of his commander. A gallant and able commander, whose own promotion is exceptionally rapid by reason of his special merits, is thus enabled to lift to higher grades the officers of his staff to whom he has become attached by companionship in the field, although these officers may be far inferior in merit and length of service to others whose duties have connected them with generals less distinguished. Promotion thus becomes with the staff a matter of hazard, dependent not on the merit of the

officer himself, but on the general with whom he serves, and heartburns, jealousy, and discontent are the natural result of so false a system.[40]

Braxton Bragg, then serving in Richmond, commented on the same bill, "The great error of the bill was in making the staff almost entirely personal—the mere creation of the general. Our present inefficiency is due almost entirely to this cause." He continued, "The staff, except personal aides of the general, should be considered as a component part of the command and remain with it without reference to change of command." Later in the same letter, General Bragg modified that position by suggesting that an army commander should have a military secretary on his personal staff besides aides and the full complement of regular staff, but his theoretical objection remained.[41]

Long before Davis and Bragg penned these comments, the adjutant general had acted to correct the obvious ills of the system. A general order published in July 1862 told the army the following: "Only aides-de-camp are to be considered as the personal staff officers of general officers; all other general staff officers assigned to the command of general officers, or who may be attached to their respective headquarters, will be regarded as forming a part of their entire command; and any change of commanding officers in such commands will not imply a change in the assignment of the general staff officer."[42]

A little more than two weeks later, Surgeon General S. P. Moore issued special instructions to his doctors in the field to ensure that they understood that the adjutant general's order covered them. The situation remained unclear, however, since there was also a standing general order issued in July 1862 proclaiming, "The appointments of general officers and officers of the General Staff in the Provisional Army, being made under special authority and for specific objectives, terminate with their commands, except in cases of assignment to other appropriate duties." Thus, technically a provisional officer on the staff either moved with his general or lost his position and commission. In some cases the new rules worked. Brigadier General William E. "Grumble" Jones wrote to W. Peters, an officer who wanted a job as AAG, that he had requested Peters but could not predict approval: "At one time such a request as I have made would have been promptly granted but now a new brigadier is allowed only his aide-de-camp. The remainder of his staff must be ready-made." However, almost a year after the original order declaring all staff officers part of the unit, the ordnance bureau found it necessary to have the adjutant general issue a general order stating, "Ordnance officers on duty in the field do not form part of the personal staff of the commanding general," and when he took command of a brigade in October 1864,

Brigadier General Sorrel found the assistant adjutant general surprised that Sorrel did not bring a staff with him.[43] Jackson's staff members' fear of losing their jobs upon the general's death in May 1863, well after the adjutant general's clarifying order on personal staffs, suggests how things really worked in the field.

Conversely, being an unattached staff officer could occasionally be an advantage. For example, Major General Isaac R. Trimble secured the formal appointment of Lieutenant McHenry Howard as his aide-de-camp when Howard's previous boss, Brigadier General Steuart, faced a lengthy recuperation from wounds. However, Howard never served a day with his new general, since Trimble was captured at Gettysburg before Howard could join him. Consequently, Lieutenant Howard eventually rejoined Steuart. He served in various positions on Steuart's staff while still formally Trimble's aide, an administrative ploy that bolstered Steuart's staff without using any authorizations.[44] Usually, however, an unattached staff officer was not so fortunate.

The combination of official professional affiliation and personal ties made the bond of the Civil War staff extremely strong. The connection between staff officer and commander was very deep and personal. This could cause turmoil in battle when a worried staff suddenly departed with their wounded commander, as frequently happened. Five aides and assistant adjutants general and the corps medical director left with Longstreet when he was wounded during the Battle of the Wilderness in early May 1864. Three of those officers accompanied their fallen general all the way to Charlottesville; Dr. J. S. Dorsey Cullen, the corps medical director, stayed with Longstreet until the end of June; Goree remained with Longstreet until he finally rejoined the army in October 1864. The confusion caused by the lack of staff officers on the field to help Stuart when he assumed command from the wounded Jackson at Chancellorsville is another example. Of the corps staff, Major Sandie Pendleton, an assistant adjutant general and chief of staff, and Colonel Porter Alexander, commanding a First Corps artillery battalion but acting as the chief of artillery in the absence of Jackson's senior artilleryman, remained on the field, but reputedly only Alexander was familiar enough with the tactical situation to be of assistance to Stuart. A year later, when Stuart fell at Yellow Tavern, his assistant adjutant general, Major Mc-Clellan, noted that he stayed on the field to assist the new commander, Fitzhugh Lee, because Stuart had often told McClellan to do so under such circumstances. McClellan's restraint was commendable, especially since the rest of the staff (including at least three couriers) accompanied the dying Stuart off the field and remained by his side until after his funeral. However, even the conscientious McClellan admitted that he rushed off to rejoin Stuart at the first opportunity.[45]

STAFF AND LINE CHANNELS

Considering the intense personal and professional connection with their commanders, the loyalty of the staff should have been assured. However, staff officers owed obeisance to two, sometimes conflicting, masters. They served their commanders first but were simultaneously members of a staff corps with allegiance to the departments in Richmond. These conflicting demands on staff loyalty were a potential source of friction, and regulations helped create that friction.

Symbolic of the tether of the staff to Richmond was the requirement for staff, engineer, and artillery officers to submit reports (separate from the commander's) to their functional departments at the end of a campaign. But regulations required staff officers to report "the state of supplies, and whatever concerns the service under their direction" and to "receive their orders" from their commander. That requirement sounds like strong support for the theory that the staff worked for the commander; however, the sentence containing the above provisions concluded with "and communicate to them those [orders] they receive from their superiors in their own [staff] corps." An order about ordnance operations read, "Chiefs of ordnance of armies and all ordnance officers in the field are attached to their respective commands, but will nevertheless conform to such orders and instructions received from the Chief of the Bureau of Ordnance in relation to their appropriate duties as do not interfere with the orders of the commanding officer in the field."[46] This statement implied that a staff officer would inform his commander of orders received through staff channels but also would obey them. There is no indication that the commander had the right to approve or disapprove such orders.

The departments in Richmond strove to gain as much control as possible over their agents in the field. Colonel Josiah Gorgas, chief of ordnance, prefaced a recommended change in the structure of the ordnance bureau with, "At present there is no responsibility on the part of officers doing ordnance duty in the field to the head of the bureau and I fear there is great waste and some neglect." An unsolicited suggestion from Major Samuel Melton of the Adjutant and Inspector General Department to Secretary of War J. A. Seddon showed Melton's perception that other departments did not hesitate to exercise control over staff officers in the field. Melton claimed that the chiefs of quartermaster, commissary, and ordnance and the surgeon general "communicate directly, and transact business personally with officers of their respective departments in the field, holding them to strict responsibility, and interfering in some measure to direct and control their discharge of duties." Melton rued that "the customs of service, founded, I suppose, in wisdom, prevent direct communication between this office and adjutants-general in the field." The bureaus had political support for their efforts to control officers of their corps in the field. In his opening message to Congress in December 1863, President Davis recommended a reorganization of the general staff to "preserve in the chief of each [bureau] the influence and control over his subordinates." Congress responded with an act legislating "that hereafter the general staff of the army shall constitute a corps."[47] Whatever the state of law and regulations, serving two masters was bound to cause tremendous tension between loyalty to the commander and staff department.

Open conflict between staff and command loyalties was not common, but it happened often enough to cause problems. An extreme case occurred in the summer of 1861. General Beauregard ordered his commissary officer, Captain W. H. Fowle, to purchase supplies from the local community. That order conflicted with Commissary General Lucius B. Northrop's plan to obtain the best prices by purchasing food elsewhere and shipping it to the army. Northrop ordered Fowle to disobey Beauregard's order. Eventually, Fowle found he could not meet demand with shipments from Richmond and began buying local food. Northrop summarily fired Fowle and replaced him with Colonel R. B. Lee. Beauregard immediately involved Lee in the squabble with the Richmond bureau, going as far as having Lee write Jefferson Davis a complaining letter. The frequent reminders to the president in Colonel Lee's letter that Beauregard ordered him to write show the precarious position the commissary chief occupied between his commander and his department. When Lee began collecting provisions locally to fill shortfalls in deliveries, Northrop fired and replaced Lee as he had Lee's predecessor. Like every story, there are at least two sides and various undercurrents to this one; however, it serves to illustrate the potential difficulty when staff officers found themselves in the middle of a conflict between their command and staff bosses.[48]

In the artillery, which did not have the pull of allegiance to a department in Richmond, there was still a potential for staff-command conflict, since the staff line was also a command line. Brigadier General Alexander noted, "A theoretical drawback, perhaps, existed in the fact that the Chief of Artillery of each Corps really had two independent commanders, namely his corps commander and the army Chief of Artillery, between whom their might arise conflicts of orders." However, such conflict did not often erupt. General William N. Pendleton, chief of artillery of the Army of Northern Virginia, transformed gracefully from an active commander to "a staff officer of the Commanding General's charged with the supervision of that rather peculiar branch of service, and only giving orders through the corps commanders, except in matters of mere routine and report."[49]

The relationship between Alexander and Pendleton provides a striking example of the dichotomy between staff and command lines. General Alexander, chief of First Corps artillery at the time of the surrender at Appomattox, got his parole from Pendleton as the chief of artillery of the Army of Northern Virginia.[50] A soldier's commanding officer or superior staff officer signed his parole. Depending on how he viewed himself and his multiple superiors, Alexander could have had Pendleton (either as his superior artillery commander or as his superior artillery staff officer) or Lieutenant General Longstreet, his corps commander, sign the parole. Considering Alexander's previous assessment of Pendleton's position, one wonders in which of the roles Alexander saw the army chief of artillery when he signed the parole.

Chapter 8

HEADQUARTERS AND HEADQUARTERS PERSONNEL

Staffs need a place—traditionally called a command post or head-quarters—to work. The essential characteristics of headquarters have not changed since time immemorial. As a minimum, such facilities must provide heat, light, and protection from the elements. Other amenities are bonuses. Headquarters also must have reasonable proximity to sub-ordinate units and to the battlefield to simplify communications, but they must maintain enough distance to ensure security from direct com-bat. Once established, headquarters attract a hodgepodge of staff offi-cers, support personnel, and personal and unit equipment that must be housed, cared for, and efficiently employed. A unit's headquarters arrangements speak volumes about the unit and its staff.

HEADQUARTERS FACILITIES

Confederate regulations did not give guidance about headquarters fa-cilities. Commanders could avail themselves of whatever the situation of-fered. The nineteenth-century norm was to take temporary possession of a farmhouse or other building and convert it into a combined office and barracks for the commander and staff. Early in the war, Confederate commanders in Virginia followed that practice. One favorite legend about the Army of Northern Virginia is that after Robert E. Lee took command, the headquarters forswore the use of buildings and instead camped humbly in tents. An observer presented a verbal picture of the idealized Lee headquarters: "A spot in the woods where five small quite plain cavalry tents with attached chimneys were grouped around a Con-federate flag." There was even a general order directing that "officers will habitually encamp with their commands and the occupation of houses is prohibited."[1] Lee partisans often present that legend to show the humility and moral superiority of their idol. Like all legends, there is some truth and some fiction in this one.

Lee had no philosophical or moral objections to using private dwellings as his headquarters. Before and immediately after taking command of the Army of Northern Virginia—through at least the peninsula campaign—Lee habitually made his headquarters in convenient houses. His military secretary, Colonel Armistead L. Long, described the comfortable houses Lee occupied in West Virginia, Charleston, and immediately after assuming command of the Army of Northern Virginia (although Long was a major contributor to the Lee myth and emphasized the simplicity of the arrangements and furniture).[2] However, Lee changed his mode of operation when the army left the peninsula. From the last half of 1862 until late in 1864, Lee worked mainly out of tents.

Foreign observers concocted or heard various reasons for the commanding general's preference for camping instead of occupying more comfortable quarters. Arthur Fremantle of the Coldstream Guards noted, "I believe [Lee] has never slept in a house since he commanded the Virginian army, and he invariably declines all offers of hospitality, for fear the person offering it may afterwards get into trouble for having sheltered the Rebel General." Pomeranian Captain Justus Scheibert thought a Confederate law prohibited using houses. Lieutenant Colonel (later Field Marshal) Garnet Wolseley, another British observer, thought Lee shunned houses to set an example for his soldiers: "A large farmhouse stands close by, which in any other army would have been the General's residence *pro tem,* but as no liberties are allowed to be taken with personal property in Lee's army, he is particular in setting an example himself." Such concerns may have figured in Lee's decision to make his midwar headquarters in tents. Alexander C. Haskell described his comfortable winter quarters in a tent and ended the passage by noting, "And in enjoying so simple a luxury as this there is the greater luxury of knowing that there is no soldier in the Army who, with a little industry in preparing his Winter Quarters, cannot have as good a bed and as good a house as General Lee himself."[3] Lee was astute enough to recognize the morale benefit of living as his soldiers did. However, the main reasons he camped in tents were much more practical and prosaic. Lee elected a headquarters under canvas for efficiency. He wrote to his wife, Mary, "As regards myself I am pretty well and comfortable enough in my tent. I should be more so I know in a house, but I have none to go to. The people are very kind in giving me invitations to take a room in their house, but they do not know what they ask. I of course cannot go alone, as a crowd is always around me." Even more explicitly, he later explained, "It is from no desire for exposure or hazard that I live in a

190

tent but from necessity. I must be where I can speedily & at all times attend to the duties of my position & be near or accessible to the officers with whom I have to act. What house could I get to hold all my staff? Our citizens are very kind in offering me a room or rooms in their houses, in which I could be sheltered, but it would separate me from the staff officers, delay the transaction of business, & turn the residence of my kind landlords into a barracks where officers, couriers, distressed women, etc., would be entering day and night."[4]

While sick and confined to a house in April 1863, Lee hinted at another reason in a letter to his daughter Agnes: "I am longing to get back to my camp but the doctors prohibit it yet awhile. You know how pleased I am at the presence of strangers. What a cheerful mood their company produces. Imagine then the expression of my face & the merry times I have." In that sarcastic passage Lee acknowledged his introverted personality and the psychological strain exacted by constantly being around strangers. When he did (or was forced to) accept invitations to quarter with civilians, he stayed in his room and avoided contact and meals with his hosts. Even camping near a house could cause unwanted attention from admirers. The commanding general wrote home that while his headquarters was near one house the owner brought buttermilk, bread, ice, and vegetables to his tent every day. "I cannot get her to desist," Lee complained, "though I have made two special visits to that effect."[5] Lee accepted the minor inconvenience of operating out of tents for efficiency and to avoid polite interaction with the residents. However, he did not maintain the practice throughout the war. His staff eventually forced him indoors.

Breaking the army commander of the habit of sheltering his headquarters in tents was difficult. The staff, worried about their general's failing health, tried various ploys. Walter Taylor reported,

> On leaving the north side the general left it to me to select an abiding-place for our party here. I, of course, selected a place where I thought he would be comfortable, although I firmly believe he concluded that I was thinking more of myself than him. I took possession of a vacant house and had his room prepared, with a cheerful fire and everything made as cozy as possible. It was entirely too pleasant for him, for he is never so uncomfortable as when comfortable. . . . So we packed up bag and baggage—books and records—and moved to a point eight miles distant, pitched our tents, and concluded that we were fixed for some days at least.

Taylor claimed the staff members finally forced Lee into a building by screwing up their courage and resorting to the stratagem of returning their boss's tent to the quartermaster while the general was visiting Richmond. Significantly, whether intentionally or accidentally, they chose unoccupied houses that precluded the need to interact with hosts for the headquarters. The stratagem with the tent may not have been as astute (or as well planned) as Taylor implied. Lee wrote to his wife, "On arriving here on the evening of the 23rd I found we had changed our camp. The house that we were occupying was wanted, indeed had been rented by a newly married couple & they had ejected Col Taylor that day. We have however a very good abode about 1½ milles from Petersburg. . . . It is dreadfully cold. I wish I had a good wood to encamp in, where I could pitch my tent. But there is none convenient. My door will not shut, so that I have a goodly company of cats and puppies around my hearth. But I shall rectify that."[6] Obviously, Lee was not pleased with the accommodations but accepted them for the same reason he usually chose tents—efficiency. He would have preferred to remain under canvas and would have insisted on it had there been a convenient spot to pitch camp.

When the headquarters of the Army of Northern Virginia occupied buildings, the front room became the assistant adjutant general's office, shared by staff officers and clerks. Lee got the best bedroom and the nicest downstairs room as a private office. The rest of the immediate staff then shared the remaining bedrooms. Colonel Taylor thought he might be relegated to "one of the miserable little back-rooms" in the Petersburg headquarters, but he ended up getting the parlor.[7] Even indoors, however, Lee's headquarters retained a modest, unobtrusive appearance and operating style.

More normal than indoor headquarters were the campsites used through most of the war. Many people commented on two aspects of Lee's headquarters—its small size and lack of ostentation. Lieutenant Colonel Wolseley marveled at a headquarters lacking "all the pomp and circumstance . . . of a european headquarters." He described it as follows:

> Lee's headquarters consisted of about seven or eight pole tents. . . . In front of the tents were some three or four wagons, drawn up without any regularity, and a number of horses roamed loose about the field. The servants—who were, of course, slaves—and the mounted soldiers called couriers, who always accompany each general of division in the field, were unprovided with tents, and slept in or under the wagons. . . . No guards or sentries were to be seen in the vicinity, no crowd of aides-de-camp loitering about, making themselves agreeable to visitors and endeavoring to save their generals from those who had no particular business. . . . [Lee's] staff are crowded together two or three in a tent, none are allowed to carry more baggage than a small box each, and his own kit is but very little larger. Everyone who approaches him does so with marked respect, al-

though there is none of that bowing and scraping and flourishing of forage caps which occurs in the presence of European generals.[8]

James Longstreet said of Lee, "He had his tents of the same kind as the other officers—perhaps a few more, to accommodate his larger staff. He made no display of position or rank. Only when he was specially engaged could a sentinel be seen at the door of his tent." Brigadier General John Imboden described Lee's headquarters at Gettysburg as "half a dozen small tents . . . a little way from the roadside to our left." Another soldier described the headquarters at Chambersburg: "The General has little of the pomp and circumstance of war about his person. A Confederate flag marks the whereabouts of his head-quarters, which are here in a little enclosure of some couple of acres of timber. There are about a half-a-dozen tents and as many baggage wagons and ambulances. The horses and mules for these, besides those of a small—very small—escort, are tied up to trees or grazing about the place." Charles Venable described the headquarters as follows: "During the winter of 1863–64 General Lee's headquarters were near Orange Court House. They were marked by the same bare simplicity and absence of military form and discipline which always characterized them. Three or four tents of ordinary size, situated on a steep hillside, made the winter quarters of himself and his personal staff. It was without sentinels or guards." Taylor, who seemed to prefer buildings but lived comfortably in camp, griped at least once about Lee's selection of headquarters sites: "and we pitched our tents in our present location, which by the way, being a bare eminence with northern exposure is by no means a pleasant one whilst this cutting wind prevails; but tis one of my commander's idiosyncracies to suffer any amount of discomfort and inconvenience sooner than to change a camp once established. So the minor lights must submit quietly, grin and endure."[9]

As if to reinforce the impression of austerity, Lee even complained politely when the quartermaster general issued him a special tent. "The tent arrived yesterday. I am now in it. It is very nice; but I fear too large, not for Comfort, but for transportation & ease of pitching on marches. . . . If however you have some foreign canvass & can make me a good tent of the Common wall size, or a little larger, I will be obliged to you."[10]

The subordinate commanders of the Army of Northern Virginia adopted their leader's style of headquarters management, although they were not as fanatic about camping as Lee and were more frequently found indoors. Before First Manassas, headquarters arrangements for subordinate units were decidedly makeshift. Thomas Goree wrote home that Longstreet's headquarters before the battle was in a pine thicket without benefit of tents or office furniture. After the battle, however, Longstreet secured more civilized accommodations in a "runaway Yankee" house equipped with furniture from other abandoned estates. The quarters were so acceptable that Goree actually called his room elegant. D. H. Hill and his staff roomed and boarded with a widow and kept two rooms as office space. When the war moved out of the Washington suburbs to the peninsula of Virginia, the divisions again found houses to shelter their headquarters. At the conclusion of that campaign, subordinate headquarters went under canvas, like Lee. Other commanders were not as hesitant to accept civilian hospitality as their boss, however, and sometimes established themselves in private dwellings while their staffs pitched tents nearby. For example, when Longstreet rejoined Lee in the spring of 1863 after the former's brief command in southern Virginia, he occupied the house of a Garnett family while his staff camped in an adjacent field. When operating independently, Longstreet used houses when available and even moved his headquarters into Petersburg during his command tenure in the Department of Virginia and North Carolina. An aide, Thomas Goree, wrote home, "For the first time since the war commenced, we have had our Hd. Qurs. in a city, and I am fast becoming very tired of it. I am boarding here in a very pleasant family at $75 per month. You no doubt think this is an enormous price, but it is less than is generally charged, and we find it cheaper than keeping up our mess with the present enormous prices of provisions."[11]

Thomas J. "Stonewall" Jackson also used both indoor and outdoor facilities for his headquarters. At Harper's Ferry in early 1861 he and his staff shared what he called an elegant mansion. Immediately before First Manassas he was quartered in "a fine, large brick house just east of the camp of the 1st Brigade." During the valley campaign he alternated between sleeping in houses and pitching camp. Rains that washed through his tent on at least one night may have influenced Jackson's choice. Heavy rains during the Second Manassas campaign forced both Jackson and A. P. Hill into houses. Jackson spent part of the last winter of his life headquartered in tents at the Boyd House south of Bunker Hill, Virginia. Inclement weather finally forced him to move the headquarters into Winchester. A. S. "Sandie" Pendleton wrote home exuberantly, "Our *hero* of many battles has succumbed and declared he must have a cessation of hostilities with the elements." After Fredericksburg, Jackson refused a room and insisted on camping in the front yard of a private home, Moss Neck, although hunger and cold weather drove the general and his staff inside on the first night, when they arrived before their wagons. However, within days an earache and doctor's orders forced Jackson into the plantation office, a three-room detached building that he occupied as both quarters and private office for many months while his staff worked out of tents on the lawn. A visitor thought "Jackson's staff seemed to be very much at home" at Moss Neck. A. P. Hill set up headquarters for the winter of 1863–64 on the lawn of Mayhurst, the twenty-room Orange County mansion of Colonel John Willis. Since Hill's wife and daughters spent the winter in the Willis mansion, the general probably slept and spent more than a few hours in the house. Richard Ewell occupied the vacant mansion of Morton Hall near Raccoon Ford as a headquarters in November 1863. Ewell, his wife, and his stepdaughter lived in part of the mansion, while the staff slept in tents and used a huge (twenty-six-by-twenty-six foot) room as an office. Mrs. Ewell reputedly got too involved with running that headquarters.[12]

Other than his penchant for social dining, J. E. B. Stuart actually seems to have been more Spartan in some ways than his infantry peers. One contemporary, John Esten Cooke, described the house Stuart used as a headquarters at Centreville in late 1861 (when Goree boasted about his elegant room) as "bare and bleak; everything about it 'looked like work.'" Cooke was more impressed by the ferocious raccoon guarding a cannon outside the house than by the headquarters facilities. Even the favorite headquarters site of the Cavalry Corps at the Bower, the home of A. Stephen Dandridge west of Charles Town, West Virginia, which Stuart used in October 1862 and again briefly in July 1863, was only a campsite on the lawn of a private home with pleasant hosts. Heros Von Borcke described the cavalry headquarters at the Bower after the Antietam campaign in these words: "This lovely *entourage* was now enlivened and diversified by the white tents of our encampment, the General's, with its fluttering battleflag, in the center, by the smoke of the camp-fire where the negroes were busily engaged in working breakfasts, by the picturesque group of officers and men who were strolling about or cleaning their arms, and by the untethered horses and mules which were quietly grazing all over the ground. . . . The long mess-table at which we dine together in the open air, was loaded with substantials."[13] Stuart and his staff spent the following winter on a hillside near Orange Courthouse. Theodore Stanford Garnett, a headquarters clerk, left a detailed description of that encampment. As a visitor entered the area, he passed the tents of the escort and couriers and the forage master's quarters with stacks of hay and piles of corn outside. A hundred yards further was a neat line of three tents about thirty feet apart connected by sawdust walks. The first tent was the assistant adjutant general's, the second was the aide's, and the third belonged to Stuart. Behind the AAG's tent was a log hut built by the clerks, and twenty yards behind that was a second line of three tents for the rest of the staff. The mess facility, a tent fly over a pine table, was beyond and downhill from Stuart's tent. Significantly absent from this picture are quarters for slaves and servants, although they certainly had accommodations. Von Borcke commented that he turned his original pup tent over to his and William Blackford's slaves, who expanded it greatly for their own use and habitually pitched it immediately behind their masters' abode. This orderly picture of neatly aligned headquarters tents was the exception rather than the rule, however.[14]

On active campaigns, headquarters facilities were neither as neatly ordered nor as picturesque as Stuart's staff described them. Lee's headquarters wagons seem to have arrived on most of their general's battlefields, but his subordinates were not always so fortunate. Brigadier General William B. Taliaferro described Jackson's headquarters at one point in the Second Manassas campaign as follows:

> Johnson's messenger . . . found the Confederate headquarters established on the shady side of an old-fashioned worm fence, in the corners of which General Jackson and his two division commanders were profoundly asleep after the fatigues of the proceeding night, notwithstanding the intense heat of that August day. There was not so much as an ambulance at those headquarters. The headquarters train was back beyond the Rappahannock (at Jeffersonton), with servants, camp-equipage, and all the arrangements for cooking and serving food. All the property of the general, the staff, and of the headquarters bureau, was strapped to the pommels and cantles of the saddles, and these formed the pillows of their weary owners.

On active campaigns, Stuart might use a house as a headquarters, but when he did the AAG usually slept on the porch, where couriers could find him easily, while Stuart and the rest of the staff slept on the ground under blankets and oilcloths. William Blackford claimed that even if the staff members slept in a house, the cavalry commander would not use a bed and made his staff officers sleep on the floor in the halls with their saddles for pillows.[15]

Accommodations were not usually so Spartan. Typically, two officers shared a wall tent or medium-sized, round Sibley tent, although finding either a single officer in a tent or three in a larger type was not uncommon. Von Borcke's first home with the Army of Northern Virginia was a pup tent (called a dog tent during the Civil War), but he quickly moved in with William Blackford. Before wounds forced him out of the Confederate army, Von Borcke had a Sibley tent of his own that was large and fancy enough to accommodate visiting members of the British Parliament (although a countryman who briefly stayed with him complained that Von Borcke's tent leaked like a sieve). Sandie Pendleton

196

described the tent he shared with Hunter McGuire (the surgeon) and Henry Kyd Douglas in October 1862 as leaky and furnished with a couple of camp stools; piles of blankets on the ground for bedding (one for Douglas and one that Pendleton and McGuire shared); a good stove liberated from the Yankees; a cross beam from the center pole to hang swords, pistol belts, spurs, and coats; and raincoats, pipes, tobacco, books, and firewood scattered about. Pendleton had earlier had to himself an eight-foot-square tent with two beds, two chairs, a table, and a trunk.[16]

When the Army of Northern Virginia went into semipermanent winter quarters, accommodations became almost luxurious. There are many accounts of two tents pitched with a fireplace between them. One tent became sleeping quarters, while the second served as combined office and sitting room. Outside, a tripod supported a washbasin for each inhabitant and a stake like a hat rack held towels and perhaps a small mirror. Inside, the accommodations, especially for winter quarters, varied widely according to the tastes and ingenuity of the occupant. Von Borcke's Sibley tent boasted a small iron stove, and the Prussian was proud of his camp furniture: "A planked floor was laid down, and over it was spread the rough resemblance of a carpet in the shape of a large square of old canvas; a packing-case which had served for the despatch of saddlery from the ordnance department did duty very efficiently for a bedstead; and with an empty whiskey-cask, which, by sawing down on one side to within a foot of the floor, stuffing the bottom with blankets, and leaving only so much of the upper portion as would comfortably support the back, became a capital easy-chair, my assemblage of 'sticks' was by no means contemptible." Cooke, another of Stuart's staff officers, described his winter quarters furnishings in great detail:

1 Table and Desk, the latter containing Macaulay's History of England, vol. V.—Recreations of Christopher North—Army Regulations—Consuelo, by George Sand—Bragelonne, by the great Dumas—The Monk's Revenge—and several official papers. A Bible and Prayer Book too. . . . Flanking the literary contents—a bag of tobacco—a laurel pipe of curious design, the gift of Bumpo—an old ink bottle—a pistol, cartridges, and sabre; the latter with rusty scabbard.

2 Wooden chairs

1 Mess chest, only half as convenient as the old cannon ammunition box, long used for a like purpose—with compartments, formerly for "Spherical case," now serving to hold coffee, sugar, and much more.

4 Blankets, neatly folded, on a bed of straw.

1 India rubber "Poncho," excellent for rainy days on horseback. . . .

1 Valise, black leather, formerly used on summer journeys to the mountains, now for a wardrobe. . . .

1 Saddle, bridle and accoutrements, on a rack, at foot of bed, in the corner.

2 Overcoats, which have been through the wars, and will cheerfully be exchanged for one which has not.

1 Pile of wood, by fire, and

1000 other things "too tedious to mention," but convenient.[17]

Division and brigade headquarters lived similarly but on a smaller scale. Major General Stephen D. Ramseur described his division headquarters in 1864 as "two small tents, rather worse for wear, several wagons drawn by thin mules, and . . . a flock of chickens and ducks that lived under the wagons."[18] Other than the chickens and ducks, this headquarters was typical.

Quartermasters, commissary officers, and ordnance officers lived separately from the rest of the headquarters and tended to quarter more often in buildings. Lee's quartermaster department kept a Richmond office, and Longstreet's quartermaster, Major Erasmus Taylor, lived in that city during the siege of Petersburg. Even some regimental quartermasters maintained Richmond offices. Forward depots rented office space, warehouses, and rooms in the towns they occupied, but life in the field with the trains was like life at the main headquarters. For example, an assistant ordnance officer in the army reserve ordnance trains shared a tent with three ordnance sergeants during the winter of 1864–65. However, some logistics staff officers were resourceful enough to escape the inconvenience of tents even in the field. At Fredericksburg, Major Raphael Moses, Longstreet's commissary officer, ate his meals with a local family (paying for them with commissary supplies) and slept in a nearby schoolhouse. The medical staff usually lived near but not necessarily immediately with the main headquarters. Von Borcke recalled visits to Longstreet's headquarters, where the three surgeons shared a large hospital tent far enough from the rest of the staff that Von Borcke often sent a mule to fetch them when socializing occurred at the main encampment.[19]

Headquarters got tents and transportation based on the size of the unit or the rank of the commander—both of which theoretically corresponded closely with the size of the staff and thus the space required. By the spring of 1863 general orders authorized a corps commander and his staff three four-horse wagons and two wall tents; a division commander and staff got two wagons and two wall tents, while a brigade commander and staff made do with one of each. Quartermaster and commissary officers had separate allocations since they lived apart from the rest of the staff, and the medical department had its own wagons and hospital tents. This was a significant reduction from the authorization contained in regulations, which allowed every general officer three tents, every staff officer above the rank of captain two tents, and every captain on the staff a tent of his own. Also, there was room for negotiation about authorizations. William Pendleton complained about his headquarters authorization under this general order, and Lee responded, "Your duties in position are more nearly allied to that of a major-general than a brigadier. If you find it necessary, therefore, the transportation and camp equipage of the former can be allowed to you." Both William Blackford and Jed Hotchkiss had special authorization for wagons to haul their mapmaking equipment. E. Porter Alexander decided, apparently on his own, that he needed more mobility as the army's chief of ordnance than he had traveling and living with the headquarters. He scrounged his own wagon, tent, driver, cook, camping equipment, and traveling desk "so as to be footloose to go & come when & where I chose." However, in the spring of 1864 the army brought even these miscellaneous officers and their transportation under control. An incredibly detailed order issued in early April (and amended to be even more restrictive before the month expired) allocated transportation and tentage to everyone from the inspector general to engineers, medical staff, and provost guards at every level from army to company.[20]

Despite the official emphasis organizational equipment received, it was far from the only necessity of a staff. Each officer also had to supply his personal uniforms and equipment.

UNIFORMS AND EQUIPMENT

Besides outlining their general duties, army regulations also described in detail the staff officers' uniform. General officers and officers of the general staff wore buff facings on the lapels of their uniforms and convex bright gilt buttons featuring a raised eagle surrounded by stars. Surgeons wore black facings. Aides-de-camp could elect whether to retain the buttons of their branch or adopt the staff uniform. Engineers wore the buff facings of the staff but had special buttons emblazoned with an E.[21]

Surviving letters and correspondence show that staff officers (like their brothers in the line) tried hard to comply with uniform requirements but apparently had only spotty success. When McHenry Howard won appointment from the ranks to be Brigadier General Charles S. Winder's aide, the best he could do for a uniform was a plain, ready-made, gray coat he picked up in Richmond. To that he added over time the red sash of a Union officer, which he liberated near Winchester from an abandoned sutler's wagon. Howard thought the sash gave his outfit a commissioned look and wore it for most of the war. To indicate his rank, Howard donned a pair of U.S. lieutenant's epaulets given him by a woman in Charles Town, West Virginia. Most staff officers, especially those with sufficient means, made more effort to clothe themselves according to regulation than did Howard, but his nonstandard outfit did not evoke criticism in the Army of Northern Virginia. Regulation uniforms were expensive, and even the best became tattered and disreputable after hard service in the field. Von Borcke reported, "My personal appearance, after so long a period of rough service in the field, was somewhat out of repair for the streets of the metropolis [Richmond]. I looked, indeed, more like a bandit than a staff officer. There were several large holes for ventilation in my hat, my coat was full of rents, and my riding-boots were soleless, so that, having worn for some time past my last pair of socks, my naked feet now touched the pavement as I walked." Von Borcke was not alone in his disreputable uniform. Even Walter Taylor at army headquarters had to write home asking for a new hat, "It being unanimously conceded that the one I now wear is a disgrace to the staff." By 1864 Goree had given up buying new clothes and was patching his old uniforms and turning the coats inside out. Field conditions were not easy on uniforms, and Confederate staff officers did not take especially good care of their clothing. Taylor was satisfied with four shirts, a quantity that allowed him to wear one a week (without ever taking it off) and wash all four once a month. Besides normal, or abnormal, wear and tear, uniforms occasionally suffered strange fates, like Captain Francis Dawson's coat, which a hungry mule ate while its owner slept on the Fredericksburg battlefield.[22]

When Stuart appointed R. Channing Price as his aide, Von Borcke sent the young man a list of necessary items of uniform and equipment to bring when he reported. At the head of the list was a good horse with a Jenifer saddle and bridle. Following closely were a saber and pistol. Von Borcke also suggested a uniform trimmed in yellow or buff in either coat or jacket style, a good pair of cavalry boots with spurs, and either a gray or a black hat. Besides those basics, Price needed a saddle blanket, another blanket for himself, an oilcloth raincoat, and miscellaneous items like combs and brushes. Cooke reported that in the winter of 1861 as an aide for Stuart he traveled in a light one-horse carriage. This unusual transportation for a cavalryman was practical for hauling around his personal gear, "which would certainly have sunk a horseman fathoms deep in the terrible mud of the region." Cooke and his fellow staff officers would not have to worry about being overburdened by personal effects for long. The Army of Northern Virginia quickly trimmed weight allowances for officers' baggage until in 1863 a general could have eighty pounds of gear, a field-grade officer sixty-five, and a company-grade officer fifty. A year later, personal baggage authorizations were down to sixty pounds for a general, fifty for a field-grade officer, and thirty for a company-grade officer.[23]

The weapons of the staff were a matter of personal preference. Like other items of personal equipment, officers usually started the war with too much and gradually trimmed down to the absolute necessities. Von Borcke may have been an extreme case, but when he joined the Army of Northern Virginia he was an "ambulating arsenal." G. Moxley Sorrel described the Prussian volunteer's initial collection of weapons:

> "[a] double-barreled rifle was strapped across his back, a Winchester carbine hung by his hip, heavy revolvers were in his belt, right and left side; an enormous straight double-edged sharp-pointed cuirasseur's saber hung together with sabertasche to his left thigh, and a short 'couteau de chasse' finished up his right side. Besides, his English army saddle bore two large holsters, one for his field-glasses, the other for still another revolver, bigger and deadlier than all the others. . . . When next I saw him he had discarded—taught by experience—all his arsenal except his good saber and a couple of handy pistols."[24]

Sorrel's description of Von Borcke's armament later in the war—a good sword and a pair of pistols—was the standard equipment for a staff officer.

Besides uniforms and weapons, staff officers needed a few specific items of equipment, primary among them a horse. Virtually every staff officer of the Army of Northern Virginia who left records of his wartime experience mentioned his horse at least in passing. There are stories about and descriptions of favorite horses. The staff inevitably commented on horses wounded or killed in battle, partly to prove the danger they personally faced. Staff officers went to great lengths to get horses from home or replacements for sick or injured mounts and told proudly of captured horses. There are even anecdotes about officers being forced to ride ornery mules until satisfactory replacements could be secured. Some memoirs comment sentimentally about the postwar lives of favorite horses in retirement. Such concern with mounts is natural. The horse was the one absolutely essential piece of equipment for a Civil War staff officer. Most general and staff officers kept more than one horse so they would always have a fresh mount and as insurance against misfortune. Slaves tended the spare horses and rode them when the headquarters moved. An unfortunate staff officer who lost his horse could generally borrow a brother officer's spare until he found a suitable remount. Officers even swapped horses so the occasional bearer of messages to the enemy could be splendidly mounted.[25] Horses were critical, and the staff went to great lengths to secure and care for them.

Another important piece of equipment was a good set of field glasses. Alexander was proud of the "long spy glass" he carried throughout the war in a special holster on his saddle. He found it "of infinite value, many times as powerful as the best glass of the opera type ever made." Most officers carried regular binoculars, however—what Alexander called opera glasses. Blackford boasted about the unusually large and powerful pair he carried and wrote derisively about the fondness of Union staff officers for wearing field glasses as status symbols. Of the loot captured from John Pope's headquarters at Catlett's Station (August 23, 1862), Blackford said, "The booty secured by the men was of great value. Officers secured many field glasses, for in those days no quartermaster or commissary in [the Union] army seemed to consider himself equipped without a splendid pair slung round his neck and a cavalry revolver in his belt." Von Borcke was one fortunate staff officer who received from the Catlett Station loot "a magnificent field-glass, which was afterward of great service."[26]

Maps, rain slickers, blankets, pencils and paper, and perhaps a small trunk or carpetbag to carry spare clothing completed the staff officer's personal equipment. It is fair to say that after the excesses of the first months of the war, staff officers traveled light. A pair of good horses, a serviceable uniform as close to regulation as he could find, a sword and a pistol or two, and a set of binoculars were all he really needed.

CLERKS

Besides the commander and his staff, all the headquarters in the Army of Northern Virginia had clerks. They were never as numerous as in the departments in Richmond, where the Adjutant and Inspector General Department alone employed sixty-one clerks and the quartermaster general eighty-eight, but they were still ever present and essential, if only to respond to all the paperwork their counterparts in the capital produced.[27]

Field headquarters got along with relatively few clerks, although because of the distributed nature of the headquarters fixing their number is difficult. Lee's headquarters paroled four soldiers (a sergeant and three privates) assigned to the 39th Virginia Cavalry Battalion who listed their duty positions as clerks in the headquarters of the Army of Northern Virginia. A fifth soldier paroled with the 12th Mississippi listed himself as detailed to the adjutant and inspector general, Army of Northern Virginia. He was probably a clerk, which would be consistent with Taylor's statement that he employed five clerks as the army assistant adjutant general. The quartermaster and commissary had their own clerks, while the army artillery headquarters had two. These were not the only clerks in the army headquarters—the engineer, ordnance, and medical departments each probably had one or two—but the total would not have been great. Corps and division headquarters also had a sprinkling of clerks. Looking only at one unit, in the spring of 1862 Stonewall Jackson had two clerks at his headquarters in the Shenandoah Valley. Shortly after that, though, at the Battle of Malvern Hill, a different clerk, Hugh McGuire, lent Jackson a novel. Jackson's division headquarters wagons were at Mechanicsville (the reason nobody else had a book), so at least one clerk was forward with the command group even if the headquarters tentage and equipment was not set up. Simultaneously, William Allan, who would eventually rise to be the corps chief of ordnance, was serving as a clerk for Jackson's quartermaster. Later, Jackson's commissary officer messed with his assistant, a courier, and four other individuals, at least some of whom were probably clerks. Hotchkiss employed a revolving staff of two or three military and civilian clerks/draftsmen in the topographical section of Jackson's engineer office.[28]

If division and corps headquarters had a few clerks in every staff section, brigades could be expected to need some, too. One clerk per brigade seems to have been the norm. Clement A. Evans described his brigade clerk as "Emery Mattox, the lean, lank, sober looking, but not always sober *acting*, clerk of the Assistant Adjutant-General."[29] Whatever a clerk's propensity to drink, brigade headquarters would have found functioning without one impossible.

An editor's footnote to D. H. Hill's article on the Battle of South Mountain (September 14, 1862) in *Battles and Leaders of the Civil War*, mentions Thomas White, the chief clerk in the Army of Northern Virginia adjutant and inspector general's office. The fact that twenty-five years after the battle White had accurate strength figures for Lee's army at Antietam illustrates what clerks did. They kept administrative files and records and made copies of correspondence. Before the invention of photocopiers, recording correspondence in a headquarters that handled the voluminous flow of paperwork Lee's did would have been a full-time job for several men. Frank Paxton, serving as an AAG on Jackson's staff before moving to command the Stonewall Brigade, wrote home, "I do scarcely any writing, leaving it all to my clerk, Mr. Figgat. If I undertook to do the writing, my eyes would not last long."[30]

Clerking was a mundane job against which the most spirited rebelled. Allan used his education and connections to move from a clerk's position into a commissioned ordnance posting. George Green, a lad of sixteen who was a clerk in Jubal Early's division headquarters, was "more fond of riding courier for him and driving spurs into the flanks of a horse than of driving pen across paper." Green captured fifty prisoners in Gettysburg at the close of the first day of fighting—not the stereotypical clerk's behavior. Robert Craighill left a cushy job as a clerk in a hospital to join the cavalry.[31] Most clerks, however, stayed at headquarters and shuffled papers.

Clerks often got their positions, like other members of the staff, based on whom they knew or to whom they were related. Allan had been a friend of Sandie Pendleton, Jackson's chief of staff. Pendleton encouraged his friend to take the ordnance examination and was probably also pivotal in getting Allan appointed to the corps staff. Dorsey Pender worked to get his wife's youngest brother assigned as a clerk where he could "learn more about office matters but less about drill." Craighill's older brother, Edward, a surgeon, secured Robert a job as a hospital clerk and later used his influence to have Robert reassigned as a clerk after recovering from a wound. Beyond considerations of nepotism, the primary qualifications for being a clerk were education and penmanship. Allan, who held a master's degree from the University of Virginia, was not atypical of clerks early in the war. Hotchkiss mentioned that the Washington College Company provided the two clerks in Jackson's headquarters during the valley campaign. Robert Craighill got his first job as a hospital clerk when the medical director "found out how bright he was and how ready with a pen." The orderly sergeant (first sergeant) of an artillery battery that was being disbanded after Antietam found himself unemployed since both batteries to which his men were moving already had orderly sergeants. The battalion commander took the sergeant as a clerk because of good penmanship and facility with filling out reports. Thus, at the beginning of the war, clerks tended to be what Pender described as "very nice gentlemen," better associates than might be found in the line. However, as the war progressed, the army needed even the nicest gentlemen in the ranks. Congress acted to prohibit hiring civilian clerks and later to prohibit detailing able-bodied men to clerical positions.[32] Those acts help explain the small number of clerks in field headquarters and mean that at the end of the war many clerks were probably unfit for combat duty.

Clerks were an important but almost invisible part of Army of Northern Virginia headquarters. Like their counterparts in modern armies, their contribution was significant in keeping the administrative wheels greased. Also like their modern counterparts, they get little credit for their unglamourous work.

COURIERS, ORDERLIES, AND ESCORTS

Other workers at headquarters in the Army of Northern Virginia who are almost historically invisible (although they get more recognition than clerks) were couriers, orderlies, and escorts. Although today each of those titles implies different duties, they were virtually interchangeable in the Civil War. The most common prewar and European term for this class of soldier was orderlies, but Johnny Reb usually called them couriers. The term was so unusual that Arthur Fremantle had to explain it to his British readers. Occasionally, especially early in the war, true escorts appeared, as when a company of infantry accompanied Jackson while he moved well ahead of his main force during the Shenandoah Valley campaign, but usually Army of Northern Virginia couriers did escort as an additional duty. Henry McClellan showed exactly that mixture of functions when he talked about "Stuart, with his staff and escort of couriers." Whatever their title, couriers, orderlies, and escorts provided invaluable service. Captain Justus Scheibert, a Pomeranian observer who accompanied the Army of Northern Virginia from Chancellorsville to Gettysburg, thought couriers were so distinct that he classified them as one of four separate types of Confederate cavalry. At least one Confederate thought couriers were the only useful form of cavalry.[33]

Army regulations told commanding generals to decide at the start of a campaign how many orderlies they needed, from what units, and for how long. These mounted soldiers were to travel with the general and perform the duties of escorts—essentially bodyguards and horse holders, although the regulations did not describe an escort's responsibilities. Oddly, the regulations said, "Mounted soldiers are to be employed to carry dispatches only in special and urgent cases." By regulation, only officers, and preferably only staff officers, carried verbal and important written orders. If a courier carried a message, commanders were supposed to mark it with the place and time of departure and the place and time of receipt.[34] As in other areas, the Army of Northern Virginia did not strictly follow regulations. Despite regulatory guidance, the primary function of couriers was carrying messages—they did escort duties as an aside.

The Army of Northern Virginia tried several methods of providing couriers. The first and simplest scheme was to detail a company or a small detachment of cavalry to each headquarters. Such companies rotated at irregular intervals. That system had advantages. It was a good way to give cavalry troopers a short break from the front lines, there was always something for the excess troopers to do, and the company's officers became additional aides for the commander. To cite an example, before he moved to Stuart's staff, Blackford's cavalry company served a detail as couriers for Jackson. Blackford acted as a staff officer—delivering orders, doing reconnaissance, and so forth—while his troopers carried messages and did the miscellaneous duties of orderlies, like carrying the general's battle flag. Similarly, Lee used twenty-five members of the Black Horse Troop, 4th Virginia Cavalry, as couriers between himself and Jackson during the maneuvering that led to Second Manassas. General Ewell used his courier company to forage during the retreat from Gettysburg.[35] Conversely, using cavalry companies as couriers diverted scarce assets from their primary function, and frequent rotation meant the couriers never really became proficient at their job.

Another method was to detail specific troopers to headquarters as couriers instead of taking entire units. That left the cavalry companies in the field at reduced strength. Under that system, some troopers who proved their worth became essentially professional couriers. Such soldiers often served as sergeants of couriers at a headquarters. It comes as no surprise that at least some of those men got courier jobs based on pre-war connections. John Gill, who served as a courier for Jackson and Fitz Lee, got both postings because of University of Virginia connections. Private DeWitt Gallaher used an old family friendship with Brigadier General Thomas L. Rosser to wrangle a detail as a courier at the general's headquarters (away from a company commander Gallaher considered tyrannical and abusive).[36] However, since detailed men also did other headquarters and support functions, the details added up to a noticeable reduction in field cavalry strength.

The Confederate army also created separate courier units. In July 1862 Secretary of War George W. Randolph authorized recruitment of special cavalry units to serve as scouts, guides, and couriers. Captain William F. Randolph organized such a company in August and reported to Major General Ewell, who may have sponsored Randolph's efforts. In September, Major John H. Richardson, formerly the colonel of the 47th Virginia Infantry Regiment, got permission to organize the 39th Virginia Cavalry Battalion as a courier unit. A company under Captain Augustus P. Pifer quickly formed and reported for duty with the Army of Northern Virginia. Their arrival aroused Lee's interest, and he wrote to Seddon that he wanted to send cavalrymen serving at headquarters back to their units and hoped Richardson's courier battalion would help accomplish that goal. Meanwhile, Lee asked for permission to mount infantry to serve as couriers. Simultaneously, the general wrote to Richardson, "I have been very anxious to get your corps of scouts and guides into service, in order to relieve the members of cavalry companies now on that duty, and return them to their regiments, where their services are much needed. Captain Pifer arrived with his company yesterday. This is the only company that I have heard of yet. Please inform me what progress you have made in your organization, and when the other companies will be ready for service."[37]

Major Richardson put another company in the field under Captain Samuel B. Brown in March 1863. Brown's company, which became known as Lee's Bodyguard but was technically C Company of the 39th Virginia Cavalry Battalion, served as couriers at Army of Northern Virginia headquarters until the end of the war. Known derisively to the staff as the "Guides, Scouts, Couriers, Detectives, and Scamps," C Company attended Lee and never camped more than a mile from headquarters. With the arrival of C Company, army headquarters issued special orders that attached Captain Randolph's original company of couriers to the 39th Virginia Cavalry Battalion as B Company. The same order moved the redesignated company from Ewell's division headquarters to the Second Corps headquarters. The formation of the battalion then stagnated. Two partially recruited detachments were diverted to enforcing conscription laws until ordered to the field in September 1863 under the mistaken impression that they were fully recruited. In November 1863 the two detachments combined to form D Company of the 39th. During February, March, and April 1864, the battalion carried a present-for-duty strength of about 130 officers and men from a total assigned strength of about 225. At war's end, Captain Brown signed paroles for seventy-eight troopers from the battalion.[38]

The 39th Virginia Cavalry Battalion was an army asset. Other than the relationship between C Company and the army headquarters, there is no specific pattern of assignment. For instance, there is no evidence that one company habitually served with each corps headquarters. B Company did work for Second Corps at least in the spring of 1863. On the other hand, Sorrel said that the First Corps used cavalry details as couriers until about May 1864, when it began using mounted infantrymen. In March 1864 Lee ordered a company of couriers to support Major General Edward Johnson in the Wilderness in attempting to intercept Judson Kilpatrick's Union cavalry returning from a raid on Richmond. Even as a last resort, Lee could not send off his own headquarters couriers, so he must have had another company of the 39th Virginia Cavalry Battalion readily available. The 39th also may have run fixed courier lines or done other duties for the army. When Lee sent help to Johnson, D Company was stationed in Henrico County, near Richmond, which was well away from the army at the time.[39] However they operated, the 39th Virginia Cavalry Battalion could not fill the army's total courier needs.

The Army of Northern Virginia finally threw courier duty open to infantrymen, who were more plentiful and thus less missed by their units than cavalrymen. Infantrymen, of course, responded eagerly and even received ten-day furloughs to secure horses and decent clothing. Time, of course, was not the major problem in converting from infantry to courier duty. Good horses were prohibitively expensive. When the youngest Goree brother, Pleasant Kittrell "Scrap" Goree, moved from the 5th Texas Infantry to courier duty at division headquarters, his brothers had to pool their money to buy him a horse and saddle. If the horse was killed in action, the government only compensated its owner a small part of the animal's value. There was no compensation for private horses that died of disease or starvation. Thus, only good luck or deep pockets kept an infantryman mounted for courier duty. Officials recognized the problem and tried to help. In June 1863 the adjutant general's office granted authority to compensate infantry soldiers detailed as couriers who provided their own horses (but did not get the cavalry's additional pay) forty cents a day for the use and risk to their horses. That provision only put couriers on the same footing as other mounted noncavalry soldiers, musicians, and artificers, who had been authorized the compensation since 1861. When even infantrymen became scarce resources, disabled soldiers whose injuries allowed them to ride replaced able-bodied soldiers on courier duty.[40]

Determining the number of couriers at any Army of Northern Virginia headquarters is as difficult as other exercises in headquarters strength accounting. Blackford estimated Stuart's couriers variously at thirty to forty and forty to fifty. Von Borcke said the cavalry commander generally had from ten to twelve couriers immediately with him. Keeping ten to twelve couriers with the commander could easily have required a detachment three times that size with the headquarters. Because of the nature of cavalry operations, Stuart needed more couriers than did the infantry commanders, so forty couriers in his headquarters is not unreasonable. Sorrel said the standard allocation of couriers for the infantry was six per corps headquarters, four per division, and two per brigade. That figure must be the absolute bottom end of the spectrum, since Second Corps headquarters paroled ten couriers and Charles W. Field's division quartermaster paroled three, not including any serving at the main headquarters. In November 1862 the company of the 7th Virginia Cavalry that served as couriers for Second Corps headquarters drew rations for twenty-five soldiers. The number at Army of Northern

Virginia headquarters was higher than either its subordinate infantry or cavalry units. C Company of the 39th Virginia Cavalry Battalion paroled one officer, one noncommissioned officer, and twenty-six privates at Appomattox. Additionally, there were couriers at the other sites that comprised the complete headquarters. For example, William Pendleton's army artillery headquarters paroled five couriers, while the quartermaster paroled eight (two of them civilians).[41] Fifty couriers is a safe estimate for the total working at all the dispersed sites that comprised the headquarters of the Army of Northern Virginia. Infantry corps probably averaged twenty-five to thirty and the cavalry corps forty.

Couriers were not a completely reliable means of communications. They got lost, killed, and captured like other soldiers and started the war as inexperienced as the rest of the army. While trying to explain why an order he sent to Ewell during First Manassas never arrived, P. G. T. Beauregard wrote, "Our guides and couriers were the worst set I ever employed, whether from ignorance or over anxiety to do well and quickly, I cannot say." However, couriers learned their duties quickly, and complaints like Beauregard's were uncommon. More common were minor transgressions like oversleeping. There were actually only two serious mistakes a courier could make. First, he could get lost or fail to locate the intended recipient of a message. That was excusable, although a courier could not often fail to deliver a message and expect to keep his job. In one such case Lee simply added as a postscript to his message, "The courier has returned with this note, having been able to learn nothing of you," followed that with supplementary instructions to update the order, and redispatched the courier. In a more serious but still correctable example, at Fredericksburg Lieutenant James P. Smith, Jackson's aide, sent a series of couriers to D. H. Hill and Early with orders to move their divisions forward as quickly as possible. None of the couriers reached the division commanders, and Smith eventually had to find them himself. The second major mistake a courier could make was passing incorrect or garbled messages. That was unforgivable. Lee told one correspondent, "If you find that your courier has given you wrong information, he must be corrected and punished." The organizational solution in either case was simple. Important messages went by multiple couriers dispatched separately at timed intervals. McClellan provided a good example in a quotation from the diary of a member of the 3d Virginia Cavalry about the battle at Kelly's Ford (February 25, 1863): "On moving back to execute this order I was met by several couriers looking for General [Fitz] Lee to inform him that a regiment of Yankees was in the woods on the right of the road facing Falmouth." Sandie Pendleton added a postscript, "I will send another courier in an hour," to a letter to advise Early to expect multiple couriers.[42] Although an extravagant use of manpower, multiple couriers carrying the same message were insurance against disaster.

Generally, though, couriers performed gallantly, and duplicate messages were unnecessary. Praise for couriers was more common than complaints. Commanders occasionally mentioned couriers either by name or as a group in reports of battles. For example, Stuart cited one of his couriers repeatedly in official reports, finally securing a commission for the trooper and putting him in charge of the headquarters couriers. A. P. Hill was impressed by the "activity and cool courage under fire" of one of his couriers. Even when cited individually, however, they often remained virtually anonymous. The First Corps official diary noted, "Hutcheson, one of our couriers, killed at 10 A.M."[43] It is interesting that the diarist thought the incident important enough to record in the corps journal and even noted the time of death but failed to capture the courier's full name or unit.

Since staff officers also delivered messages, their duties often overlapped those of couriers. Although couriers theoretically only carried written communications while staff officers delivered all verbal messages and orders, that rule was not inviolable. Couriers often did much more than deliver written notes. Stuart cited a courier who was killed when "sent to post a battery from his native State" and another for being "of great service in showing the first Kentucky its place in line." On the retreat from Gettysburg the cavalryman "sent a trusty and intelligent soldier (Private Robert W. Goode, 1st Virginia Cavalry) to reach the commanding general by a route across the country, and relate to him what I knew as well as what he might discover *en route*." Even more explicitly, Stuart commended his "personal escort, composed of privates from the ranks" for "acting as they did in the capacity of bearers of dispatches, both oral and written." A bystander at Jericho Mills (May 23, 1864) on the North Anna line heard Robert E. Lee tell a courier, "Orderly, go back and tell General A. P. Hill to leave his men in camp; this is nothing but a feint, the enemy is preparing to cross below." That was exactly the type of message—important and likely to evoke questions—a staff officer should have carried. A more stark example is that of Private Gill, who reported for duty as a courier for Jackson before the Seven Days' Battles. Gill found Jackson pacing on the porch of his headquarters.

> I told him I had come to report to him for duty as a courier by order of Captain [Sandie] Pendleton, and was ready to receive any orders he might give me. . . . General Jackson's first order directed me to go to each

210

Brigade headquarters and deliver to each commanding officer positive instructions to move their respective commands that evening not later than 9 o'clock on the road to Louisa C[ourt] H[ouse], and when in line to await further orders.

I got back to headquarters about 10 o'clock. I had had some ten brigade commanders to interview, which was no easy task for a green courier like myself. I accomplished the work, however, and reported to General Jackson that the army was moving in accordance with his instructions.[44]

Conversely, staff officers often carried written messages. In routine situations it was easy to mistake them for couriers. Major J. W. Ratchford, at the time D. H. Hill's assistant adjutant general, reported, "One evening, while on this march from Williamsburg, I was sent by General Hill to headquarters with a written message for General [Joseph E.] Johnston. Staff officers ordinarily carried only verbal messages, written ones being sent by courier. I wore no badge of rank, and General Johnston, not recognizing me, ordered me to report to a sergeant and wait his time to formulate a reply." The incident offended Ratchford, although when someone pointed out the mistake to the commander, "General Johnston . . . apologized for not recognizing me." However, occasional embarrassment could not get officers out of the courier business. Staff officers usually delivered important orders whether verbal or written. Kyd Douglas related the harrowing twenty-hour, 105–mile journey he made over the Blue Ridge Mountains carrying the order for Ewell to join Jackson at the start of the valley campaign. Douglas swapped horses five times (riding one horse to death) and had to be taken to a hotel by ambulance to sleep for twenty-four hours after the ride, but he delivered the message. Although that was an unusual case, Jackson sent Douglas because the message was critical, not because a courier could not take it. Douglas said, "While my heart stood still with amazement, [Jackson] told me the contents of the paper and added that, as it was very important, he did not care to send it by courier." In fact, there was a regular courier line between Jackson and Ewell, and one of the places Douglas swapped horses was the courier station at Madison Courthouse. In another example, in June 1864 as the Union army maneuvered south after Cold Harbor, P. G. T. Beauregard sent three staff officers, two colonels and a major, in a two-hour period to convince Lee that Ulysses S. Grant's whole army threatened Petersburg. That was a critical message unsuitable for transmission by courier. As a subset of important communications, staff officers also did courier duty when the mission involved correspondence with the enemy (although they usually took a courier along, if only to carry the white flag).[45]

Despite sometimes performing the same duties, staff officers saw a vast difference between themselves and couriers—a difference as much social as functional. Randolph McKim, a newly appointed aide wearing a sergeant's uniform and riding a borrowed horse without even spurs, was also mistaken for a courier. He recalled, "I was very angry and felt the blood suffuse my face." Lieutenant Robert Stiles, sent to Early as an engineer, found himself shunned by the irascible Early: "I saw clearly that I was neither needed nor desired on the division staff and that, if I remained, the best I could expect would be the position and duty of a sort of upper courier, which I was not willing to assume." Couriers also recognized the difference in status but believed they contributed as much as the staff. Private Gill noted, "From that time on until after the great battles around Richmond [the Seven Days' Battles] I was constantly in the saddle at the great General's [Jackson's] side and I feel that I at least rendered service quite equal if not fully equal, to that of some of the staff." One courier of better-than-average social status thought he really was a staff officer. He wrote, "General Rosser had me detailed to be at his head-quarters, nominally as a 'courier' but really with all the privileges of a staff officer—riding and messing with him." More typical of the social gulf between staff officers and couriers, however, was Theodore S. Garnett's assessment of his stint as a clerk and courier before his selection as Stuart's aide: "My position as a courier, of course, debarred me in great measure from the society and intercourse of the Staff Officers, tho' I will say that there were few of Genl. Stuart's staff who made distinctions between [the staff and couriers]."[46]

At headquarters, a sergeant typically supervised the couriers. That individual organized the system, assigned missions, and oversaw the care of men and horses. A. P. Hill's couriers followed what were probably common procedures. Individual couriers took turns based on a duty roster and got missions randomly as they rose to the top of the list. At night two horses were often kept saddled for emergency duty.[47] In battle, couriers took messages in turn and fell in at the end of the line when they returned from a mission, although on the battlefield the line of waiting messengers was seldom long and all pretense of a duty roster succumbed to the necessity of the moment.

To now, couriers have been discussed in their primary element, providing tactical communications, and, at least in the Confederate army, they were virtually the sole element of the system. However, couriers also acted as part of the operational and strategic communications systems and had to be integrated with and complement other means of communications. The telegraph and semaphore were tremendous tools for strategic communications, but they did not perform that function alone.

Basing couriers at telegraph and signal stations to deliver incoming messages immediately was standard practice. However, delivering messages from the end of the line to the recipient was not the only way couriers interacted with the other systems; often, couriers backed up or duplicated other communications means. A volunteer aide-de-camp sent to establish a courier line between Louisa Courthouse and Charlottesville found his orders to emplace a backup system puzzling: "Although at first I saw no occasion for couriers between the two points in question where we had telegraph stations, the necessity for them became abundantly apparent" when Union raiders cut the telegraph wires. Couriers also served as backups for semaphore lines when weather prevented visibility between stations. As a supplementary system couriers sometimes outperformed the primary systems. Only couriers could carry large or bulky items, and neither the telegraph nor the semaphore was especially efficient for large documents or very long messages. Lee told his wife to send some socks she had knitted to the quartermaster for forwarding to the army because "our little couriers have as much as they can carry ordinarily." The normal courier load must have been significant if a rider could not find room for a few dozen socks. Even with items suitable for the telegraph or semaphore, couriers had an advantage over short distances. In the final phase of the war, when the Army of Northern Virginia headquarters was close to the capital, Lee commented to Braxton Bragg, "Couriers seem to reach me from Richmond more promptly than telegrams." Sending couriers avoided several intermediate processing steps that the other means required. Thus, despite the presence of the telegraph and semaphore systems and throughout the war but especially when it operated in the Richmond-Petersburg area, the Army of Northern Virginia established regular courier routes between the quartermaster's office in the capital, various stops in the city, and the field headquarters.[48]

Besides carrying messages and more in line with the functions of orderlies and escorts, couriers did miscellaneous duties for their generals. Probably most common of these was holding horses—somebody had to control the officers' steeds when they dismounted, and couriers got the duty by default. Officers seldom mentioned that service and probably considered it so standard as not to merit comment. And if anybody stood guard at the tent of a commander, it was usually a courier—called in the performance of that duty an orderly—although in one case an Irishman from the provost guard proudly guarded Jackson's door. More interesting and exciting were unusual assignments or orders to accompany staff officers on special missions. One thirteen-year-old courier, Charlie Randoph, distinguished himself by herding stragglers to the front at Antietam. Hotchkiss always took one or two couriers with him to run errands on mapping missions, a duty for which he apparently had eager volunteers. Von Borcke mentioned "a trusty young courier, named Chanceller, in whom I had the fullest confidence, and who had always accompanied me on expeditions of particular peril." The Prussian later told of couriers taking the headquarters wagons out to gather supplies for Christmas dinner. Couriers also occasionally conducted reconnaissance. As one example, Jackson sent the commander of his couriers and one trooper forward to pinpoint the enemy at Chancellorsville.[49] Another miscellaneous mission was serving as guides. Guides might be posted at critical points to steer units in the right direction, or they might accompany individuals or units unfamiliar with the terrain. Depending on the situation, a staff officer, a single courier, or several couriers might act as guides.

The escort function really only became an issue when the general and staff suddenly confronted the enemy. Several stories survive of the staff and couriers forming line of battle at the unexpected approach of the enemy. For example, during the march to Second Manassas, federal cavalry surprised Lee and his staff. The staff and couriers, ten to twelve total horsemen, hastily formed line and confronted the Yankees. Believing they faced organized Rebel cavalry, the Union squadron withdrew. Another example comes from the account of George W. Tucker, A. P. Hill's courier sergeant, about the death of his general. On April 2, 1865, Tucker and another courier accompanied Hill in an attempt to reach the crumbling lines of Third Corps south of Petersburg. The party met two Union soldiers and conned them into surrendering. One courier ushered the prisoners to the rear while the others went on. When Hill and Tucker met two more Yankees, they tried to bluff them as well but were unsuccessful. Tucker claimed he tried to get in front of Hill, but the general was mortally wounded despite his effort. Once, during the Bristoe Station campaign, Stuart even committed his couriers to an attack against retreating Union infantry. Similarly, during the Seven Days' Battles, Jackson ordered his staff and couriers to attack a twenty-man federal outpost they bumped into during the night. Less dramatic but equally vital, Ewell's escort company stood mounted picket in front of Second Corps all night on July 4, 1863, as the corps withdrew from the Gettysburg battlefield. Taylor summed up the escort function with a certain sarcasm when he wrote home, "Don't be alarmed. We aides will shield [Lee] from all danger. Ma appeals to me most pathetically to see to this for the country's sake. I couldn't help reading this to my brother staff officers. We were considerably entertained because of her evident but unnecessary anxiety. . . . Rest assured ladies. I pledge you my word the Tycoon shall not be kidnapped."[50]

SLAVES AND SERVANTS

Servants were as ubiquitous as couriers at all the headquarters in the Army of Northern Virginia. Lee, Jackson, Longstreet, A. P. Hill, Ewell, William Pendleton, and hundreds of lesser officers had one or more servants. Most were slaves, either from the officer's personal estate or hired annually from their owners, but some were free blacks and a few were white. Jackson's servant was Jim Lewis, a free black from Lexington, Virginia. Pender hired two servants, both probably free blacks. Pender admonished his wife "not to neglect to get me a cheaper boy than Joe unless his father will consent to let him stay for less. He is very anxious to remain but in these times when servants are so low I cannot begin to pay $15 per month for what Joe does." Simultaneously, Pender was trying to convince his other servant, Harris, to get by on less than fifteen dollars a month, a wage negotiation not commonly conducted with slaves. Captain Blackford commented on the servant of one of his acquaintances who was "the most perfect Irishman in every respect I have ever seen." There were also cases of women serving as cooks and laundresses. For example, Henry Heth acquired his uncle's old cook, Lavinia, and kept her as his headquarters cook for the rest of the war.[51] Such examples, however, were a tiny minority in a category dominated by male, African-American slaves. Whatever their legal status, servants played the important role of keeping the headquarters life-support systems running.

Servants pitched and broke camp, cooked, did laundry, tended horses, drove wagons, and did the myriad functions necessary to sustain day-to-day life in the headquarters. Their rations and quarters were sparse but not significantly different from those of their masters. Slaves slept in or under the wagons when the headquarters was involved in active campaigning and improvised their own tents or huts for winter quarters. In unusual circumstances, they shared their masters' blankets. They always shared their masters' food. At least on some occasions, lucky ones got a share of captured booty. Army regulations required that servants with the army wear civilian clothes rather than uniforms. They also had to have certificates from their employers or owners to prove their status with the army. Servants had to have passes to move about the army (as did everyone), and the assistant adjutants general accounted for them using special procedures, mainly to protect the property rights of their owners.[52] Servants even got passes and furloughs to return home for visits, traveling either alone or with their masters.

The biggest trouble with slaves and servants was feeding them. When the Confederate Congress in 1864 rescinded the authorization for officers to buy food from the commissary and began issuing them rations like enlisted soldiers, the legislation made no provision for servants. The howl of complaint from the army was tremendous. A standard ration was not enough for one man, much less two, and feeding slaves by purchasing food locally (the only alternative) was prohibitively expensive. A lieutenant aide-de-camp, whose pay was $130 a month and whose regular monthly expenses included $100 for his mess bill and ten dollars pay to his servant, simply could not buy the servant's rations. People tried to work around the provisions of the new law. One brigade commander, James H. Lane, wrote, "I addressed General Lee an official communication asking that I be allowed to report officer's servants as *laundresses;* as I looked upon the act as a very unjust one; and he replied that officers' servants could not be reported as *laundresses,* nor could the servants of enlisted men be so reported unless they were *mustered* in as *laundresses* for the use of ALL the *men.*" That crisis eventually resolved itself when Congress relented. The government continued to issue officers' rations but allowed them to purchase additional food for their servants. Officers through the grade of colonel could buy one additional ration equivalent to that of the common soldier; generals could buy two or three additional rations depending on rank.[53]

Relations between masters and slaves varied; the masters, of course, determined that relationship. Some servants satisfied their masters and some did not. Porter Alexander had a body servant/groom/cook throughout the war and a second who served as a wagon driver from just before Second Manassas until the Yankees captured both driver and wagon days before Appomattox. Alexander was pleased with (and proud of) both. He mentioned that Lee knew his groom, Charley, by name, and Charley felt confident enough to take the commanding general a Christmas present. But even Alexander's relation with his slaves was not idyllic. Officers were responsible for their servants' deportment and discipline. Infractions generally resulted in beatings. Alexander wrote, "I had hired for an [h]ostler & servant a 15 year old darkey named Charley—a medium tall & slender, ginger-cake colored, & well behaved & good dispositioned boy. In all the 3½ years I had him with me I had to give him a little licking but twice—once for robbing a pear tree in the garden of the Keach house, in which we were staying on the outskirts of Richmond below Rocketts, & once in Pa. just before Gettysburg, for stealing apple-brandy & getting tight on it." Despite the rare breaches of discipline, Alexander appreciated Charley's service. He paid Charley's annual rental fee to a Richmond bank. Since the owner never drew on the account, Alexander closed it in early 1865 and gave Charley the ten-dollar gold piece he had earned during the war.[54]

Not all master-slave relations in the headquarters were as satisfactory as Alexander's with Charley. Surgeon Spencer G. Welch wrote to his wife that her brother's servant, Tony, "stole some syrup to give to a negro girl who lives near our camp, and Ed gave him a pretty thorough thrashing for it. He says Tony is too much of a thief to suit him and he intends to send him back home. I had to give Gabriel a little thrashing this morning for 'jawing' me. I hate very much to raise a violent hand against a person as old as Gabriel, although he is black and a slave. He is too slow for me, and I intend to send him back by Billy [Welch's brother] when he goes home on furlough." Within months, Welch replaced Gabriel with a new slave, Alick, who was more acceptable and even made money on the side doing laundry for the troops. Officers who did not beat their slaves were not always satisfied with their performance either. Hotchkiss felt so responsible for his rented servant's involvement with alcohol that he bought the man. Lee wrote home, "I want a good servant badly but I do not think it is worth while to commence with Fleming at this late date. He would have to learn a good deal before he would be useful, & on the 31st of December I wish to liberate all of them. . . . Perry is very willing and I believe does as well as he can. You know he is slow & inefficient & moves much like his father Lawrence, whom he resembles very much. He is also very fond of his blankets in the morning. The time I most require him out. He is not very strong either." Perry stayed with Lee despite his shortcomings but received additional help. The general commented in another letter home, "I have George as cook now. He is quite subdued but has only been here a day. I give him & Perry each [$]8.20 per month. I hope they will be able to lay up something for themselves." Of course, it was not always the masters who complained, although slaves had to be more circumspect in their protests. William Pendleton noted, "George of Oakland, who waits upon us, is very complaining. He says he is 'broke down' and can't stand being here in this 'wide ocean.'" But slaves and servants did not generally complain, and Pendleton may have been right that many of them enjoyed being with the army: "It is a life they like vastly." Stonewall Jackson's death devastated his servant and cook, a free mulatto named Jim. He had formed strong attachments during the war and liked his job. Jim attached himself to Sandie Pendleton after Jackson's death and then broke down completely when Pendleton also fell. Jim became depressed and went home to Lexington for a short visit, intending eventually to serve another of Jackson's old staff. He died before he could return to the army.[55]

Whether or not slaves and servants liked the duty, their masters found them indispensable. Brigadier General Evans wrote a whole series of letters asking that Moses, who had gone home to visit his wife and stayed longer than Evans anticipated, be sent back as soon as possible. Evans waxed eloquent in his journal when Moses finally returned to duty: "The day's history would be incomplete without mention of the advent of Moses to his accustomed place of cook, hostler & servitor-general." Major Eugene Blackford, William's brother, wrote, "I am put to all manner of inconveniences for want of a servant, no child missed its nurse more than I miss George." John Hampden Chamberlayne did not have a servant when he rejoined the army after being exchanged as a prisoner. Without someone to wait on him, he faced an uncomfortable future. Chamberlayne made temporary arrangements and reassured his mother that she did not need to rush sending a servant: "I am yet on general staff duty with Col. R. Lindsay W[alker]—Have a horse and all trappings—am waited on by Col. W's boy & am more comfortable than you have any idea of—Do not send any boy up, except by some gentleman whom you can trust—I shd like to have one of the three—But be careful to send him so he can't get lost." A few days later, Chamberlayne reiterated that there was no rush sending a servant since he was borrowing one of Colonel William J. Pegram's. Pegram had both his own servant and his brother's (Brigadier General John Pegram was wounded at the Wilderness and did not return to the army until July 1864) and could not use both.[56] Such arrangements were strictly temporary, though, and Chamberlayne soon got his own slave from home.

Servants did not live an unremittingly dull life confined at headquarters under close supervision, as one might expect. There are stereotypical anecdotes about singing and dancing around camp, but slaves also roamed the countryside with a surprising degree of freedom. That was not a reflection of liberal enlightenment in the Army of Northern Virginia but a comment on the habitual shortage of rations. Most servants had horses or mules or access to their owners' mounts and used the resulting mobility to scour the neighborhood for food. Foraging was a major duty, but it was also an opportunity to have a social life away from camp. The incident involving Tony, the slave who was beaten for stealing syrup for a local girl, gives a hint of one way servants spent their time away from camp when not actively foraging. Some slaves were more successful in their off-duty adventures than was Tony. William Pendleton conducted the wedding of a black from the army quartermaster trains to a local woman. Pendleton mentioned a large gathering and a bountiful wedding supper before the ceremony.[57] Some members of

218

that large wedding party were probably attached to the army, since it is hard to believe they were all friends of the bride.

Servants' lives in the Army of Northern Virginia also were not necessarily as safe as their noncombatant status would imply. They went on campaigns, sometimes followed their masters into battle, and occasionally faced enemy fire even in the headquarters. For example, Stuart's servant, Bob, accompanied his master on the Chambersburg raid in October 1862. Possibly under the influence of alcohol, Bob fell asleep in a fence corner. The column was gone when he awoke, and the Yankees almost captured him and the two spare horses he was leading. A. P. Hill's servant led his master's horse in the early stages of the Battle of Cedar Mountain until Hill (who had been walking at the head of Branch's brigade) needed the horse. Presumably, the servant made a judicious exit once relieved of the horse. Beauregard's headquarters at the McLean house during First Manassas came under Union artillery fire. One round hit the kitchen, where the headquarters slaves were preparing dinner. Fortunately, nobody was hurt. After Chancellorsville, Lee, Stuart, and A. P. Hill all set up headquarters, complete with servants, on Fairview Hill, where Union artillery "repeatedly forced us day and night to leave the field for half an hour."[58]

Considering their relative freedom of movement, access to horses, and proximity to safety in the Union lines, perhaps the most surprising thing about headquarters slaves is how few of them seem to have run away. Typical comments about servants, although they may reflect the postwar phenomenon of romanticizing slavery, emphasize their faithfulness. General Evans claimed that his slave was content and utterly spoiled. As a result, "He went through the Pennsylvania Campaign last year, being fully apprised that he had but to remain in order to be free. I offered him there the choice of remaining or returning and he scouted the idea of living among Yankees. While Moses thinks he is not so good as a Southern white man, yet he feels immeasurable superiority over the Yankee whites." According to Evans, "the attentions of some Dutch damsels . . . [and] the familiarity they had presumed to treat him with" offended Moses. Another typical postwar reminiscence about a faithful slave came from William Blackford: "I got as a servant Gilbert, the son of 'Aunt Charlotte,' my wife's 'Mammy,' and a more faithful attendant never was. He remained with me until the end of the war, and was with me in both campaigns north of the Potomac where he could, at any time he chose, have secured his freedom by leaving me. But he not only never showed any disposition to do so but on several occasions, while out foraging for our mess, ran the risk of his life in escaping from foraging parties of the enemy." Alexander Haskell thought the tale of his servant,

July, escaping from a Union cavalry patrol while on an expedition to secure buttermilk from a farmhouse near the route of march was a good story. He did not comment as Blackford had on how easy it would have been for July to surrender and gain freedom instead of risking his life by fleeing. Bob, Stuart's slave, rode into camp several days after the other raiders returned. Bob had been hiding in the woods and feeding the horses at night while he eluded Union patrols to make his way home. Kyd Douglas said that at Appomattox his servant, Buck, suddenly disappeared with spare horse, saddle, bridle, and trunk containing all of Douglas's clothing. Douglas thought Buck had run away, but he reappeared later with all the equipment. Buck believed the Yankees had captured Douglas and hid to save the gear.[59]

However, all servants were not as faithful as their masters thought. Von Borcke granted his rented slave a leave to visit a sick wife. The slave took most of Von Borcke's wardrobe and disappeared forever. Captain Francis W. Dawson's servant, Aleck, disappeared with Dawson's spare horses in late 1864 when Dawson was the Cavalry Corps ordnance officer. A long pursuit failed to apprehend the runaway. Dawson met Aleck after the war in Petersburg and accepted a story that the previously faithful servant had gone to see a girlfriend in Winchester and the Yankees captured the horses, leaving him no way to return to the army. Surgeon Spencer Welch thought his servant, Wilson, was trustworthy and dependable. He and Wilson had experienced many trying ordeals together, including sharing blankets on terrible battlefields. Wilson told Welch during the march to Gettysburg that he did not like Pennsylvania because he "sees no black folks," so Welch was surprised when the slave disappeared on the return march: "My servant got lost in Maryland. I do not think it was his intention to leave, but he was negligent about keeping up and got in rear of the army and found it too late to cross the river." Imagine Welch's surprise when a black soldier captured in the Crater at Petersburg gave his name as William Wilson and claimed to have once belonged to a surgeon in McGowan's brigade, where Welch served. The doctor reluctantly admitted that the black Union soldier was probably Wilson, his faithful servant who had gotten "lost" in Maryland.[60]

MESSING AND OFF-DUTY ACTIVITIES

With so many officers and soldiers at headquarters, there had to be a system for meals. The soldiers drew rations from the commissary and cooked in small groups using unit equipment. Cooking duties rotated, unless someone volunteered to assume that function permanently. Officers, however, had to provide for themselves. The standard solution was to band together in groups (often including enlisted men) called messes, to pool money to purchase supplies, and to prepare and share common meals. Headquarters sometimes split into two or more messes, although normally all the officers (especially in smaller units) comprised the mess. Of course, elements of the headquarters that usually lived and operated separately, like the quartermaster, commissary, ordnance, and artillery, formed their own messes. Servants cooked, served, and often procured the meals for the officers' mess. Responsibility for running the mess, which involved collecting money, purchasing supplies, and overseeing the general operation, either rotated or was a permanent duty, depending on the mess. For example, Major John Fairfax, a wealthy, pious bon vivant who was renowned for his ability to obtain supplies (especially whiskey), ran Longstreet's headquarters mess for the entire war; Stuart's portly medical director, Talcott Eliason, ran that general's headquarters mess; and Pender's mess was the responsibility of Harris, the commander's slave. Conversely, both Lee's and Jackson's messes rotated what they called the caterer position among the officers.[61]

Whatever the decision on administration of the mess, common feeding and the exigencies of military life dictated a fairly standard meal schedule with built-in flexibility. Captain Justus Scheibert recorded the messing procedure and typical fare at Stuart's headquarters:

Two meals, breakfast at seven in the morning in inactive periods, at four o'clock on marches, served in the mess tent (a piece of sailcloth which protects against sun and rain), and dinner at six o'clock in the evening, or taken after the march constituted the highly practical method of feeding. The courses were simple, the same in the mornings as in the evenings: cornbread (bread baked from maize) and wheatbread lay on the table, the latter often prepared as crackers. There was also coffee mixed with parched wheat or corn, and some tea, also sassafras tea, meat and molasses (a type of syrup cooked from sugarcane). Butter was a rare delicacy, as were eggs. . . . On many days there was naturally nothing but bacon and crackers.

Scheibert's description conforms well with Sandie Pendleton's picture of the routine at Ewell's headquarters:

Our life is monotonous enough now, but I am moderately busy & manage to exist without ennui. In the morning, after a moderately late breakfast, say 8 o'clock, read my Bible & smoke my pipe, then a stroll & some talking, after which I have my [official] papers to fix up. Then I read an hour, if I have any bks [books] or Yankee papers. This brings me to a late dinner and then my pipe helps me to get thru the afternoon until the mail comes, with an occasional assistance of chess; and then at night I have all my papers to go over with the Gen., which makes the hours go until bed time.[62]

Sharing was a norm within the mess. In periods of scarce rations, boxes of goodies from home became communal property. Pender illustrated that norm when he wrote to his wife, "I have gotten so that I cannot bear Dr. Holt [the brigade surgeon] about me. He is getting rather odious to all the mess. He showed so much selfishness." Pender went on to explain that Holt had not shared some butter he got from home but ate both the mess's supply (taking big helpings) and what another staff officer brought from home. In extremis, sharing could become formalized. The morning of the surrender at Appomattox, Longstreet and Gordon's staffs were collocated: "Somebody had a little cornmeal, and somebody else had a tin can, such as is used to hold hot water for shaving. A fire was kindled, and each man in his turn, according to rank and seniority, made a can of cornmeal gruel and was allowed to keep the can until the gruel became cool enough to drink."[63]

But times were not always bad, and headquarters were places for more than working, sleeping, and eating. There is a famous adage that war is characterized by long periods of boredom interspersed with brief moments of sheer terror. The Civil War was no exception. Staffs of the Army of Northern Virginia found all kinds of ways to relieve the boredom and occupy their off-duty hours.

Visiting was probably the most frequent leisure activity. Confederate staffs enjoyed social company. Officers individually or in groups as large as the entire staff visited anybody and everybody. They sought out friends in other units, visited nearby headquarters, and took jaunts to see local civilians. When not out visiting, they were often entertaining impromptu guests of their own. Sometimes these were just social calls; sometimes they were a prelude to other activities. For example, Longstreet frequently entertained some poker buddies. When women were available, staffs arranged dances, ranging from informal affairs in a parlor with the ladies of the house as partners to huge gala balls that attracted people from miles around. One officer, J. P. Smith, remembered, "While General Stuart slept on the parlor sofa, his staff, by the music his own couriers supplied, danced until the 'wee sma' hours' with the fairest of the fair." In winter quarters, units and staffs built theaters to stage dramatic and minstrel productions. Of course, such theatrical performances drew large crowds and were a great reason to get out and see people.[64]

To supplement the internal socializing there was the occasional requirement to entertain an important visitor, newspaper correspondent, or foreign guest. Although Lee tolerated brief visits to his headquarters by important or influential civilians, he did not allow them to stay long. Even Francis C. Lawley, a politically important and sympathetic London *Times* correspondent, could not stay at the army headquarters; lesser lights stood no chance at all. Von Borcke's memoirs make a reader think that all such visitors went to cavalry headquarters, and many did. Stuart had the winning personality to entertain official guests, but others also got random visitors shuffled off from Lee's headquarters. For example, Longstreet had a whole gaggle of foreign observers traveling with his headquarters during the invasion of Pennsylvania. Lawley and the London *Illustrated News* correspondent spent time at Jackson's headquarters, while the Marquis of Hartington and a Colonel Leslie also spent a week there.[65] Of course, guests were an excuse for all sorts of entertainment and social activities. Most Army of Northern Virginia headquarters welcomed them.

When not visiting or entertaining, the staff found other ways to while away the time in camp. Stuart liked to gather his whole headquarters around campfires for conversation, storytelling, music, singing, and dancing. Sitting around fires or in tents talking to comrades helped pass time quickly and pleasantly. Reading was also a favorite pastime, and the literary fare available in the Army of Northern Virginia was both surprisingly varied and erudite. During the evacuation of Richmond, McHenry Howard had to leave behind copies of Virgil and the tragedies of Aeschylus, while Hotchkiss and Allan spent four days reading aloud to each other from the *Life of Lorenzo de Medici*. Sandie Pendleton, Stapleton Crutchfield (the chief of artillery), and Hunter McGuire (the medical director) read aloud Shakespeare, *Vanity Fair*, *The Pickwick Papers*, *A Tale of Two Cities*, and eighteenth-century Irish comedies. Books passed from hand to hand so that everyone got a chance to read them. Their absence evoked comments like "We have quite a dull time in camp, no books, no papers, and few letters."[66] Even captured Yankee letters, read out of a mix of duty and curiosity, provided diversion. Besides reading, writing letters home or keeping diaries or journals occupied many an idle hour. Headquarters generally had access to paper and ink, so those pastimes (sometimes avocations) were easier for the staff than for common soldiers—finding staff officers writing home on the official letterhead stationery of their units is not at all uncommon.

Religious services also rated high as off-duty activities. Many headquarters had nightly prayer meetings, and Sunday services were virtually universal. Staffs often went as a group into the nearest town to attend the local church. Even the religiously indifferent attended, and many officers commented on the subject and quality of sermons they heard. Although not strictly recreation, church occupied a significant place in the off-duty activities at headquarters.

Outdoor pursuits included hunting and a variety of equestrian and military sports. Hunting had the benefit of providing meat for the mess, and several officers practiced the sport regularly. Von Borcke wrote about hunting rabbits, squirrels, and even bullfrogs, although he admitted he could never overcome his prejudice against frogs despite their good taste. Porter Alexander was an inveterate hunter. He shot quail wherever he found them and always carried an old musket filled with bird shot so he could shoot birds kicked up unexpectedly on the march. Alexander claimed to have killed 120 quail in a single two-acre field—the mess must have fed well on such bounty. The primary equestrian sports were races and jumping. During the first winter of the war, Longstreet's headquarters was a Mecca for horse-jumping contests. Unseated riders paid a fine for "the entertainment and amusement" of the staff. William Blackwood said that at cavalry headquarters, "pistol practice from the saddle at a gallop was our favorite amusement on the staff and it is surprising how accurately one can shoot in this way." Brigadier General Lane described an elaborate tournament held in his brigade in April 1864. Thirteen mounted "knights" armed with swords attempted within ten seconds to cut the head off a dummy, snatch a suspended ring, strike a head-sized target on the ground, and pierce another on a pole. A unit band played at intervals during the contest, and wags burlesqued the performance from the sidelines. Mounted pistol-firing and jumping contests followed the main event. Such activities continued almost to the end of the war. In late December 1864 Taylor wrote to his fiancée about a tournament conducted at Heth's headquarters in which visiting ladies sponsored officer riders, an acquaintance of theirs was elected Queen of Love and Beauty, and the subsequent ball lasted all night.[67]

The occasional snows of Northern Virginia winters added variety to outdoor recreation, and the army responded giddily. Sorrel and Peyton Manning built a two-horse sleigh and had a great time until it flipped dangerously. Snowball fights, some of them elaborate quasi-military maneuvers of up to brigade or division size, broke out spontaneously and universally across the army whenever it snowed. Commenting on a snowball fight between Edward Johnson's and Robert Rodes's divisions in March 1864, chaplain James B. Sheeran claimed that there were eight thousand participants, the combat raged back and forth over a half a mile of terrain, and "our boys came back home as proud as if they had gained a victory over the Yankees." Scheibert was amazed that officers passing through the Texas brigade to reach Lee's headquarters after a snowfall in April 1863 did not take offense when pelted with snowballs. He considered this insubordination a striking contrast to the harsh discipline and undeniable valor of the Texans on campaign.[68] Everybody else probably considered it simply good-natured high jinks by troops for whom snow was a novelty.

However, despite the inevitability and importance of off-duty pursuits, headquarters were primarily places for work, not play. Facilities, quarters, messing arrangements, and leisure activities are all secondary to the main function of any headquarters—commanding and administering the units under its control. What was most important about an Army of Northern Virginia headquarters was the business it conducted and the procedures it used to conduct that business.

Chapter 9

STAFF PROCEDURES

MEETINGS

Staffs in the Army of Northern Virginia functioned without the countless meetings that plague modern staffs. Regulations directed daily visits by staff officers to headquarters at specified times: "The orderly hours being fixed at each head-quarters, the staff officers and chiefs of special services either attend in person, or send their assistants to obtain the orders of the day."[1] However, there was nothing like the formal morning and/or evening briefings that are universal in modern armies. Nevertheless, staffs had regular interaction with commanders when they could raise issues, receive guidance, and transact the business of their departments.

It was not always that way. Upon assuming command of the army, Robert E. Lee began a unique form of the staff meeting. The staff formed a large semicircle in the front room of the house that served as headquarters while the commander read all the incoming correspondence for the day. When Lee finished reading an item, he handed it to a staff officer—Walter Taylor said "in regular order," which implies that Lee distributed the load without consideration of subject matter—with guidance on how to handle the issue. Lee thus acted as his own adjutant and chief of staff and assumed responsibility for even the most petty details of administering the army. That technique had myriad drawbacks, not the least of which was the inordinate amount of the commander's time it consumed. Lee quickly recognized the deficiencies and stopped the practice. He delegated responsibility for paperwork to his assistant adjutant general and expected to see only the "knotty and difficult" cases and those dealing with very high-ranking officers. After the procedural change, Taylor, the AAG who received responsibility for routine paperwork, remembered occasions when there were no issues vital enough to take to the commander for several days in a row, and even then the number was always small.[2]

Thus, Lee relieved himself of the burden of paperwork; however, without scheduled meetings, he might easily have become isolated from his staff. The army commander sidestepped the possibility of isolation through techniques other than meetings. Lee was generally available to see anyone except friends of soldiers condemned by courts-martial and officers complaining about promotion. He does not seem to have established routine interviews with his staff, like some of his subordinates, but saw his staff officers when either he or they had business to transact. Taylor mentioned being summoned "at the usual hour . . . to his presence to know if there were any matters of army routine upon which his judgment and action were required," so the AAG probably always conducted what business he had at a standard time. However, Taylor also felt free to visit the boss as the need arose—"with my accustomed freedom [I] entered his tent without announcement or ceremony." In any case, mornings were Lee's preferred time for staff matters. That routine left the rest of the day free so he could ride the lines. In winter, when the flow of paperwork was heaviest, administration often took from breakfast until three in the afternoon, although that estimate comes from the period when Lee was confined to quarters and was probably personally handling more administration than usual.[3]

Subordinate commanders in the Army of Northern Virginia instituted daily meetings with their staff officers, although they took the form of sequential individual appointments rather than meetings of the whole staff. For example, Thomas J. Jackson met his quartermaster, commissary, ordnance, and medical officers every morning after breakfast. They came armed with written reports of the condition and needs of their departments. Jackson dealt with each in turn, giving guidance, issuing orders, and making decisions. The assistant adjutant general followed the rest of the staff. He presented Jackson with two stacks of papers—those from army headquarters or the War Department and those that originated in the lower echelons of the command. Jackson dealt with the papers while the AAG took notes on the response, endorsement, or action required for each. Next came discussion of inspector general reports, military court cases, and directions to miscellaneous staff sections as necessary. With routine matters completed, Jackson personally wrote letters to Lee, the secretary of war, and committees of Congress. In slack operational periods, he worked on official reports of battles before going for a walk or ride. While Jackson did other things, the staff translated his guidance into correspondence. In the evening, the assistant adjutant general brought back "great stacks of papers prepared by his own direction" for signature, and Jackson "signed his name until sometimes he would fall asleep over his table; he often wrote T. J. Jakson in his haste and weariness." Richard Ewell maintained a similar schedule when he succeeded Jackson in command of the Second Corps. Ewell's nightly paper-signing sessions routinely lasted two hours. Besides the normal morning interviews, Jackson habitually called on his staff at all hours of the day or night for information, sometimes asking the same question several times or demanding the answer in writing.[4]

Taking care of staff business in the morning was standard at all Army of Northern Virginia headquarters, although some commanders expected to sign papers at that time rather than later. For example, William Pendleton twice mentioned doing all his paperwork early in the morning to free the rest of the day for other matters. D. H. Hill also did his office work in the morning and used afternoons to inspect his command. When commanders broke the morning routine, staffs saw it as an ill omen. The afternoon before starting on the Chambersburg raid, J. E. B. Stuart ordered his adjutant to prepare all official papers requiring his attention and retired to his tent with them. This caused "a more than unusual stir at cavalry headquarters [and] aroused suspicions on the part of those who were somewhat behind the scenes." Since commanders handled staff matters in the morning, it was natural for assistant staff officers also to receive their instructions at that time. Frederick M. Colston, an assistant ordnance officer with the reserve ordnance train, noted, "The next morning I rode to the courthouse to get my orders for the day from Colonel [Briscoe] Baldwin."[5] A morning ride to get orders would have been standard fare for junior staff officers.

COORDINATION

A basic staff activity, coordination by Army of Northern Virginia staffs varied from good to abysmal. Part of the problem was the need to preserve the secrecy of military operations. The best way to keep a secret, of course, was not to tell anyone anything, and the Army of Northern Virginia practiced that technique aggressively. The downside of keeping secrets was that staff coordination was impossible without open exchange of information. Staff officers grumbled that commanders impaired efficiency by keeping them in the dark about impending operations. Surgeon Lafayette Guild did not know of upcoming maneuvers in time to replenish medical supplies or provide additional doctors. He complained that "everything is done hurriedly and mysteriously." Lieutenant Francis Dawson, acting as chief of ordnance for James Longstreet while Peyton Manning recovered from wounds, noted that no one told him about the corps' impending move from Chattanooga to Knoxville. Only Dawson's instinctive feeling that something was in the wind, hard work to overcome bureaucratic obstacles placed by the Army of Tennessee staff, and the fortuitous presence of a shipment of Enfield rifles he had brought from Virginia kept the corps supplied with ordnance during that campaign.[6] Stringent security measures are as old as warfare itself. Army of Northern Virginia commanders were aware of the problems caused by limiting knowledge of their plans, but they consciously accepted decreased staff efficiency for the sake of security.

However, secrecy was not the only inhibitor to effective staff coordination. Even after battles, when secrecy was no longer an issue, staff coordination was often poor. Medical directors were notoriously unable to coordinate with other staff agencies, especially the critical commissary and quartermaster. The only effective means found of feeding the wounded was assigning assistant commissary officers directly to division field hospitals under the direction of the senior surgeon. By the end of the war, quartermaster officers may also have been assigned to medical trains. One captain's parole listed his duty as assistant quartermaster and his unit as the Reserve Medical Train of the Third Corps. He may have been serving as a medical purveyor, or he may have been a permanent quartermaster representative to the medical trains. Other staff sections also had difficulty coordinating, or at least difficulty achieving results from coordination. For example, while serving as the Army of Northern Virginia Chief of Ordnance, E. Porter Alexander complained that his reserve ordnance trains waited more than a week for transportation after he submitted the required requisition to the quartermaster. The delay may have resulted from any number of factors, but Alexander's frustration shows a lack of coordination among staff agencies. Sometimes even when they coordinated, staffs did not communicate effectively. When the Army of Northern Virginia was swapping two worn-out Mississippi regiments for two fresher North Carolina regiments from another department in the fall of 1862, the army quartermaster made an inaccurate report to Lee based on miscommunication with a subordinate quartermaster. John B. Hood's quartermaster reported to Colonel James L. Corley that the two Mississippi regiments had departed. Corley told Lee the same, and Lee notified the receiving commander that the regiments were on the way. To Hood's quartermaster, "departed" meant the units had left the division area. To Colonel Corley, "departed" meant they were on trains heading south. Actually, the regiments were at the railroad station but still waiting for a train. Corley and Lee had to correct their reports.[7] Better staff coordination and communication could have prevented the embarrassment.

229

On the other hand, staffs did try to coordinate their activities. Occasionally a chief of staff even issued what would now be called formal staff-planning guidance. In one such case, Colonel Thomas Jordan wrote to his chief of commissary, W. H. Fowle, "Captain—The general commanding directs that you take prompt and effective measures to provide forthwith, at your depot near these headquarters, ample provisions—including fat cattle—for twenty-five thousand men for two weeks, and that amount, at least, must be constantly maintained on hand, subject to requisition, until otherwise ordered."[8] When units moved from one major command to another, the receiving command issued instructions to ease the transfer. For example, when responsibility for A. C. Haskell's cavalry brigade moved from Second Corps to First Corps in February 1865, the First Corps staff sent Haskell administrative instructions. The instructions included a promise that the staff would forward copies of all of the corps' general orders as soon as possible, direction that all future official correspondence would go through Longstreet's headquarters, and special procedures for the expeditious handling of requests to visit Richmond, along with the warning that "the number [of such requests] will be limited." Similarly, staffs coordinated temporary command arrangements when a commander was unavailable. For example, when Lee planned to be absent a few days in Richmond, his staff wrote to Richard Ewell that General Robert Chilton would remain with the headquarters. Chilton would run routine matters and consult Ewell (the temporary commander) on important subjects. In an emergency, Ewell could either move to the army headquarters or have it moved to him as he desired. Staff officers also coordinated with supporting agencies. In November 1862 Jackson's chief of commissary, Major W. J. Hawks, exchanged illustrative correspondence with Captain S. L. Stuart, the officer in charge of the cattle depot responsible for supplying Jackson's corps. They discussed consumption rates (about four hundred cows per week), the availability of hogs, and whether one recent cattle shipment had been double-invoiced.[9] These sorts of issues are the basics of staff coordination. Routine reports and all the forms and instructions devoted to them are another example of staff coordination. If the Army of Northern Virginia did not shine in those areas, it expended significant energy trying.

One significant activity that the staff generally coordinated well was marches and movements. Although cases abound of units waiting in formation for hours for other elements to pass so they could join the column, of the whole army using a single road when alternates were available, and of trains improperly mixing with combat units, the Army of Northern Virginia habitually moved large numbers of troops, guns, and wagons efficiently. March instructions varied from minimal to infinitely complex. An example of the former variety read simply, "Have your cmd. ready to move at 15 min. notice. Strike camp & trains follow when you move." Another more thorough but still terse example was, "General: Move at sunrise to-morrow to Winchester. Colonel [William] Allan will move his trains, following your lead division. Take your artillery." A specimen of the complex variety laid out essentially standard operating procedures for marches. It detailed march times, rest halt procedures, straggler control, the location of company commanders and ambulances in the column, disposition of broken-down vehicles, and procedures for clearing old and occupying new camps. Another detailed order went so far as to direct that "the colors will be carried displayed." Colonel Alexander R. Boteler's notes to himself about coordinating the movement of Jackson's force from the Shenandoah Valley to the peninsula are another illustration. Boteler was to go to Charlottesville, see the superintendent of the Central Railroad, arrange to move brigades in a specified order, check on the type and capacity of the cars, confirm the march rate, and arrange for the subsequent movement of wagons. At the opening of the Second Manassas campaign, G. Moxley Sorrel sent the brigade commanders in Longstreet's division orders with the route, departure time, individual equipment and rations to carry, disposition of sick soldiers, procedures for specific items of equipment, and coordinating instructions that artillery batteries would receive separate orders and brigade quartermasters should report to the division quartermaster immediately. Sorrel then followed the original orders with modifications as departure times and other details changed. Even moving prisoners of war was usually coordinated well. In a letter directing one of his subordinates to escort four hundred prisoners to Richmond, Jackson included guidance about notifying the Richmond provost marshal of the number to expect, authority to buy food for prisoners and guards en route, and instructions to contact a specific commissary captain to fill immediate ration needs.[10]

Another area where the Army of Northern Virginia generally did well was communicating its needs to Richmond; however, the procedures frequently used to accomplish that task were symptomatic of poor staff coordination with higher headquarters. Commanding generals did too much business with the capital and their staffs too little, while everyone preferred to go in person or send an envoy rather than write letters or submit reports. That tendency started early and continued throughout the war. P. G. T. Beauregard had a habit of dispatching staff officers, often politically powerful volunteer aides, to Richmond to see the president. He sent Colonel John S. Preston, "a gentleman of ability and much personal weight," to urge a concentration of forces before First Manassas. Beauregard immediately followed Preston with Colonel James R. Chesnut to reinforce the idea. Chesnut even went armed with written instructions "to assist his memory, and prevent any misconception as to the main features of the projected campaign." When Beauregard did not receive adequate quartermaster support, he sent letters to powerful members of Congress complaining that "to obtain anything with despatch, I have to send a special messenger to Richmond." Beauregard's technique of going straight to the top and bypassing the staff with his complaints provoked a firestorm of protest. The quartermaster general complained that he did not know of any shortages in Beauregard's command and added, "The military operations and manoeuvers of your army are never divulged, and it is utterly impossible for me to know how to anticipate your wants. . . . You should write me often, if only a line, when anything is required, and you shall be provided if possible." Beauregard responded in part, "Major [W. L.] Cabell says that, 'Knowing your inability to comply with his former requisitions for wagons, etc., he thought it was useless to make new ones upon you, hence he was trying to get them from around here.[']" In answer to a mild censure from Jefferson Davis about submitting "timely requisitions and estimates," Beauregard wrote, "With regard to making timely requisitions on the Quartermaster and Commissary Departments, not knowing what number of troops the War Department intended at any time to concentrate here, it was impossible to make proper requisitions until after the arrival of the troops."[11] Those exchanges show a complete lack of staff coordination between the army in the field and the supporting departments in Richmond. Effective communications and coordination between the field and departmental staffs would have provided the necessary strength figures or produced acceptable supply calculations based on estimates of projected personnel strength. Inexperience, lack of training, and lack of initiative by staff officers caused potentially preventable problems.

Staff coordination problems with the capital continued under Joseph E. Johnston. When the army moved to the peninsula, close to Richmond, the technique of sending envoys to the capital got completely out of hand. Adjutant General Samuel Cooper finally prohibited any officers other than commanding generals themselves from visiting "the seat of government for transaction of business in person, as it may be done by correspondence." Of course, that directive could not stop the practice, and officers often visited Richmond on furlough or official duty. In either status they were not hesitant to conduct personal or unit business. For example, two years after the original order banning trips to Richmond, Brigadier General William Pendleton sent his aide to present opinions directly to President Davis rather than writing a letter.[12] In that instance, Pendleton was not only disobeying orders about personal visits to the capital but also violating orders about sending all correspondence through official channels.

It is more difficult to determine how effectively Lee managed staff co-ordination with Richmond. He signed hundreds of letters on detailed staff issues, which critics use to show that his staff was ineffective—little more than clerks and couriers—and that he had to micromanage the details of the army. Some of Lee's letters were to Davis or to the secretary of war and some were to the heads of the Richmond staff departments. Because Lee personally signed most of the letters leaving the army for Richmond (a regulatory requirement), it is hard to tell which he wrote on his own initiative and which the staff proposed or even drafted. For example, a letter to the quartermaster general said, "The Chief Quartermaster of the Army brought me this morning a sample of the shoes recently sent from Richmond. One pair was of Richmond manufacture and another from Columbus, Georgia. . . . Neither could compare with the shoes made in this army." Colonel Corley provoked that letter, even if he did not actually suggest or draft it. He was looking for support for his scheme of making shoes locally. That was a case, typical of the way the staff officers operated, of getting the commander involved in their problems. Lee was the officers' big gun. When they wanted results, they frequently used his prestige. In another instance, Lee wrote to Davis immediately after Corley received an unsatisfactory answer from the quartermaster general about the forecast for delivery of forage.[13] In that case, Lee seems to have taken the initiative, since he mentioned that he told Corley to present the issue to the quartermaster general and that he wrote to Davis only after his quartermaster reported back.

As these examples show, it is difficult to determine if Lee's letters on staff issues were simply legitimate staff correspondence over the commander's signature, personal intervention inspired by the staff, or strictly self-generated attempts to solve staff problems (evidence of staff inefficiency and poor coordination). He wrote on a variety of subjects from strategy to personnel policy to logistics. Some letters were in response to questions from the capital; others were generated in the field. The ones that most obviously impinge on staff areas are those dealing with logistics. However, the logistics posture of the Army of Northern Virginia was always so tenuous (and not exclusively due to staff inefficiency) that it was a legitimate command concern. Lee would have been negligent had he ignored the issues. Nevertheless, Lee's correspondence with Richmond on staff issues was extensive enough to suggest poor routine coordination by his staff.

CORRESPONDENCE

During the Civil War, there was one basic form of military correspondence—the letter. Regulations explained exactly how to format,
write, and address letters, including the correct paper size and how to
fold it. Staff officers could write to people below their headquarters in
the chain of command, but the commander was supposed to sign correspondence to anyone above him. Regulations required commanders to
write to an appropriate staff officer at higher headquarters rather than
to the commander, while they told staff officers writing a subordinate to
say that the communication was "by order" and state by whose order.
The regulatory requirements produced some incongruous results. Commanders writing to superiors addressed their letters to staff officers and
then wrote for the consumption of the general. Sometimes commanders
played it safe and wrote both the higher commander and a staff officer.
For example, Stuart's report on the Chambersburg raid was addressed
"To General R. E. Lee, Through Colonel R. H. Chilton, A. A. General,
Army of Northern Virginia," and opened "Colonel,—I have the honor
to report." Staff officers habitually wrote in the third person, often with
excessive reference to their commanding officers. They even included excuses when forwarding letters to higher headquarters under their own
signature rather than the general's. For example, a letter from General
W. H. F. "Rooney" Lee's AAG sending time-sensitive information to
army headquarters from a recently returned scout opened with, "In the
absence of General Lee at the front, I have the honor to inform you."
Charles Marshall, R. E. Lee's aide, sent a letter to Secretary of War
Breckinridge with the explanation, "General Lee having left camp before
the original of the inclosed letter was ready for his signature, instructed
me to send an official copy of it." But all the regulatory guidance did not
standardize correspondence. By regulation, the addressee's name would
have always been in the bottom left corner of the letter; however, many
letters opened with the addressee in the salutation, which was standard
for civilian letters. Closings varied from the polite "Very respectfully,
Your obedient servant" to the more official "By order of General Lee."[14]
Despite irregularities in format, the military letter served as the basic vehicle for correspondence in the army.

Letters to multiple addressees often became a special category of correspondence called circulars. These were sometimes copies forwarded simultaneously to all addressees; however, in theory a circular went from
one addressee to the next in turn, with each showing by endorsement
that he had seen it.[15] The circular was a useful technique for delivering

orders when distances between recipients were short and subjects routine.

All subsequent correspondence directly about the topic of the original letter (other than an answering letter) was done by endorsement on the outside of the folded letter. The receiving headquarters noted the subject and author of the letter in a first endorsement; subsequent endorsements, separated by lines, followed below the first. Some actions received as many as eleven endorsements from company to army headquarters, although normally five to six sufficed.[16] Generally, endorsements were terse comments like "forwarded" or "approved" with a responsible individual's signature. Occasionally, however, endorsements might contain lengthy details. For example, Taylor returned a request for a medical board with the endorsement, "Req. returned approved. The attention of the Examining Board is called to Par. VII G O No. 71 Adj GO 1864 [Paragraph VII, Adjutant and Inspector General's Office General Order Number 71, 1864 series]. If unfit for duty in the field, but capable of performing duty in some department of the service, the Board will specify for what position he is best qualified & if he has heretofore been detailed upon any light duty the Board will state how & where employed & if his services are still desirable in such position."[17] An endorsement might also contain requests for additional information or instructions for the originator to appear in person to discuss the action. Another Taylor endorsement provides a good example: "The general wishes to see General Pendleton early after breakfast on the morning of the 18th instance (tomorrow)." Army of Northern Virginia headquarters were not shy about returning correspondence that arrived from subordinates without proper endorsement. An example from cavalry headquarters told the subordinate, "The general [Stuart] further directs me to call your attention to the order requiring all official papers to be properly indorsed before being sent to these headquarters for action."[18]

One important aspect of correspondence was keeping copies for future reference. All units maintained copies of their own orders and those of the headquarters above them. Regulations also required each headquarters to maintain extensive files of letters sent and received. Since endorsements always appeared on the original correspondence and might not remain in the headquarters, keeping copies of them was impossible. The approved solution was to log the subject and substance of each endorsement. In all, there was a very rational, if administratively burdensome, system for keeping records of correspondence. It worked well, although not perfectly. For example, in January 1865 Robert E. Lee signed a letter to the adjutant general asking for copies of special orders about cavalry assignments. Obviously, the army headquarters had not kept copies of all orders received, and since Lee could only identify the orders as "the special orders issued last spring," they lacked even a good log. In late 1861 President Davis had to send a special emissary to Joe Johnston, Beauregard, and Gustavus W. Smith with the admission "I have habitually neglected to keep copies of my letters and telegrams addressed to you since you entered on duty with the Army of the Potomac." Davis made two assumptions—that originators routinely kept copies of their letters and that addressees kept the originals. In the case of presidential correspondence, that may have been true; however, those assumptions often would have been bad. Important correspondence sometimes left a headquarters without being copied. For example, Johnston wrote to one of his subordinates during the Battle of Seven Pines, "I fear that in my note of last evening, of which there is no copy, I was too positive on the subject of your attacking the enemy's left flank." Beauregard tried to mollify Ewell, who was offended over criticism for not advancing at First Manassas when he had received no order to do so, with the excuse: "Unfortunately no copy, in the hurry of the moment, was kept of said order, and so many guides—about a dozen or more—were sent out in different directions, that it is impossible to find out who was the bearer of the order referred to." The failure to keep copies of even important orders during battle was understandable and not unusual. A type of carbon paper called field note paper existed that produced a copy as the note was written, but most orders during battle were written on small scraps of paper torn from memorandum books. John D. Imboden even claimed during the Shenandoah Valley campaign, "About ten o'clock at night I received a note from Jackson written in pencil on the blank margin of a newspaper."[19] Obviously, the only record of such correspondence would be the original, saved by the recipient.

One of the most persistent bureaucratic problems in the Army of Northern Virginia (and the Confederacy as a whole) was the Confederate habit of writing to Richmond—to the president, the War Department, or Congress—directly, without submitting the correspondence through the chain of command. The adjutant general's office explained the problem and chided the field at length in a general order.

The attention of officers is called to the thirty-fourth article of Army Regulations, and especially to those paragraphs of the article which relate to the channel of military correspondence. It is no exaggeration to state that nearly one-third of the correspondence received at the War Department and this office from officers of the Army and others in the military service comes directly from the writers without passing through the prescribed channel. Therefore, all indirect communication with the Department is prohibited, and where it is attempted, either in person or by letter, the application will be referred to the proper military commander before action is taken on it, and instructions will at the same time be given to bring the offender to trial for violation of the regulations and orders respecting military correspondence. These regulations were made after long experience. They have been found indispensable and must be observed.

Not only are all papers and applications to be forwarded through regular channels of communication, but the officers through whom they come, and who are generally supposed to be informed on the merits of the case presented, are required to express their opinions thereon, either approval or disapproval. These opinions are frequently important to the Department, and the rule which prescribes them must not be overlooked.

Richmond had to repeat that warning in October 1864 and again in March 1865, so the problem never went away.[20]

Commanders dictated directly or outlined for staff preparation a large part of the correspondence coming from their headquarters. Before First Manassas, General Beauregard dictated a letter of instruction for a member of his staff he was sending to Richmond to urge his ideas on the government. After that battle, Colonel Thomas Jordan, Beauregard's chief of staff, took a dictated order for pursuit from President Davis. Lee did much of his work by dictation. Charles Venable, Walter Taylor, and Armistead Long from his personal staff all frequently took dictated letters. R. Channing Price, Stuart's AAG, was famous for his ability to listen to Stuart as they rode, digest complicated instructions, stop briefly to prepare letters, and obtain the general's signature on the correspondence without alteration. Henry McClellan claimed to have done the same for Stuart during the retreat from Gettysburg. McClellan had to wake and correct a groggy Stuart when the general tried to change destinations for the artillery to places that were "manifestly absurd." Thomas Goree and Moxley Sorrel both prepared orders for Longstreet, although the evidence does not show whether by dictation or transcription of verbal instruction. Typically, a staff officer working from guidance rather than straight dictation would write a draft, submit the draft to the commander for editing, give the approved product to a clerk for final rewrite in ink, obtain the commander's signature, and return the signed original to the clerks for copying and distribution. Of course, not all correspondence prepared by the staff, whether dictated or drafted from guidance, emerged exactly as the general intended. Joseph E. Johnston said a written order that he relied on Beauregard's staff to prepare after Johnston assumed command at Manassas "differed greatly from the order sketched the day before." Results were not much better when commanders wrote their own material. Corrections were frequent, and occasionally the staff had to translate the boss's handwriting for intermediaries. For example, Venable added a postscript to a telegram Lee wrote in 1864 telling the telegraph operator to "read [the] last sentence 'by light to-morrow.' "[21]

Besides procedures for preparing correspondence, the Army of Northern Virginia had routines for receiving, opening, and reading incoming letters. Generally, the chief of staff or assistant adjutant general received and sorted the mail. He weeded out the private letters and opened most of the official correspondence. Couriers delivered immediate dispatches to the assistant adjutant general at night; routine matters waited for the morning. Should a correspondent need to keep the contents of a letter secret from staff minions, he could mark it "confidential" or "private." Such markings, used singly or in combination, generally stopped even an aggressive AAG from opening a letter. Occasionally though, mistakes occurred, or the markings failed to provide the desired deterrent. Once, Captain James P. Smith opened a sealed message for Jackson thinking it was simply a report from the pickets. He was surprised to discover a message from Lee. Smith immediately sent the letter into Jackson's room. Minutes later, Jackson emerged to ask who had opened the letter. Smith admitted he had, and Jackson took him and Sandie Pendleton into his room. Smith wrote later that Jackson had divulged the contents of the letter to the two staff officers, and he probably also administered more than a gentle reprimand for opening the private letter. McClellan received a message marked "confidential" for Stuart from headquarters late one rainy night at the opening of the Gettysburg campaign. He said, "Under normal circumstances I would not have ventured to break the seal; but the rain poured down so steadily that I was unwilling to disturb the general unnecessarily, and yet it might be important that he should immediately be acquainted with the contents of the despatch. It was a lengthy communication from General Lee, containing the directions upon which Stuart was to act. I at once carried it to the general and read it to him as he lay under the dripping tree. With a mild reproof for having opened such a document, the order was committed to my charge for the night and Stuart was soon asleep."[22] Such bold disregard of confidential markings was likely rare.

ORDERS

Although the military letter was the basic form of correspondence, the most important means of passing information in the Army of Northern Virginia was through formal orders. They came, by regulation, in two varieties: general and special. General orders contained information of interest to the entire command, or at least multiple segments of it. Special orders pertained to individuals or single units. The distinguishing factor between the two types was whether the whole command needed to know the information. Army regulations gave as examples of appropriate subjects for general orders the hours for roll calls, the number and kinds of orderlies the general needed, police requirements, returns to be made and the appropriate forms for such reports, laws and regulations, and promotions and appointments. The issuing headquarters numbered orders sequentially in an annual series. Regulations required commanders to read and approve all general orders and important special orders before the staff issued them. Headquarters at all levels maintained files of orders received and forwarded to higher headquarters copies of orders issued.[23]

In practice, the line between the two types of orders was occasionally fuzzy. The vast majority of special orders dealt with individual assignments or details; however, there are also examples of special orders directing the commissary to issue red pepper if available (and black if not) and suggesting the appropriate ration for that condiment. Additionally, the adjutant and inspector general's office used special orders to issue instructions revoking the provisions of a regulation about substitutes and to give guidance about shipping the bodies of deceased soldiers. Both those subjects met the standard for general orders and should have been published as such. In lower headquarters, special orders were the vehicle for recording and authorizing individual activities like furloughs. They were also occasionally used for combat orders like the famous "lost order" of the Antietam campaign, Army of Northern Virginia Special Order 191. Lower-level units used special orders much like general orders. In those cases, special orders served essentially as orders of the day. For example, one cavalry brigade special order contained movement instructions for the next day, directions to use the current period of rest to prepare muster rolls, an edict to ensure that officers and soldiers sharpened their sabers, and a directive to inspect to ensure enforcement of recent baggage reductions. The same brigade used its special orders to assign picket duty.[24]

The subject matter of general orders varied widely, and a single order might contain many paragraphs on different topics. One order dealt with subjects as diverse as an announcement that sheriffs would get bounties for arresting deserters, the policy on transferring from line to partisan units, directions for withdrawing ammunition if forced to evacuate a fort, procedures for physical examinations for recruits, the requirement to report names of surgeons who lost their medical kits, and promotion procedures for company officers of reorganized regiments. Early in the war, before the Confederacy published its own army regulations, general orders informed subordinates about regulatory requirements. They published uniform guidelines; leave, discharge, and furlough policies; standards for correspondence; and procedures for reports and returns. They even directed commanders to follow the provisions of the 1857 edition of U.S. Army regulations. As Virginia turned over its state forces to the Confederacy, general orders provided coordinating instructions on accounting for money, equipment, personnel, and units. Reprinting regulatory guidance did not stop with the publication of Confederate regulations. Months after the publication of the first Confederate regulations, the adjutant and inspector general's office issued a general order reprinting sections on muster and pay procedures, correspondence policies, annual returns, returns of deceased soldiers, after-action reports, and substitutes. And even when disseminating regulations was no longer necessary, general orders remained the approved technique for changing, amending, or revoking specific regulatory provisions. For example, General Order 17 of the 1861 series modified two paragraphs of the army regulations about procedures for invaliding and discharging soldiers. Months later, another general order revoked General Order 17, simultaneously revoked two paragraphs in the 1862 version of regulations, and substituted new provisions on medical discharges. The failure of the Confederacy to edit early versions of its regulations meant that some provisions had to be changed almost immediately. The 1862 version of army regulations were approved in mid-March. By the end of May, barely enough time to print and distribute copies, general orders started modifying the new regulations. Besides changing regulations, general orders also modified earlier orders. For example, one general order in September 1862 revoked two paragraphs of an earlier order and changed a clause in another.[25] Posting and keeping current with changes must have been challenging.

A recurring topic in general orders was requirements for submission of reports and what they should contain. Commanders and staffs required constant prodding to produce the necessary information. No type of report was exempt, although rations accountability and strength reports were favorites for frequent reminders. General orders either explicitly demanding reports or containing reminders about their submission somewhere in the text came out early in the war and continued throughout. Surgeon Lafayette Guild explained the necessity for repeating orders and expressed the sentiment of everyone involved when he wrote, "I find it necessary to reiterate orders every few months, or they become obsolete, or rather they are disregarded."[26]

Another recurring theme was the publication "for the information of the Army" of recently passed legislation. General orders reprinted virtually every applicable law from acts to punish drunkenness in the army to the bill to organize the Signal Corps. Some of these reprints were quite lengthy. An order in November 1862 reprinted twenty-six laws; another in March 1864 reprinted nineteen laws and was followed three months later by an order publishing another twenty-six laws. Of course, reprinting laws was not always sufficient. Most new legislation required implementing instructions, and general orders were the vehicle for their distribution as well. The implementing instructions for four laws on conscription, exemptions, and conscription camps covered about three times as much space as the laws themselves.[27]

General orders were also a convenient place to reward valiant effort and congratulate commanders and troops for victories. For example, Johnston used a general order to announce the victory at Ball's Bluff, briefly describe the battle and booty, and thank the troops involved. As the corps commander, Beauregard reprinted Johnston's order and added his own flowery praise in a subsequent corps general order. In another instance, Longstreet congratulated his troops in a general order after the victory at Fredericksburg. And Lee used a general order to reprint for general consumption President Davis's congratulatory letter thanking the army for its performance at Chancellorsville. These congratulations were not just a hollow administrative exercise. Troops—or at least officers—appreciated mention in orders. Eugene Blackford, William's brother and an officer in the 5th Alabama Infantry Regiment, mentioned Stuart praising the regiment on the Chancellorsville field and added proudly, "We will get due credit in general orders." Of course, all general orders offering praise were not necessarily welcome. Army of Northern Virginia General Order 61 of the 1863 series lauded Stonewall Jackson and announced his death.[28]

Units maintained copies of orders and other important documents in orders books, which became collections of miscellaneous unit orders, higher headquarters orders, implementing instructions, and circulars. Hampton's Cavalry Brigade's orders book contained certified copies of the brigade's special orders and Cavalry Division general orders. It also had brigade and division circulars, such as warning orders and movement instructions. Some division general orders had brigade implementing instructions immediately below the order. For example, the implementing instructions for a division order to maintain a regiment on constant alert with horses saddled as a "Grand Force" included directions for when the regiments would take the duty and when and how they would be relieved.[29] The orders book also contained copies of Army of Northern Virginia ordnance and commissary circulars, the latter included because the brigade commissary officer knew there had been complaints on the subject.

AFTER-ACTION REPORTS

Army regulations required commanders of regiments, batteries, separate squadrons, and all higher headquarters to submit reports to their immediate superior headquarters after every battle. Anyone wanting to recognize individual valor or achievement could forward a separate report, and the commanding general would consider whether to include such recognition in his report to the government. The procedure was to submit the after-action report on the battle before the special report recognizing individuals, thus limiting the official report to accounts of the action and general praise or blame. Additionally, regulations required staff officers to submit separate reports on the activities of their staff sections to the respective departments in Richmond.[30] As with everything else, the Adjutant and Inspector General Department had to send out additional instructions on the content of official after-action reports, which read, "Officers of the Army are directed in all official reports, whether of sieges, campaigns, or battles, to confine their statements to the facts and events connected with the matter on which they report. No extraneous subject, whether of speculation or of collateral narrative, has a proper place in the official reports of military operations. As much conciseness as is consistent with perspicuity and fullness of statement will be observed in such communications."[31]

Those regulatory provisions kept soldiers all over the South busy writing reports. Even a casual glance at one of the volumes of reports in the *Official Records* will convince a skeptic that Confederates took after-action reports seriously. Regardless how serious or important, however, after-action reporting in the Army of Northern Virginia was not always the most timely process. In fact, the army was often extraordinarily late in submitting such reports. Early in the war the authorities clamored for timely reports. Adjutant General Cooper wrote to Johnston less than a month after the first Battle of Manassas, "The Secretary of War directs that your attention be called to the fact that no reports of the battle of Manassas have been forwarded to this office and to state that before this it was contemplated that full reports would have been received respecting that engagement and its results." That chiding must have affected Johnston, since a consolidated sixty-day report that included Manassas went to Richmond a little less than two months later. And the effect of the reminder lasted until the army's next big battles under Johnston.

There was a spate of report writing immediately after the Battle of Williamsburg. Reports from that battle (including those from regiments that submitted) were generally done in a week, although Longstreet took eleven days, Jubal Early two months, and D. H. Hill until January 1863. Another frenzy of report writing followed the fighting at Seven Pines on May 31–June 1, 1862. Most of the reports on that battle were submitted within a week. Only Cadmus Wilcox's brigade report, Gustavus Smith's Left Wing report, and Johnston's army report took much more than a week, and all were dated on or before June 24, 1862.[32] However, Johnston's wounding and removal from the eastern army brought a screeching halt to timely after-action reporting.

Under Lee, the Army of Northern Virginia took its time informing the government about the detailed results of battles and campaigns. Typical of the new attitude was Jackson, who submitted a nine-line report containing little detail about the battles of the Shenandoah Valley campaign on May 26, 1862, and did not forward complete reports with enclosures until April 10, 1863. Cooper prodded Lee for reports, as he had Johnston, this time using as a club a resolution of the House of Representatives asking for all of the Army of Northern Virginia's battle reports. Lee complained that he tried to keep the department informed, but constant movement and the loss or change of leaders from death or wounds had made it impossible to prepare the required detailed reports. At the time of this exchange in January 1863, Lee did not even have all the input from subordinate units for the Seven Days' Battles, which had occurred six months earlier. The army commander promised to send reports when he could. Despite Lee's excuses, Cooper's plea did have the desired effect. The army immediately began a period of intense writing as leaders at all echelons tried to catch up on delinquent after-action reports. The result was a flurry of reports on the battles of the previous year. However, Lee, who had to wait for input from everyone else to do his reports, did not completely catch up. He sent a bundle of subordinate unit reports to the adjutant general's office for safekeeping during the Gettysburg campaign that he had to retrieve later so he could finish his work.[33]

Reports were tardy not only because they were difficult to write and considered of lower priority than other activities. Commanders also objected to them—or at least to having them published—on grounds of operational security. Jackson did not like publishing his reasons for undertaking certain endeavors (a significant component of an after-action report) because it showed the enemy the thought process behind his maneuvers. In April 1864 Lee warned Seddon about the evils of publishing reports by asserting that it was wrong to assume that no harm could be done because reports covered past events. Lee said he tried to

explain in reports why he did things, and the same reasoning could apply
again later. Especially since future action was likely to be on the same
ground as past battles, the enemy might learn what influenced Lee and
thus limit his responses. He closed by asking the secretary and Congress
not to publish battle reports, by 1864 a case of closing the barn door
after the horses had escaped.[34]

The process of preparing reports influenced their content. Higher-
level unit commanders seldom wrote their own reports. Members of the
staff gathered the information and prepared drafts for the commander's
consideration. Jackson constantly reminded the staff to gather information about his battles but never got around to writing reports. He eventually asked for Lieutenant Colonel Charles J. Faulkner, recently
returned from being the U.S. minister to France, as his assistant adjutant
general specifically so that Faulkner could write after-action reports.
That move caused friction on Jackson's staff, where old-timers like
Henry Kyd Douglas considered Faulkner unqualified either as an AAG
or as an author of reports. Douglas thought Sandie Pendleton deserved
promotion to the lieutenant colonel's spot on the staff and would have
done a better job on the reports than Faulkner since Pendleton had been
in the battles. Had Jackson lived to fight more campaigns after Faulkner
joined the staff, the impact on Second Corps official reports might have
been interesting. Jackson planned to use Faulkner like a medieval chron-
icler or modern official historian, telling the AAG, "I want you to get
where you can see all that is going on, and, with paper and pencil in
hand, write it down, . . . and then write up the Report at once after the
battle." A. P. Hill also entrusted writing reports to his staff but did not
always like the results. He considered the initial report the staff prepared
on Chancellorsville "very imperfect." Lieutenant Colonel Charles Marshall wrote most of Lee's official reports, but there is no indication that
Lee was less than pleased with the product.[35]

Whoever the author, the process of writing official reports was fairly
standard. The author gathered material (mainly from subordinate unit
reports), organized it, investigated to reconcile inconsistencies, and
wrote a draft report. The commander then edited the draft until he was
satisfied. Marshall gave a good description of the process he and General
Lee used to prepare the Gettysburg official report:

> That report was prepared by myself with every facility to make it accurate
> which General Lee could give me. I had the official reports of the Corps,
> Division, and Brigade Commanders, those of the Artillery and Cavalry
> Commanders, and of the Medical staff. I had an opportunity of convers-
> ing with the authors of these reports, and of getting explanations of what

was doubtful, and declining that which was conflicting or contradictory. I had General Lee's private correspondence with the officers of his army, with the President and Departments, his orders, general and special, public and confidential, and more than all, I had the advantage of full and frank explanations of his own plans and purposes from General Lee himself. When from the various sources I have mentioned I had compiled a continuous narrative it was submitted to him for examination. He would peruse it carefully, make such alterations as his personal knowledge suggested, and when there was a material difference in the statements contained in the reports, he required it to be brought particularly to his notice, read the conflicting reports himself, sought every opportunity by conversation or correspondence of reconciling the discrepancies, and in some instances changed his own report to such a statement of the general outlines of the facts as to omit entirely those things which his efforts could not render altogether free from doubt. He weighed every sentence I wrote, frequently making minute verbal alteration, and questioned me closely as to the evidence on which I based all statements which he did not know to be correct. In short, he spared no pains to make his official reports as truthful as possible, and for whatever errors they contain I can safely say he is wholly free from responsibility.[36]

As Marshall said, sources of information for reports varied. They were not always as easy to get or reconcile as he implied in this quotation. Subordinate reports often arrived late. Marshall himself admitted at a dinner party long after the war that he had trouble getting the Gettysburg campaign report from Stuart and that he wrote the first draft of the army report without any input from the cavalry commander, a technique Lee would not accept. Marshall thought Lee either spoke or wrote to Stuart and finally coaxed the report from him. Most high-level official reports included maps, which of course required time to prepare. In his journal Jed Hotchkiss frequently mentioned gathering data or preparing maps to accompany Second Corps reports. Those, of course, drew as much attention from the commander as the written product. Jackson peremptorily rejected Hotchkiss's first map of Cedar Mountain. Hotchkiss noted, "The Gen. was out of humor in the morning about the position of the forces on the field on the map. [James K.] Boswell took him the map against my wishes, and he gave vent to considerable displeasure." Jackson also did not like another Cedar Mountain map and sent Hotchkiss off to check sources. The topographer took five days to interview regimental commanders and check with A. P. Hill's staff about unit locations before he resubmitted the map to Jackson. That attempt won approval with only the minor editorial change of "Valley Army" to "Army of the Valley." Report authors also used sources other than the commander to edit and check their work. Colonel Faulkner often

245

showed Hotchkiss draft official reports and even read them aloud at night to Hotchkiss and Boswell. All the checking and questioning helped clear up details. In one case, Boswell said it even showed the commander what had really happened during the battle. He noted, "Had a long talk with Gen'l. Jackson about the operations around Richmond; explained to him the battle of Cold Harbor [Gaines's Mill]. He says he never before had a clear idea of that fight."[37]

Commanders tried hard to weed out controversial material (and often even justifiable criticism) from their reports. Joseph Johnston returned part of Gustavus Smith's Seven Pines report that was critical of Longstreet with the admonition, "I inclose herewith the first three sheets of your report, to ask a modification—or omission, rather. They contain two subjects which I never intended to make generally known, and which I have mentioned to no one but yourself." Jackson crossed out a laudatory mention of Brigadier General Charles S. Winder from Lieutenant Colonel Faulkner's draft report on Cedar Mountain because he thought it might reflect poorly on E. F. Paxton, Winder's replacement. Hotchkiss and Faulkner could not agree on exactly which companies or battalions from what regiments had done a particular maneuver during the Battle of Winchester. Jackson decided to call them "some of Taylor's Brig. . . . as he would allow nothing that could be a matter of controversy to enter the report."[38] Lee deleted many controversial remarks from Marshall's draft Gettysburg official report. Marshall explained, "He struck from the original draft many statements which he thought might affect others injuriously, his sense of justice frequently leading him to what many consider too great a degree of lenience. . . . He declined to embody in his report anything that might seem to cast the blame upon others . . . he said he disliked in such communications to say aught to the prejudice of others, unless the truth of such statements had been established by an investigation in which those affected by them had been afforded an opportunity to defend or justify their actions." Elsewhere, Marshall wrote on the same subject, "Sometimes in the course of my work it seemed to me necessary to speak strongly of events that were calculated to call forth words of praise or blame. [Lee] often struck out observations of mine on subjects that aroused my liveliest interest and excited my feelings, saying in a playful way, 'Colonel, if you speak so strongly of this you will have nothing left to say of something better.' "[39]

However, all the data in the world and all the efforts to check facts and remove contentious statements could not eliminate controversy. Johnston did not use Lee's system of correlating and reconciling reports, and consequently several subordinates challenged him about the accuracy of his reports or those from other subordinates. Brigadier General

Benjamin Huger wrote to both Johnston and President Davis to object to parts of Longstreet's report on Seven Pines. When Lee's brief initial report from the Fredericksburg battlefield appeared in print, a subordinate complained: "I have just this moment read the official report of General Lee of the battle on last Saturday," wrote Robert Ransom, who felt slighted because his brigade was not mentioned. Longstreet, the brigadier's corps commander, responded sympathetically,

> The communication from the commanding general to the War Department made on the 14th instant, was not intended as an official report of the battle of the 13th. It was written on the field, and was intended to explain our position more than anything else, and was dictated at a time when we were hourly in expectation of a general battle. . . . The general commanding had no thought that it would ever be published, much less that it would go out to the world as his official report of the battle.
>
> He particularly regrets that injustice has been done your command, as first reports are more apt to make lasting impressions than later and more truthful ones.
>
> I trust that your gallant and devoted command will be satisfied to await for truth in the official reports.[40]

Lieutenant Colonel Faulkner did not finish all of Jackson's reports before the general died. Kyd Douglas complained that Faulkner produced a rough copy of the last report without the traditional paragraph mentioning the staff and then hastily resigned from the army. Douglas thought that the staff had been terribly injured by the failure to acknowledge its performance. But not everybody was displeased with official reports. Soldiers liked to see their units and leaders mentioned. As J. A. Englehard, a brigade AAG, noted proudly in a letter to a friend, "It was a 'Tar Heel' fight and you see we got Genl. Lee to *thanking* God, which you know means something brilliant."[41]

Army of Northern Virginia staffs clearly demonstrated the staff characteristic of having standard methods or procedures by which they performed routine specified duties. They had well-established procedures to interact with the commander, to correspond with superiors and subordinates, to distribute orders and instructions, and to coordinate the activities of the army. There was a logical, systematic process to issue and track orders and a tremendous amount of effort expended in writing after-action reports. All of that, however, was meaningless if the staff did not perform as expected in battle.

247

Chapter 10

THE STAFF IN BATTLE

Intelligence and Combat Functions

INTELLIGENCE

The Confederacy had an eighteenth-century intelligence apparatus unsuited to the semimodern war it fought. An organization in Richmond bore the promising title of Intelligence Office, but that agency provided information to families about sick and wounded soldiers and had nothing to do with intelligence in the military sense. The only dedicated Confederate intelligence bureau was a small branch of the Signal Corps that conducted limited strategic intelligence from its Richmond office—an effort confined largely to smuggling agents into Northern cities and gathering Union newspapers. The Signal Corps's collection effort was hit or miss and not well coordinated or focused. Field armies mirrored the national government's lack of system; however, despite the lack of formal structure, the Confederate military did gather and refine information. The Army of Northern Virginia used multiple means to collect information but relied on premodern techniques both to coordinate collection and to evaluate the information gathered. Staff officers played various roles in that process and were critical in many respects to its success. However, there was no staff officer responsible for intelligence, and staff intelligence functions were generally additional or collateral duties. Commanders served as their own intelligence officers. They developed their own informal collection plans, assigned individual and unit intelligence collection tasks, received raw information from sources, evaluated the data for accuracy and the source for reliability, combined the various bits of information into a coherent whole, and acted on the resulting intelligence. The process was not modern or even consistently efficient, but it existed and suited both the individuals and the times.

Confederate regulations gave little guidance on intelligence operations. In fact, they used the word *intelligence* not in the modern sense of a processed, evaluated product but as a synonym for *information*. The only regulatory guidance on intelligence was a short section on tactical reconnaissance that was heavy on patrol techniques and lacked discussion of processing or evaluating the resulting information. Respected theorists like Dennis Hart Mahan considered the collection and ordering of military information a vital duty. He claimed good intelligence solved half a commander's problem. Mahan's influential theoretical works gave detailed instruction on organizing patrols, told what reconnaissance officers should look for, and even proposed techniques of estimating distances and angles; however, they did not give practical advice on how commanders or staffs should control the collection process or analyze the resulting information.[1] Without guidance from above or acceptable doctrine, the Army of Northern Virginia developed its own intelligence system.

The two primary sources of strategic information were spies or agents and Union newspapers. Those sources usually supplied an amazingly clear picture of the overall strategic situation. Northern newspapers were a tremendous source of strategic information throughout the war. Even thirty-nine years after the fact, Thomas T. Munford considered his find of Northern newspapers in discarded Union knapsacks at White Oak Swamp a significant coup. When Stonewall Jackson complained about being cut off from news in the Shenandoah Valley, Richard Ewell began sending him newspapers by courier. J. E. B. Stuart included captured newspapers in his reports to headquarters. Robert E. Lee considered Union newspapers valuable enough sources of information to forward them to Jefferson Davis. When he did not send actual papers or clippings, Lee wrote long letters summarizing news of strategic importance. One example from July 1864 shows what information the army commander thought would interest the president. In the letter Lee summarized articles on Union losses at Kenesaw Mountain (June 27, 1864) and other battles in the West, changes in Union draft laws, and market news, including the price of gold in New York, and noted the absence of anything about Jubal Early's activities in the valley, from which Lee inferred that they remained undetected. In the later stages of the war, the Army of Northern Virginia got a regular and dependable supply of Union newspapers by the simple expedient of trading for them across the lines. Occasional interruption of that source raised suspicions in the Confederate camp. Lee commented in a postscript to a letter to Davis, "To-day we could get no papers from the enemy, from which I inferred there was some good news they wished to withold. The one [newspaper] sent was captured. You must excuse its condition."[2]

Spies, although more glamorous, were a less reliable source of strategic intelligence than newspapers. In the parlance of the day, spies were stationary agents. Federal authorities rounded up the Army of Northern Virginia's spy network in Washington (several women supported by Signal Corps couriers) fairly quickly. Conversely, Southern sympathizers in the border states and almost everybody in occupied portions of the Confederacy volunteered information. Their intelligence was often valuable, but informal sources were not reliable in terms of frequency, quantity, or quality. Soldiers and volunteer or paid civilians who moved in and out of Confederate lines on specific missions were more successful than stationary spy networks. Soldiers performing that function, called scouts as opposed to spies, operated out of uniform. They were usually recruited from cavalry units and were organized and directed by Stuart. Scouts worked individually or in small groups, and their total number was surprisingly small. Theodore Garnett, Stuart's aide, claimed that the cavalry commander "owed much of success in war" to just four scouts. Scouts penetrated Union picket lines and gathered information of immediate tactical value either by snatching prisoners or by watching camps. Alternatively, the scouts leaked to the rear of the army, where they might determine general force locations and composition. One group of four or five scouts operating behind Union lines in April 1864 forwarded a report of troop movements, road conditions, U. S. Grant's personal movements, and various rumors they had heard along with a request that the courier bearing the report be returned to his unit and replaced. As part of the initial jockeying before Chancellorsville, Lee sent a scout to observe the Baltimore and Ohio Railroad. The scout reported that Burnside's Ninth Corps of five divisions was being shipped west in forty-seven trains. The scout had confirmed unit identifications and low troop morale by talking with soldiers at stops. Three weeks later, another of Lee's scouts gave detailed information about Union shipping on the Potomac River over a ten-day period that helped Lee estimate enemy intentions.[3]

Occasionally, staff officers served as scouts. Before Chancellorsville, Richard H. Anderson wrote, "I have the honor to report that yesterday General [Ambrose R.] Wright sent his assistant adjutant-general, Captain [V. J. B.] Girardey, across the river, at the United States Ford, to examine the country opposite. The Captain returned last night, having carefully executed his instructions, and reports the enemy altogether removed from that neighborhood. Citizens informed him that they had been moving for some time past and had gone to Aquia Creek. The river was swimming in the deepest part of the channel."[4] Such information was important but could not satisfy the intelligence needs of the entire army. Corps commanders used their own intelligence assets to supplement the work of army scouts.

James Longstreet was an early devotee of scouting. He used two volunteer aides, Frank Terry and Thomas Lubbock, as scouts after First Manassas. Those two Texans specialized in nightly penetration of Union lines to snatch prisoners for interrogation. The resulting intelligence would have been primarily tactical in nature. E. Porter Alexander sent a young boy into the Union camp on the peninsula. Alexander inserted the boy by boat at night and recovered him a week later. He was pleased to receive "a very full, accurate, & valuable report of the force the enemy had & how they were disposed & what they were doing." That was also tactical information. Later scouts became bolder and made significant incursions into Union territory that would have produced more generalized intelligence. Some Confederate scouts ventured as far north as New York City, collecting rumors and general impressions of conditions. More common were scouting missions to Washington, Aquia Creek, and along the Potomac River that produced both operational and strategic intelligence.[5]

The Army of Northern Virginia maintained a fund in greenbacks to pay spies and scouts, either as fees for service or as reimbursement for expenses. Longstreet paid his famous scout, Thomas Harrison, the princely sum of $150 monthly in U.S. greenbacks. Longstreet appreciated Harrison's work, but not enough to retain him indefinitely, releasing the former actor from service and later regretting the move. Of course, some spies may not have been exactly what they seemed. One, identified in correspondence only as Langley, purportedly worked for Jackson and gave A. P. Hill information during the Maryland campaign. He got $200 Union and $500 Confederate to defray expenses in December 1863 but was back asking for $1,000 Union and $1,500 Confederate in February 1864. Langley had a pass from the federals to move in and out of the lines as an agent to get copies of Southern newspapers for the Northern press. He may have been working for one side or the other, both, or just himself. Langley was probably typical of a whole class of agents. Funds available to pay for intelligence varied but must have been significant since there was enough left in the army kitty at Appomattox to divide among the staff to pay for their journeys home.[6]

The Signal Corps' role in operational intelligence gathering was examined in chapter 4. The only other unique collection system was a brief experiment with observation balloons. The Union army exploited balloons sooner, longer, and more extensively then the Confederates, but the Rebels did not ignore the "air war" completely. Using a jury-rigged balloon that legend claims was made from the silk dresses of patriotic Southern women (but was actually created from bolts of silk), Alexander hovered over the battlefield of Gaines's Mill. Alexander had devised and disseminated a signal system using four large balls hanging beneath the balloon to report what he saw. What he saw and reported was the movement of Slocum's division of Sixth Corps across the Chickahominy River to reinforce the Union right flank. A subsequent attempt to operate the balloon from a ship ended in disaster when the ship grounded and fell prey to a Union gunboat. The Confederacy did not attempt to resurrect military ballooning—it was simply too expensive. The Confederates did learn a valuable lesson, though. Alexander's later assessment was that "the observers in the balloons should be *trained staff officers,* not the ignorant class of ordinary balloonists, which I think were generally in charge of Federal balloons."[7]

Another secondary source of information was the occasional seizure of official Union documents from intercepted couriers and captured headquarters or trains. Couriers, of course, fell into hostile hands with some regularity; however, the value of the information they carried varied considerably. Capturing documents at headquarters produced great intelligence but was difficult and depended on extremely good luck. Stuart's cavalry experienced such luck during the Catlett Station raid when they captured John Pope's "private despatch book with copies of his most important correspondence with [Abraham] Lincoln, [Henry] Halleck and others."[8] Every Confederate would have liked to repeat that experience often enough to make it a reliable source of intelligence, but such success was discouragingly infrequent. The loss of friendly intelligence when Confederate documents fell into enemy hands also offset such windfalls witness the loss of a saddlebag full of Stuart's documents when the Yankees captured one of his aides at Verdiersville only five days before the Catlett Station raid.

The primary source of tactical and battlefield intelligence was local reconnaissance. Cavalry, infantry patrols, and pickets conducted the bulk of tactical reconnaissance, but staff officers also performed that function as a primary part of their duties. In fact, staffers criticized commanders, both Union and Confederate, who did personal reconnaissance instead of leaving that to the experts. For example, Alexander criticized Irvin McDowell for conducting a personal reconnaissance before First Manassas ("a duty he might have more wisely confided to his staff") and Lee for his reconnaissance at Malvern Hill ("This should have been done earlier that morning, not by Lee in person, but by staff-officers under cavalry escort.").[9] As discussed in chapter 4, engineer officers were presumed to have special aptitude for reconnaissance, but all officers—and especially all staff officers—performed that function.

Staff reconnaissance techniques ranged from almost amateurishly crude to fairly sophisticated. At the low end of the scale were the officers who, alone or accompanied by one or two couriers, simply rode forward until they bumped into the enemy and returned (if they managed to avoid capture) to report what they discovered. As dangerous and guileless as that tactic may seem, it was sometimes necessary, especially in situations where the commander desperately needed to know exactly where the enemy was. Garnett used a variation of that basic technique when Stuart sent him and two couriers to the picket line with instructions not to report or return until they located the enemy. William Blackford described a more sophisticated procedure he habitually used. Blackford had three soldiers whose judgment and courage he trusted detailed to accompany him on all reconnaissance missions. He limited the size of the party because four men could ride close to the enemy without attracting attention. When they reached a good observation point, all would dismount. One man held the horses while Blackford and the others crept forward under cover. Blackford used his binoculars to examine the terrain and enemy, while his companions watched the flanks, provided local security, and pointed out anything they saw. The whole party returned to report at the end of the mission. When the situation permitted, Blackford converted his normal small scouting party into a semipermanent observation post. He and his regular companions still did the reconnaissance, but they took couriers with them to carry messages so they could remain at their observation post. Blackford described that technique in operation during the Battle of Fredericksburg. He found a hilltop that overlooked the right flank of the battlefield and "reported the fact to Stuart, proposing that I should occupy this hill as a post of observation. He was delighted with the idea, and sent twenty couriers with me, telling me to send him a report every fifteen or twenty minutes. . . . I gave notice of each attack they made by sending a report in writing to General Stuart, which he forwarded to Jackson. . . . When the last general attack was about to start, having sent off all the couriers, I went myself to General Stuart to inform him." Heros Von Borcke used the same technique of a stationary observation post supported by couriers at Antietam. Jed Hotchkiss may have been doing the same thing as he and a mounted escort atop Massanutten Mountain watched Turner Ashby maneuvering against Nathaniel P. Banks in the Shenandoah Valley during the opening phases of Jackson's valley campaign, although Hotchkiss did not specifically record sending couriers with reports of what he observed.[10]

Processing the information from newspapers, spies and scouts, balloonists, captured documents, battlefield reconnaissance, and other sources fell mainly to commanders. Lee gave a brief glimpse of the commander processing his own intelligence when he wrote, "I have for some time been doubtful of the intentions of the enemy. His movements could be accounted for on several suppositions."[11] The staff's role in the intelligence system—other than as direct information collectors—was one of administration rather than substance. That trend emerged early in the war.

The Army of Northern Virginia began exploiting spies and Union newspapers long before it assumed its legendary name. P. G. T. Beauregard credited Colonel Thomas Jordan, his assistant adjutant general and chief of staff, with organizing (before the general joined the Rebel army facing Washington) an efficient spy network that "receive[d] regularly from private persons at the Federal Capital, most accurate information of which politicians high in council, as well as War Department clerks, were the unconscious ducts." Beauregard's semiofficial biographer, Alfred Roman, explained that Jordan's spy network provided not only government information but also the other source of strategic intelligence, newspapers: "During the period a thorough secret-service communication was maintained between Washington and the Confederate headquarters at Manassas, whereby trustworthy private information was received through cipher despatches, while regular files of all the important Northern journals reached our lines in the same way; those from New York, particularly, rendering unconscious assistance to our cause." Beauregard admitted that he used Union newspapers to verify and confirm federal strength figures obtained from a War Department clerk captured shortly before First Manassas. After that battle, Alexander, in his role as signal officer, assumed some of Jordan's duties as spymaster and newspaper collector for the army. As a minimum, Jordan asked Alexander to devise better means of communicating with agents, which Alexander used as his entree into the intelligence business. However, the energetic Alexander's contribution to Army of Northern Virginia intelligence system was one of refinement on the margins rather than innovation. He concocted a variety of schemes to communicate better with agents in Washington and had one agent whose primary duty was collecting and forwarding newspapers (which Alexander claimed gave the Rebels their best information on Union strengths and movements), but he did not develop new sources or methods or in any way institute a modern system of analysis and distribution.[12] Staff officers handled the details of recruiting, paying, and communicating with agents, but commanders personally debriefed returning agents, read reports, and perused enemy newspapers.

Extensive research found only one case of a staff officer doing classic staff intelligence analysis. Alexander said he developed an order of battle of the Union army from reports of spies in Washington and information from Northern newspapers:

> The one thing we had done for us by our friends in Washn. City was to keep & send us regularly arrivals & departures of all Federal troops, & clippings from newspapers which mentioned troops brigaded or associated together. From information of this sort I was able quite soon to construct a roster of the Federal army, showing every division of it with the brigades in each division & the regts. in each brigade. This of course enabled us to estimate the force of the enemy very accurately.

Incidentally, Alexander also provides the only example of a staff officer running a deliberate counterintelligence operation. Two attempts by that resourceful staff officer to pass messages to George B. McClellan failed when patriotic Southerners intercepted the messages. Alexander hoped to establish himself (using a code name) as a traitor and thus uncover Union agents inside the Army of Northern Virginia when they tried to contact him. The plans were good and quite involved—one required Stuart's cavalry to drive in the Union pickets and clandestinely drop a letter—but execution fell afoul of well-intentioned Confederates who were not privy to the scheme.[13]

Absence of aggressive staff participation in intelligence analysis was not as detrimental to efficiency as a modern observer might expect. The available intelligence sources simply did not produce more information than a single individual could digest. When Lee complained about a dearth of information, he mentioned surprisingly few resources: "Some of my best scouts are absent; one was killed in a skirmish a short time since, two have been captured, and Captain [E. P.] Bryon, of the signal corps, whom I sent into Maryland to watch the river on that side was, without my knowledge . . . ordered to report to General Beauregard in Charleston. The scouts report that it is very difficult to get within the enemy's lines, as their pickets are posted within 50 steps of each other. These circumstances may account for my getting no information."[14] An army commander whose intelligence apparatus was crippled by the loss or capture of four scouts and effective enemy picketing was not depending on more assets than would tax his personal analytic powers. An intelligent commander could read reports and newspapers, debrief agents, do his own analysis, and arrive at conclusions as well as any member of his staff. In fact, a major factor in Lee's success was his ability to perform the intelligence function better than either his staff or the enemy. He was remarkably good (or lucky) at divining enemy intentions from the fragments of available information, and he certainly outshone his opponents in using the intelligence he gleaned. Detailing the administration of collection management to the staff and subordinates relieved the major commanders of the most onerous part of Civil War intelligence operations. The system worked to the satisfaction of the individuals involved. Where it failed, it did so because the normal sources of intelligence dried up, not because of poor analysis or lack of system. For example, during offensive maneuvers into enemy territory such as the Gettysburg campaign, the friendly civilian spies and strategically located signal stations that aided Lee's defensive operations in Northern Virginia were not available. Scouts could not efficiently fill the void, and Lee made poor use of his other intelligence assets, such as his cavalry.[15] Army of Northern Virginia commanders complained about the lack of intelligence but not about how that intelligence was collected, processed, or analyzed.

STAFF ORGANIZATION FOR COMBAT

The staff's primary combat function was as a critical element in the command and control system on the battlefield. Commanders used staff officers to transmit orders, coordinate and supervise execution, conduct liaison with other units and commanders, maneuver units, and provide information about conditions on the field. These activities were accomplished in a typically informal fashion—there was no doctrine or disciplined system for staff battlefield activities. A symptom of that lack of doctrine was the unsystematic way staffs organized for combat. It was impossible to predict which officers would accompany the commander on the field or what duties they might perform there.

Normally, quartermaster, commissary, ordnance, and medical chiefs stayed with their respective trains or hospitals, while aides and assistant adjutants general accompanied the commander on the field. There were standing orders (or at least customary practices) that kept quartermasters, commissaries, and surgeons in the rear. Joseph E. Johnston and Beauregard followed tradition at First Manassas and had only their aides accompany them on the field, leaving even chiefs of staff and AAGs at headquarters to hurry forward arriving troops and greet visitors (like President Davis). Beauregard thought that was the doctrinal way to operate—the general staff belonged in the rear. He commented in his report on the battle, "The general staff attached to the [Confederate] Army of the Potomac, were necessarily engaged severally with their responsible duties, at my headquarters at Camp Pickens." Lee usually used his staff in the same way, although some or all of his AAGs frequently accompanied him to the field. As a typical example, Lee's report on Chancellorsville cited Lieutenant Colonel James L. Corley (quartermaster) for taking care of his trains and Lieutenant Colonels Robert G. Cole (commissary) and Briscoe G. Baldwin (ordnance) for "attending the wants of their departments." In contrast, Lee cited the assistant adjutants general, engineers, and aides for being "active in seeing to the execution of orders," "reconnoitering the enemy and constructing batteries," and "watching operations and carrying orders." Lieutenant Colonel Walter Taylor, the AAG, generally stayed at headquarters until he was sure there would be a battle and headquarters preparatory functions were complete; then he joined Lee on the field.[16] Such a rational staff organization for combat was, however, neither consistently practiced nor standard throughout the army.

Officers who should have been in the rear taking care of their assigned duties showed up on the field. Examples are too numerous to detail comprehensively, but the following give the flavor. As the Army of Northern Virginia's chief of ordnance during both Seven Pines and the Seven Days' Battles, Alexander left his ordnance trains to venture forward onto the field. At Gaines's Mill during the Seven Days' Battles, Major John Haskell, commissary chief for Major General D. R. "Neighbor" Jones at the time, not only operated forward with his commander but carried messages, placed troops, and rallied regiments for Longstreet, R. H. Anderson, and W. H. C. Whiting before joining John B. Hood's troops in an attack. Jackson was short of staff at Second Manassas, so he used his medical director as an aide-de-camp to carry orders. During the same campaign, Lee commandeered Stuart's quartermaster and dispatched him in command of a cavalry detachment to conduct a reconnaissance of Warrenton. A story exists about Ewell accosting an elegantly dressed officer at Cedar Mountain: "'I say, you man with the fine clothes on! Who are you, and where do you belong?' Being informed, with all possible dignity, that he was 'Captain ———, Quartermaster of the ——— Virginia regiment,' the grim old soldier threw up both hands and exclaimed: 'Great heavens! a Quartermaster in a battle-field; who ever heard of such a thing before? But as you are here I will make you useful as well as ornamental.'" Ewell sent the quartermaster officer off with a message: "The gallant Quartermaster carried the message and brought the answer, but . . . soon discovered that his trains needed looking after, and never ventured near General Ewell during a battle again." D. H. Hill had a reputation for "every now and then '*treating*' the non-combatant officers of his staff—the quartermasters, commissaries, and doctors—to what he

257

called 'a little airing in a fight' when he thought they stood in need of it."[17]

The lack of disciplined staff organization for combat did not manifest itself solely in officers coming forward from the rear to watch or participate. The opposite was also true—staff officers who should have been attending their commanders often got sidetracked into extraneous missions. Captain William D. Farley of Stuart's cavalry staff rode ahead of Stuart at Gaines's Mill and began following the sound of the guns. He had no idea where he was going, so he dismounted, left his horse with an ambulance, and tried to find some action. Farley first joined a Louisiana regiment and worked with them for a while before migrating to a North Carolina regiment. The wandering aide left the Tar Heels to join Hood's Texans, but nothing was happening on their front, so he went on to a South Carolina regiment and joined them in a late-afternoon attack. Farley claimed to have fired eighty rounds that day—mostly in sniping. He did not rejoin Stuart until late at night. During the same battle, McHenry Howard, Brigadier General Charles S. Winder's aide, spent his day rallying regiments and trying to convince flanking units from different commands to join his brigade's attacks. Howard did not see Winder from the start of the action until after dark, when he stumbled onto the general almost accidentally.[18] Farley and Howard had a good time and arguably contributed to the total effort, but they were of no direct use to their commanders throughout the battle.

At South Mountain, before Antietam, Alexander spotted some people on a hill overlooking the battlefield. Lee agreed with Alexander's suggestion that he take a few men to investigate, and Alexander scrounged up eight infantrymen for the mission. The onlookers proved to be nothing more menacing than curious civilians. Instead of returning to Lee, however, Alexander found a rock where he could snipe at the enemy in the valley below while his detail kept him supplied with loaded muskets. Only after an hour or so of sniping did Alexander release the soldiers and return to Lee. Hotchkiss, the topographical engineer, was off on business at the start of the Antietam battle. He judged his horse too tired to participate, so he stayed in Shepherdstown, where he spent the night—as did Sandie Pendleton and Hunter McGuire—while their boss, Jackson, slept on the field. At least both Pendleton and McGuire had participated in the battle. At Chancellorsville, Henry Kyd Douglas, at the time a company commander and acting assistant inspector general in the Stonewall Brigade, preceded his unit to the field. In Douglas's words, "my brigade not being up, I joined General A. P. Hill, at his request." He might have been useful to his unit as it moved into the battle. In a similar vein, Arthur Fremantle commented about the early hours of the second day's fighting at Gettysburg, "As the whole of the morning was evidently to be occupied in disposing the troops for the attack, I rode to the extreme right with Colonel [Peyton] Manning and Major [Thomas] Walton [of Longstreet's staff], where we ate quantities of cherries, and got a feed of corn for our horses. We also bathed in a small stream, but not without some trepidation on my part, for we were almost beyond the lines and were exposed to the enemy's cavalry."[19] The British observer could do as he pleased; the two staff officers accompanying him might have been useful to Longstreet that morning when the corps was marching and countermarching and in sore need of staff supervision. These may have been harmless, valorous, or inconsequential activities and were usually more interesting than performing standard staff duties, but officers not being where they were supposed to be detracted from the staff's combat effectiveness.

The potential for mischief from lack of doctrine on how staffs operated in battle increased when commanders ranged widely over battlefields or took off without their staffs. Staff officers frequently returned from a mission to find their commanders vanished without a trace. Blackford commented that Stuart had a habit of "riding about the field in every direction, sending first one and then another of his staff off on some duty from which it was often difficult to rejoin him." Von Borcke said that he and most of the staff and couriers were separated from Stuart for two days during the Second Manassas campaign. Stuart's aide, Garnett, spent a full day separated from his boss during the Mine Run campaign. Longstreet had a habit of riding off without telling his staff and simply expecting them to follow. Lee was frequently unaccompanied by staff at critical points in battles. He often left much of his staff at headquarters and ventured onto the field with either no escort or one so small it quickly evaporated as he dispatched aides on missions. Alexander recorded his surprise when a solitary Lee joined him at the forward artillery positions covering Pickett's retreating troops after their charge at Gettysburg. Alexander mentioned tearing down fence rails to cross the Emmitsburg Road, so the commanding general was well forward, but without his staff he could not exercise command or influence the action. At Antietam, Lee borrowed staff officers because "none of my staff are present."[20] In a time when tactical command and control depended on messengers, a commander alone had little chance of influencing a battle.

Ideally, considering the command and control system available to the Army of Northern Virginia, commanders should have picked a position that afforded a good view of the field and remained there, which happened when terrain and situation permitted. Lee's position at Fredericksburg is an example, and William Pendleton's position during the defense of the Potomac River fords after Antietam is another. Pendleton's description of his command arrangements could have been extracted from a textbook: "My own position was chosen at a point central, moderately protected by conformation of ground, at the same time commanding the general view and accessible from every direction, with as little exposure of messengers as any one place in such a scene could be. And here, except when some personal inspection or order had to be given requiring temporary absence, I remained for best service throughout the day."[21] Unfortunately, the personalities of the commanders, the command ethos of the day, and the situation and terrain on most battlefields did not favor such rational arrangements.

COMMAND AND CONTROL

Despite faulty organization for combat, staffs in the Army of Northern Virginia performed invaluable command and control functions. Obviously, they carried messages and delivered orders. Examples of that necessary command function are so common—in fact, it is the only duty for which they are universally given credit—that it does not require explication. However, if all staff officers did in battle was deliver messages, they would have been merely high-paid couriers. Such was not the case. They had other functions that required intelligence, expertise, trust, and judgment. One such duty was liaison.

In the liaison role, commanders used staff officers to clarify orders, determine the situation of flank and supporting units, and generally to stay abreast of the friendly situation. Brigadier General Alfred Iverson's Gettysburg report gives excellent examples of all these uses:

> During the cannonading that ensued, my brigade was in support of the battery, and, having received instructions from General [Robert] Rodes to advance gradually to the support of a battery he intended placing in front and not understanding the exact time at which the advance was to take place, I dispatched a staff officer to him, to learn at what time I was to move forward, and received instructions not to move until my skirmishers became hotly engaged. . . . [When orders arrived] I immediately dispatched a staff officer to inform Brigadier-General [Junius] Daniel [who was in support] that I was about to advance, and one to notify my regiments, and to observe when the brigade on my left [Edward A. O'Neal's] commenced to move.[22]

Iverson's efforts did not properly coordinate his advance or mitigate the disastrous results of his attack, but at least he used liaison officers in a textbook fashion.

An officer on a liaison mission might shuttle back and forth between his commander and other headquarters, or he might remain semipermanently with the unit with which he was to liaise. Captain Andrew G. Dickinson, John B. Magruder's AAG, performed such a function at Malvern Hill. Dickinson shuttled information and messages between Magruder and Lee—going as far as writing down verbal instructions, apparently so he would not forget them. Also during the Seven Days' Battles, Stuart sent Blackford as a liaison officer to Jackson. Blackford explained his mission as follows: "Wishing to keep General Jackson informed of his movements, General Stuart now sent me with a small escort of picked men and a guide, for the country was full of scouting parties of the enemy, to inform him of his whereabouts." Blackford remained with Jackson overnight and informally joined his staff until he could rejoin Stuart. During the federal probing attacks in October 1862 following Stuart's Chambersburg raid, the cavalry commander sent Von Borcke out on a dual intelligence and liaison mission: "At this time I received orders from General Stuart to proceed with a number of couriers at once to the little town of Smithfield, about twelve miles distant, where we had a small body of cavalry, to watch the enemy's movements on our right, and establish frequent communications with Jackson at Bunker Hill only a few miles off." At Fredericksburg, Stuart's aide, Lieutenant R. Channing Price, liaised between Stuart and Jackson to keep Jackson informed of developments on his flank. On the Chancellorsville battlefield, Jackson left Douglas with Brigadier General Fitzhugh Lee with instructions "to remain with General Lee and bring in person any report General Lee might wish to make." Jackson also left his aide, Captain James P. Smith, at the starting point for his famous attack on the Union's right flank. Smith "was ordered to remain at the point where the advance began, to be a center of communication between the general and the cavalry on the flanks, and to deliver orders to detachments of artillery still moving up from the rear." At Gettysburg, Ewell sent Campbell Brown, his AAG, to find Stuart (who was picketing Ewell's left flank) or any general of cavalry to find out what they knew about the situation. The AAG found Stuart, sent an immediate message to Ewell, remained with Stuart for two or three hours to keep current, and left a courier with Stuart when he returned to Ewell. Stuart assigned Garnett as a liaison officer to Cadmus Wilcox's division during the Mine Run campaign with orders to remain until the federal attack (expected soon) began and then to keep Stuart fully informed on the progress of the battle. During the Battle of the Wilderness, Early said, "I posted my Adjutant General, Major John W. Daniel, with a courier, in a position to be communicated with by [John B.] Gordon, so as to inform me of the success attending the movement, and enable me to put in the other brigades at the right time." Besides keeping Early informed, Daniel was also supposed to coordinate the actions of the three brigades making that dusk attack. His wounding may have contributed to the unraveling of the operation. During the same battle, Harry Hays sent his aide, William Seymour, to coordinate the simultaneous advance of Hays's unit and the Stonewall Brigade.[23]

These are all examples of using a staff officer to acquire friendly information or to facilitate cooperation between units. Such duty requires skill and intelligence. The liaison officer must know his commander's thoughts, plans, and information needs. Liaison requires judgment—without command authority but with the ability to speak responsibly for the commander—and was thus a perfect job for a Civil War staff officer.

Another common command and control function of Army of Northern Virginia staff officers was coordination and supervision. Alexander caught the essence of those functions when he wrote, "An army is like a great machine, and in putting it into battle it is not enough for its commander to merely issue the necessary orders. He should have a staff ample to supervise the execution of each step, & to promptly report any difficulty or misunderstanding." Elsewhere, Alexander's comments about a Union action reinforce the concept of staff supervision: "And Hooker took a further precaution, most desirable whenever important orders are issued. He despatched a competent staff-officer, Gen. [Gouverneur K.] Warren, his chief engineer, to supervise their execution."[24]

Assistant inspectors general had a special role in supervision. Their responsibility for enforcing discipline necessarily placed them in a direct supervisory role. Instructions for inspectors general in battle told them to watch and report a variety of activities and made them responsible for policing some of the most vexing battlefield problems, like straggling and drifting off the front line. One long sentence from those instructions is instructive about the scope of an inspector's supervisory duties on the field:

> Preparatory to battle inspectors will locate their provost guard at eligible points for arresting all stragglers; acquaint themselves with the locality of the ordnance, supply, and ambulance trains, and the field hospitals, the character of the grounds in the vicinity of their commands, front and rear, and of all roads to and from the line of battle, and connecting with the main traveled roads in rear; the troops supporting both flanks; the position of reserves; the watchfulness observed by pickets and skirmishers thrown to the front, and report this, and all other information, derived from the examination of prisoners or other sources, which may prove im-

portant in aiding his commander in the intelligent performance of his duty.[25]

Critics reproach Lee for failing to use his staff to supervise. Typical, if more blunt than most, of such criticism is this assessment by Jeffry D. Wert: "Once Lee's orders were conveyed, his influence dissipated because he did not possess a staff capable of keeping him informed of problems or even guiding the fighting in accord with Lee's wishes." In the main, such criticism is deserved—Lee did not make good use of the supervisory talent of his staff. The problem was not that Lee's staff did not supervise at all; it was that their supervisory efforts were spotty and inefficient. The blame, however, was not the staff's. Lee did not understand the duties of an army commander to include detailed supervision of the execution of orders. He told a Pomeranian observer, Captain Justus Scheibert, "I plan and work with all my might to bring the troops to the right place at the right time; with that I have done my duty. As soon as I order the troops forward into battle, I lay the fate of my army in the hands of God; It is my generals' turn to perform their duty."[26] Thus, Lee delegated tactical responsibility to his subordinate leaders. The burden for supervision might have transferred with that responsibility. If that was Lee's thinking, he was wrong. A leader who delegates extensively still needs to supervise to ensure that his subordinates understand and execute the intended plan. Lee retained responsibility even if he delegated authority and should have used his staff to supervise more aggressively than they did. Nevertheless, the staff of the Army of Northern Virginia was a complete system, not just the army headquarters staff. The lower staff echelons did supervise and coordinate. A few examples illustrate common techniques and procedures.

Staff officers accompanied different units or columns when large units moved or fought separately. Jackson used that technique when he was unsatisfied with the march discipline of his corps. Stuart also used the technique during the attack on Catlett Station, as Blackford described: "A member of the staff was assigned to each attacking column with orders to see that everything was done to secure the general objective in view and to report progress frequently to the General [Stuart] at the reserve." Stuart employed the same technique in the preliminary maneuvering before Yellow Tavern when he sent Garnett to accompany one column while he traveled with another. Alternatively, a commander might send a staff officer to watch several units or a specific part of the field. When heavy firing broke out on the Confederate left at First Manassas, Beauregard sent a staff officer with half a dozen couriers to observe the action and report its progress every ten minutes. That technique was not as common or as systematized in the Army of Northern Virginia as it became in the Union's Army of the Potomac (where aides spent entire battles with subordinate commands serving as a second set of eyes, reporting separately from subordinate commanders, and returning at night to headquarters to review notes and get additional instructions), but it was a recognized practice. A staff officer might also be given a special assignment to supervise a specific activity. Douglas described such a procedure at Antietam: "At the suggestion of [Lee], General Jackson directed me to ascertain the position of all the artillery which would be engaged, to refamiliarize myself with all the roads leading to and from their positions to Sharpsburg and the rear, so as to direct in what manner to get ammunition, to take off disabled guns or caissons and bring up new ones, and to get any reports that needed attention; and for this purpose to visit them frequently as possible. He relieved me from personal duty with himself for the day."[27] Douglas, who had no artillery connections or experience, wore out three horses that day and eventually fainted from lack of food and water. He was invaluable in his special mission at Antietam because he was a Sharpsburg native and knew the ground well. Normally, however, artillery, ordnance, quartermaster, commissary, and medical trains had sufficient staff supervision in their own structure—most staff supervision focused on the infantry. And very hands-on supervision it was. Army of Northern Virginia staff supervision went well beyond observing and reporting; staff officers were expected to lead when circumstances required.

During the main battle on the Confederate left at First Manassas, Captain Samuel W. Ferguson, one of Beauregard's aides, busied himself directing regiments. He changed their positions, reordered them, and ordered halts or advances based on his understanding of his commander's desires. Longstreet cited Peyton Manning for bravely leading an attack, regimental flag in hand, and personally killing three Yankees at Williamsburg. In the fight at Port Republic (June 9, 1862), Douglas reported that Jackson "directed me to ride rapidly for the first regiment I could get (he had sent Pendleton to put Taliaferro under arms), to bring it quickly and to 'take that piece.'" At Second Manassas, Jackson sent Douglas to get support from Longstreet, a request with which Longstreet concurred: Longstreet "hurried off a staff officer for D. R. Jones' division, and just then two batteries came galloping up the hill. He requested me while waiting for Jones' division to direct the placing and firing of one of them." During the same battle, Von Borcke was on a mission for Stuart: "After a rapid gallop of a few minutes, I met two brigades of A. P. Hill's division, which I ordered to proceed at a double-quick to the point of danger. Very soon I encountered General Hill himself, to whom

I made the necessary explanations, and who at once proceeded in person to the threatened position." In June 1864 in the Shenandoah Valley, Major General W. H. F. "Rooney" Lee dispatched his aide, Garnett, at the head of a squadron of the 3d North Carolina Cavalry to assist Brigadier General Bradley T. Johnson. The regimental commander requested permission to accompany the squadron, since the rest of his regiment was momentarily unemployed, but it is clear that Garnett led the expedition. Later the same day, Lee sent Garnett off at the head of the 5th North Carolina Cavalry in an attack.[28]

Brigadier General Clement A. Evans's praise of his brigade assistant adjutant general at Fredericksburg gives a good idea of what commanders expected from their staff officers. Evans cited Captain Edward P. Lawton for "cheering the men, leading this regiment, or restoring the line of another, encouraging officers, he was everywhere along the whole line the bravest of the brave." Even more clearly demonstrating staff use in battle is the example of James L. Kemper's aide, Captain John Beckham, at Turner's Gap (September 14, 1862). Kemper and his staff arrived at the gap late in the day, ahead of their brigade. Kemper sent Beckham back to bring the brigade forward. The aide deployed the small brigade and led it into the attack until General Kemper took command. As the battle progressed, the regiments lost contact with each other. Kemper sent Beckham to correct the situation, which he did by recalling a stalled regiment and redeploying it on the opposite side of its flank unit.[29] Deploying a brigade for battle and redeploying regiments during a battle are critical command functions. General Kemper, like his peers, felt no hesitation about delegating that function to his staff.

A more dramatic example comes to us from Douglas's explanation of his activities as AAG of Major General Edward "Allegheny" Johnson's division during the attack on Culp's Hill on the third day at Gettysburg. Douglas went to hurry forward Brigadier General William "Extra Billy" Smith's brigade and virtually assumed command of it in the process:

> In my impatience I perhaps forgot the proprieties and told [Smith] that, as I was familiar with the exact situation, I would, if he would permit me, lead his brigade in at the right place. To this he courteously assented. . . . I was riding in front of the lines on "Ashby" and officers and men cried to me to dismount. I saw that I was alone on horseback. But I was about to turn the brigade over to its commander, and then it did not seem proper for a staff officer to dismount, although I knew I could not go far on horseback up that breakneck hill. I had given the order to throw out some skirmishers to the front as we moved on, and was pointing with my sword, directing the line to the left oblique.[30]

Douglas (with the commander's assent) not only led the brigade forward and positioned it for the attack but even deployed the skirmishers. General Smith might as well have been totally absent. A day before that incident, in the same general area of Culp's Hill, Randolph McKim as an aide-de-camp ordered a regiment to fire. The target turned out to be another Confederate regiment. McKim consoled himself with the belief that nobody was killed (he did not mention wounded). During and after Pickett's charge, Longstreet's staff scurried about the battlefield trying to support the attack, rally and reform broken lines, and reestablish defensive positions. For much of that time Longstreet remained lethargic, so the staff virtually commanded the corps. During the mainly dismounted cavalry battle at Haw's Shop (May 29, 1864), even a courier got into the mode of direct leadership in battle. John Gill remembered delivering orders to withdraw the Charleston Dragoons: "I had not time to address the Colonel, I gave the order, as I broke into their ranks, 'Right about face, double quick, march,' and succeeded in extricating them from a very dangerous position. General [Fitzhugh] Lee complimented me for the prompt manner in which I acted."[31]

PLANS AND ORDERS

Staff participation in tactical and operational planning was strictly limited. That is to be expected, since most Army of Northern Virginia commanders had vastly more military training and experience than their staffs. There are no instances like the Army of the Potomac's planning for the Wilderness campaign, when the army chief of staff, Andrew A. Humphreys, submitted two courses of action to the commander, George G. Meade, and then translated the decision into detailed orders. In the Army of Northern Virginia, when the staff had a direct role in planning operations, its participation usually reflected personal knowledge of the immediate terrain more than tactical expertise. For example, Captain James K. Boswell, Jackson's chief of engineers, played a major role in selecting maneuver routes during the Second Manassas campaign. On August 13, 1862, during the preliminary maneuvering along the Rappahannock, Boswell noted, "General Jackson then directed me to examine and on the following day to report to him, the most desirable route for passing around the enemy's flank and reaching Warrenton." That instance relied on Boswell's reconnaissance ability; however, a later incident in the same campaign found the young captain making recommendations based on map work and personal knowledge as a local native. "About 3 P.M. [August 24, 1862] I received an order from General Jackson to report immediately to him at Jeffersonton, which being done, he directed me to select the most direct and covered route to Manassas."[32] Jackson approved Boswell's suggestion and ordered him to guide the lead division on what was to become one of the brilliant operational maneuvers of the war. However, examples like this one are rare.

If staff participation in planning was minimal, it was critical to preparing and issuing orders. Elaborate written orders were rare in the Army of Northern Virginia and when produced were occasionally poorly drafted, vague, and confusing. Beauregard issued written orders for First Manassas that were detailed and explicit. However, subsequent orders that day deteriorated significantly. For example, a staff officer delivered the following verbally to Stuart: "Colonel Stuart, General Beauregard directs that you bring your command into action at once and that you attack where the firing is hottest." That statement was neither clear nor very helpful to the cavalry commander. Early described with some irritation a series of vague, confusing orders for moves, attacks, counterattacks, and withdrawals he received during the same battle. One was as a scrawled "Send Early to me" on the bottom of orders to someone else without indication of Beauregard's location or intent. Johnston did not do much better nearly a year later at Seven Pines. He failed to communicate his plan clearly to Longstreet and did not follow the verbal orders with written confirmation. The result was a confused, mismanaged battle in which Longstreet's division took a wrong road and fouled the movement of two other divisions. Johnston did not improve his performance during the battle. Cadmus Wilcox's brigade received four sets of orders—at least one in writing—that caused it to march back and forth and eventually made it very late joining the fight.[33] It took time for the Army of Northern Virginia to learn acceptable orders techniques, but it eventually did.

When Lee used written operations orders, he generally drafted them himself and had his staff prepare and dispatch the necessary copies. When he intervened in tactical matters after the commencement of battle, Lee usually issued verbal orders directly to divisional and corps commanders either in person or through his staff. For example, after a conference with his senior commanders before the Seven Days' Battles, Lee spent the rest of the day in his room, eventually emerging to hand his staff "the confidential order of battle, with instructions to prepare copies themselves, and forward them at once to the several division commanders." The result was a general order with detailed instructions, sometimes for units as low as individual regiments (especially for the cavalry), signed by Robert Chilton as assistant adjutant general. The staff must have interpreted its commander's instructions liberally, since copies went to heads of staff departments as well as to division commanders. In that case, staff participation in the orders process was limited to clerical work. At other times, however, the staff translated general guidance from Lee into written instructions. Brigadier General Imboden described such a process after Gettysburg. Lee summoned Imboden to his tent about two o'clock in the morning on July 4, 1863.

> After a good deal of conversation about roads, and the best disposition of my forces to cover and protect the vast train, [Lee] directed that the chiefs of his staff departments should be waked up to receive, in my presence, his orders to collect as early the next day as possible all the wagons and ambulances which I was to convoy, and have them in readiness for me to take command of them. His medical director (Dr. Lafayette Guild) was charged to see that all the wounded who could bear the rough journey should be placed in empty wagons and ambulances. He then remarked to me that his general instructions would be sent to me in writing the following morning.

The staff prepared a general order for the withdrawal that night and issued it in the morning. In that case, the staff took the commander's intent (and perhaps some specific provisions) but had to flesh out the details and translate it into a written order.[34] That is typical staff process of order writing in any period.

Army of Northern Virginia orders for major campaigns could be detailed—at least detailed enough to give commanders what they needed—but they were neither long nor complicated. The order to initiate the Second Manassas campaign had movement instructions with starting times, provisions for a reserve for the army and each wing, logistics instructions, and coordinating instructions about miscellaneous subjects like straggling, but that was all. Similarly, the order for Chancellorsville was a brief, four-paragraph document with movement and tactical instructions for the infantry and artillery plus a paragraph covering logistic and administrative details.[35]

But even the mature system for writing orders for the Army of Northern Virginia was not foolproof. Colonel Charles Marshall composed and wrote the loose and unclear order that allowed Stuart to take off on his ill-fated Gettysburg ride, and Lee approved the order by signing it. Controversy arose after the war about the unclear nature of the orders for the concentration and conduct of that famous battle. Nevertheless, at army level, written orders for battles improved significantly under Lee and his staff. Battlefield orders could still be confusing and not well thought out, though. At Malvern Hill, Lee sent Magruder, Benjamin Huger, and D. H. Hill orders reading, "Batteries have been established to rake the enemy's line. If it is broken, as is probable, [Lewis A.] Armistead, who can witness the effect of the fire, has been ordered to charge with a yell. Do the same." That was a poorly conceived order without a hint of the coordination required for a multibrigade attack. It resulted in a brave but bobbled assault. Perhaps it was best that Lee usually left tactical details to his corps commanders, although he did not adhere steadfastly to that routine. As late as Chancellorsville, when he had a trusted and capable command team under him, Lee wrote division commanders detailed letters ordering tactical shifts, passing intelligence, directing minute logistical arrangements, and reminding the commanders to take care of their men and animals. In one case, he even got into the details of who would relieve pickets.[36] In Lee's defense, in that case Longstreet and most of his corps were absent and Lee had assumed direct command of the two First Corps divisions on the field.

Lee's major subordinates used procedures similar to his in issuing their orders. Longstreet wrote some or many of his orders personally. In at least one instance, he got verbal orders from Lee, returned to his tent, prepared his own corps order, and passed it to his staff for processing and distribution while the general slept. On other occasions though, G. Moxley Sorrel, as chief of staff, drafted warning orders and composed movement orders while the corps commander was handling other matters. Longstreet, however, did not always confirm directions by issuing written versions of verbal orders. In November 1862 Sorrel sent messages to Anderson, Hood, and G. E. Pickett saying, "The general commanding directs that you proceed without delay to execute the movement, verbal orders and instructions for which you received from him yesterday."[37] That effectively initiated execution but did not ensure that all parties had the same understanding of the verbal orders.

The quality of Jackson's orders was inconsistent. At Gaines's Mill, Jackson used an aide to relay complicated verbal orders, including contingency plans, to his subordinate commands. Execution went astray due to a misinterpretation by the aide. In other instances, he issued such imprecise orders as "Order forward the whole line. The battle is won." Historian James I. Robertson Jr. called Jackson's orders throughout the battle at Cedar Mountain "garbled and incomprehensible." Sandie Pendleton gave Early an order that day that read, "Gen. Jackson sends compliments to Gen. Early and says advance on the enemy and you will be supported by Gen. Winder," which is little more explicit than "Tell Gen. Ewell to drive the enemy" (June 27, 1862) or "Tell my column to cross that road," issued at Chancellorsville. As to Jackson's written prebattle orders, much of their success seems to have depended on the ability of his assistant adjutant general and later chief of staff Sandie Pendleton. William Gleason Bean, Pendleton's biographer, noted that a planned night counterattack at Fredericksburg aborted when Pendleton received a temporarily incapacitating wound. The order-preparation process, which had been going smoothly, broke down like a wagon that lost a wheel. Jackson eventually called off the attack when he realized that subordinate units would not receive their orders in time.[38]

The other way staff officers influenced tactical orders was by offering suggestions or asking questions. Sometimes they proposed specific maneuvers. As an example, Brigadier General Robert Toombs related that at Malvern Hill, "My adjutant, Capt. [Dudley M.] DuBose, proposed to him [Joseph B. Kershaw] to unite that, and some other companies of other regiments, with his command in the attack on the enemy's batteries, to which he assented; and this command, under Cols. [Edgar M.] Butt and [William R.] Holmes, accompanied by Capt. DuBose and Maj. [Willliam F.] Alexander (my quartermaster, who acted as one of my aides on the field), advanced with Gen. Kershaw's brigade." Or consider the incident at Chancellorsville when Captain Alexander C. Haskell proposed a counter to a plan already espoused by Brigadier General Henry Heth. Haskell suggested sending two regiments as skirmishers in front of the advancing column. Heth took the suggestion and gave Haskell command of the two skirmisher regiments. The maneuver proved successful. During the final day of fighting in the Wilderness, Howard, an aide to a brigade commander, made a series of suggestions to his division commander, Edward Johnson, that materially changed the nature, intent, and result of the fight. By Howard's account,

> I was at the right of the brigade line, General [George] Steuart being toward the centre, when Major-General Johnson rode by in some haste and called out to me [meaning it for General Steuart], that it was not intended to bring on a general engagement that day. When he presently rode up a second time and called out, "Remember, Captain Howard, it is not meant to have a general engagement," I said, "But, General, it is evident that the two lines will come together in a few minutes, and whether it is intended to have a general engagement or not, will it not be better for our men to have the impetus of a forward movement in the collision?" "Very well," said he, "let them go ahead a little." I looked down the line for General Steuart (I do not remember now—1911—whether he was in sight, but the bullets were flying thicker and the men were getting restive and the moment seemed critical), and raising my sword, I called out "Forward!" The men responded with alacrity and almost immediately a tremendous fire rolled along the line. . . . [Later in the engagement] Major-General Johnson rode by again and I said to him, "General, if it is not intended to have a general engagement, the edge of the woods, with the open space in front will be an excellent place to form our line," and he replied, "Yes, let it be done." I communicated it to General Stuart, and it was so done.

Of course, sometimes suggestions from the staff fell on deaf ears. During a skirmish at Catoctin Mountain (September 13, 1862) Von Borcke tried to tell Stuart that Union skirmishers were advancing on the howitzer Stuart was using to shell the enemy in the valley below and that it was time to withdraw. Stuart did not listen and instead dispatched Von Borcke with orders for the advancing troops, whom he believed to be Confederate cavalry, to hold their fire. Von Borcke was almost killed trying to deliver that message. It is not surprising that later the same day at Middletown, Von Borcke refrained from suggesting a withdrawal when Stuart again held his position longer (and thus took more casualties) than the Prussian staff officer thought advisable.[39]

It was only natural for staff officers to participate on the fringes of tactical planning. They almost had to. As a primary source of reconnaissance, they would have had to debrief their commanders and would have been useful to have nearby to answer questions as the plan developed. In that light, a remark by Beauregard is instructive. While arguing after the war about why he should have been in command at First Manassas, Beauregard wrote (in the third person), "Having been attached . . . to the staff of the Commander-in-chief, General [Winfield] Scott, in the Mexican War, General Beauregard had taken a leading part in the reconnaissances and conferences that had led and determined the marches and battles of that campaign."[40] Beauregard contended that he gained valuable experience from that participation. He overstated his case when he claimed to have been a leading player in Scott's campaign planning, but it is quite likely that he participated peripherally and perhaps materially in the process. Staff officers in the Civil War did the same. Commanders would have asked about terrain or enemy dispositions a staff officer had reconnoitered. Judgments like whether there was enough room to deploy a brigade on a certain piece of ground—a logical question to ask an officer who had seen the area—gave a junior officer plenty of room to express his tactical opinion.

Occasionally, staff officers got a chance to have a real impact on operational matters by serving as confidants of the commander. Taylor described being called to Lee's tent for lengthy discussions about the Union army's probable movements and intentions. Taylor mentioned the incident not because it was unusual but because he thought Lee's closing comments showed that the general was psychologically ready for the approaching campaign—such talks between commanders and their principal staff officers were almost certainly common. Regardless of frequency, the incident shows Lee using Taylor not merely as an administrator or glorified clerk but as a confidant, adviser, consultant, or sounding board for operational matters. Taylor seemed to think he served those purposes, lamenting, "I wish the old chief had some older, wiser, more temperate head near him, for I daily become more and more convinced of my inability to fill the position I occupy."[41] Taylor was explaining a falling-out he had with Lee, but the implication of the comment is significant. Unfortunately, Taylor, who was supremely egotistic but humble enough not to openly brag about such things as his personal exploits in battles, did not expound on that aspect of his relationship with Lee, perhaps because he thought it obvious.

Staff officers could also influence orders just by asking for clarification. Porter Alexander documented such a case during First Manassas when directed to issue an order with which he disagreed: "About 6 P.M. I happened to be the only one of [Beauregard's] personal staff with him. Rather abruptly and apropos of nothing that I saw or heard, he said to me: 'Ride across the Stone Bridge and find Col. Kershaw, who is conducting the pursuit along the pike. Order him to advance very carefully and not to attack.' . . . 'Shall I tell him not to attack under *any circumstances*, no matter *what* the condition of the enemy in his front?' "[42] Beauregard modified his instructions so that Kershaw could attack if he had a battery in support and a decided advantage. By making suggestions or questioning orders, staff officers had an impact on tactical maneuvers. It was subtle and well within the limits of the senior-subordinate relationship but should not be discounted.

MISCELLANEOUS FUNCTIONS

Another combat function of the staff was as a convenient pool of officers for special missions, which often put them in direct combat leadership roles. This chapter previously discussed how Haskell received command of two regiments of skirmishers at Chancellorsville in response to a suggestion he made, and he was only one of many staff officers who performed similar duties. A few examples show the variety of such assignments. At First Manassas, Johnston's chief of ordnance, colonel F. J. Thomas, took command of "a battalion formed of fragments of all commands" and led it until he was killed. Among other adventures, Von Borcke led special patrols to cut telegraph lines and at one point commanded the left wing of Stuart's cavalry. As Jackson's aide, Kyd Douglas led a fifty-man detachment that secured Nicodemus Hill throughout the night after the Battle of Antietam. In 1864, when he was a division assistant adjutant general, Douglas took charge of a skirmish line and cleared Winchester when Early reached that town. Douglas also seems to have gained a reputation as an efficient rear-guard commander by the later stages of the war. He commanded the two hundred–man detachment that covered Early's withdrawal from the out-skirts of Washington and the division's rear guard at other times during the general's 1864 campaign in the Shenandoah Valley. A brigade quartermaster, Captain R. E. B. Hervetson, formed a pickup unit of teamsters to help defend the trains against Union cavalry at Williamsport, after Gettysburg. At a critical time in the Wilderness battle, Longstreet sent his assistant adjutant general, Moxley Sorrel, into a virtual jungle to find, rally, form, and lead a large body of troops in an attack that would require an intricate maneuver. Sorrel gathered three brigades (George T. Anderson's, William Mahone's, and William T. Wofford's), organized them, and launched an extremely successful flank attack. At almost the same time, Major General M. L. Smith, Lee's chief engineer, was forming brigades to attempt a similar move as a follow-up to Sorrel's attack, a maneuver that aborted with Longstreet's wounding. Two staff officers led an attack earlier in that battle to capture an artillery piece stranded between the lines, and Robert Stiles as the adjutant of an artillery battalion led a night patrol to retrieve a gun isolated during the fighting at Cold Harbor. Even couriers occasionally received leadership roles. In September 1864 near Port Republic, Brigadier General William C. Wickham assigned John Gill, a Signal Corps sergeant serving as a courier, to command of a cavalry skirmish line when the officer commanding the skirmishers was hit.[43]

Besides such instances of providing a talent pool, staffs also served as a small in extremis force for the commander. They were frequently found manning artillery in critical situations, a task suitable for their numbers. Two of Beauregard's aides, Ferguson and Chisolm, turned captured federal guns on their former owners at First Manassas; Louis F. Terrill, a volunteer aide to Brigadier General Beverly H. Robertson, improvised lanyards at Manassas depot during the Second Manassas campaign; Longstreet's staff members briefly manned guns on the field at Antietam while the corps commander held their horses and commented on their shooting; McKim carried and loaded canister rounds for a hard-pressed battery at Stephenson's Depot (June 15, 1863) before racing off to look for help; Stuart's staff and couriers attacked a federal cavalry camp during the Mine Run campaign; and three members of Alexander's First Corps artillery staff fought a gun on the edge of the Crater at Petersburg until relieved by reinforcements from a nearby hospital and infantry volunteers. Even chaplains occasionally took a combat leadership role in extremis. At Second Manassas, Father James B. Sheeran of the 14th Louisiana stopped panicked ambulance drivers and formed a gaggle of stragglers into a rough line to repel a rumored federal attack. The priest admitted he was crestfallen to later discover Isaac Trimble's brigade deployed nearby for the same purpose. He relinquished his brief command and retired a few hundred yards to await the outcome of the fight. And of course, since the staff served as the personal bodyguard for the commander, stories of the staff forming to protect their leader—as Lee's staff and couriers did during the Second Manassas campaign, when the army commander unexpectedly encountered federal cavalry—are common. All in all, it seems unlikely that the average staff officer only fired his sidearm once during the war as Campbell Brown, from Ewell's staff, claimed he did.[44]

In summary, a staff officer's role in battle was varied, to say the least, and he rarely had the luxury of knowing in advance exactly what functions he might have to perform on the field. In a unique case, Beauregard had his aides write after-action reports on their participation in First Manassas. The reports give a taste of what staff officers experienced in battle. A. R. Chisolm wrote several orders by dictation before carrying orders to Jackson and guiding his brigade into position. Chisolm reported ex post facto to Beauregard about alterations Jackson made in his original deployment and then took messages to the ordnance and commissary officers to establish stockpiles of supplies at the Lewis house. Chisolm then carried orders to the three brigades guarding the fords on the right flank to pull back to the near side of the stream. Chisolm returned to headquarters but was unable to locate General Beauregard (who left while his aide was changing horses). While looking for Beauregard, Chisolm rallied a broken regiment and then ran into a captain whose unit had been driven off a captured battery. Chisolm found Philip St. George Cocke's brigade and ordered it to attack the battery. The wandering aide next encountered Jackson and offered him assistance. Jackson had him place a battery and some supporting infantry. Chisolm subsequently joined Johnston for a while and guided some cavalry into the attack, then sensed confusion among some men guarding prisoners and took charge of the detail. Chisolm finally located Beauregard at the Lewis house and was dispatched with orders for General Arnold Elzey. Chisolm finally returned to headquarters about ten o'clock that night after a long and busy day.[45]

At sunrise, Chisolm's counterpart, Lieutenant Samuel W. Ferguson, carried orders to Francis S. Bartow and Barnard E. Bee about positioning their brigades. He then carried orders to Early and Jackson before being dispatched to lead one of Longstreet's aides to Early's position. By nine o'clock, Ferguson was off on a mission to locate D. R. Jones and his brigade. Before noon, Ferguson rode to deliver orders to Stuart and simultaneously to investigate what was happening on the left and whether the quartermaster and commissary had stockpiled ammunition and food at the Lewis house as ordered. During the main fight on the left, Ferguson delivered several orders, changed the position of regiments, and ordered halts or attacks. When the federal retreat began, Beauregard sent Ferguson to recall the troops and stop the pursuit.

Unfortunately, the third aide who submitted a report, J. Heyward, was not as meticulous about accounting for his activities as his peers. Nevertheless, we know that Heyward led regiments into position, delivered orders, and brought units back into camp after the battle.[46] Whatever staff officers did, it is safe to say that in the Army of Northern Virginia they were more than administrative functionaries and had more responsibilities on the field than simply delivering orders.

COMBAT LOGISTICS

The logistics and special staff oversaw several necessary battlefield support systems. Most quartermaster and commissary functions were accomplished before battle—soldiers carried their own food and equipment and had little prospect of resupply until after the fight—but other logistical systems had to function smoothly in combat. Primary among those was the medical evacuation system.

Regulations established the basic structure of the medical evacuation system, although that procedure changed over time as the army gained experience. Technically, quartermasters in coordination with medical directors established ambulance depots at the first convenient building behind the lines and arranged for ambulances that would "follow the troops engaged to succor the wounded and remove them to the depots." The medical director was supposed to distribute his doctors to the depots and send what medical personnel he could spare to accompany the ambulances. In fact, the surgeons quickly found that they had to control their own ambulances and assumed responsibility for all aspects of the medical evacuation system. It also became apparent that ambulances alone would not suffice for evacuation. Ambulances were too vulnerable to reach the wounded under fire, and traditional expedients like using bandsmen as litter bearers could not service the number of wounded on the typical battlefield. The Army of Northern Virginia resorted to detailing soldiers as litter bearers. In preparation for the Seven Days' Battles, A. P. Hill issued the following order: "The infirmary corps of two men and one non-commissioned officer from each company, the men without arms, under charge of a lieutenant from each regiment, will be detailed and ordered to report to regimental surgeons." Two months later, general orders mandated that system across the army by directing the formal detail (signed by the company commander and countersigned by the regimental commander) of two men from each company to care for the wounded in battle. Carrying a litter, water, and rudimentary first-aid supplies, these soldiers, under the direction of the assistant surgeon of their regiment, hauled the wounded off the field to what might be called a casualty-collection point, a convenient spot to gather the wounded out of direct fire. There, the assistant surgeon, equipped with a "hospital knapsack . . . [of] such instruments, dressings, and medicines as may be needed in an emergency on the march or in the field," bandaged and administered stimulants (when available). From the casualty-collection point, the wounded moved by ambulance—or by litter to ambulance, depending on the situation—to a brigade or division field hospital. Normally in an occupied house or barn identified by a flag since there was seldom time to erect hospital tents (even if they were available), these field hospitals became legendary sites of horror. Sorrel described his evacuation after being stunned by a shell fragment at Antietam while delivering a message to the front lines. Other than the attention he received from other officers, his account is typical. Litter bearers "carried [him] off on a stretcher to a less exposed place." There, Thomas Fairfax, also of Longstreet's staff, found him and administered whiskey. An ambulance evacuated Sorrel and another wounded staff officer to "the army field-infirmary." Medical director Lafayette Guild examined Sorrel's injuries and proclaimed him only lightly wounded but out of action for two weeks. Sorrel moved by ambulance across the Potomac to convalesce with a local family while his companion, who was more severely wounded, continued on to a Richmond hospital.[47]

Of course, that system did not operate automatically—it required planning and coordination. General Imboden's casual comment, quoted earlier in this chapter, about the two o'clock evacuation order after Gettysburg is full of implied tasks for the medical corps. Doctor Guild "was charged to see that all the wounded who could bear the rough journey should be placed in empty wagons and ambulances." That responsibility presupposed an efficient system to communicate with the corps and division medical staffs, to triage the wounded to identify those strong enough to travel, to transport the wounded to the collection point, to gather the available transportation, to assign wounded to specific wagons, and to arrange for their care during the trip as well as for care for those left behind. In that specific case, getting the column moving did not end Guild's problems. He also had to organize a ferry system across the swollen Potomac, an ambulance shuttle from the river to the railhead in Staunton, and rail transportation to the Richmond hospitals. And of course, there was the constant worry that the enemy might overrun the field hospitals. Doctor Hunter McGuire, the Second Corps medical director, contrived the excuse of taking a saddlebag full of peaches to Jackson at the Dunker Church during the fighting at Antietam to see what was going on and to assure himself of the safety of his hospital.[48]

The evacuation system suffered from the same vagaries of human conduct as any other battlefield system. Surgeons, litter bearers, and ambulance corpsmen were cited for their brave conduct and disregard for danger while caring for the wounded under fire. Conversely, some doctors refused to go onto the field, and ambulance drivers more than once abandoned their vehicles or refused to perform their duties except under direct threat.[49] Lack of doctors, medicine, and transportation hampered the operation. The evacuation system saved many soldiers, but many others died for lack of care. As a staff-organized and -executed battlefield system, though, the medical evacuation system of the Army of Northern Virginia was reasonably efficient.

The other major battlefield logistics system of the Army of Northern Virginia was the ordnance resupply system. Resupplying artillery ammunition, although a major task and a headache, was uncomplicated. Since each gun had a caisson that could shuttle ammunition back and forth from the trains to the battery, the only trick was establishing the trains in an accessible spot, keeping track of the location of various types of ammunition, and issuing it on demand. Conversely, getting ammunition to infantry in combat posed problems. The Confederate *Field Manual for Use of the Officer on Ordnance Duty* told each brigade ordnance officer to procure one or more wagons under the control of an ordnance sergeant for each regiment strictly for use as ordnance vehicles. Before every battle, commanders were supposed to detail six men per regiment as an augmentation to the normal ordnance staff. One man followed the regiment to determine its needs and to communicate them to the regimental ordnance wagon, which either waited at a division ordnance depot or followed the regiment as closely as the situation permitted.[50] That was an excellent plan and should have provided efficient ammunition resupply on demand.

In reality, the system does not appear to have functioned as smoothly as the manual envisioned. Ordnance wagons did not often follow the troops and, even when ordered to do so, occasionally went astray, as happened to Rodes's divisional ordnance officer during the third Battle of Winchester (September 19, 1864). The ordnance officer, Captain James M. Garnett, ordered an ordnance wagon per brigade under the control of one of his assistants forward from the trains when he heard the battle begin. He then occupied himself with rallying stragglers until he received a plea for ammunition from the front. Yankee cavalry had diverted the wagons he had sent forward, so Garnett had to scrounge up additional ammunition. There are also enough stories about gleaning cartridges from fallen companions (or from the enemy) and about people hurrying to the rear to get emergency resupplies of ammunition to suggest that the system was not as responsive as intended. A. P. Hill is supposed to have sent his staff and couriers off to fill their pockets and haversacks with cartridges to resupply Maxcy Gregg's brigade, which had been reduced to throwing stones, at Second Manassas. And as an aide-de-camp at Gettysburg, McKim had to conduct an emergency resupply for his brigade. McKim took a detail back about a mile to the trains, where they got three cases of ammunition, which they carried forward slung in blankets under fence rails.[51] A truly efficient ammunition supply system would have prevented such incidents. Nevertheless, there is no case of Army of Northern Virginia units running completely out of ammunition, so criticism cannot be too harsh. The system could have been a lot better, but it worked.

CONCLUSION

The staffs of an army comprise a system—they work vertically as well as horizontally, and each depends on those above, below, and beside it for efficient operation. Looking at any specific staff in isolation will produce misleading results. A weak link anywhere can be fatal to the entire system; conversely, a particularly energetic and efficient staff officer can often overcome weakness in other parts of the system. The Army of Northern Virginia's staffs are a case in point.

Considered as a system rather than as a collection of individual entities, the staffs in the Army of Northern Virginia accomplished most of the functions demanded of modern staffs. They secured and provided the commander with information, data, and advice. Staffs transmitted orders to the command and notified commanders of matters requiring his action. They supervised, within their authority, the execution of orders, and they took the initiative to carry out the commander's intent. Staffs prepared detailed orders according to the commander's decisions and guidance, although they did not prepare plans or do contingency planning and usually had minor substantive input into the orders they issued. As for the characteristics of a modern staff, commanders delegated authority to their staffs (formally and informally), supervised execution of orders, and had set methods and procedures to divide labor and perform specified duties. The system was never as clearly defined as modern doctrine would like, and individual staffs performed those functions and exhibited those characteristics to differing degrees, but the system as a whole did what was required. The major area where the Army of Northern Virginia staff system failed to meet modern criteria was its lack of an education system to develop staff officers. Selection based on ill-defined criteria or nepotism without the benefit of formal training meant that the staff system could not be completely modern. The major functional deficiencies were in operational planning and intelligence analysis. In these areas, Army of Northern Virginia staffs were behind the most developed staffs of their day, but they remained on a par with most of their international counterparts.

It is easy to criticize Army of Northern Virginia staffs for inefficiency—one need only point to their failures. For example, the logistics staff can be held responsible for the army's chronic and legendary shortages. Confederate logisticians did not measure up to the standards set by their enemy; however, given resources equal to their Union counterparts, there is no evidence that Army of Northern Virginia logisticians would not have performed equally well. An abundance of resources covers a multitude of sins. Key logistical decisions made by the national government (especially with respect to control and use of railroads and procurement and distribution of supplies) hamstrung the system. Even a logistical genius might not have overcome the difficulties Army of Northern Virginia quartermasters and commissary officers faced. Given that fact, it would be equally valid to praise them for doing as well as they did—a classic case of a half-full instead of a half-empty glass. The assistant adjutants general, aides-de-camp, and assistant inspectors general, who receive criticism because they did not invent the modern staff system or even imitate contemporary European staffs, did about all that could be expected of them. There was no training, procedure, or precedent for a major operational role for staff officers. Most had little or no military experience. They did what their commanders asked and generally did it very well. In combat, they were aggressive about their battlefield supervision role as they understood it. That understanding placed emphasis on reliably delivering orders and messages under fire and unhesitatingly exercising initiative and assuming direct leadership when required. Lower-level staffs appear to have been more directly involved in nonadministrative duties, more a reflection of leadership style than of staff competence.

In accordance with basic staff theory, the commander will always be key to how his staff behaves and what they do. If a staff performed poorly, the commander deserves the blame unless he asked for more and the staff did not deliver. Lee never asked his staff for more; his subordinates sometimes did (to different extents) and got varied results. It is also true that some individuals did better than others. Taylor, Sorrel, Alexander, Sandie Pendleton, and Price each turned in stellar performances for their bosses. Each was an energetic, intelligent individual, but none had more than on-the-job training for his position. Others with the same opportunity might have done as well.

Much of the performance, good and bad, of Army of Northern Virginia staffs—in true traditional fashion—relied on the commander-staff relationship. Evidence suggests that staff officers had sufficient authority and were intelligent enough to have performed operational planning or intelligence analysis. They simply were not asked to do so. Commanders who used their staffs effectively got good returns; those who did not ask as much received less. Nobody thought to involve the staff deeply in operational issues. It was not something Confederate commanders of the Civil War even seriously contemplated. This was, after all, a war on the border between the traditional and the modern eras, and the leaders were largely products of the traditional. Grady McWhiney and Perry D. Jamieson argue that the primary influence on Civil War generals, especially Confederate leaders, was their Mexican War experience. Their thesis specifically concerns tactics and is controversial because of an assertion that southern cultural aggressiveness also influenced tactics. However, if tactical thinking was "fossilized by what [Confederate generals] saw and did while under the command of [Zachary] Taylor and [Winfield] Scott," one should not expect radical changes in staff doctrine from the Mexican War model. Still, considered as a system, the staffs of the Army of Northern Virginia do not deserve the judgment of critics who believe their duties were limited to reconnaissance, transcribing and transmitting orders, and preparing reports and returns—functions of "detail, not ideas." One authority on staffs, Kenneth C. Allard, issued a harsh verdict about Civil War staffs that is a matter of judgment and a demand for perfection seldom achieved by any staff: "When the task at hand was purely operational, there were many instances in which the staff was simply incapable of extending either the control or the will of the commander."[52] A contemporary critic, S. W. Melton, made a good point when he wrote, "The staff deserves earnest consideration. My limited experience in the service has been sufficient to convince me that the importance of an efficient staff has been much underestimated, and that it cannot be overestimated. In the work of discipline, in the matters of supply, in the successful pursuit of the campaign, well-nigh everything depends upon a competent, earnest and laborious staff. The Army is childlike, utterly dependent. The general cannot be ubiquitous—is indeed but a man. The staff must make up the complement."[53] Twentieth-century observers like to think that commanders who tended toward modernity were somehow superior and that the Union eventually cornered the market on them, but such is not necessarily the case. Despite its traditional staff system, the Army of Northern Virginia stayed in the field for four years against a better armed, better equipped, numerically superior foe and won its share of battles, strong testimony on behalf of the effectiveness of the staff system. The glass was at least half full.

NOTES

Introduction

1. Richard A. Gabriel and Karen S. Metz, *From Sumer to Rome: The Military Capabilities of Ancient Armies* (New York: Greenwood Press, 1991), 40–41, 23; Yigael Yadin, *The Art of Warfare in Biblical Lands in the Light of Archaeological Study* (New York: McGraw-Hill Book Co., 1963), 1:113; Chaim Herzog and Mordechai Gichon, *Battles of the Bible* (New York: Random House, 1978), 170; John Frederick Charles Fuller, *The Generalship of Alexander the Great* (1906; reprint, New York: Da Capo Press, 1993), 52; Peter Connolly, *Greece and Rome at War* (Englewood Cliffs, N.J.: Prentice-Hall, 1981), 223.

2. François Ferdinand Philippe, Prince de Joinville, *The Army of the Potomac, Its Organization, Its Commander, and Its Campaign*, trans. William Henry Hurlburt (New York: Anson D. F. Randolph, 1862), 52.

3. See Jay Luvaas, *The Military Legacy of the Civil War: The European Inheritance* (1959; reprint, Lawrence: University of Kansas Press, 1988); T. Harry Williams, *Lincoln and His Generals* (New York: Alfred A. Knopf, 1952), 313; Jeffry D. Wert, "The Tycoon: Lee and His Staff," *Civil War Times Illustrated* 11 (July 1972): 12, 18.

4. U.S. Department of the Army, *FM 101–5: Command and Control for Commanders and Staff*, coord. draft, July 1992 (Washington, D.C.: Headquarters Department of the Army, 1992), 2–2.

5. James Donald Hittle, *The Military Staff: Its History and Development*, 3d ed. (Harrisburg, Pa.: Stackpole Co., 1961), 10–11.

6. J. Davis to Senate and House, Mar. 24, 1864, in James D. Richardson, comp., *Messages and Papers of the Confederacy* (Nashville, Tenn.: U.S. Publishing Co., 1905), 1:458.

Notes

Chapter 1: Staff Organization

1. James M. Matthews, ed., *Statutes at Large of the Provisional Government of the Confederate States of America* (Richmond, Va.: R. M. Smith, Printer to Congress, 1864), 38–39, 43–44.

2. Ibid., 45–47.

3. Ibid., 47–52; on the regular army of the Confederacy, see Richard P. Weinert, *The Confederate Regular Army* (Shippensburg, Pa.: White Mane Publishing Co., 1991).

4. J. Davis to Senate and House, Mar. 24, 1864, and J. Davis to Senate, Mar. 11, 1865, in Richardson, comp., *Messages and Papers*, 1:457–65, 540; James M. Matthews, ed., *Public Laws of the Confederate States of America* (Richmond, Va.: R. M. Smith, Printer to Congress, 1862–64), 281–82; A&IGO G.O. #44, Apr. 24, 1864, in U.S. War Department, *The War of the Rebellion: A Compilation of the Records of the Union and Confederate Armies* (hereafter OR) (1880–1901; reprint, Harrisburg, Pa.: Historical Times, 1985), ser. 4, 3:352–53. Amended to add staff to cavalry divisions by A&IGO G.O. #67, Aug. 16, 1864, in OR, ser. 4, 3:592–94.

5. Confederate States of America War Department, *Regulations for the Army of the Confederate States, 1863. Corrected and Enlarged with Revised Index (the Only Correct Copy)* (1863; reprint, Harrisburg, Pa.: National Historical Society, 1980), 10–11, 7.

6. Gilbert Moxley Sorrel, *Recollections of a Confederate Staff Officer* (1905; reprint, New York: Bantam Books, 1992), 52.

7. Ibid., 51.

8. Walter Herron Taylor, *General Lee, His Campaigns in Virginia, 1861–1865* (Brooklyn, N.Y.: Press of Braunworth and Co., 1906), 55, 57.

9. R. E. Lee to S. Cooper, Mar. 6, 1863, and R. E. Lee to G. W. C. Lee, Mar. 29, 1864, in Clifford Dowdey and Louis H. Manarin, eds., *The Wartime Papers of R. E. Lee* (Boston: Little, Brown, and Co., 1961), 222, 686; R. E. Lee to J. Davis, Mar. 21, 1863, in Douglas Southall Freeman, ed., *Lee's Dispatches to Jefferson Davis, 1862–1865. From the private collection of Jones de Renne* (New York: G.P. Putnam's Sons, 1915, 1957), 82.

10. Sorrel, *Recollections*, 97–98; William Gilham, *Manual of Instruction for the Volunteers and Militia of the Confederate States* (Richmond, Va.: West and Johnston, 1862), 43.

11. J. A. Seddon to the president [J. Davis], Dec. 16, 1864, in OR, ser. 4, 3:943; Abstract of field returns of ANV, Dec. 10, 1862, and Dec. 20, 1862, in OR, ser. 1, 21:1057, 1075.

12. Sorrel, *Recollections*, 51.

13. Frank E. Vandiver, *Rebel Brass: The Confederate Command System* (Baton Rouge: Louisiana State University Press, 1956), 18; James Longstreet, *From Manassas to Appomattox: Memoirs of the Civil War in America* (Philadelphia: J. B. Lippincott Co., 1896), 333; Henry Kyd Douglas, *I Rode with Stonewall* (Chapel Hill: University of North Carolina Press, 1940), 101; Edward

Porter Alexander, *Military Memoirs of a Confederate* (1907; reprint, New York: Da Capo Press, 1993), 378.

14. C. M. Blackford to wife, July 18, 1863, in Susan Leigh Colton Blackford, comp., *Letters from Lee's Army; or Memoirs of Life in and out of the Army in Virginia during the War between the States*, ed. and abr. Charles M. Blackford III (1894–96; reprint, New York: C. Scribner's Sons, 1947), 193.

15. R. E. Lee to J. Davis, Mar. 21, 1863, in Freeman, ed., *Lee's Dispatches*, 81–82.

16. J. Davis to Senate and House, Mar. 28, 1864, in Richardson, comp., *Messages and Papers*, 1:464.

17. J. Tyler to S. Price, June 7, 1864, in OR, ser. 1, vol. 51, pt. 2, p. 994.

18. Alexander, *Military Memoirs*, 618; *Paroles of the Army of Northern Virginia*, vol. 15 of *Southern Historical Society Papers* (1876–1959; reprint, Wilmington, N.C.: Broadfoot Publishing Co., 1990–92), 1–3, 449, 458, 464–65; tabular list of Appomattox paroles, in OR, ser. 1, vol. 46, pt. 1, p. 1277; Walter Herron Taylor, *General Lee*, 172–85; Jennings Cropper Wise, *The Long Arm of Lee: The History of the Artillery of the Army of Northern Virginia* (1915; reprint, Richmond, Va.: Owens Publishing Co., 1988), 2:952.

19. Abstract of field returns of ANV, Nov. 10, 1862, in OR, ser. 1, vol. 19, pt. 2, p. 713; Walter Herron Taylor, *Four Years with General Lee* (1878; reprint, Bloomington: Indiana University Press, 1962), 172–76; Kenneth Radley, *Rebel Watchdog: The Confederate Army Provost Guard* (Baton Rouge: Louisiana State University Press, 1989), 45.

20. Abstract of field returns, ANV, Nov. 20, 1862, and Dec. 10, 1862, in OR, ser. 1, 21:1025, 1057; *Paroles of the Army of Northern Virginia*, 15:69–70, 41, 43–45, 454–55, 185–89, 273; tabular list of Appomattox paroles, in OR, ser. 1, vol. 46, pt. 1, pp. 1277–78; "Stonewall's Commissary General, Maj. Wells J. Hawks," *Confederate Veteran* 34 (Aug. 1926): 286; Wise, *Long Arm of Lee*, 2:952; Robert J. Trout, *They Followed the Plume: The Story of J. E. B. Stuart and His Staff* (Mechanicsburg, Pa.: Stackpole Books, 1993), 11, 16, 3; William Willis Blackford, *War Years with Jeb Stuart* (New York: C. Scribner's Sons, 1945), 92–93; Theodore Stanford Garnett, *Riding with Stuart: Reminiscences of an Aide-de-Camp*, ed. Robert J. Trout (Shippensburg, Pa.: White Mane Publishing Co., 1995), 19.

21. Abstract from field returns of ANV, Nov. 20, 1862, in OR, ser. 1, 21:1025; T. J. Goree to mother, Aug. 20, 1864, in Thomas W. Cutrer, ed., *Longstreet's Aide: The Civil War Letters of Thomas J. Goree* (Charlottesville: University Press of Virginia, 1995), 132; James Fitz John Caldwell, *The History of a Brigade of South Carolinians Known First as Gregg's and Subsequently as McGowan's Brigade* (1866; reprint, Marietta, Ga.: Continental Book Co., 1951), 105; *Paroles of the Army of Northern Virginia*, 15:486–87.

22. Edward Porter Alexander, *Fighting for the Confederacy*, ed. Gary W. Gallagher (Chapel Hill: University of North Carolina Press, 1989), 53; John G. Walker, "Sharpsburg," in *Battles and Leaders of the Civil War*, ed. Robert Underwood Johnson and Clarence Clough Buel (New York: Century Co., 1887),

2:680; J. M. Goggins to J. Longstreet, Aug. 15, 1887, James M. Goggins Folder, Civil War Miscellaneous Collection, U.S. Army Military History Institute, Carlisle Barracks, Pa.

23. J. H. Chamberlayne to M. B. Chamberlayne, Oct. 9, 1862, in John Hampden Chamberlayne, *Ham Chamberlayne—Virginian: Letters and Papers of an Artillery Officer in the War for Southern Independence*, ed. Churchill Gibson Chamberlayne (Richmond, Va.: Press of the Dietz Printing Co., 1932), 120.

Chapter 2—The General Staff in the Army of Northern Virginia: Chief of Staff, Adjutant General, and Inspector General

1. Report on the Battle of Bull Run, Aug. 26 [Oct. 14], 1861, in *OR*, ser. 1, 2:491; ANV G.O. #61, June 4, 1862, in *OR*, ser. 1, 2:574; Douglas, *I Rode with Stonewall*, 101; report of Lt. Gen. Richard S. Ewell, 1863, in *OR*, ser. 1, vol. 27, pt. 2, p. 452; Sorrel, *Recollections*, 100; report of Brig. Gen. J. E. B. Stuart, May 10, 1862, in *OR*, ser. 1, 11:573; Heros Von Borcke, *Memoirs of the Confederate War for Independence* (1867; reprint, Gaithersburg, Md.: Butternut Press, 1985), title page; E. Johnson to A. S. Pendleton, Aug. 22, 1863, in *OR*, ser. 1, vol. 27, pt. 2, p. 505; Dept. of North Carolina G.O. #1, Sept. 24, 1863, in *OR*, ser. 1, vol. 51, pt. 2, p. 769; Gilham, *Manual*, 44; Matthews, ed., *Public Laws*, 281.

2. Matthews, ed. *Public Laws*, 281; *Proceedings of the First Confederate Congress, Fourth Session. 7 December 1863–18 February 1864*, ed. Frank E. Vandiver, vol. 50 of *Southern Historical Society Papers*, 420; Pierre Gustave Toutant Beauregard, "The First Battle of Bull Run," in *Battles and Leaders of the Civil War*, ed. Robert Underwood Johnson and Clarence Clough Buel (New York: Century Co., 1887) 1:203; report on the Battle of Bull Run, Aug. 26 [Oct. 14], 1861, in *OR*, ser. 1, vol. 2, pp. 491, 501.

3. ANV G.O. #124, Oct. 28, 1862, in *OR*, ser. 1, vol. 19, pt. 2, p. 688; J. D. Imboden to R. H. Chilton, Feb. 12, 1864, in *OR*, ser. 1, 33:1167; Sorrel, *Recollections*, 52; Walter Herron Taylor, *General Lee*, 56.

4. W. H. Taylor to Bettie Saunders, Mar., 15, 1864, and W. H. Taylor to mother, Mar. 23, 1865, in R. Lockwood Tower, ed., *Lee's Adjutant: The Wartime Letters of Walter Herron Taylor, 1862–1865* (Columbia: University of South Carolina Press, 1995), 139–40, 141–42; Douglas, *I Rode with Stonewall*, 101.

5. Von Borcke, *Memoirs*, 89, 204.

6. Sorrel, *Recollections*, 100.

7. Daniel H. Hill, "Lee's Attack North of the Chickahominy," in *Battles and Leaders*, ed. Johnson and Buel, 3:348.

8. R. E. Lee to J. Davis, Mar. 21, 1863, in Freeman, ed., *Lee's Dispatches*, 82.

9. William Willis Blackford, *War Years*, 159–60.

10. Matthews, ed., *Public Laws*, 281–82; A&IGO G.O. #44, Apr. 29, 1864, in *OR*, ser. 4, 3:352.

11. Gilham, *Manual*, 492–94; Confederate States of America War Department, *Regulations, 1863*, 47–49; A&IGO G.O. #46½, Feb. 26, 1864, in *OR*, ser. 4, 2:170–71.

12. A. S. Pendleton to mother, Apr. 23, 1862, in William G. Bean, *Stonewall's Man: Sandie Pendleton* (Chapel Hill: University of North Carolina Press, 1959), 62; E. F. Paxton to wife, Oct. 5 and 12, 1862, in Elisha Franklin Paxton, *The Civil War Letters of General Frank "Bull" Paxton, CSA, a Lieutenant of Lee and Jackson*, ed. John Gallatin Paxton (Hillsboro, Tex.: Hill Junior College Press, 1978), 58.

13. Walter Herron Taylor, *General Lee*, 55.

14. W. H. Taylor to Lucien, Oct. 24, 1864, book 2, Lewis Leigh Collection, U.S. Army Military History Institute, Carlisle Barracks, Pa.

15. W. H. Taylor to Bettie Saunders, Nov. 21, 1863, in Tower, ed., *Lee's Adjutant*, 90.

16. See Louise Haskell Daly, *Alexander Cheves Haskell, the Portrait of a Man* (1934; reprint, Wilmington, N.C.: Broadfoot Publishing Co., 1989), 74, 82–83; P. T. Vaughn to W. H. Taylor, Oct. 24, 1864, book 50, Leigh Collection.

17. Matthews, ed., *Public Laws*, 89–90.

18. A. S. Pendleton to mother, Oct. 8, 1862, in Susan Pendleton Lee, ed., *Memoirs of William Nelson Pendleton, D.D.* (1893; reprint, Harrisburg, Va.: Sprinkle Publications, 1991), 230; Daly, *Alexander Cheves Haskell*, 122.

19. R. E. Lee to E. A. Lee, Feb. 6, 1863, in Dowdey and Manarin, eds., *Wartime Papers*, 400.

20. Ibid., xi.

21. Confederate States of America War Department, *Regulations, 1863*, 8–9; E. Blackford to mother, May 26, 1863, book 33, Leigh Collection.

22. R. E. Lee to G. W. Randolph, July 11, 1862, and R. E. Lee to secretary of war [J. A. Seddon], July 12, 1862, in Dowdey and Manarin, eds., *Wartime Papers*, 230–31.

23. Wise, *Long Arm of Lee*, 2:924; R. E. Lee to secretary of war [G. W. Randolph], Jan. 27, 1865, in *OR*, ser. 1, vol. 46, pt. 2, pp. 1143–50.

24. Robert Stiles, *Four Years under Marse Robert* (New York: Neale Publishing Co., 1903), 187–88; Jedediah Hotchkiss, *Make Me a Map of the Valley: The Civil War Journal of Stonewall Jackson's Topographer*, ed. Archie P. McDonald (Dallas, Tex.: Southern Methodist University Press, 1973), 118–19.

25. James I. Robertson Jr., *General A. P. Hill: The Story of a Confederate Warrior* (1987; reprint, New York: Vintage Books, 1992), 131–33, 152–54, 171–75.

26. Matthews, ed., *Public Laws*, 89; A&IGO G.O.s #131, 64, and 87, Oct. 3, 1863, Aug. 10, 1864, and Dec. 10, 1864, in *OR*, ser. 1, 2:992–94.

27. A&IGO G.O. #63, Sept. 4, 1862, in *OR*, ser. 4, 2:76.

28. A&IGO G.O. #71, Sept. 6, 1864, in ibid., 3:623–24.

29. Sorrel, *Recollections*, 64; Jeffry D. Wert, *General James Longstreet: The Confederacy's Most Controversial General* (New York: Simon and Schuster,

1993), 373; R. E. Lee to J. Davis, Oct. 2, 1862, and May 20, 1863, in *OR*, ser. 1, vol. 19, pt. 2, pp. 643–44; vol. 25, pt. 2, pp. 810–11.

30. Henry Brainerd McClellan, *The Life and Campaigns of J. E. B. Stuart, Commander of the Cavalry of the Army of Northern Virginia* (1885; reprint, Little Rock, Ark.: Eagle Press of Little Rock, 1987), 69; J. P. Benjamin to J. E. Johnston, Jan. 27, 1862, in *OR*, ser. 1, 5:1049; see *OR*, ser. 1, vol. 29, pt. 2, p. 839, and vol. 33, p. 1193.

31. Quoted in Wise, *Long Arm of Lee*, 1:423.

32. See papers in Chamberlayne, *Ham Chamberlayne*, 233–51.

33. R. L. Walker to S. Cooper, May 13, 1863, and W. H. Gibbs to J. A. Seddon, July 10, 1864, in ibid., 179, 233.

34. Matthews, ed., *Public Laws*, 85–86.

35. R. E. Lee to S. Cooper, Jan. 20, 1865, in *OR*, ser. 1, vol. 46, pt. 2, p. 1110; R. E. Lee to J. A. Seddon, Apr. 5, 1864, in *OR*, ser. 1, 33:1261–62; J. Davis to R. E. Lee, June 1, 1864, in *OR*, ser. 1, vol. 51, pt. 2, p. 976.

36. Sorrel, *Recollections*, 208–9; Daly, *Alexander Cheves Haskell*, 112; Charles S. Venable, "General Lee in the Wilderness Campaign," in *Battles and Leaders*, ed. Johnson and Buel, 4:240.

37. Confederate States of America War Department, *Regulations, 1863*, 47–49, 15, 8.

38. J. Longstreet to T. Jordan, Sept. 26, 1861, in *OR*, ser. 1, vol. 51, pt. 2, p. 314; A. T. Caperton to the president [J. Davis], Dec. 1, 1864, in *OR*, ser. 1, vol. 46, pt. 2, p. 1201; list of detailed men from the 13th South Carolina Volunteers, undated, book 3, Leigh Collection.

39. R. E. Lee to J. A. Seddon, Feb. 15, 1864, in *OR*, ser. 1, 33:1173.

40. Randolph Harrison McKim, *A Soldier's Recollections: Leaves from the Diary of a Young Confederate* (New York: Longmans, Green, and Co., 1910), 135.

41. Quoted in Wise, *Long Arm of Lee*, 2:590.

42. ANV G.O. #63, May 14, 1863, in *OR*, ser. 1, vol. 25, pt. 2, p. 798.

43. A. S. Pendleton to J. C. Breckinridge, July 23, 1864, in *OR*, ser. 1, vol. 37, pt. 2, p. 600; Robertson, *General A. P. Hill*, 147.

44. Virginia Army Headquarters, G.O. #15, May 13, 1861, in Edgar R. Luhn Jr., ed., *Luhn's Edition, C.S. Army General Orders* (Newville, Pa.: Civil War Source Book Publishers, 1992), 1:29; A&IGO G.O. #14, Oct. 21, 1861, in Luhn, ed., *C.S. Army General Orders*, 1:18–19; ANV G.O. #68, June 14, 1862, in *OR*, ser. 1, vol. 2, pt. 3, p. 599; A&IGO G.O. #64, Sept. 8, 1862, in *OR*, ser. 4, 2:78.

45. R. H. Chilton to Gens. Longstreet and Jackson, Sept. 22, 1862, in *OR*, ser. 1, vol. 19, pt. 2, p. 618.

46. S. Cooper to J. A. Seddon, Dec. 16, 1863, in *OR*, ser. 4, 2:1059.

47. R. E. Lee to M. C. Lee, Nov. 30, 1864, and R. E. Lee to G. W. C. Lee, May 11, 1863, in Dowdey and Manarin, eds., *Wartime Papers*, 872, 484; Tower, ed., *Lee's Adjutant*, 242; R. E. Lee to B. Bragg, June 9, 1864, in Tower, ed., *Lee's Adjutant*, 770; T. J. Jackson to J. E. Johnston, Mar. 27, 1862, and

T. J. Jackson to R. S. Ewell, Apr. 10, 1862, in *OR*, ser. 1, vol. 12, pt. 3, pp. 840, 845.

48. Matthews, ed., *Statutes*, 167–68; C. A. Evans to wife, June 17, 1863, 6:00 A.M., and June 17, 1863, in Clement Anselm Evans, *Intrepid Warrior: Clement Anselm Evans, Confederate General from Georgia*, comp. and ed. Robert Grier Stephens Jr. (Dayton, Ohio: Morningside Bookshop, 1992), 204–5, 206; E. Blackford to father, June 28, 1963, book 3, Leigh Collection; A. S. Cunningham to R. H. Chilton, Jan. 27, 1865, in *OR*, ser. 1, vol. 46, pt. 2, p. 1150; W. D. Pender to wife, May 27, 1863, in William Dorsey Pender, *The General to His Lady: The Civil War Letters of William Dorsey Pender to Fanny Pender*, ed. William Woods Hassler (1965; reprint, Gaithersburg, Md.: Ron R. Van Sickle Military Books, 1988), 241; P. J. Semmes to wife, Sept. 8, 1862, L-S Box, General Paul Semmes Folder, Leigh Collection.

49. Diary entry, Jan. 8, 1864, Alexander Davis Betts, *Experiences of a Confederate Chaplain, 1861–1864, by Rev. A. D. Betts, Chaplain 30th N.C. Troops*, ed. W. A. Betts (190?; reprint, Ann Arbor, Mich.: University Microfilms, 1973), 53.

50. S. G. Welch to wife, Nov. 28, 1864, in Spencer Glasgow Welch, *A Confederate Surgeon's Letters to His Wife* (New York: Neale Publishing Co., 1911), 116.

51. W. H. Taylor to Bettie Saunders, Jan. 28, 1864, in Tower, ed., *Lee's Adjutant*, 110; T. J. Goree to "Sister Frank" [Mary Francis Kittrell], Oct. 5, 1861, in Cutrer, ed., *Longstreet's Aide*, 46; R. E. Lee to postmaster general [John H. Reagan], Nov. 27, 1862, in *OR*, ser. 1, 21:1036.

52. McHenry Howard, *Recollections of a Maryland Confederate Soldier and Staff Officer* (1914; reprint, Dayton, Ohio: Morningside Bookshop, 1975), 225–27.

53. Confederate States of America War Department, *Regulations, 1863*, 8, 105; A&IGO G.O. #39, May 26, 1862, in *OR*, ser. 4, 1:1128; Alexander, *Fighting for the Confederacy*, 62; A&IGO G.O. #61, Aug. 23, 1862, in *OR*, ser. 4, 2:69; R. E. Lee to T. J. Jackson, Nov. 27, 1862, in Dowdey and Manarin, eds., *Wartime Papers*, 347.

54. Hotchkiss, *Make Me a Map*, 153; Wert, *General James Longstreet*, 379; Daly, *Alexander Cheves Haskell*, 100.

55. Daly, *Alexander Cheves Haskell*, 118.

56. A. S. Pendleton to K. Pendleton, Feb. 9, 1864, in Bean, *Stonewall's Man*, 187; see "Official Diary of First Corps, A.N.V., while Commanded by Lt-General R. H. Anderson, from June 1st to October 18, 1864," in *Southern Historical Society Papers*, 7:503–12.

57. S. W. Melton to J. A. Seddon, Nov. 11, 1863, in *OR*, ser. 4, 2:945.

58. J. Davis to Senate and House, Mar. 28, 1864, in Richardson, comp., *Messages and Papers*, 1:459–60.

59. Matthews, ed., *Public Laws*, 281–82; A&IGO G.O.s #44 and #67, Apr. 29, 1864, and Aug. 16, 1864, in *OR*, ser. 4, 3:352–53, 593; ANV G.O. #65, May 21, 1863, in *OR*, ser. 1, vol. 25, pt. 2, p. 815; HQ Hampton's Cav. Bde.

S.O.s #17 and #23, May 24, 1863, and June 1, 1863, Hampton's Brigade Order Book, book 41, Leigh Collection; ANV Arty. unnumbered HQ order, Jan. 14, 1863, included in W. N. Pendleton to R. H. Chilton, Feb. 11, 1863, in OR, ser. 1, vol. 25, pt. 2, p. 613.

60. R. H. Chilton to J. B. Hood, Nov. 14, 1862, in OR, ser. 1, vol. 19, pt. 2, p. 719; Right Wing, ANV G.O. #40, Oct. 3, 1862, in OR, ser. 1, vol. 51, pt. 2, p. 631.

61. Confederate States of America War Department, *Regulations, 1863*, 49–50.

62. Ibid., 31–32.

63. A&IGO circular, June 4, 1864, in OR, ser. 4, 3:466–71.

64. Ibid., 468.

65. ANV Arty. unnumbered HQ order, Jan. 14, 1863, in ibid., ser. 1, vol. 25, pt. 2, p. 613; HQ Cav. Div. G.O. #13, book 41, Leigh Collection.

66. A&IGO G.O. #42, Apr. 14, 1864, in OR, ser. 4, 3:297–99.

67. J. P. Harrison to wife, Sept. 1, 1861, book 1, Leigh Collection.

68. R. H. Chilton to J. B. Hood, Nov. 14, 1862, in OR, ser. 1, vol. 19, pt. 2, pp. 718–19; Howard, Recollections, 252.

69. R. E. Lee to T. J. Jackson, Oct. 1, 1862, in OR, ser. 1, vol. 19, pt. 2, p. 641; B. Bragg to W. H. Taylor, Jan. 6, 1865, in OR, ser. 1, vol. 46, pt. 2, p. 1018; Wise, *Long Arm of Lee*, 2:731–35; ANV G.O. #26, Apr. 3, 1863, in OR, ser. 1, vol. 51, pt. 2, pp. 847–48.

70. J. Davis to Speaker of the House [Thomas S. Bobcock], Mar. 1, 1862, in Richardson, comp., *Messages and Papers*, 1:193.

71. R. E. Lee to J. Davis, Mar. 21, 1863, in Freeman, ed., *Lee's Dispatches*, 81–82; R. E. Lee to J. Davis, Sept. 7, 1862, in OR, ser. 1, vol. 19, pt. 2, p. 597.

72. Howard, *Recollections*, 220.

73. Ibid., 359–60; William J. Seymour, Diary-Memoir, June 23 and 27, 1863, Gregory A. Coco Collection, Harrisburg Civil War Roundtable Collection, U.S. Army Military History Institute, Carlisle Barracks, Pa.

74. Robertson, *General A. P. Hill*, 110; Daly, *Alexander Cheves Haskell*, 77; Sorrel, *Recollections*, 32, 374.

75. A&IGO circular, June 4, 1864, in OR, ser. 1, 3:469; Bryan Grimes, *Extracts of Letters of Major-General Bryan Grimes to His Wife*, comp. Pulaski Cowper (1884; reprint, Wilmington, N.C.: Broadfoot Publishing Co., 1986), 83; J. E. B. Stuart to R. H. Chilton, Aug. 20, 1863, in OR, ser. 1, vol. 27, pt. 2, p. 710; W. Mahone to [A. P. Hill], June 22, 1864, 7:20 p.m., in OR, ser. 1, vol. 51, pt. 2, p. 1026; John Cabell Early, "A Southern Boy's Experience at Gettysburg," *Journal of the Military Service Institution* 43 (Jan.–Feb. 1911): 418–19.

76. W. H. Taylor to R. H. Anderson, May 31, 1864, in Dowdey and Manarin, eds., *Wartime Papers*, 759.

77. Howard, *Recollections*, 260.

78. Douglas, *I Rode with Stonewall*, 40, 277; Howard, *Recollections*, 260; R. E. Lee to J. Davis, June 29, 1862, in Freeman, ed., *Lee's Dispatches*, 22.

Chapter 3—The General Staff in the Army of Northern Virginia: Quartermaster, Commissary, and Medical Director

1. Confederate States of America War Department, *Regulations, 1863*, 97.

2. Ibid., 190; Richard D. Goff, *Confederate Supply* (Durham, N.C.: Duke University Press, 1969), 84–85; Matthews, ed., *Public Laws*, 196–97.

3. J. P. Benjamin to the president [J. Davis], Nov. 30, 1861, in OR, ser. 4, 1:760; J. A. Seddon to J. Davis, Nov. 26, 1863, in OR, ser. 4, 2:1004; Matthews, ed., *Public Laws*, 278–79.

4. Confederate States of America War Department, *Regulations, 1863*, 90; C. A. Evans to wife, Dec. 26, 1863, in Evans, *Intrepid Warrior*, 311; A&IGO G.O. #121, Sept. 9, 1863, in OR, ser. 4, 2:797.

5. Confederate States of America War Department, *Regulations, 1863*, 90–97, 108–9, 113–89; Confederate States of America War Department, *Regulations for the Army of the Confederate States for the Quartermaster's Department Including the Pay Branch Thereof* (Richmond, Va.: Ritchie and Dunnavant, 1862) 190–233, esp. 197, 194, 190–92; Goff, *Confederate Supply*, 131.

6. Goff, *Conferderate Supply*, 130.

7. John Cheves Haskell, *The Haskell Memoirs*, ed. Gilbert E. Govan and James W. Livingood (New York: Putnam, 1960), 28–29.

8. S. L. Stuart to H. J. Hawls, Nov. 8, 1862, book 50, Leigh Collection.

9. Theodore Stanford Garnett, *Riding with Stuart*, 75; J. H. Chamberlayne to M. B. Chamberlayne, Oct. 24, 1861, in Chamberlayne, *Ham Chamberlayne*, 48.

10. W. L. Ritter, "Sketches of the Third Maryland Artillery," in *Southern Historical Society Papers*, 9:443.

11. T. J. Goree to brother [R. D. Goree], Dec. 18, 1864, in Cutrer, ed., *Longstreet's Aide*, 141.

12. *Proceedings of the Second Confederate Congress. First Session, Second Session in Part. 2 May–14 June 1864, 7 November–14 December 1864*, ed. Frank E. Vandiver, vol. 51 of *Southern Historical Society Papers*, 252.

13. *Proceedings of the First Confederate Congress*, 50:31, 386, 23–24.

14. *Proceedings of the Second Confederate Congress. Second Session in Part. 2 December 15, 1864–March 18, 1865*, ed. Frank E. Vandiver, vol. 52 of *Southern Historical Society Papers*, 71.

15. Caldwell, *History of a Brigade*, 86–87.

16. *Proceedings of the First Confederate Congress*, 50:30, 211–14; *Proceedings of the Second Confederate Congress*, 51:274.

17. Goff, *Confederate Supply*, 34, 75–76, 84; QM Gen.'s Office circular, Mar. 24, 1863, in OR, ser. 1, vol. 25, pt. 4, pp.638–86.

18. Alexander, *Military Memoirs*, 279.

19. C. A. Evans to wife, Sept. 23, 1864, in Evans, *Intrepid Warrior*, 446.

20. H. B. Davidson to S. Cooper, June 29, 1863, in OR, ser. 1, vol. 51, pt. 2, p. 730.

21. Caldwell, *History of a Brigade*, 15; return of captures and abstracts of prisoners taken, OR, ser. 1, 2:571; Alexander, *Military Memoirs*, 102.

22. Edward McCrady Jr., "Gregg's Brigade of South Carolinians in the Second Battle of Manassas," in *Southern Historical Society Papers*, 13:12.

23. Robertson, *General A. P. Hill*, 113–14; J. H. Lane to unknown, Oct. 12, 1864, in James H. Lane, "Glimpses of Army Life in 1864: Extracts from Letters Written by Brigadier-General J. H. Lane," in *Southern Historical Society Papers*, 18:414.

24. Edwin B. Coddington, *The Gettysburg Campaign: A Study in Command* (New York: Charles Scribner's Sons, 1968), 153; C. Price to mother, Oct. 15, 1862, in Channing Price, "Stuart's Chambersburg Raid, an Eyewitness Account," *Civil War Times Illustrated* 4 (Jan. 1966): 10.

25. R. S. Ewell to R. H. Chilton, 1863, and report of Maj. Gen. R. E. Rodes, 1863, in OR, ser. 1, vol. 27, pt. 2, pp. 442, 550; Coddington, *Gettysburg Campaign*, 164.

26. Report of Maj. Gen. Jubal Early, Aug. 22, 1863, in OR, ser. 1, vol. 27, pt. 2, p. 466.

27. Stiles, *Four Years*, 199.

28. E. Blackford to father, June 21, 1863, book 33, Leigh Collection; Chamberlayne, *Ham Chamberlayne*, 191.

29. J. A. Early to J. C. Breckinridge, July 3, 1864, in OR, ser. 1, vol. 37, pt. 2, p. 591.

30. Everard H. Smith, "Chambersburg: Anatomy of a Confederate Reprisal," *American Historical Review* 96 (Apr. 1991): 438, 440.

31. QM Gen. circular, Nov. 1861, in OR, ser. 4, 1:767; ANV G.O. #2, Jan. 3, 1862, in OR, ser. 1, vol. 51, pt. 2, p. 430.

32. P. H. Powers to wife, May 15, 1862, book 19, Leigh Collection.

33. Matthews, ed., *Public Laws*, 102–4; A&IGO G.O. #30, Mar. 7, 1864, in OR, ser. 4, 3:198–200. See price lists in OR, ser. 4, 2:453, 616–17, 631–32, 836–38, 843–46; H. M. Bell to J. C. Breckinridge, May 15, 1864, in OR, ser. 1, vol. 37, pt. 1, p. 737.

34. Goff, *Confederate Supply*, 66; A&IGO G.O. #97, Dec. 1, 1862, in OR, ser. 4, 2:219; R. E. Lee to G. W. Randolph, Nov. 14, 1862, in OR, ser. 1, vol. 19, pt. 2, p. 718; A. R. Lawton to R. E. Lee, Apr. 26, 1864, in OR, ser. 1, 33:1313; R. E. Lee to M. C. Lee, Jan. 17, 1865, in Dowdey and Manarin, eds., *Wartime Papers*, 884.

35. Report of Maj. John A. Harmon, C.S. Army, chief quartermaster, of captured property during the second and third quarters, 1862, in OR, ser. 1, vol. 19, pt. 1, p. 960.

36. J. H. New to J. Perkins Jr., Jan. 19, 1863, with endorsements, in OR, ser. 1, 21:1097–99; A. C. Myers endorsement on R. E. Lee to G. W. Randolph, Nov. 14, 1862, in OR, ser. 1, vol. 19, pt. 2, p. 718; A. R. Lawton to B. Bragg, Jan. 3, 1865, in OR, ser. 1, vol. 46, pt. 2, p. 1009.

37. P. H. Powers to wife, May 12, 1862, book 19, Leigh Collection.

38. R. E. Lee to T. J. Jackson, Nov. 19, 1862, 9:00 A.M., and R. E. Lee to J. E. B. Stuart, Dec. 23, 1862, in *OR*, ser. 1, 21:1021, 1076; W. J. Hawks to R. G. Cole, Mar. 17, 1863, drawer 3, Leigh Collection; ANV G.O. #43, Mar. 21, 1863, in *OR*, ser. 1, vol. 25, pt. 2, p. 681; see P. H. Powers to wife, Apr. 14, 1862, book 19, Leigh Collection.

39. Evans, *Intrepid Warrior*, 339.

40. S. G. Welch to wife, Aug. 18, 1862, in Welch, *Confederate Surgeon's Letters*, 20.

41. Report of Brig. Gen. John R. Jones, in *OR*, ser. 1, vol. 19, pt. 1, p. 1007.

42. Matthews, ed., *Public Laws*, 69; Confederate States of America War Department, *Regulations, 1863*, 107–8; A&IGO G.O.s #100 and #13, Dec. 8, 1862, and Feb. 3, 1864, in *OR*, ser. 4, 2:229–30, 74.

43. James Lynn Nichols, *The Confederate Quartermaster in the Trans-Mississippi* (Austin: University of Texas Press, 1964), 19; Goff, *Confederate Supply*, 67; Matthews, ed., *Public Laws*, 72; R. E. Lee to S. Cooper, Nov. 15, 1862, in *OR*, ser. 1, 21:1012–13; William B. B. Cross, "Memorandum of Resources of Department—Clothing, Camp Equipment, and Miscellaneous Stores," in *Southern Historical Society Papers*, 2:120; C. A. Hege to mother, May 10, 1863, book 11, Leigh Collection.

44. Von Borcke, *Memoirs*, 199; Alexander R. Lawton, "Letter to Hon. Mr. Miller, Richmond, Va., January 27, 1865," in *Southern Historical Society Papers*, 2:117; James H. Lane, "History of Lane's North Carolina Brigade," in *Southern Historical Society Papers*, 10:208; Wert, *General James Longstreet*, 366; R. E. Lee to M. C. Lee, Nov. 25, 1864, in Dowdey and Manarin, eds., *Wartime Papers*, 871.

45. Right Wing, ANV G.O. #47, Nov. 7, 1862, in *OR*, ser. 1, vol. 51, pt. 2, p. 642; Wert, *General James Longstreet*, 366; R. E. Lee to A. R. Lawton, Jan. 19, 1864, A. R. Lawton to R. E. Lee, Feb. 5, 1864, and R. E. Lee to J. A. Early, Feb. 11, 1864, in *OR*, ser. 1, 33:198–99, 1146, 1159–60.

46. J. H. Lane to unknown, Feb. 5, 1864, in Lane, "Glimpses of Army Life in 1864," 18:407.

47. Lane, "History of Lane's North Carolina Brigade," 10:208.

48. Gary W. Gallagher, *Stephen Dodson Ramseur, Lee's Gallant General* (Chapel Hill: University of North Carolina Press, 1985), 139; Matthews, ed., *Statutes*, 38–39; Confederate States of America War Department, *Regulations, 1863*, 109–12.

49. *Proceedings of the First Confederate Congress, First Session Completed, Second Session in Part*, vol. 45 of *Southern Historical Society Papers*, 270.

50. J. Davis to House of Representatives, Sept. 6, 1862, in Richardson, comp., *Messages and Papers*, 1:243.

51. P. H. Powers to wife, Dec. 25, 1862, book 19, Leigh Collection; Hotchkiss, *Make Me a Map*, 130; A&IGO G.O. #1, Jan. 6, 1865, in *OR*, ser. 4, 3:1000; *Paroles of the Army of Northern Virginia*, 15:2, 70, 94, 212, 303, 402.

52. James A. Seddon, *Report of the Secretary of War*, April 28, 1864 (Richmond, Va.: n.p., 1864), 18–19; Goff, *Confederate Supply*, 17; A&IGO G.O.

#98, Dec. 3, 1862, A. C. Myers to J. A. Seddon, Dec. 9, 1862, and A&IGO G.O. #2, Jan. 3, 1863, in *OR*, ser. 4, 2:225, 231–32, 295–96; Alexander, *Military Memoirs*, 481; A&IGO G.O. #15, Feb. 5, 1864, in *OR*, ser. 4, 3:77; "Field Telegrams from Headquarters A.N.V.," in *Southern Historical Society Papers*, 4:190–91.

    53. J. E. Johnston to J. Davis, Mar. 13, 1862, in *OR*, ser. 1, vol. 51, pt. 2, p. 1074.

    54. Stiles, *Four Years*, 46.

    55. Susan Leigh Colton Blackford, comp., *Letters*, 7.

    56. HQ Virginia Forces, G.O. #32, July 12, 1861, in *OR*, ser. 1, vol. 51, pt. 2, p. 163; Pierre Gustave Toutant Beauregard, "The First Battle of Bull Run," in *Battles and Leaders*, ed. Johnson and Buel, 1:220; P. G. T. Beauregard to A. C. Myers, Aug. 1, 1861, and A. C. Myers to P. G. T. Beauregard, Aug. 1, 1861, in Alfred Roman, *The Military Operations of General Beauregard in the War between the States, 1861 to 1865, Including a Brief Personal Sketch and a Narrative of His Services in the War with Mexico, 1846–48* (New York: Harper and Brothers, 1883), 1:122, 125.

    57. R. E. Lee to T. J. Jackson, Oct. 1, 1862, in *OR*, ser. 1, vol. 19, pt. 2, p. 641; extracts from the journal of Lt. Col. E. P. Alexander, chief of ordnance, ANV, Oct. 1–Nov. 15, [1862], in *OR*, ser. 1, vol. 119, pt. 1, p. 155; A&IGO G.O. #61, Aug. 23, 1862, in *OR*, ser. 4, 2:69; ANV G.O. #58, Apr. 20, 1863, and S. Crutchfield to W. N. Pendleton, Apr. 16, 1863, in *OR*, ser. 1, vol. 25, pt. 2, pp. 739–40, 726; Wise, *Long Arm of Lee*, 1:429; Hotchkiss, *Make Me a Map*, 162; C. M. Blackford to S. C. Blackford, July 19, 1863, in Susan Leigh Colton Blackford, comp., *Letters*, 196; HQs Valley District unnumbered G.O., June 27, 1864, in *OR*, ser. 1, vol. 37, pt. 1, p. 768.

    58. Charles W. Ramsdell, "Lee's Horse Supply, 1861–1865," *American Historical Review* 35 (1929–30): 773, 759; ANV G.O. #115, Oct. 1, 1862, in *OR*, ser. 1, vol. 19, pt. 2, pp. 642–43.

    59. Susan Pendleton Lee, ed., *Memoirs*, 218; HQ Cav. Div. ANV, G.O. #25, July 29, 1863, in *OR*, ser. 1, vol. 27, pt. 3, p. 1049; W. N. Pendleton to R. E. Lee, Feb. 11, 1863, in *OR*, ser. 1, vol. 25, pt. 2, p. 618; Ramsdell, "Lee's Horse Supply," 772–73; G. W. Imboden to wife, Nov. 27, 1864, book 28, Leigh Collection.

    60. J. T. Brown to W. N. Pendleton, May 11, 1863, J. L. Corley to W. N. Pendleton, May 20, 1863, J. F. Gilmer to R. E. Lee, Apr. 19, 1863, and J. L. Corley to W. N. Pendleton, May 20, 1863, in *OR*, ser. 1, vol. 25, pt. 2, pp. 793, 812–13, 735; A. H. Cole to J. L. Corley, Feb. 20, 1865, in *OR*, ser. 1, vol. 46, pt. 2, p. 1242.

    61. Matthews, ed., *Statutes*, 45–46; See Treasury Department authorization, book 59, J. B. Phillips Folder, and extract ANV S.O. #71, Sept. 10, 1864, book 50, Leigh Collection; R. E. Lee to J. A. Randolph, Nov. 10, 1862, in *OR*, ser. 2, 19:709; Douglas, *I Rode with Stonewall*, 135, 279.

    62. R. E. Lee to S. Cooper, Nov. 18, 1862, in *OR*, ser. 1, 21:1018; Goff, *Confederate Supply*, 74; R. E. Lee to T. J. Jackson, Feb. 7, 1863, in *OR*, ser. 1, vol.

51, pt. 2, pp. 678–79; HQ Arty. Corps [ANV] unnumbered S.O., Jan. 29, 1863, in *OR*, ser. 1, vol. 25, pt. 2, p. 599; Hotchkiss, *Make Me a Map*, 121–22; Confederate States of America War Department, *Regulations, 1863*, 103.

63. W. N. Pendleton to E. P. Alexander, May 19, 1863, in *OR*, ser. 1, vol. 25, pt. 2, p. 808.

64. Goff, *Confederate Supply*, 198; Wise, *Long Arm of Lee*, 2:718; *Proceedings of the Second Confederate Congress*, 51:34.

65. Alexander, *Fighting for the Confederacy*, 446; endorsement by J. A. Early, Feb. 3, 1865, in *OR*, ser. 1, vol. 46. pt. 2, p. 1135.

66. Alexander, *Fighting for the Confederacy*, 308; Roman, *Military Operations*, 1:72, 120–21; Beauregard, "First Battle of Bull Run," 1:202–3; L. B. Northrop, "The Confederate Commissariat at Manassas," in *Battles and Leaders*, ed. Johnson and Buel, 1:261; Goff, *Confederate Supply*, 21–22, 36; Joseph E. Johnston, "Responsibilities of the First Bull Run," in *Battles and Leaders*, ed. Johnson and Buel, 1:256–57.

67. Venable, "General Lee," 2:240; L. B. Northrop to R. E. Lee, July 23, 1863, in *OR*, ser. 1, vol. 51, pt. 2, p. 738; J. R. Crenshaw to L. B. Northrop, Jan. 12, 1863, in *OR*, ser. 1, vol. 21, pp. 1088–90; W. H. Taylor to Bettie Saunders, Jan. 28, 1864, in Tower, ed., *Lee's Adjutant*, 110.

68. L. B. Northrop endorsement on R. E. Lee to J. A. Seddon, Jan. 28, 1863, in *OR*, ser. 1, vol. 51, pt. 2, pp. 674–5; G. W. Randolph to R. E. Lee, Nov. 14, 1862, in *OR*, ser. 1. vol. 19, pt. 2, p. 717; R. E. Lee to G. W. Randolph, Nov. 17, 1862, 6:30 P.M., in *OR*, ser. 1, 21:1016; R. E. Lee to J. A. Seddon, Mar. 27, 1863, in Dowdey and Manarin, eds., *Wartime Papers*, 418–19; L.B. Northrop to J. A. Seddon, Mar. 2, 1863, in *OR*, ser. 4, 2:414; Goff, *Confederate Supply*, 79–80; Jerrold Northrop Moore, *Confederate Commissary General; Lucius Bellinger Northrop and the Subsistence Bureau of the Southern Army* (Shippensburg, Pa.: White Man Publishing Co., 1996), 169–70, 197, 199; R. E. Lee to J. Davis, Aug. 9, 1864, in Freeman, ed., *Lee's Dispatches*, 288–89.

69. R. E. Lee to J. A. Seddon, Jan. 20, 1863, in *OR*, ser. 1, 21:1100–1101; L. B. Northrop to R. E. Lee, Nov. 22, 1863, R. E. Lee to L. B. Northrop, Nov. 23, 1863, R. E. Lee to J. A. Seddon, Nov. 19, 1863, and J. A. Seddon to R. E. Lee, Nov. 20, 1863, in *OR*, ser. 1, vol. 29, pt. 2, pp. 843–44, 837, 838; J. A. Seddon to R. E. Lee, Jan. 11, 1865, R. E. Lee to J. A. Seddon, Jan. 11, 1865, L. B. Northrop to J. A. Seddon, Jan. 12, 1865, and R. E. Lee to J. A. Seddon, Jan. 19, 1865, in *OR*, ser. 1, vol. 46, pt. 2, pp. 1034–35, 1040, 1074–75.

70. L. B. Northrop to G. W. Randolph, Nov. 13, 1862, and R. E. Lee to G. W. Randolph, Nov. 7, 1862, in *OR*, ser. 1, vol. 19, pt. 2, pp. 699–700; Hotchkiss, *Make Me a Map*, 79; C. A. Evans to wife, June 20, 1863, in Evans, *Intrepid Warrior*, 210; Jubal Anderson Early, *A Memoir of the Last Year of the War for Independence in the Confederate States of America* (Lynchburg, Va.: C. W. Button, 1867), 81; R. E. Lee to L. B. Northrop, Jan. 5, 1864, in Dowdey and Manarin, eds., *Wartime Papers*, 648; C. M. Blackford to S. C. Blackford, June 18, 1863, in Susan Leigh Colton Blackford, comp., *Letters*, 232–33; Arthur James Lyon Fremantle, *Three Months in the Southern States, April–June, 1863*

(New York: John Bradburn, 1864), 241–44; Wert, *General James Longstreet*, 344; F. W. Dawson to mother, Oct. 13, 1864, in Francis W. Dawson, *Reminiscences of Confederate Service, 1861–1865*, ed. Bell I. Wiley (Baton Rouge: Louisiana State University Press, 1980), 203.

71. Goff, *Confederate Supply*, 167.

72. W. H. Taylor to Bettie Saunders, Mar. 8, 1864, in Tower, ed., *Lee's Adjutant*, 133.

73. Confederate States of America War Department, *Regulations, 1863*, 234; Matthews, ed., *Public Laws*, 281–82.

74. Confederate States of America War Department, *Regulations, 1863*, 234–85.

75. W. N. Pendleton to wife, Nov. 2, 1861, in Susan Pendleton Lee, ed., *Memoirs*, 161; R. S. Young to brother, June 18, 1862, book 17, Leigh Collection; Lane, "History of Lane's North Carolina Brigade," 10:209; Horace Herndon Cunningham, *Doctors in Gray: The Confederate Medical Service* (Baton Rouge: Louisiana State University Press, 1958), 252–55; J. Davis to Congress, Aug. 22, 1861, in Richardson, comp., *Messages and Papers*, 1:130–31; Confederate States of America War Department, *Regulations, 1863*, 240.

76. Quoted in Cunningham, *Doctors in Gray*, 261; L. Guild to surgeon general [Samuel P. Moore], July 5, 1862, in OR, ser. 1, vol. 2, pt. 3, pp. 633–34.

77. "Surgeons of the Confederacy: Dr. Hunter Holmes McGuire, of Virginia," *Confederate Veteran* 34 (Apr. 1926): 141.

78. Army of the Potomac [Confederate] G.O. #2, Aug. 11, 1861, in Luhn, ed., *C.S. Army General Orders*, 96; report of surgeon Lafayette Guild, Aug. 17, 1862, in OR, ser. 1, vol. 11, pt. 2, pp. 501–10; Cunningham, *Doctors in Gray*, 257, 259, 118; L. Guild to S. P. Moore, Oct. 9, 1862, in OR, ser. 1, vol. 19, pt. 3, p. 659.

79. L. Guild to S. P. Moore, Jan. 9, 1863, in OR, ser. 1, 21:1085.

80. Sorrel, *Recollections*, 97; Fremantle, *Three Months*, 241; *Paroles of the Army of Northern Virginia*, 15:1–3; A&IGO G.O. #124, Sept. 22, 1863, in OR, ser. 4, 2:822.

81. J. Davis to Congress, Aug. 22, 1861, in Richardson, comp., *Messages and Papers*, 1:130–31; Cunningham, *Doctors in Gray*, 116–17.

82. HQ Valley District, G.O. #51, May 22, 1862, and ANV G.O. #94, Aug. 11, 1862, in OR, ser. 1, vol. 12, pt. 3, pp. 898, 928; report of surgeon Lafayette Guild, Aug. 16, 1862, in OR, ser. 1, vol. 11, pt. 2, p. 501; J. Davis to House, Oct. 13, 1862, in Richardson, comp., *Messages and Papers*, 1:263–66; Fremantle, *Three Months*, 234.

83. L. Guild to S. P. Moore, Oct. 9, 1862, in OR, ser. 1, vol. 19, pt. 2, pp. 659–60; Cunningham, *Doctors in Gray*, 119; Confederate States of America War Department, *Regulations, 1863*, 281; P. J. Semmes to wife, Sept. 8, 1862, L-S Box, General Paul Semmes Folder, Leigh Collection; A&IGO G.O. #61, Aug. 23, 1862, in OR, ser. 4, vol. 2:69; Daly, *Alexander Cheves Haskell*, 82.

84. Cunningham, *Doctors in Gray*, 121–22; *Paroles of the Army of Northern Virginia*, 15:1–3.

85. Confederate States of America War Department, *Regulations, 1863,* 237–38, 282; Office of the Chief of Commissary circular, Dec. 28, 1863, in *OR,* ser. 4, 3:61.

86. ANV S.O. #196, Sept. 21, 1862, and L. Guild to S. P. Moore, Oct. 9, 1862, in *OR,* ser. 1, vol. 19, pt. 2, p. 615; pt. 3, p. 660; Matthews, ed., *Public Laws,* 63–65; A&IGO G.O. #78, Oct. 28, 1862, and A&IGO G.O. #28, Mar. 12, 1863, in *OR,* ser. 4, 2:149, 425.

87. Confederate States of America War Department, *Regulations, 1863,* 235; R. E. Lee to G. W. Randolph, Sept. 21, 1862, in *OR,* ser. 1, vol. 19, pt. 2, p. 614; A&IGO G.O. #73, Oct. 1, 1862, in *OR,* ser. 4, 2:105.

88. Confederate States of America War Department, *Regulations, 1863,* 234; Right Wing, ANV G.O. #43, Oct. 4, 1863, in *OR,* ser. 1, vol. 5, pt. 2, p. 631; *Paroles of the Army of Northern Virginia,* 15:1–3.

89. Cunningham, *Doctors in Gray,* 108, 265; Alexander, *Military Memoirs,* 56–57, 318.

90. Cunningham, *Doctors in Gray,* 129–32; Douglas, *I Rode with Stonewall,* 252; W. H. Taylor to R. H. Anderson, May 8, 1863, and W. H. Taylor to L. McLaws, May 8, 1863, in *OR,* ser. 1, vol. 25, pt. 2, p. 786.

Chapter 4—Special Staff in the Army of Northern Virginia

1. Alexander, *Fighting for the Confederacy,* 168; Matthews, ed., *Statutes,* 48; Edward Porter Alexander, "Confederate Artillery Service," in *Southern Historical Society Papers,* 11:99; Wise, *Long Arm of Lee,* 1:143, 146.

2. W. N. Pendleton to R. E. Lee, June 21, 1862, in *OR,* ser. 1, vol. 51, pt. 2, p. 577. Pendleton suggested this reorganization as early as June 5 (Susan Pendleton Lee, ed., *Memoirs,* 198).

3. Alexander, "Confederate Artillery Service," 11:102; ANV G.O. #71, June 22, 1862, in *OR,* ser. 1, vol. 11, pt. 3, pp. 612–13.

4. *OR,* ser. 1, vol. 11, pt. 3, p. 613.

5. Alexander, *Military Memoirs,* 90, 147, 158.

6. Alexander, "Confederate Artillery Service," 11:103–4.

7. Fourth endorsement of J. H. Chamberlayne to G. W. Randolph, June 4, 1862, in Chamberlayne, *Ham Chamberlayne,* 83.

8. Alexander, "Confederate Artillery Service," 11:104; S. Crutchfield to J. H. Chamberlayne, Jan. 31, 1863, in Chamberlayne, *Ham Chamberlayne,* 153; A. L. Long to W. N. Pendleton, Oct. 1, 1862, in *OR,* ser. 1, vol. 19, pt. 2, p. 642.

9. W. N. Pendleton to R. E. Lee, Oct. 2, 1862, ANV S.O. #29, Oct. 4, 1862, and ANV G.O. #115, Oct. 1, 1862, in *OR,* ser. 1, vol. 19, pt. 2, pp. 647–54, 642; Alexander, *Fighting for the Confederacy,* 168.

10. J. H. Chamberlayne to M. B. Chamberlayne, Oct. 9, 1862, in Chamberlayne, *Ham Chamberlayne,* 121.

11. W. N. Pendleton to R. E. Lee, Feb. 11, 1863, and R. E. Lee to W. N. Pendleton, Apr. 6, 1863, in *OR,* ser. 1, vol. 25, pt. 2, pp. 614–18, 709; Alexander, *Military Memoirs,* 370; R. E. Lee to J. Davis, Mar. 7, 1863, in Freeman, ed.,

Lee's Dispatches, 74–75; ANV G.O. #20, Feb. 15, 1863, in *OR*, ser. 1, vol. 24, pt. 2, p. 625.

12. W. N. Pendleton to H. C. Cabell, May 19, 1863, in *OR*, ser. 1, vol. 25, pt. 2, p. 808.

13. ANV G.O. #69, June 4, 1863, in *OR*, ser. 1, vol. 51, pt. 2, p. 721; Alexander, "Confederate Artillery Service," 11:103.

14. W. S. Pendleton to wife, Jan. 7, 1863, in Susan Pendleton Lee, ed., *Memoirs*, 276.

15. William N. Pendleton, "Official Report of General W. N. Pendleton, Chief of Artillery ANV, Sept. 12, 1862[3]" in *Southern Historical Society Papers*, 5:195–96; T. J. Goree to J. Longstreet, May 17, 1875, in Cutrer, ed., *Longstreet's Aide*, 159; William Miller Owen, *In Camp and Battle with the Washington Artillery of New Orleans* (1885; reprint, Gaithersburg, Md.: Butternut Press, 1982), 258–59; HQ Arty., ANV S.O. #18, Apr. 14, 1864, in *OR*, ser. 1, 33:1282; Alexander, *Fighting for the Confederacy*, 251.

16. Wise, *Long Arm of Lee*, 2:704, 560–61; Alexander, "Confederate Artillery Service," 11:103; Alexander, *Fighting for the Confederacy*, 337–38.

17. W. N. Pendleton, "Abstract of a Bill to Organize the Artillery of the Confederate States," Oct. 29, 1864, and R. E. Lee to W. N. Pendleton, Nov. 7, 1864, in *OR*, ser. 1, vol. 51, pt. 2, pp. 1049–52; W. N. Pendleton to J. A. Seddon, Nov. 8, 1864, in *OR*, ser. 1, vol. 42, pt. 3, pp. 1205–6.

18. Alexander, "Confederate Artillery Service," 11:103; Cav. Corps ANV S.O. #18, Nov. 2, 1863, in *OR*, ser. 1, vol. 51, pt. 2, p. 783; Alexander, *Fighting for the Confederacy*, 337–38; HQ Arty., ANV S.O. #13, Apr. 7, 1864, in *OR*, ser. 1, 33:1267.

19. Wise, *Long Arm of Lee*, 2:579.

20. Susan Pendleton Lee, ed., *Memoirs*, 168–69; Wise, *Long Arm of Lee*, 1:74–79; McClellan, *Life and Campaigns*, 154; A&IGO G.O. #90, Nov. 19, 1862, in *OR*, ser. 4, 2:194.

21. Confederate States of America War Department, *Regulations, 1863*, 286–365; Confederate States of America Ordnance Bureau, *The Field Manual for Use of the Officers on Ordnance Duty* (1862; reprint, Ardentsville, Pa.: D. S. Thomas, 1984), 144.

22. Matthews, ed., *Statutes*, 28–29, 47–52; A&IGO S.O. #17, Apr. 8, 1861, in *OR*, ser. 4, 1:211; William Allan, "Reminiscences of Field Ordnance Service with the Army of Northern Virginia," in *Southern Historical Society Papers*, 14:137; Alexander, *Military Memoirs*, 52–53; Alexander, *Fighting for the Confederacy*, 60.

23. Matthews, ed., *Public Laws*, 39, 57–58, 281–82; Confederate States of America War Department, *Regulations, 1863*, 294; A&IGO G.O. #24, Apr. 16, 1862, in *OR*, ser. 4, 1:1065–66; instructions to ordnance officers in the field, May 20, 1862, in *OR*, ser. 4, 1:1124–25; A&IGO G.O.s #46 and #110, July 1, 1862, and Aug. 12, 1863, in *OR*, ser. 4, 2:1, 707; Alexander, *Fighting for the Confederacy*, 61, 126; Allan, "Reminiscences," 14:141; Dawson, *Reminiscences*, 62; *Paroles of the Army of Northern Virginia*, 15:1–3.

24. Josiah Gorgas, "Notes on the Ordnance Department of the Confederate Government," in *Southern Historical Society Papers*, 12:90; A&IGO G.O.s #68, #70, and #71, Sept. 17, 1862, Sept. 23, 1862, and Sept. 26, 1862, in *OR*, ser. 4, 2:85, 92, 96–97; Frank E. Vandiver, *Plowshares into Swords: Josiah Gorgas and Confederate Ordnance* (Austin: University of Texas Press, 1952), n. 21, 142–43, 207; Dawson, *Reminiscences*, 112–13; Howard, *Recollections*, 179; Frederick M. Colston, "Recollections of the Last Months in the Army of Northern Virginia," in *Southern Historical Society Papers*, 38:1.

25. Alexander, *Military Memoirs*, 232; Alexander, *Fighting for the Confederacy*, 126, 76; Alexander, "Confederate Artillery Service," 11:104; P. G. T. Beauregard to L. P. Walker, June 23, 1861, in Roman, *Military Operations*, 1:74.

26. Allan, "Reminiscences," 14:141.

27. William Allan, *The Army of Northern Virginia in 1862* (1892; reprint, with introduction by John C. Ropes, Dayton, Ohio: Press of Morningside Bookshop, 1984), xiii.

28. Alexander, *Military Memoirs*, 172, 219, 232.

29. Allan, "Reminiscences," 14:143.

30. Ibid., 14:143–44; Pendleton, "Official Report," 5:199.

31. George Michael Neese, *Three Years in the Confederate Horse Artillery* (New York: Neale Publishing Co., 1911), 179; Wise, *Long Arm of Lee*, 2:657, 692; John Gill, *Reminiscences of Four Years as a Private Soldier in the Confederate Army, 1861–1865* (Baltimore: Sun Printing Office, 1904), 59; Vandiver, *Plowshares into Swords*, 74; Gorgas, "Notes on the Ordnance Department," 12:92; Josiah Gorgas, "Special Report No. 2, C.S.A. War Department Ordnance Bureau, Richmond, Va., December 31, 1864," in *Southern Historical Society Papers*, 2:62; War Department circular, July 22, 1863, in *OR*, ser. 1, vol. 27, pt. 3, pp. 1091–92.

32. Allan, "Reminiscences," 14:139.

33. A&IGO G.O. #6, Jan. 14, 1864, in *OR*, ser. 4, 3:27–28; R. E. Lee to B. Bragg, Dec. 30, 1864, Braxton Bragg Papers, U.S. Army Military History Institute, Carlisle Barracks, Pa.

34. A&IGO G.O. #148, Nov. 18, 1863, in *OR*, ser. 4, 2:965.

35. R. E. Lee to J. Gorgas, June 5, 1862, and R. E. Lee to S. R. Mallory, June 21, 1862, in Dowdey and Manarin, eds., *Wartime Papers*, 185, 196; A. L. Long to J. Gorgas, Nov. 10, 1862, in *OR*, ser. 1, vol. 19, pt. 2, p. 712; W. N. Pendleton to B. G. Baldwin, June 10, 1864, in *OR*, ser. 1, vol. 36, pt. 3, pp. 888–89; Alexander, *Fighting for the Confederacy*, 413, 443–44, 500.

36. Extracts from the journal of Lt. Col. E. P. Alexander, chief of ordnance, ANV, Oct. 1–Nov. 15, [1862], in *OR*, ser. 1, vol. 19, pt. 1, p. 154.

37. Confederate States of America War Department, *Regulations, 1863*, 73; Fremantle, *Three Months*, 241–42; A&IGO G.O. #19, Feb. 17, 1863, in *OR*, ser. 4, 2:401.

38. C. A. Evans to wife, Aug. 10, 1861, in Evans, *Intrepid Warrior*, 67; Alexander, *Military Memoirs*, 176, 182; Alexander, *Fighting for the Confederacy*, 148; Allan, "Reminiscences," 14:142.

39. Extract from B. G. Baldwin to J. Gorgas, May 7, 1863, in J. Gorgas to J. A. Seddon, May 12, 1863, in *OR*, ser. 1, vol. 25, pt. 2, p. 795

40. Josiah Gorgas, "Annual Report No. 1, Ordnance Office, Richmond, Va., October 13, 1864," in *Southern Historical Society Papers*, 2:59.

41. HQ Cav. Div. G.O. #14, Apr. 23, 1863, book 41, and requisition, June 26, 1861, unmarked box, Col. I. I. Seibles Folder, Leigh Collection.

42. Allan, "Reminiscences," 14:141.

43. Ibid., 141–42, 144–46; James M. Garnett, "Diary of Captain James M. Garnett, Ordnance Officer, Rodes's Division, 2d Corps, Army of Northern Virginia," in *Southern Historical Society Papers*, 27:4.

44. Confederate States of America War Department, *Regulations, 1863, 366.*

45. Ibid., 415, 366–83, 78–84, 4–5.

46. A&IGO G.O. #90, June 26, 1863, in *OR*, ser. 4, 2:609.

47. Matthews, ed., *Public Laws*, 49, 98–99; Stiles, *Four Years*, 183–84; Seddon, *Report*, 9.

48. William Willis Blackford, *War Years*, 251.

49. J. F. Gilmer, "Letter to Hon. J. C. Breckinridge, Secretary of War, Richmond, Virginia, 16th February 1865," in *Southern Historical Society Papers*, 2:123.

50. A. L. Rives to J. E. Johnston, Feb. 25, 1861, in *OR*, ser. 1, 5:1081–82; James Lynn Nichols, *Confederate Engineers* (Tuscaloosa, Ala.: Confederate Publishing Co, 1957), 28.

51. R. E. Lee to J. F. Gilmer, Mar. 27, 1863, in *OR*, ser. 1, vol. 25, pt. 2, p. 686; R. E. Lee to A. L. Rives, Mar. 30, 1864, in *OR*, ser. 1, 33:1245; R. E. Lee to G. W. C. Lee, Mar. 30, 1864, in Dowdey and Manarin, eds., *Wartime Papers*, 686.

52. Daly, *Alexander Cheves Haskell*, 124.

53. William Willis Blackford, *War Years*, 127; J. E. B. Stuart to R. H. Chilton, July 14, 1862, in *OR*, ser. 1, vol. 11, pt. 2, p. 522.

54. Roman, *Military Operations*, 1:80–81; C. W. Howard to R. E. Lee, Dec. 2, 1862, in *OR*, ser. 1, 21:1042; William Willis Blackford, *War Years*, 210.

55. Douglas, *I Rode with Stonewall*, 220.

56. Jubal Anderson Early, *Memoir*, 101.

57. Hotchkiss, *Make Me a Map*, 150; Douglas Southall Freeman, *Lee's Lieutenants: A Study in Command* (New York: Charles Scribner's Sons, 1942, 1970), 1:498.

58. William Willis Blackford, *War Years*, 152.

59. James Lynn Nichols, "Confederate Map Supply," *Military Engineer* 46 (Jan.–Feb. 1954), 28, 29, 31; James Keith Boswell, "The Diary of a Confederate Staff Officer," *Civil War Times Illustrated* 15 (Apr. 1976): 37.

60. Frederick M. Colston, "Recollections," 38:7.

61. Hotchkiss, *Make Me a Map*, 20, 63–64, 78, 98, 108, 109–11, 142–44, 68; William Willis Blackford, *War Years*, 165; W. G. Atkinson to P. G. T. Beauregard, July 5, 1861, book 17, Leigh Collection; Nichols, *Confederate Engineers*, 81.

62. Hotchkiss, *Make Me a Map*, 107, 164; J. Hotchkiss to J. H. Alexander, Dec. 31, 1864, in *OR*, ser. 1, vol. 43, pt. 2, p. 947.

63. William Willis Blackford, *War Years*, 200; Nichols, *Confederate Engineers*, 87; Hotchkiss, *Make Me a Map*, 251–67.

64. Longstreet, *From Manassas to Appomattox*, 254–55.

65. J. Hotchkiss to G. F. R. Henderson, quoted in Nichols, *Confederate Engineers*, 81–82.

66. Hotchkiss, *Make Me a Map*, 39.

67. Stiles, *Four Years*, 276; Alexander, *Fighting for the Confederacy*, 72; Hotchkiss, *Make Me a Map*, 26, 46; William Willis Blackford, *War Years*, 105.

68. Longstreet, *From Manassas to Appomattox*, 113; R. E. Lee to W. H. Smith, June 3, 1862, and June 4, 1862, in Dowdey and Manarin, eds., *Wartime Papers*, 182–83; Alexander, *Military Memoirs*, 475; Boswell, "Diary," 31, 34; Alexander, *Fighting for the Confederacy*, 167–68.

69. William Willis Blackford, *War Years*, 257.

70. Slave labor receipt, Sept. 23, 1863, Peters Collection, Slave Requisition Folder, Leigh Collection; HQ Engineer Troops, July 15, 1864, in *OR*, ser. 1, vol. 40, pt. 3, pp. 776–78.

71. A&IGO G.O. #41, Feb. 18, 1864, in *OR*, ser. 1, 33:1190; Hotchkiss, *Make Me a Map*, 235; Stiles, *Four Years*, 187.

72. Matthews, ed., *Public Laws*, 38; A&IGO G.O. #40, May 29, 1862, in *OR*, ser. 4, 1:1132; Edward H. Cummins, "The Signal Corps in the Confederate States Army," in *Southern Historical Society Papers*, 16:93–107.

73. J. F. Milligan to S. Cooper, July 1, 1862, in *OR*, ser. 1, vol. 2, pt. 3, p. 629; Alexander, *Military Memoirs*, 14–16.

74. Alexander, *Military Memoirs*, 14–16, 30–32, 38, 52; Alexander, *Fighting for the Confederacy*, 49–50, 66, 71–72.

75. T. J. Jackson to J. Longstreet, Apr. 5, 1862, 9:10 A.M., T. J. Jackson to R. E. Lee, Apr. 29, 1862, and R. E. Lee to T. J. Jackson, May 1, 1862, in *OR*, ser. 1, vol. 12, pt. 3, pp. 843, 872, 878; Matthews, ed., *Public Laws*, 61; Charles E. Taylor, *Signal and Secret Service of the Confederate States* (1903; reprint, Harmans, Md.: Toomey Press, 1986), v–vi; A&IGO G.O.s #40 and #10, May 29, 1862, and Jan. 24, 1863, in *OR*, ser. 4, 1:1132, 2:371.

76. Alexander, *Fighting for the Confederacy*, 75; report of Cpt. Joseph L. Bartlett, Aug. 20, 1862, in Dowdey and Manarin, eds., *Wartime Papers*, 267–68; John G. Walker, "Jackson's Capture of Harper's Ferry," in *Battles and Leaders*, ed. Johnson and Buel, 2:608–9; Henry Kyd Douglas, "Stonewall Jackson's Intentions at Harper's Ferry," in *Battles and Leaders*, ed. Johnson and Buel, 2:617; R. E. Lee to T. J. Jackson, Nov. 10, 1862, 7:00 P.M., in *OR*, ser. 1, vol. 19, pt. 2, p. 710.

77. Jubal Anderson Early, *Memoir*, 72.

78. Gallagher, *Stephen Dodson Ramseur*, 155.

79. Jay Luvaas, "The Role of Intelligence in the Chancellorsville Campaign, April–May, 1863," in *Intelligence and Military Operations*, ed. Michael I. Handel (Portland, Oreg.: Frank Cass, 1990), 104.

80. Charles E. Taylor, *Signal and Secret Service*, v, 8; Fremantle, *Three Months*, 202; R. E. Lee to J. Longstreet, Apr. 27, 1863, in Dowdey and Manarin, eds., *Wartime Papers*, 440–41; R. E. Lee to J. A. Seddon, Feb. 14, 1863, in *OR*, ser. 1, vol. 25, pt. 2, pp. 622–23; Alexander, *Fighting for the Confederacy*, 66; R. E. Lee to A. P. Hill, June 8, 1863, in *OR*, ser. 1, vol. 27, pt. 3, p. 869.

81. Alexander, *Military Memoirs*, 189; A. Pleasanton to S. Williams, June 20, 1863, 7:00 A.M., in *OR*, ser. 1, vol. 27, pt. 3, p. 224; W. N. Pendleton to wife, Sept. 18, 1863, in Susan Pendleton Lee, *Memoirs*, 302; Wert, *General James Longstreet*, 379; Longstreet, *From Manassas to Appomattox*, 471; McClellan, *Life and Campaigns*, 154–55.

82. Luvaas, "Role of Intelligence," 104–5; report on the Battle of Bull Run, Aug. 26 [Oct. 14], 1861, in *OR*, ser. 1, 2:500; James E. B. Stuart, "Report of General J. E. B. Stuart of Cavalry Operations on First Maryland Campaign, from August 30th to September 18th 1862," in *Southern Historical Society Papers*, 3:294; G. M. Sorrel to L. McLaws, Dec. 10, 1862, in *OR*, ser. 1, vol. 51, pt. 2, p. 659.

83. Cummins, "Signal Corps," 16:98; Alexander, *Fighting for the Confederacy*, 205.

84. McClellan, *Life and Campaigns*, 139, 107–8; Jubal Anderson Early, *Memoir*, 72.

85. J. P. Benjamin to J. E. Johnston, Oct. 27, 1861, in *OR*, ser. 1, 5:923.

86. T. Jordan to J. P. Benjamin, Oct. 29, 1861, in ibid., 928.

87. G. W. Randolph to J. Davis, Aug. 12, 1862, in ibid., ser. 4, 2:47; Cummins, "Signal Corps," 16:101, 98; A&IGO G.O. #40, May 29, 1862, in *OR*, ser. 4, 1:1132; Walter Herron Taylor, *Four Years*, 139; W. H. Taylor to Bettie Saunders, Feb. 8, 1864, in Tower, ed., *Lee's Adjutant*, 116.

88. Walter H. Taylor, "Telegram to Gen. G. W. C. Lee, 11 Aug 1864," in *Southern Historical Society Papers*, 14:573; R. E. Lee to J. A. Seddon, May 10, 1863, in *OR*, ser. 1, vol. 25, pt. 2, p. 790; W. Taylor to Cpt. Fisher, May 4, 1864, in *OR*, ser. 1, vol. 36, pt. 2, p. 372; C. Marshall to J. A. Early, Aug. 31, 1864, in *OR*, ser. 1, vol. 25, pt. 1, p. 1009.

89. *OR*, ser. 1, vol. 25, pt. 1, pp. 1009–10.

90. Cummins, "Signal Corps," 16:103; Robertson, *General A. P. Hill*, 147.

91. See, for example, messages when ANV HQ was at Chaffin's Bluff in Dowdey and Manarin, eds., *Wartime Papers*, 856–67; A&IGO G.O. #44, June 17, 1862, in *OR*, ser. 4, 1:1155; R. E. Lee to B. Bragg, May 28, 1864, in Freeman, ed., *Lee's Dispatches*, 201; A&IGO G.O. #88, June 24, 1863, in *OR*, ser. 4, 2:607.

92. Roman, *Military Operations*, 153; William Mahone Memoir (typescript), William Mahone Folder, Civil War Times Illustrated Collection, U.S. Army Military History Institute, Carlisle Barracks, Pa., 2; Von Borcke, *Memoirs*, 336–37;

J. E. B. Stuart to R. H. Chilton, Aug. 20, 1863, in *OR*, ser. 1, vol. 27, pt. 2, p. 314; Trout, *They Followed the Plume*, 319–20; *Paroles of the Army of Northern Virginia*, 15:465.

Chapter 5—Personal Staff in the Army of Northern Virginia

1. Confederate States of America War Department, *Regulations, 1863*, 4; Matthews, ed., *Public Laws*, 281–82.

2. Report on the Battle of Bull Run, Aug. 26 [Oct. 14], 1861, in *OR*, ser. 1, 2:500; D. H. Hill to wife, July 10, 1861, Daniel Harvey Hill Papers, U.S. Army Military History Institute, Carlisle Barracks, Pa.

3. R. E. Lee to E. Sparrow, Mar. 20, 1863, in *OR*, ser. 4, 2:447.

4. W. H. Taylor to Bettie Saunders, Jan. 28, 1864, and Feb. 5, 1865, in Tower, ed., *Lee's Adjutant*, 109, 110.

5. T. J. Goree to S. W. K. Goree, Aug. 27, 1861, in Langston James Goree, ed., *The Thomas Jewitt Goree Letters*, vol. 1, *The Civil War Correspondence* (Bryan, Tex.: Family History Foundation, 1981), 76.

6. R. S. Ewell to L. O. Branch, May 14, 1862, in *OR*, ser. 1, vol. 12, pt. 3, p. 890.

7. B. Bragg to W. P. Johnston, Apr. 22, 1864, in ibid., ser. 4, 3:316; *Proceedings of the Second Confederate Congress*, 52:229.

8. J. Davis to Senate, Mar. 11, 1865, and Mar. 28, 1864, in Richardson, comp., *Messages and Papers*, 1:540, 1:464.

9. *Proceedings of the First Confederate Congress*, 45:239.

10. Jon L. Wakelyn, *Biographical Dictionary of the Confederacy* (Westport, Conn.: Greenwood Press, 1977), 129–30, 319; Alexander, *Fighting for the Confederacy*, 38; U.S. War Department, *List of Staff Officers of the Confederate Army, 1861–1865* (Washington, D.C.: U.S. Government Printing Office, 1891), 31–32, 114, 17; Owen, *In Camp and Battle*, 52; Douglas, *I Rode with Stonewall*, 21.

11. P. G. T. Beauregard to E. P. Alexander, Aug. 27, 1861, P. G. T. Beauregard to J. Davis, Aug. 10, 1861, and P. G. T. Beauregard to J. E. Johnston, Sept. 5, 1861, in *OR*, ser. 1, vol. 51, pt. 2, pp. 255, 1071, 272.

12. Douglas, *I Rode with Stonewall*, 32; see A. R. Boteler to J. P. Benjamin, Jan. 18, 1862, in *OR*, ser. 1, vol. 51, pt. 2, p. 443; G. F. R. Henderson, *Stonewall Jackson and the American Civil War* (1898; reprint, New York: David McKay Co., 1961), 397.

13. A. R. Boteler to J. A. Seddon, Aug. 15, 1863, in *OR*, ser. 4, 2:718.

14. Alexander R. Boteler, "Stonewall Jackson in the Campaign of 1862," in *Southern Historical Society Papers*, 40:177–78.

15. Douglas, *I Rode with Stonewall*, 152; report of Maj. Gen. Jubal A. Early, Aug. 22, 1863, in *OR*, ser. 1, vol. 27, pt. 2, p. 464.

16. J. Tyler to S. Price, June 7, 1864, in *OR*, ser. 1, vol. 51, pt. 2, p. 993; Sorrel, *Recollections*, 3–4; T. J. Goree to S. W. K. Goree, Jan. 18, 1862, in Goree, ed., *Thomas Jewitt Goree Letters*, 1:125; Wert, *General James Longstreet*, 63, 75, 83; J. E. B. Stuart to R. H. Chilton, Aug. 20, 1863, in *OR*, ser. 1, vol. 27, pt.

2, p. 702; HQ Dept. of Northern Virginia, S.O. #156, July 6, 1864, book 59, Walter H. Taylor Folder, Leigh Collection.

17. Von Borcke, *Memoirs*, 228–29; Stuart, "Report of General J. E. B. Stuart," 3:294; Wert, *General James Longstreet*, 154.

18. E. Blackford to father, [winter 1863], book 33, Leigh Collection.

19. Confederate States of America War Department, *Regulations, 1863*, 87–89, 407–20; Matthews, ed., *Public Laws*, 71–72; Seddon, *Report*, 9–10; E. P. Alexander to H. E. Young, Mar. 10, 1865, in OR, ser. 1, vol. 46. pt. 2, p. 1300; William G. Nine and Ronald G. Wilson, eds., *The Appomattox Paroles, April 9–15, 1865*, 2d ed. (Lynchburg, Va.: H. E. Howard, 1989), 26.

20. R. E. Lee to secretary of war [J. A. Seddon], Mar. 23, 1864, in OR, ser. 4, 3:246; J. Davis to Senate and House, Sept. 11, 1862, in Richardson, comp., *Messages and Papers*, 1:244; A&IGO G.O. #109, Dec. 20, 1862. in OR, ser. 4, 2:248; Matthews, ed., *Public Laws*, 72, 157, 193, 194, 183, 280.

21. Alexander, *Fighting for the Confederacy*, 338–39; C. M. Blackford to wife, Feb. 1, 1863, and July 30, 1863, in Susan Leigh Colton Blackford, comp., *Letters*, 164–65, 198.

22. Charles Henry Lee, *Judge Advocate's Vade Mecum*, 2d ed. (Richmond, Va.: West and Johnston, 1864), 48–91; Susan Leigh Colton Blackford, comp., *Letters*, passim.

23. E. P. Alexander to H. E. Young, Mar. 10, 1865, in OR, ser. 1, vol. 46, pt. 2, pp. 1300–1301; for original circular see H. E. Young to W. McGowan, Mar. 7, 1865, book 28, Leigh Collection; R. E. Lee to secretary of war [J. A. Seddon], Mar. 23, 1864, and A&IGO G.O. #44, Apr. 29, 1864, in OR, ser. 4, 3:246–47, 352; Seddon, *Report*, 10.

24. Evans, *Intrepid Warrior*, 159–79, 318–21, 330; D. Pender to wife, Mar. 28, 1863, in Pender, *The General to His Lady*, 213.

25. Hotchkiss, *Make Me a Map*, 115–16.

26. Sorrel, *Recollections*, 70.

27. O. Latrobe to J. B. Kershaw, Mar. 28, 1865, and J. Longstreet to W. H. Taylor, Mar. 30, 1865, in OR, ser. 1, vol. 46, pt. 3, pp. 1361, 1367.

28. G. M. Sorrel to division commanders, June 26, 1863, and ANV G.O. #82, Aug. 12, 1863, in ibid., vol. 51, pt. 2, pp. 727–28, 754; R. E. Lee to J. Davis, Apr. 7, 1864, ANV S.O. #96, Apr. 7, 1864, and R. E. Lee to J. Davis, Apr. 13, 1864, in Freeman, ed., *Lee's Dispatches*, 149–50, 151–54, 156.

29. See Sorrel, *Recollections*, 63; Wert, *General James Longstreet*, 374–76; Douglas, *I Rode with Stonewall*, 158; Alexander, *Fighting for the Confederacy*, 191–92; journal entry, Jan. 2, 1864, and C. A. Evans to wife, Jan. 15, 1864, in Evans, *Intrepid Warrior*, 330, 321.

30. C. M. Blackford to wife, Feb. 20, 1863, Jan. 10, 1863, June 28, 1863, May 23, 1864, and May 26, 1864, in Susan Leigh Colton Blackford, comp., *Letters*, 167, 157, 184, 247.

31. Confederate States of America War Department, *Regulations, 1863*, 407, 149, 198; J. Davis to Congress, Apr. 29, 1861, in Richardson, comp., *Messages and Papers*, 1:80–81; Sidney J. Romero, *Religion in the Rebel Ranks* (Lanham,

Md.: University Press of America, 1983), 19–20; *Proceedings of the First Confederate Congress*, vol. 47 of *Southern Historical Society Papers*, 43.

32. Matthews, ed., *Statutes*, 116; Romero, *Religion in the Rebel Ranks*, 12; Matthews, ed., *Public Laws*, 45, 175; *Proceedings of the First Confederate Congress*, 50:224; Bean, *Stonewall's Man*, 146–48.

33. Romero, *Religion in the Rebel Ranks*, 37–38.

34. McKim, *Soldier's Recollections*, 215–16.

35. E. Blackford to mother, May 26, 1863, book 33, Leigh Collection; Romero, *Religion in the Rebel Ranks*, 16–17; D. H. Hill to wife, Oct. 6, 1862, Hill Papers.

36. John William Jones, *Christ in the Camp, or Religion in Lee's Army* (Richmond, Va.: B. F. Johnson and Co., 1887), 382–83; Romero, *Religion in the Rebel Ranks*, 9–10.

37. Jones, *Christ in the Camp*, 96; A. S. Pendleton to mother, Mar. 10, 1863, in Susan Pendleton Lee, ed., *Memoirs*, 254; A. C. Hopkins to J. W. Jones, Mar. 22, 1867, in Jones, *Christ in the Camp*, 475.

38. On chaplains' duties, see Romero, *Religion in the Rebel Ranks*, 24–29 (appendix, 147–62, lists surviving tracts); for samples of many chaplains' activities, see Betts, *Experiences*, 8–10, 43, 50–51, 66, 70; on writing to Union families, see description of Chaplain Owens, 17th Mississippi, in Stiles, *Four Years*, 144, 30; Nicholas A. Davis, *The Campaign from Texas to Maryland with the Battle of Fredericksburg* (1863; reprint, Austin, Tex.: Steck Co., 1961), 93–94, 96, 130; A. C. Hopkins to J. W. Jones, Mar. 22, 1867 in Jones, *Christ in the Camp*, 469; McKim, *Soldier's Recollections*, 238, 221; James B. Sheeran, *Confederate Chaplain: A War Journal of Rev. James B. Sheeran, c.ss.r, 14th Louisiana, C.S.A.*, ed. Joseph T. Durkin (Milwaukee, Wis.: Bruce Publishing Co., 1960), 8, 76, 36–37.

39. J. W. Jones to A. E. Dickinson, Oct. 1, 1864, and A. C. Hopkins to J. W. Jones, Mar. 22, 1867, in Jones, *Christ in the Camp*, 96, 354, 475; E. Blackford to mother, May 26, 1863, book 33, Leigh Collection.

40. Sheeran, *Confederate Chaplain*, 39, 63, 83, 42–43; Betts, *Experiences*, 42, 35.

41. Sheeran, *Confederate Chaplain*, 32–33.

42. Romero, *Religion in the Rebel Ranks*, 23–24; A. C. Hopkins to J. W. Jones, Mar. 22, 1867, in Jones, *Christ in the Camp*, 466; Sheeran, *Confederate Chaplain*, 52.

43. Jones, *Christ in the Camp*, 325; W. N. Pendleton to wife, Apr. 15, 1863, in Susan Pendleton Lee, ed., *Memoirs*, 255; John William Jones, "A Reminiscence of an Official Interview with General R. E. Lee," in *Southern Historical Society Papers*, 10:92; John William Jones, "The Old Virginia Town, Lexington," *Confederate Veteran* 1 (Jan. 1893): 20; Henry Brainerd McClellan, "Tenth Annual Reunion of the Virginia Division Army of Northern Virginia Association. Address by Major H. B. McClellan, of Lexington, Ky., on the Life, Campaigns, and Character of J. E. B. Stuart," in *Southern Historical Society Papers*, 8:453;

"The Death of Major-General J. E. B. Stuart," in *Southern Historical Society Papers*, 7:107.

44. Minutes of Chaplains' Association of 2d and 3d Corps, ANV, Round Oak Church, Va., Mar. 16–Apr. 25, 1863, in Jones, *Christ in the Camp*, 515–22; B. T. Lacy, "An Address of the Chaplains of the Second Corps ("Stonewall" Jackson's), Army of Northern Virginia, to the Churches of the Confederate States, March 24, 1863," in *Southern Historical Society Papers*, 14:348–56; Jones, *Christ in the Camp*, 49.

45. Betts, *Experiences*, 31.

46. Jones, *Christ in the Camp*, 94–95.

47. Sheeran, *Confederate Chaplain*, 54.

48. Jones, *Christ in the Camp*, 49–50; ANV G.O. #15, Feb. 7, 1864, in *OR*, ser. 1, 33:1150; C. A. Evans to wife, May 1, 1864, in Evans, *Intrepid Warrior*, 379; Romero, *Religion in the Rebel Ranks*, 9–10, 14, 57; W. N. Pendleton to wife, June 19, 1862, in Susan Pendleton Lee, ed., *Memoirs*, 191; W. H. Taylor to Bettie Saunders, Aug. 28, 1864, in Tower, ed., *Lee's Adjutant*, 186; Hotchkiss, *Make Me a Map*, 56, 133; McKim, *Soldier's Recollections*, 139.

49. Confederate States of America War Department, *Regulations, 1863*, 77; Radley, *Rebel Watchdog*, 50–51; *OR*, ser. 1, vol. 23, pt. 2, p. 744.

50. ANV G.O.s #102 and #103, Sept. 17, 1862, and Sept. 6, 1863, in *OR*, ser. 1, vol. 19, pt. 2, pp. 592, 596; *OR*, ser. 1, vol. 11, pt. 3, pp. 576–77; vol. 12, pt. 3, pp. 928–29; vol. 19, pt. 2, pp. 618–19; vol. 27, pt. 3, p. 1050; ANV G.O. #63, June 5, 1862, in *OR*, ser. 1, vol. 11, pt. 3, p. 577; H. H. Howard to mother and brothers, Oct. 9, 1862, book 2, Leigh Collection.

51. Theodore Stanford Garnett, *Riding with Stuart*, 76.

52. Radley, *Rebel Watchdog*, 302, 297, 291, 46; ANV S.O. #151, June 4, 1863, in *OR*, ser. 1, vol. 51, pt. 2, p. 721; see D. B. Bridgford to W. H. Palmer, Oct. 3, 1864, in *OR*, ser. 1, vol. 42, pt. 1, p. 870, and *Paroles of the Army of Northern Virginia*, 15:453–58, 449–51; R. P. Blount to J. Davis, Nov. 20, 1862, in *OR*, ser. 2, 4:950; U.S. War Department, *List of Staff Officers*, 16; U.S. War Department, *List of Field Officers, Regiments, and Battalions in the Confederate States Army, 1861–1865* (189?; reprint, Bryan, Tex.: J. M. Carroll and Co., 1983), 13; Stewart Sifakis, *Compendium of the Confederate Armies: Alabama* (New York: Facts on File, 1992), 62, 67.

53. Radley, *Rebel Watchdog*, 50–51; Robertson, *General A. P. Hill*, 259.

54. ANV G.O. #21, Feb. 16, 1863, in *OR*, ser. 1, vol. 25, pt. 2, p. 629; ANV G.O. #94, Aug. 11, 1862, in *OR*, ser. 1, vol. 12, pt. 3, p. 928; report of Maj. D. B. Bridgford, chief provost marshal, HQ, Provost Marshal, 2d Corps, Jan. 9, 1863, in *OR*, ser. 1, 21:641.

55. Reprt of Maj. D. B. Bridgford, Jan. 9, 1863, in *OR*, ser. 1, 21:641; Longstreet, *From Manassas to Appomattox*, 129; D. B. Bridgford to W. H. Palmer, Oct. 3, 1864, in *OR*, ser. 1, vol. 42, pt. 1, p. 870; McClellan, *Life and Campaigns*, 396; John H. Worsham, *One of Jackson's Foot Cavalry, His Experiences and What He Saw during the War, 1861–1865* (New York: Neale Publishing Co., 1912), 139.

Chapter 6—Staff Selection and Training

1. Jones, *Christ in the Camp*, 229.

2. B. Bragg to W. P. Johnston, Apr. 22, 1864, and S. W. Melton to J. A. Seddon, Nov. 11, 1863, in *OR*, ser. 4, 3:316, 2:951.

3. Seddon, *Report*, 5.

4. J. H. Chamberlayne to M. B. Chamberlayne, Feb. 23, 1862, in Chamberlayne, *Ham Chamberlayne*, 67–68.

5. Freeman, *Lee's Lieutenants*, 3:332.

6. R. E. Lee to J. Davis, Mar. 21, 1863, in Freeman, ed., *Lee's Dispatches*, 82–83; R. E. Lee to M. C. Lee, Feb. 14, 1864, in Dowdey and Manarin, eds., *Wartime Papers*, 671.

7. D. H. Hill to wife, Dec. 19, 1861, Hill Papers; John Cabell Early, "A Southern Boy's Experience at Gettysburg," 415; W. D. Pender to wife, June 6, 1861, and June 25, 1862, in Pender, *The General to His Lady*, 24–25, 159; report of Brig. Gen. William Barksdale, May 15, 1863, in *OR*, ser. 1, vol. 25, pt. 1, p. 841; C. A. Evans to wife, Nov. 18, 1864, and Dec. 23, 1864, in Evans, *Intrepid Warrior*, 518, 528; Lane, "History of Lane's North Carolina Brigade," 10:213; Alexander, *Fighting for the Confederacy*, 338; R. E. Lee to G. W. C. Lee, Mar. 29, 1864, in Dowdey and Manarin, eds., *Wartime Papers*, 686.

8. Susan Leigh Colton Blackford, comp., *Letters*, 164; Sorrel, *Recollections*, 26; "Stonewall's Commissary General," 286; T. J. Goree to mother, Feb. 18, 1864, and n. 2, in Cutrer, ed., *Longstreet's Aide*, 114.

9. G. W. Peterkin to S. P. Lee, Apr. 29, 1887, in Susan Pendleton Lee, ed., *Memoirs*, 291; J. Davis to J. E. Johnston, July 13, 1861, in *OR*, ser. 1, 2:977; Wise, *Long Arm of Lee*, 1:170; Bean, *Stonewall's Man*, 43; W. D. Pender to wife, Sept. 11, 1861, in Pender, *The General to His Lady*, 58; Vandiver, *Plowshares into Swords*, 113; Douglas, *I Rode with Stonewall*, 301.

10. Longstreet, *From Manassas to Appomattox*, 32; Sorrel, *Recollections*, 2–4; T. J. Goree to S. W. K. Goree, Jan. 18, 1862, in Goree, ed., *Thomas Jewitt Goree Letters*, 1:125.

11. Sorrel, *Recollections*, 21–22; D. Pender to wife, Mar. 28, 1863, in Pender, *The General to His Lady*, 213; D. H. Hill to wife, Oct. 18, 1862, Hill Papers.

12. John Keegan, *The Mask of Command* (New York: Penguin Books, 1988), 195, 198. I accept Keegan's characterization of Grant's staff with some trepidation. The 21st Illinois was not from Galena, and Grant fired the only officer (Lt. Col. B. Lagow) that he definitely took from the 21st; nevertheless, his chief of staff (Brig. Gen. J. A. Rawlins) was from Galena, and other staff officers were prewar acquaintances. Conversely, at least by the Vicksburg campaign, both Grant's chief of quartermaster and chief of commissary were West Point graduates. See Ulysses Simpson Grant, *The Personal Memoirs of U. S. Grant*, ed. with notes by E. B. Long (1952; reprint, New York: Da Capo Press, 1982), 130, 280.

13. Bean, *Stonewall's Man*, 76n; Sorrel, *Recollections*, 231; McClellan, *Life and Campaigns*, 62; Hotchkiss, *Make Me a Map*, 3; McKim, *Soldier's Recollections*, 110; Henderson, *Stonewall Jackson*, 138.

14. William Willis Blackford, *War Years*, 11–12, 17–19; Romero, *Religion in the Rebel Ranks*, 41; Owen, *In Camp and Battle*, 51; Evans, *Intrepid Warrior*, 328, 340; Lane, "History of Lane's North Carolina Brigade," 10:212–13; William Willis Blackford, *War Years*, 90; J. E. B. Stuart to T. R. Price, Mar. 30, 1863, in Harry J. Warthen Jr., ed., "Family Ties: Letters from J. E. B. Stuart," *Civil War Times Illustrated* 23 (Oct. 1983), 34.

15. C. A. Evans to wife, Dec. 23, 1864, in Evans, *Intrepid Warrior*, 528; R. E. Lee to M. C. Lee, Dec. 30, 1864, in Dowdey and Manarin, eds., *Wartime Papers*, 880; Sorrel, *Recollections*, 16, 98; quoted in Romero, *Religion in the Rebel Ranks*, 9.

16. W. H. Taylor to [M. L. Taylor], Aug. 1, 1863, in Tower, ed., *Lee's Adjutant*, 110; Wert, *General James Longstreet*, 83; Sorrel, *Recollections*, 17; Trout, *They Followed the Plume*, 28.

17. William Willis Blackford, *War Years*, 90.

18. McClellan, *Life and Campaigns*, 375–76 n. 1.

19. Sorrel, *Recollections*, 48.

20. Trout, *They Followed the Plume*, 29; Grant, *Personal Memoirs*, 145; Alexander, *Military Memoirs*, 451–52.

21. Biographical data largely from Ezra J. Warner, *Generals in Gray: Lives of the Confederate Commanders* (Baton Rouge: Louisiana State University Press, 1959, 1993), passim; Sorrel, *Recollections*, 14; Dawson, *Reminiscences*, 56.

22. Charles Granton, "Some Reminiscences of Camp Life with Stonewall Jackson—Before he was known to fame" (typescript), [1900?], Charles Granton Folder, Civil War Times Illustrated Collection.

23. Douglas, *I Rode with Stonewall*, 101.

24. Alexander, *Military Memoirs*, 417; J. Davis to Senate and House, Mar. 28, 1864, in Richardson, comp., *Messages and Papers*, 1:458.

25. See Georgia, *Regulations for the Quartermaster's Department of the State of Georgia, 1861* (Milledgeville, Ga.: Boughton, Nisbet, and Barnes, State Printers, 1861); Georgia, *Regulations for the Commissariat of the State of Georgia, 1861* (Milledgeville, Ga.: Boughton, Nisbet, and Barnes, State Printers, 1861); Gilham, *Manual*, iv.

26. Confederate States of America War Department, *Regulations for the Army of the Confederate States for the Quartermaster's Department*; W. LeRoy Brown, "The Red Artillery," in *Southern Historical Society Papers*, 26:366; Confederate States of America Ordnance Bureau, *Field Manual*, passim, 66; G. W. Randolph to J. Davis, Aug. 12, 1862, in *OR*, ser. 4, 2:47; David Winfred Gaddy, "William Norris and the Confederate Signal and Secret Service," *Maryland Historical Magazine* 70 (summer 1975): 172, 184–85; Boswell, "Diary," Apr. 14, 1863, 37; Dennis Hart Mahan, *A Treatise on Field Fortifications: Containing Instructions on the Methods of Laying out, Constructing, Defending, and Attacking Intrenchments: With the General Outlines Also of the Arrangement, the Attack, and Defence of Permanent Fortifications*, 3d ed., rev. and enl. (New York: John Wiley, 1862); Dennis Hart Mahan, *Summary of the Course of Permanent Fortifications and of the Attack and Defence of Permanent Works for*

the Use of the Cadets of the U.S. Military Academy (Richmond, Va.: West and Johnston, 1863).

27. C. Blackford to wife, Oct. 25, 1863, in Susan Leigh Colton Blackford, comp., *Letters*, 223; Charles H. Lee, *Judge Advocate's Vade Mecum.*

28. M. Schuppert, *A Treatise on Gun-Shot Wounds* (1861; reprint, American Civil War Surgery Series, no. 9, San Francisco: Norman Publishing, 1990); Julian John Chisolm, *A Manual of Military Surgery for the Use of Surgeons in the Confederate States Army: With an Appendix of the Rules and Regulations of the Medical Department of the Confederate States Army* (1861; reprint, American Civil War Surgery Series, no. 4, San Francisco: Norman Publishing, 1989); Edward Warren, *An Epitome of Practical Surgery for Field and Hospital* (1863; reprint, American Civil War Surgery Series, no. 6, San Francisco: Norman Publishing, 1989); Felix Formento Jr., *Notes and Observations on Army Surgery* (1863; reprint, American Civil War Surgery Series, no. 9, San Francisco: Norman Publishing, 1990); Cunningham, *Doctors in Gray*, 148–49; Francis Peyre Porcher, *Resources of the Southern Fields and Forests, Medical, Economical, and Agricultural: Being Also a Medical Botany of the Confederate States with Practical Information on the Useful Properties of Trees, Plants, and Shrubs* (1863; reprint, American Civil War Medical Series no. 4, San Francisco: Norman Publishing, 1991); James B. McCaw, ed., *Confederate States Medical and Surgical Journal* (1864–65; reprint, American Civil War Medical Series, no. 12, San Francisco: Norman Publishing, 1992), 26; Francis Peyre Porcher, "Confederate Surgeon," in *Southern Historical Society Papers*, 17:17.

29. William Willis Blackford, *War Years*, 13, 279; see Stiles, *Four Years*, 111; Douglas, *I Rode with Stonewall*, 14, 209; Confederate States of America War Department, *Regulations for the Army of the Confederate States for the Quartermaster's Department*, annotated copy, Civil War Miscellaneous Collection; J. H. Chamberlayne to G. W. Bagby, June 4, 1863, in Chamberlayne, *Ham Chamberlayne*, 183; Robert Lewis Dabney, *Life and Campaigns of Lieut.-Gen. Thomas J. Jackson* (New York: Blelock and Co., 1866), 288–89.

30. John W. Daniel, introduction to the original edition, Sorrel, *Recollections*, xxx.

Chapter 7—Staff Authority and Relations with the Commander

1. Walter Herron Taylor, *General Lee*, 56.

2. ANV G.O. #130, Dec. 4, 1862, in *OR*, ser. 1, 21:1046; Right Wing, ANV G.O. #28, June 20, 1863, in *OR*, ser. 1, vol. 51, pt. 2, p. 576.

3. Army of the Potomac Confederate G.O. #41, July 17, 1861, in *OR*, ser. 1, vol. 51, pt. 2, pp. 175–76; Alexander, *Fighting for the Confederacy*, 55; Douglas, *I Rode with Stonewall*, 45.

4. ANV G.O. #124, Oct. 28, 1862, in *OR*, ser. 1, vol. 19, pt. 2, p. 688; Frederick M. Colston, "Recollections," 37:3.

5. Walter Herron Taylor, *Four Years*, 134; Freeman, *Lee's Lieutenants*, 3:330.

6. Robertson, *General A. P. Hill*, 173–75.

7. R. E. Lee to A. P. Hill, May 8, 1863, in *OR*, ser. 1, vol. 25, pt. 2, pp. 786–87.

8. R. E. Lee to T. J. Jackson, Oct. 1, 1862, in ibid., vol. 19, pt. 2, p. 641.

9. Grimes, *Extracts*, 31.

10. Charges and specifications against Brig. Gen. J. B. Robertson, in *OR*, ser. 1, vol. 31, pt. 1, p. 470.

11. Gordon C. Rhea, *The Battle of the Wilderness, May 5–6, 1864* (Baton Rouge: Louisiana State University Press, 1994), 275.

12. McKim, *Soldier's Recollections*, 151.

13. George Lemmon, "Letter to Fitzhugh Lee, 26 Jan. 1881," in *Southern Historical Society Papers*, 9:141–42.

14. Enclosure by A. S. Pendleton, 1862, to T. J. Jackson to R. H. Chilton, Apr. 10, 1863, in *OR*, ser. 1, vol. 12, pt. 1, pp. 709–10.

15. Sorrel, *Recollections*, 168.

16. Douglas, *I Rode with Stonewall*, 53–54; Evans, *Intrepid Warrior*, 426; Von Borcke, *Memoirs*, 204; Haskell, *Haskell Memoirs*, 10–11; Dawson, *Reminiscences*, 101–2.

17. W. H. Taylor to Bettie Saunders, Dec. 13, 1863, in Tower, ed., *Lee's Adjutant*, 96–97.

18. W. H. Taylor to Bettie Saunders, Feb. 28, 1864, and Mar. 4, 1864, in ibid., 128, 129–30.

19. Longstreet, *From Manassas to Appomattox*, 52.

20. Wise, *Long Arm of Lee*, 2:515–17; G. M. Sorrel to W. T. Martin, Nov. 14, 1862, in *OR*, ser. 1, vol. 51, pt. 2, p. 645; Lafayette McLaws, Lafayette McLaws Manuscript (copy from Lafayette McLaws Papers, Perkins Library, Duke University), Box 6 (Confederate Commanders and Staffs), Robert L. Brake Collection, U.S. Army Military History Institute, Carlisle Barracks, Pa.; Bean, *Stonewall's Man*, 203–4; William Mahone, William Mahone Memoir (typescript), 5–6, William Mahone Folder, Civil War Times Illustrated Collection.

21. Douglas, *I Rode with Stonewall*, 236; Pender, *The General to His Lady*, 164; J. T. L. Preston, Dec. 5, 1861, quoted in Bean, *Stonewall's Man*, 50; Hunter H. McGuire, "General T. J. ("Stonewall") Jackson, His Career and Character. Address Delivered June 23, 1897," in *Southern Historical Society Papers*, 25:106.

22. Henderson, *Stonewall Jackson*, 557.

23. John William Jones, *Personal Reminiscences of General Robert E. Lee* (1874; reprint, Richmond, Va.: U.S. Historical Society Press, 1989); James Power Smith, "Stonewall Jackson's Last Battle," in *Battles and Leaders*, ed. Johnson and Buel, 3:203–5.

24. Robertson, *General A. P. Hill*, 62; Bean, *Stonewall's Man*, 91; D. H. Hill to wife, Feb. 5, 1862, Hill Papers; Daly, *Alexander Cheves Haskell*, 113.

25. Sorrel, *Recollections*, 66; Douglas, *I Rode with Stonewall*, 75; Hotchkiss, *Make Me a Map*, 80; McClellan, *Life and Campaigns*, 364; McKim, *Soldier's Recollections*, 115.

26. McClellan, *Life and Campaigns*, 411.

27. Owen, *In Camp and Battle*, 113; T. J. Goree to mother, Dec. 14, 1861, in Cutrer, ed., *Longstreet's Aide*, 60.

28. W. D. Pender to wife, June 23, 1863, in Pender, *The General to His Lady*, 251; John William Jones, "The Career of General Jackson," in *Southern Historical Society Papers*, 35:88.

29. Douglas, *I Rode with Stonewall*, 97, 68.

30. Alexander, *Fighting for the Confederacy*, 481–82; Walter Herron Taylor, *Four Years*, 77; W. H. Taylor to Bettie Saunders, Aug. 15, 1864, Aug. 8, 1863, Jan. 28, 1864, Nov. 14, 1864, Feb. 2, 1864, in Tower, ed., *Lee's Adjutant*, 182, 68–69, 109, 83, 115.

31. Susan Pendleton Lee, ed., *Memoirs*, 295; Dawson, *Reminiscences*, 125.

32. Sorrel, *Recollections*, 61–64, 231–32.

33. Dawson, *Reminiscences*, 102–3, 128, 132; W. H. Taylor to Bettie Saunders, Nov. 15, 1863, Dec. 13, 1863, Dec. 27, 1863, Feb. 21, 1864, and Mar. 4, 1864, in Tower, ed., *Lee's Adjutant*, 89, 97–98, 105, 123, 132.

34. Daly, *Alexander Cheves Haskell*, 94, 88; Dawson, *Reminiscences*, 116; R. E. Wilbourn to J. A. Early, Feb. 19, 1873, in *Southern Historical Society Papers*, 9:273; P. H. Powers to wife, May 15, 1864, book 19, Leigh Collection; A. S. Pendleton to mother, Nov. 25, 1863, in Bean, *Stonewall's Man*, 151.

35. Walter Herron Taylor, *General Lee*, 157; D. L. Cross to sister, Mar. 3, 1865, book 5, Leigh Collection; Dawson, *Reminiscences*, 138; Keegan, *Mask of Command*, 198.

36. Fremantle, *Three Months*, 240–41n.

37. S. Y. T. [Samuel Y. Tupper] to brother, July 18, 1861, book 19, Leigh Collection; Howard, *Recollections*, 176; Theodore Stanford Garnett, *Riding with Stuart*, 73–74; McKim, *Soldier's Recollections*, 117, 123.

38. Matthews, ed., *Public Laws*, 281; Dawson, *Reminiscences*, 128–29; Walter Herron Taylor, *General Lee*, 55–57; Hotchkiss, *Make Me a Map*, 145; A. S. Pendleton to mother, May 16, 1863, in Susan Pendleton Lee, ed., *Memoirs*, 273; P. H. Powers to wife, May 17, 1864, book 19, Leigh Collection; A&IGO S.O. #72, Mar. 24, 1863, in *OR*, ser. 1, vol. 25, pt. 2, p. 683; C. S. Venable to unknown, Jan. 15, 1864, in *OR*, ser. 1, 33:1091; ANV S.O. #188, Sept. 5, 1862, in *OR*, ser. 1, vol. 19, pt. 2, p. 595; Williamson biography, 24–25, Elbert Madison Williamson Folder, Harrisburg Civil War Roundtable Collection.

39. S. W. Melton to J. A. Seddon, Nov. 11, 1863, in *OR*, ser. 4, 2:951.

40. J. Davis to Senate and House, Mar. 28, 1864, in Richardson, comp., *Messages and Papers*, 1:458–59.

41. B. Bragg to W. P. Johnston, Apr. 22, 1864, in *OR*, ser. 4, 3:316.

42. A&IGO G.O. #53, July 31, 1862, in ibid., 2:26.

43. S. P. Moore to [field medical officers], Aug. 18, 1862, A&IGO G.O.s #48 and #84, July 11, 1862, and June 15, 1863, in ibid., 2:56, 3, 593; W. E. Jones to W. Peters, Dec. 11, 1862, Peters Collection, William E. Jones Folder, Leigh Collection; Sorrel, *Recollections*, 233.

44. Howard, *Recollections*, viii, 201–2, 206, 214–15.

45. Wert, *General James Longstreet*, 389–91; Wise, *Long Arm of Lee*, 2:553; McClellan, *Life and Campaigns*, 236; Theodore Stanford Garnett, *Riding with Stuart*, 73, 414.

46. Confederate States of America War Department, *Regulations, 1863*, 51; A&IGO G.O. #24, Apr. 16, 1862, in *OR*, ser. 4, 1:1066.

47. J. Gorgas to J. P. Benjamin, Mar. 12, 1862, and S. W. Melton to J. A. Seddon, Nov. 11, 1863, in ibid., 1:990, 2:945; J. Davis to Senate and House, Dec. 7, 1863, in Richardson, comp., *Messages and Papers*, 2:373; Matthews, ed., *Public Laws*, 281.

48. Roman, *Military Operations*, 1:72, 121; for Northrop's rebuttal, see Northrop, "Confederate Commissariat," 1:261.

49. Alexander, "Confederate Artillery Service," 11:103.

50. Alexander, *Military Memoirs*, 613.

Chapter 8—Headquarters and Headquarters Personnel

1. Justus Scheibert, *Seven Months in the Rebel States during the North American War, 1863*, ed. with intro. by William Stanley Hoole, trans. Joseph C. Hayes (Tuscaloosa, Ala.: Confederate Publishing Co., 1958), 35; ANV G.O. #27, Apr. 5, 1864, in *OR*, ser. 1, 33:1262.

2. Armistead Lindsay Long, *Memoirs of Robert E. Lee: His Military and Personal History* (New York: J. M. Stoddard and Co., 1887), 112, 142, 166.

3. Fremantle, *Three Months*, 249; Scheibert, *Seven Months*, 110; Garnet Wolseley, "A Month's Visit to the Confederate Head Quarters," *Blackwood's Edinburgh Magazine* 93 (Jan. 1863), quoted in Sir Frederick Maurice, ed., *An Aide-de-Camp of Lee: Being the Papers of Colonel Charles Marshall, Sometime Aide-de-Camp, Military Secretary, and Assistant Adjutant General on the Staff of Robert E. Lee, 1862–1865* (Boston: Little, Brown, and Co., 1927), xx; Daly, *Alexander Cheves Haskell*, 120.

4. R. E. Lee to M. C. Lee, Jan. 15, 1863, Sept. 18, 1864, in Dowdey and Manarin, eds., *Wartime Papers*, 652, 855.

5. R. E. Lee to A. Lee, Apr. 11, 1863, in ibid., 431–32; R. E. Lee to M. C. Lee, Aug. 23, 1863, in Robert E. Lee [Jr.], *Recollections and Letters of General Robert E. Lee* (Garden City, N.Y.: Garden City Publishing Co., 1924), 109–10.

6. Walter Herron Taylor, *Four Years*, 141, 150; R. E. Lee to M. C. Lee, Nov. 25, 1864, in Dowdey and Manarin, eds., *Wartime Papers*, 871–72.

7. Walter Herron Taylor, *Four Years*, 141.

8. Wolseley, "A Month's Visit," quoted in Maurice, ed., *An Aide-de-Camp of Lee*, xx–xxi.

9. James Longstreet, "Our March against Pope," in *Battles and Leaders*, ed. Johnson and Buel, 3:524; John Daniel Imboden, "The Confederate Retreat from Gettysburg," in *Battles and Leaders*, ed. Johnson and Buel, 3:421; Owen, *In Camp and Battle*, 242; Venable, "General Lee," 2:240; W. H. Taylor to Bettie Saunders, Oct. 25, 1863, in Tower, ed., *Lee's Adjutant*, 79.

10. R. E. Lee to A. R. Lawton, July 27, 1864, book 41, Leigh Collection.

11. T. J. Goree to S. W. K. Goree, July 20, 1861, Sept. 27, 1861, Mar. 13, 1863, in Goree, ed., *Thomas Jewitt Goree Letters*, 1:52, 87, 179; D. H. Hill to wife, Dec. 26, 1861, Hill Papers; Wert, *General James Longstreet*, 242.

12. T. J. Jackson to wife, May 8, 1861, quoted in Dabney, *Life and Campaigns*, 191; E. G. Lee to wife, July 13, 1861, L-S Box, Brig. Gen. Edwin G. Lee Folder, Leigh Collection; Douglas, *I Rode with Stonewall*, 74–75; Robertson, *General A. P. Hill*, 110, 154, 246; A. S. Pendleton to mother, Nov. 19, 1862, in Bean, *Stonewall's Man*, 84, 153–54; Howard, *Recollections*, 191; James Power Smith, "With Stonewall Jackson in the Army of Northern Virginia," *Southern Historical Society Papers*, vol. 43, pt. 1, pp. 35–36, 38–39; Roberta Cary Corbin Kinsolving, "Stonewall Jackson in Winter Quarters: Memories of Moss Neck in the Winter of 1862–63," *Confederate Veteran* 20 (Jan. 1912): 26; E. Blackford to father, [winter 1863], book 33, Leigh Collection; Freeman, *Lee's Lieutenants*, 3:331.

13. John Esten Cooke, *Wearing of the Gray: Being Personal Portraits, Scenes, and Adventures of the War* (1867; reprint, Gaithersburg, Md.: Olde Soldier Books, 1988), 185; Von Borcke, *Memoirs*, 185.

14. Theodore Stanford Garnett, quoted in Trout, *They Followed the Plume*, 34; Von Borcke, *Memoirs*, 188; Theodore Stanford Garnett, *Riding with Stuart*, 27.

15. William Booth Taliaferro, "Jackson's Raid around Pope," in *Battles and Leaders*, ed. Johnson and Buel, 3:507–8; McClellan, *Life and Campaigns*, 316; William Willis Blackford, *War Years*, 147.

16. Von Borcke, *Memoirs*, 187, 334; Scheibert, *Seven Months*, 42; A. S. Pendleton to Nancy, Oct. 26, 1862, in Bean, *Stonewall's Man*, 82–83; A. S. Pendleton to Rose [sister], Oct. 23, 1861, book 50, Leigh Collection.

17. William Willis Blackford, *War Years*, 160; Von Borcke, *Memoirs*, 338; John Esten Cooke, *Outlines from the Outpost*, ed. Richard Harwell (Chicago: R. R. Donnelley and Sons, 1961), 15–16.

18. Gallagher, *Stephen Dodson Ramseur*, 138.

19. See address on O. Latrobe to E. Taylor, Dec. 22, 1864, in *OR*, ser. 1, vol. 43, pt. 2, p. 943; See Davis, *Campaign*, 130; Frederick M. Colston, "Recollections," 38:4; Wert, *General James Longstreet*, 224; Von Borcke, *Memoirs*, 332.

20. ANV G.O. #58, Apr. 20, 1863, and R. E. Lee to W. N. Pendleton, Apr. 25, 1863, in *OR*, ser. 1, vol. 25, pt. 2, pp. 739, 749; Confederate States of America War Department, *Regulations, 1863*, 106; William Willis Blackford, *War Years*, 88; Hotchkiss, *Make Me a Map*, 10; Alexander, *Fighting for the Confederacy*, 127; ANV G.O.s #27 and #32, Apr. 5, 1864, and Apr. 19, 1864, in *OR*, ser. 1, 33:1262–64, 1295–96.

21. Confederate States of America War Department, *Regulations, 1863*, 402–3.

22. Howard, *Recollections*, 83, 107, 113; Von Borcke, *Memoirs*, 268; W. H. Taylor to sister, May 8, 1863, in Tower, ed., *Lee's Adjutant*, 54; T. J. Goree to mother, Feb. 8, 1864, in Cutrer, ed., *Longstreet's Aide*, 116; Dawson, *Reminiscences*, 80.

23. Quoted in Trout, *They Followed the Plume*, 30–31; Cooke, *Wearing of the Gray*, 322; ANV G.O. #58, Apr. 20, 1863, in OR, ser. 1, vol. 25, pt. 2, p. 739; ANV G.O. #27, Apr. 5, 1864, in OR, ser. 1, 33:1262.

24. Sorrel, *Recollections*, 48.

25. Douglas, *I Rode with Stonewall*, 279; Von Borcke, *Memoirs*, 191.

26. Alexander, *Fighting for the Confederacy*, 183; William Willis Blackford, *War Years*, 148, 107; Von Borcke, *Memoirs*, 85.

27. Goff, *Confederate Supply*, 127.

28. *Paroles of the Army of Northern Virginia*, 15:7–9, 327, 154–55, 27–28; W. H. Taylor to Bettie Saunders, Jan. 28, 1864, in Tower, ed., *Lee's Adjutant*, 64; J. Hotchkiss to wife, Apr. 14, 1862, in Hotchkiss, *Make Me a Map*, 22, 158, 162, 167, 197, 252; Douglas, *I Rode with Stonewall*, 115; Allan, *Army of Northern Virginia*, xii; "Stonewall's Commissary General," 286.

29. Journal entry, Jan. 1, 1864, in Evans, *Intrepid Warrior*, 328.

30. Daniel Harvey Hill, "The Battle of South Mountain, or Boonsboro," in *Battles and Leaders*, ed. Johnson and Buel, 2:565n; E. F. Paxton to wife, Oct. 5, 1862, in Paxton, *Civil War Letters*, 58.

31. Allan, *Army of Northern Virginia*, xii; Stiles, *Four Years*, 212; Edward A. Craighill, *Confederate Surgeon: The Personal Recollections of E. A. Craighill*, ed. Peter W. Houck (Lynchburg, Va.: H. E. Howard, 1989), 33–34.

32. W. D. Pender to wife, Mar. 11, 1862, in Pender, *The General to His Lady*, 121; Craighill, *Confederate Surgeon*, 33–34; Hotchkiss, *Make Me a Map*, 22; Williamson biography, 12, Elbert Madison Williamson Folder, Harrisburg Civil War Roundtable Collection; Matthews, ed., *Statutes*, 275; Matthews, ed., *Public Laws*, 114–15.

33. Fremantle, *Three Months*, 143; Douglas, *I Rode with Stonewall*, 53; Mc-Clellan, *Life and Campaigns*, 147; Scheibert, *Seven Months*, 44; E. Blackford to father, Mar. 8, 1863, book 33, Leigh Collection.

34. Confederate States of America War Department, *Regulations, 1863*, 51–52, 57.

35. William Willis Blackford, *War Years*, 81–127, passim, esp. 117–18; John Hennessy Jr., *Return to Bull Run: The Campaign and Battle of Second Manassas* (New York: Simon and Schuster, 1994), 94; Campbell Brown, Campbell Brown Manuscript (typescript), [1869–70], Box 6 (Confederate Commanders and Staffs), Brake Collection.

36. See entry on Benjamin Franklin Weller in Trout, *They Followed the Plume*, 325; Gill, *Reminiscences*, 63, 92; DeWitt Clinton Gallaher, *A Diary Depicting the Experiences of DeWitt Clinton Gallaher in the War between the States while Serving in the Confederate Army* ([Charleston, W.Va.?]: privately published, [1945?]), 12.

37. Lee A. Wallace, *A Guide to Virginia Military Organizations, 1861–1865*, Rev. 2d ed. (Lynchburg, Va.: H. E. Howard, 1986), 68; R. E. Lee to J. A. Seddon, Dec. 1, 1862, in OR, ser. 1, 22:1040–41; R. E. Lee to J. H. Richardson, Nov. 30, 1862, in OR, ser. 1, 21:1039.

38. W. H. Taylor to sister, Nov. 14, 1863, in Tower, ed., *Lee's Adjutant*, 85; Wallace, *Guide*, 68; Jubal Anderson Early, *Lieutenant General Jubal Anderson Early: Autobiographical Sketch and Narrative of the War between the States* (Philadelphia: J. B. Lippincott Co., 1912), 188; William F. Randolph, "Chancellorsville," in *Southern Historical Society Papers*, 29:329; abstracts of returns of ANV, Feb. 10, Mar. 20, Apr. 10, and Apr. 20, 1864, in OR, ser. 1, 33:1157, 1158, 1271, 1289; *Paroles of the Army of Northern Virginia*, 15:7–9.

39. Sorrel, *Recollections*, 198–99; Stewart Sifakis, *Compendium of the Confederate Armies: Virginia* (New York: Facts on File, 1992), 142; R. E. Lee to E. Johnson, Mar. 2, 1864, in OR, ser. 1, 33:1205.

40. William Youngblood, "Personal Observations at Gettysburg," *Confederate Veteran* 19 (June 1911): 286; T. J. Goree to mother, Feb. 8, 1864, and Aug. 20, 1864, in Cutrer, ed., *Longstreet's Aide*, 116, 132; A&IGO G.O. #77, June 6, 1863, in OR, ser. 4, 2:580; Matthews, ed., *Statutes*, 45; Sorrel, *Recollections*, 199.

41. William Willis Blackford, *War Years*, 92, 159; Heros Von Borcke and Justus Scheibert, *The Great Cavalry Battle of Brandy Station, 9 June 1863*, trans. Stuart T. Wright and F. D. Bridgewater (Winston-Salem, N.C.: Palaemon Press, 1976), 39; *Paroles of the Army of Northern Virginia*, 15:186, 465, 7–8, 27; provision return for Cpt. S. B. Meyer's Company, 7th Virginia Cav., Nov. 25, 1862, Union Folder Box, Confederate Troops, etc., Miscellaneous Folder, Leigh Collection.

42. P. G. T. Beauregard to R. S. Ewell, July 26, 1861, in OR, ser. 1, vol. 46, pt. 2, p. 199; R. E. Lee to R. S. Ewell, Apr. 3, 1865, in Dowdey and Manarin, eds., *Wartime Papers*, 929; see Randolph, "Chancellorsville," 29:330; James Power Smith, "With Stonewall Jackson," 43:28; R. E. Lee to W. B. Ball, Nov. 15, 1862, in OR, ser. 1, 21:1014; diary of W. R. Carter, quoted in McClellan, *Life and Campaigns*, 205; Alexander S. Pendleton, "Letter to General Early, July 23, 1863," in *Southern Historical Society Papers*, 9:121.

43. Trout, *They Followed the Plume*, 6, 8, 37–38; report of Brig. Gen. Ambrose P. Hill, May 10, 1862, in OR, ser. 1, vol. 2, pt. 1, p. 578; "Official Diary of First Corps, A.N.V., while Commanded by Lieutenant General R. H. Anderson, from May 7th to 31st, 1864," in *Southern Historical Society Papers*, 7:492.

44. Report of Maj. Gen. J. E. B. Stuart of operations, Sept. 2–20, [1862], in OR, ser. 1, vol. 19, pt. 2, p. 294; J. E. B. Stuart to T. A. Pratt, Dec. 23, 1861, in OR, ser. 1, 5:493–94; J. E. B. Stuart to R. H. Chilton, Aug. 20, 1863, and report of J. E. B. Stuart, June 13, 1863, in OR, ser. 1, vol. 27, pt. 2, pp. 701, 685; Neese, *Three Years*, 275; Gill, *Reminiscences*, 63–64.

45. James W. Ratchford, *Some Reminiscences of Persons and Incidents of the Civil War* (1909; reprint, Austin, Tex.: Shoal Creek Publishers, 1971), 41; Douglas, *I Rode with Stonewall*, 42–45; Henry Kyd Douglas, "A Ride for Stonewall," in *Southern Historical Society Papers*, 21:206–11; T. J. Jackson to R. S. Ewell, Apr. 10, 1862, in OR, ser. 1, vol. 12. pt. 3, p. 845; Alexander, *Military Memoirs*, 551–52; see Von Borcke, *Memoirs*, 191, and Douglas, *I Rode with Stonewall*, 162.

46. McKim, *Soldier's Recollections*, 111–12; Stiles, *Four Years*, 184; Gill, *Reminiscences*, 65; Gallaher, *Diary*, 12; Theodore Stanford Garnett, *Riding with Stuart*, 31.

47. George W. Tucker, "Death of General A. P. Hill," in *Southern Historical Society Papers*, 9:566.

48. See [G. M. Sorrel] to J. B. Hood, May 31, 1863, in *OR*, ser. 1, vol. 25, pt. 2, p. 845, and O. Latrobe to G. H. Steuart and M. D. Corse, Mar. 25, 1865, in *OR*, ser. 1, vol. 46, pt. 3, p. 1351; Boteler, "Stonewall Jackson," 40:179; R. E. Lee to M. C. Lee, Dec. 17, 1864, Nov. 30, 1864, and R. E. Lee to B. Bragg, June 9, 1864, in Dowdey and Manarin, eds., *Wartime Papers*, 878, 872, 770.

49. Douglas, *I Rode with Stonewall*, 119, 132; Stiles, *Four Years*, 99, 260; William Willis Blackford, *War Years*, 182; J. Hotchkiss to J. A. Early, Jan. 21, 1864, in *OR*, ser. 1, 33:112; Von Borcke, *Memoirs*, 181, 333; Randolph, "Chancellorsville," 29:331.

50. Alexander, *Military Memoirs*, 196; Tucker, "Death of General A. P. Hill," 9:564–69; Cooke, *Wearing of the Gray*, 378; Gill, *Reminiscences*, 66, 90; W. H. Taylor to sister, Nov. 14, 1863, in Tower, ed., *Lee's Adjutant*, 85.

51. Bean, *Stonewall's Man*, 69; W. D. Pender to wife, May 4, 1862, in Pender, *The General to His Lady*, 117; William Willis Blackford, *War Years*, 46; Henry Heth, *The Memoirs of Henry Heth*, ed. James L. Morrison Jr. (Westport, Conn.: Greenwood Press, 1974), 192.

52. S. G. Welch to wife, Sept. 3, 1862, in Welch, *Confederate Surgeon's Letters*, 29; Sheeran, *Confederate Chaplain*, 12; Confederate States of America War Department, *Regulations, 1863*, 77; A&IGO G.O. #69, Sept. 19, 1862, in *OR*, ser. 4, 2:86; Matthews, ed., *Public Laws*, 89.

53. Theodore Stanford Garnett, *Riding with Stuart*, 48; J. H. Lane to unknown, Apr. 9, 1864, in Lane, "Glimpses of Army Life in 1864," 18:409; Matthews, ed., *Public Laws*, 260.

54. Alexander, *Fighting for the Confederacy*, 127, 156, 187, 76–77, 508.

55. S. G. Welch to wife, Jan. 16, 1864, May 4, 1864, in Welch, *Confederate Surgeon's Letters*, 87–88, 92; journal entry, Jan. 2, 1865, in Hotchkiss, *Make Me a Map*, 251, 318n; R. E. Lee to M. C. Lee, Dec. 7, 1862, Feb. 8, 1863, in Dowdey and Manarin, eds., *Wartime Papers*, 353, 402; W. N. Pendleton to wife, Nov. 17, 1862, in Susan Pendleton Lee, ed., *Memoirs*, 233; Douglas, *I Rode with Stonewall*, 154–55.

56. Evans, *Intrepid Warrior*, 297, 310, 336; E. Blackford to mother, July 27, 1864, book 33, Leigh Collection; J. H. Chamberlayne to mother, May 17, 1864, May 21, 1864, in Chamberlayne, *Ham Chamberlayne*, 221, 222.

57. W. N. Pendleton to wife, undated, in Susan Pendleton Lee, ed., *Memoirs*, 306.

58. McClellan, *Life and Campaigns*, 161; William Willis Blackford, *War Years*, 179; Alexander, *Fighting for the Confederacy*, 46; Robertson, *General A. P. Hill*, 105; Scheibert, *Seven Months*, 77.

59. Journal entry, Jan. 5–9, 1864, in Evans, *Intrepid Warrior*, 336; William Willis Blackford, *War Years*, 48; Daly, *Alexander Cheves Haskell*, 111–12;

James Power Smith, "With Stonewall Jackson," 43:21; Douglas, *I Rode with Stonewall*, 333–35.

60. Von Borcke, *Memoirs*, 69; Dawson, *Reminiscences*, 123–24; S. G. Welch to wife, Sept. 3, 1862, June 28, 1863, July 17, 1863, and Aug. 4, 1864, in Welch, *Confederate Surgeon's Letters*, 29, 58, 60, 104.

61. Sorrel, *Recollections*, 16–17, 66; Von Borcke, *Memoirs*, 224–25; W. D. Pender to wife, Dec. 7, 1861, in Pender, *The General to His Lady*, 108; James Power Smith, "With Stonewall Jackson," 43:37; W. H. Taylor to sister, May 8, 1863, in Tower, ed., *Lee's Adjutant*, 54.

62. Scheibert, *Seven Months*, 78–79; A. S. Pendleton to Mary, Apr. 30, 1864, in Bean, *Stonewall's Man*, 198.

63. W. D. Pender to wife, Apr. 11, 1863, in *The General to His Lady*, 223; Maurice, ed., *An Aide-de-Camp of Lee*, 260.

64. Wert, *General James Longstreet*, 225; Von Borcke, *Memoirs*, 133–34; James Power Smith, "With Stonewall Jackson," 43:22; Sorrel, *Recollections*, 17.

65. Scheibert, *Seven Months*, 36; James Power Smith, "With Stonewall Jackson," 43:41.

66. William Willis Blackford, *War Years*, 93; Howard, *Recollections*, 365; Hotchkiss, *Make Me a Map*, 105–6; Bean, *Stonewall's Man*, 84–85, 104, 192; D. H. Hill to wife, Oct. 9, 1862, Hill Papers.

67. Von Borcke, *Memoirs*, 58, 68; Alexander, *Fighting for the Confederacy*, 156; Haskell, *Haskell Memoirs*, 14; Blackwood, *War Years*, 217; Lane, "Glimpses of Army Life in 1864," 18:411; W. H. Taylor to Bettie Saunders, Dec. 26, 1864, in Tower, ed., *Lee's Adjutant*, 214.

68. Sorrel, *Recollections*, 19–20; Sheeran, *Confederate Chaplain*, 79; Scheibert, *Seven Months*, 36.

Chapter 9—Staff Procedures

1. Confederate States of America War Department, *Regulations, 1863*, 46.

2. Walter Herron Taylor, *General Lee*, 56; "Col. Walter H. Taylor, A.A.G.," in *Southern Historical Society Papers*, 41:83; Walter Herron Taylor, *Four Years*, 77.

3. Venable, "General Lee," 2:240; Walter Herron Taylor, *Four Years*, 76; R. E. Lee to M. C. Lee, Apr. 5, 1863, in Dowdey and Manarin, eds., *Wartime Papers*, 427.

4. James Power Smith, "With Stonewall Jackson," 43:39–40; A. S. Pendleton to Kate [wife], [Feb. 1864], in Bean, *Stonewall's Man*, 189; Douglas, *I Rode with Stonewall*, 40.

5. W. N. Pendleton to wife, June 17, 1862, and Aug. 6, 1864, in Susan Pendleton Lee, ed., *Memoirs*, 190, 365; D. H. Hill to wife, Jan. 23, 1862, Hill Papers; McClellan, *Life and Campaigns*, 136; Frederick M. Colston, "Recollections," 38:9.

6. Quoted in Cunningham, *Doctors in Gray*, 126; Dawson, *Reminiscences*, 104–5.

7. Commissary circular, Dec. 28, 1863, in *OR*, ser. 4, 3:61; *Paroles of the Army of Northern Virginia*, 15:70; E. P. Alexander to P. G. T. Beauregard, Sept. 7, 1861, in Roman, *Military Operations*, 1:477; R. E. Lee to G. W. Smith, Nov. 10, 1862, in *OR*, ser. 1, vol. 19, pt. 2, pp. 709–10.

8. T. Jordan to W. H. Fowle, July 7, 1861, in Roman, *Military Operations*, 1:129.

9. O. Latrobe to A. C. Haskell, Feb. 3, 1865, in *OR*, ser. 1, vol. 46, pt. 2, p. 1195; C. S. Venable to R. S. Ewell, Feb. 22, 1864, in Dowdey and Manarin, eds., *Wartime Papers*, 675; S. L. Stuart to W. J. Hawks, Nov. 8 and 12, 1862, book 50, Leigh Collection.

10. H. B. McClellan to R. J. Beckham, June 6, 1863, book 50, Leigh Collection; A. S. Pendleton to J. C. Breckinridge, Aug. 9, 1864, and HQs II Corps G.O. #26, Apr. 13, 1863, in *OR*, ser. 1, vol. 25, pt. 2, pp. 992, 719–20; W. H. C. Whiting to W. Hampton, Mar. 7, 1862, in *OR*, ser. 1, 5:532; Boteler, "Stonewall Jackson," 40:175–76; G. M. Sorrel to C. M. Wilcox, Aug. 9, 1862, and others, in *OR*, ser. 1, vol. 51, pt. 2, pp. 604–6; Thomas J. Jackson, "Letter to Colonel Munford, June 10, 1862," in *Southern Historical Society Papers*, 7:530–31.

11. Roman, *Military Operations*, 1:84, 82, 121–25.

12. A&IGO G.O. #17, Mar. 27, 1862, in *OR*, ser. 1, 1:1028; W. N. Pendleton to wife, May 17, 1864, in Susan Pendleton Lee, ed., *Memoirs*, 332.

13. See Wert, "The Tycoon," 18; R. E. Lee to A. R. Lawton, Jan. 30, 1864, in Dowdey and Manarin, eds., *Wartime Papers*, 664–65; R. E. Lee to J. Davis, June 16, 1864 in Freeman, ed., *Lee's Dispatches*, 46–47.

14. Confederate States of America War Department, *Regulations, 1863*, 47; Von Borcke, *Memoirs*, 207; L. T. Brien to W. H. Taylor, Aug. 22, 1864, in *OR*, ser. 1, vol. 51, pt. 2, p. 1036; C. Marshall to J. C. Breckinridge, May 20, 1864, in *OR*, ser. 1, vol. 37, pt. 1, p. 744; See, for example, letters from ANV headquarters to Brig. Gen. Grimes in Grimes, *Extracts*, 91, 94.

15. Howard, *Recollections*, 295; see for example ANV Arty. movement order, Apr. 7, 1865, in Wise, *Long Arm of Lee*, 2:953–54.

16. For examples of eleven endorsements, see HQ 1st Regt. Tennessee Volunteers, application for transfer, Feb. 2, 1863, book 2, item 22, Leigh Collection.

17. W. H. Taylor endorsement on P. T. Vaughn to W. H. Taylor, Oct. 24, 1864, Book 50, Leigh Collection.

18. W. H. Taylor endorsement on W. N. Pendleton to W. H. Taylor, Mar. 17, 1865, in *OR*, ser. 1, vol. 46, pt. 3, p. 1320; N. E. Fitzhugh to W. Hampton, Nov. 28, 1862, in *OR*, ser. 1, vol. 51, pt. 2, p. 653.

19. Confederate States of America War Department, *Regulations, 1863*, 8–9; R. E. Lee to S. Cooper, Jan. 26, 1865, in *OR*, ser. 1, vol. 46, pt. 2, p. 1140; J. Davis to P. G. T. Beauregard, Nov. 9, 1861, and letters of the same date to Johnston and Smith in *OR*, ser. 1, 5:944; Joseph E. Johnston, "Letter to MG Huger, May 31, 1862," in *Southern Historical Society Papers*, 10:274; P. G. T. Beauregard to R. S. Ewell, July 26, 1861, in *OR*, ser. 1, vol. 46, pt. 2, p. 199; Maurice, ed., *An Aide-de-Camp of Lee*, 270; Owen, *In Camp and Battle*, 127; see R. E. Lee to R. H. Anderson, June 29, 1864, and H. B. McClellan to R. J. Beckham,

June 6, 1863, book 50, Leigh Collection; John Daniel Imboden, "Stonewall Jackson in the Shenandoah," *Century Magazine* 30 (June 1885): 290.

20. A&IGO G.O. #3, Jan. 9, 1863, in *OR*, ser. 4, 2:308; A&IGO G.O.s #78 and #10, Oct. 11, 1864, and Mar. 17, 1865, in ibid., ser. 4, 3:720–21, 1152.

21. Roman, *Military Operations*, 84; Alexander, *Military Memoirs*, 49; Sorrel, *Recollections*, 51–52, 32; Long, *Memoirs*, 204; William Willis Blackford, *War Years*, 204–5; McClellan, *Life and Campaigns*, 365; T. J. Goree to M. F. G. Kitrell, Aug. 23, 1861, in Goree, ed., *Thomas Jewitt Goree Letters*, 1:73; Maurice, ed., *An Aide-de-Camp of Lee*, 278; Johnston, "Responsibilities," 1:246; C. S. V.[enable] endorsement to telegram from R. E. Lee to P. G. T. Beauregard, May 30, 1864, in Venable, "General Lee," 2:244.

22. Walter Herron Taylor, *Four Years*, 76; William Willis Blackford, *War Years*, 111; Von Borcke, *Memoirs*, 255; Raleigh E. Colston, "Lee's Knowledge of Hooker's Movements," in *Battles and Leaders*, ed. Johnson and Buel, 3:233; James Power Smith, "With Stonewall Jackson," 43:23; McClellan, *Life and Campaigns*, 316–17.

23. Confederate States of America War Department, *Regulations, 1863*, 45–47.

24. Army of the Potomac [Confederate] S.O. #95, Aug. 8, 1861, in Luhn, ed., *C.S. Army Special Orders,* 3 vols. (Newville, Pa.: Civil War Source Book Publishers, 1992) 2:178; A&IGO S.O.s #51 and #254, Mar. 5, 1862, and Dec. 4, 1861, in *OR*, ser. 4, 1:97, 776; ANV S.O. #71 extract, Sept. 10, 1864, book 50, Leigh Collection; ANV S.O. #191, Sept. 9, 1862, in *OR*, ser. 1, vol. 19, pt. 2, pp. 603–4; HQ Hampton's Cav. Bde. S.O.s #12 and #16, May 14, 1863, and May 20, 1863, book 41, Leigh Collection.

25. A&IGO G.O.s #43, #9, and #9 [duplicate], June 13, 1862, June 6, 1861, and June 25, 1861, in *OR*, ser. 4, 1:1151, 369–73, 398–400; Virginia Army HQ G.O. #15, May 13, 1861, and HQ Virginia State Forces G.O.s #4, #25, #27, and #29, Apr. 29, 1861, June 8, 1861, June 17, 1861, and June 24, 1861, in Luhn, ed., *C.S. Army General Orders*, 1:29, 28, 32; A&IGO G.O. #14, Oct. 21, 1861, in Luhn, ed., *C.S. Army General Orders*, 1:18–19; A&IGO G.O.s #17 and #41, Nov. 7, 1861, and May 31, 1862, in *OR*, ser. 4, 1:723, 1139; A&IGO G.O.s #48 and #72, July 11, 1862, and Sept. 29, 1862, in *OR*, ser. 4, 2:3–4, 98.

26. See, for example, A&IGO G.O. #12, Mar. 10, 1862, in *OR*, ser. 4, 1:984; HQ Dept. of Northern Virginia G.O. #68, June 14, 1862, in *OR*, ser. 1, vol. 2, pt. 3, p. 599; A&IGO G.O.s #64 and #20, Sept. 8, 1862, and Feb. 19, 1863, in *OR*, ser. 4, 2:78, 406; L. Guild to S. P. Moore, June 6, 1863, in *OR*, ser. 1, vol. 27, pt. 3, p. 864.

27. A&IGO G.O.s #1, #38, and #40, Jan. 1, 1862, May 22, 1862, and May 29, 1862, in *OR*, ser. 4, 1:825, 1126–27, 1131–33; A&IGO G.O. #93, Nov. 22, 1862, in *OR*, ser. 4, 2:198–207; A&IGO G.O.s #29 and #53, Mar. 25, 1864, and June 17, 1864, in *OR*, ser. 4, 3:189–94, 491–99; A&IGO G.O. #1, Jan. 1, 1862, in *OR*, ser. 1, 5:1016–17, or A&IGO G.O.s #37 and #82, Apr. 6, 1863, and Nov. 3, 1862, in *OR*, ser. 4, 2:469–72, 160–68.

28. HQ Army of the Potomac [Confederate] G.O. #47, Oct. 22, 1861, and HQ 1st Corps, Army of the Potomac G.O. #64, Oct. 23, 1861, in *OR*, ser. 1, 5:348; HQ I Corps G.O. #53, Dec. 1862, in *OR*, ser. 1, vol. 51, pt. 2, p. 663; ANV G.O. #59, May 7, 1863, in *OR*, ser. 1, vol. 25, pt. 1, p. 805; E. Blackford to mother, [May 4, 1863], book 33, Leigh Collection; ANV G.O. #61, May 11, 1863, in *OR*, ser. 1, vol. 25, pt. 2, p. 798.

29. HQ Cav. Div. G.O. #17, May 20, 1863, in HQ Hampton's Cav. Bde. Orders Book, book 41, Leigh Collection.

30. Confederate States of America War Department, *Regulations, 1863*, 73, 51.

31. A&IGO G.O. #76, June 5, 1863, in *OR*, ser. 4, 2:579.

32. S. Cooper to J. E. Johnston, Aug. 17, 1861, in ibid., ser. 1, vol. 51, pt. 2, p. 240; reports of General Joseph E. Johnston of operations from May 23 to Jul. 22 [1861], Oct. 14, 1861, in *OR*, ser. 1, 2:470–79; *OR*, ser. 1, vol. 11, pt. 1, pp. 564–606, 933–94.

33. T. J. Jackson to S. Cooper, May 26, 1862, and T. J. Jackson to R. H. Chilton, Apr. 10, 1863, in *OR*, ser. 1, vol. 12, pt. 1, pp. 701–10; R. E. Lee to S. Cooper, Jan. 26, 1863, in *OR*, ser. 1, 21:1113–14; R. E. Lee to S. Cooper, July 20, 1863, in Dowdey and Manarin, eds., *Wartime Papers*, 555.

34. Hotchkiss, *Make Me a Map*, 125; R. E. Lee to secretary of war [J. A. Seddon], Apr. 30, 1864, in *OR*, ser. 1, 33:1330–31.

35. Douglas, *I Rode with Stonewall*, 210; Henderson, *Stonewall Jackson*, 627, 123; report of Maj. Gen. Ambrose P. Hill, May 8, 1863, in *OR*, ser. 1, vol. 25, pt. 1, p. 885; Maurice, ed., *An Aide-de-Camp of Lee*, 178.

36. Maurice, ed., *An Aide-de-Camp of Lee*, 179–80.

37. David G. McIntosh, "Review of the *Gettysburg Campaign*," in *Southern Historical Society Papers*, 37:94–95; Maurice, ed., *An Aide-de-Camp of Lee*, 214–15; Hotchkiss, *Make Me a Map*, 108, 112, 115, 117, 119–27, 135; Boswell, "Diary," 34.

38. Gustavus W. Smith, "Two Days of Battle at Seven Pines (Fair Oaks)," in *Battles and Leaders*, ed. Johnson and Buel, 2:243; Hotchkiss, *Make Me a Map*, 124–25.

39. Maurice, ed., *An Aide-de-Camp of Lee*, 180–81, 178.

40. B. Huger to J. E. Johnston, Sept. 20, 1862, and B. Huger to J. Davis, Sept. 21, 1862, in *OR*, ser. 1, vol. 11, pt. 1, pp. 935–38; R. Ransom to R. H. Chilton, Dec. 17, 1862, in *OR*, ser. 1, 21:1124; J. Longstreet to R. Ransom, Dec. 19, 1862, in *OR*, ser. 1, 21:1125.

41. Douglas, *I Rode with Stonewall*, 210–11; J. A. Englehard to "Friend Ruf," Aug. 28, 1864, Wiley Sword Collection, U.S. Army Military History Institute, Carlisle Barracks, Pa.

Chapter 10—The Staff in Battle: Intelligence and Combat Functions

1. Confederate States of America War Department, *Regulations, 1863*, 67; Dennis Hart Mahan, *An Elementary Treatise on Advanced-Guard, Out-Post*

and Detachment Service of Troops, and the Manner of Posting and Handling Them in the Presence of an Enemy (New York: John Wiley, 1861), 105–16.

2. T. T. Munford to W. Hampton, Mar. 23, 1901, quoted in Alexander, *Fighting for the Confederacy*, 149; T. J. Jackson to R. S. Ewell, Apr. 10, 1862, in *OR*, ser. 1, vol. 12, pt. 3, pp. 845, 848–69, and passim; R. E. Lee to J. E. B. Stuart, May 31, 1863, in *OR*, ser. 1, vol. 12, pt. 2, p. 844; see R. E. Lee to J. Davis, Nov. 19, 1862, in *OR*, ser. 1, 21:1021; R. E. Lee to J. Davis, July 1, 1864, in Freeman, ed., *Lee's Dispatches*, 265–67, and passim, esp. 272, 279, 283, 362, and 363; R. E. Lee to J. Davis, July 12, 1864, in Freeman, ed., *Lee's Dispatches*, 284.

3. Alexander, *Fighting for the Confederacy*, 69; Theodore Stanford Garnett, *Riding with Stuart*, 38; C. M. Smith to J. E. B. Stuart, Apr. 10, 1864, in Trout, *They Followed the Plume*, 296–97; R. E. Lee to J. Davis, Apr. 4, 1863, and R. E. Lee to J. A. Seddon, Apr. 28, 1863, in *OR*, ser. 1, vol. 25, pt. 2, pp. 103–4, 646.

4. R. H. Anderson to W. H. Taylor, Feb. 24, 1863, in *OR*, ser. 1, vol. 25, pt. 2, p. 641.

5. Sorrel, *Recollections*, 10; Alexander, *Fighting for the Confederacy*, 75; see R. E. Lee to J. Davis, Dec. 8, 1862, and Jan. 21, 1863, in *OR*, ser. 1, 21:1052–54, 1103–4.

6. Alexander, *Fighting for the Confederacy*, 140; Sorrel, *Recollections*, 126; R. E. Lee to J. A. Early, Feb. 15, 1864, and R. E. Lee to J. D. Imboden, Mar. 19, 1864, in *OR*, ser. 1, 33:1174, 1233; Frederick M. Colston, "Recollections," 38:14.

7. Alexander, *Fighting for the Confederacy*, 115–17; Alexander, *Military Memoirs*, 172.

8. Alexander, *Military Memoirs*, 189.

9. Ibid., 22, 161.

10. Theodore Stanford Garnett, *Riding with Stuart*, 65; William Willis Blackford, *War Years*, 82–83, 192–93; Von Borcke, *Memoirs*, 151–52; Hotchkiss, *Make Me a Map*, 34.

11. R. E. Lee to J. Davis, Feb. 26, 1863, in *OR*, ser. 1, vol. 25, pt. 2, p. 642.

12. Beauregard, "First Battle of Bull Run," 1:197; Roman, *Military Operations*, 1:75; Alexander, *Fighting for the Confederacy*, 69; Alexander, *Military Memoirs*, 55.

13. Alexander, *Fighting for the Confederacy*, 68–69, 70–71.

14. R. E. Lee to J. A. Seddon, Mar. 29, 1863, in *OR*, ser. 1, vol. 25, pt. 2, p. 691.

15. Jay Luvaas, "Lee: A General without Intelligence," in *Intelligence and Military Operations*, ed. Michael I. Handel (Portland, Oreg.: Frank Cass, 1990), 124–25, 133.

16. W. Gordon McCabe, "Major Andrew Reid Venable, Jr.," in *Southern Historical Society Papers*, 37:63; Beauregard, "First Battle of Bull Run," 1:211, 214–16; report on the Battle of Bull Run, Aug. 25, 1861, in Roman, *Military Operations*, 1:446; R. E. Lee to S. Cooper, Sept. 21, 1863, in *OR*, ser. 1, vol. 25,

pt. 1, pp. 804–5; W. H. Taylor to Bettie Saunders, Aug. 15, 1864, in Tower, ed., *Lee's Adjutant*, 87.

17. Alexander, *Military Memoirs*, 92, 140; Haskell, *Haskell Memoirs*, 31–34; Douglas, *I Rode with Stonewall*, 137; J. E. B. Stuart to R. H. Chilton, Feb. 28, 1863, in *OR*, ser. 1, vol. 12, pt. 2, p. 738; John William Jones, "Reminiscences of the Army of Northern Virginia, Paper no. 9," in *Southern Historical Society Papers*, 10:89; Stiles, *Four Years*, 66.

18. Cooke, *Outlines*, 352–56; Howard, *Recollections*, 140–45.

19. Alexander, *Fighting for the Confederacy*, 142–43; Hotchkiss, *Make Me a Map*, 82–83; Douglas, *I Rode with Stonewall*, 221; Fremantle, *Three Months*, 258.

20. William Willis Blackford, *War Years*, 149; Von Borcke, *Memoirs*, 96–98; Theodore Stanford Garnett, *Riding with Stuart*, 23; Alexander, *Fighting for the Confederacy*, 265; Owen, *In Camp and Battle*, 150.

21. Report of Brig. Gen. William N. Pendleton of operations Aug. 20–Sept. 24 [1862], Sept. 24, 1862, *OR*, ser. 1, vol. 19, pt. 1, p. 832.

22. Reports of Brig. Gen. Alfred Iverson, July 17, 1863, in *OR*, ser. 1, vol. 27, pt. 2, p. 579.

23. Alexander, *Military Memoirs*, 162; William Willis Blackford, *War Years*, 78–80; Von Borcke, *Memoirs*, 216; McClellan, *Life and Campaigns*, 194; Douglas, *I Rode with Stonewall*, 221; James Power Smith, "Stonewall Jackson's Last Battle," 3:209; portion of Campbell Brown manuscript from Tennessee Historical Commission files, 73, 75, Box 6 (Confederate Commanders and Staffs), Brake Collection; Theodore Stanford Garnett, *Riding with Stuart*, 24; Jubal Anderson Early, *Memoir*, 18–19; Rhea, *Battle of the Wilderness*, 423, 182.

24. Alexander, *Fighting for the Confederacy*, 236; Alexander, *Military Memoirs*, 345.

25. A&IGO circular, June 4, 1864, in *OR*, ser. 4, 3:469.

26. Wert, "The Tycoon," 16; Scheibert, *Seven Months*, n. 75.

27. William Willis Blackford, *War Years*, 102; Theodore Stanford Garnett, *Riding with Stuart*, 63; Alexander, *Military Memoirs*, 34; See, for example, in Army of the Potomac, T. Lyman to family, May 15, 16, 1864, in Theodore Lyman, *With Grant and Meade from the Wilderness to Appomattox*, ed. George R. Agassiz; originally published as *Meade's Headquarters, 1863–1865* (1922; reprint, Lincoln: University of Nebraska Press, 1994), 91, 93; Douglas, *I Rode with Stonewall*, 169.

28. S. W. Ferguson to P. G. T. Beauregard, Aug. 1, 1861, in *OR*, ser. 1, vol. 51, pt. 2, p. 212; report of Maj. Gen. James Longstreet, May 16, 1862, in *OR*, ser. 1, vol. 11, pt. 1, p. 568; Douglas, *I Rode with Stonewall*, 86, 140; Von Borcke, *Memoirs*, 101; Theodore Stanford Garnett, *Riding with Stuart*, 77–78.

29. Evans, *Intrepid Warrior*, 137–38; John Michael Priest, *Before Antietam: The Battle for South Mountain* (Shippensburg, Pa.: White Mane Publishing Co., 1992), 252–53.

30. Douglas, *I Rode with Stonewall*, 249–50.

31. McKim, *Soldier's Recollections*, 196; Longstreet, *From Manassas to Appomattox*, 393–95; Gill, *Reminiscences*, 100.

32. Andrew A. Humphreys, *The Campaign in Virginia of '64 and '65* (New York: Charles Scribner's Sons, 1908), 12; report of Capt. J. K. Boswell of operations Aug. 13–28 [1862], Feb. 12, 1863, in *OR*, ser. 1, vol. 12, pt. 2, pp. 648–50.

33. HQ Army of the Potomac [Confederate] unnumbered S.O., July 20, 1861, in *OR*, ser. 1, 2:479–80; William Willis Blackford, *War Years*, 27; Jubal Anderson Early, *Lieutenant General Jubal Anderson Early*, 17–20; Alexander, *Military Memoirs*, 83–84.

34. Maurice, ed., *An Aide-de-Camp of Lee*, xxvi, 86; HQ Dept. of Northern Virginia G.O. #75, June 24, 1862, in Dowdey and Manarin, eds., *Wartime Papers*, 198–200; Alexander, *Fighting for the Confederacy*, 93; Imboden, "Confederate Retreat," 3:422; see ANV G.O. #74, July 4, 1863, in Dowdey and Manarin, eds., *Wartime Papers*, 539–40.

35. ANV S.O. #185, Aug. 19, 1862, in ibid., 259–60; ANV S.O. #121, Apr. 30, 1863, in *OR*, ser. 1, vol. 25, pt. 762.

36. Wert, "The Tycoon," 15; see Walter Herron Taylor, *Four Years*, 97–98, 103–9, and Isaac Trimble, "The Campaign and Battle of Gettysburg," *Confederate Veteran* 25 (1917):211; Wise, *Long Arm of Lee*, 1:225; R. E. Lee to L. McLaws, Apr. 29, 1863, and R. E. Lee to R. H. Anderson, Apr. 29 and Apr. 30, 1863, in Dowdey and Manarin, eds., *Wartime Papers*, 444, 445, 446, and 447–48.

37. Wert, *General James Longstreet*, 188, 379; G. M. Sorrel to R. H. Anderson, Nov. 19, 1862, in *OR*, ser. 1, vol. 51, pt. 2, p. 649.

38. Henderson, *Stonewall Jackson*, 363; Douglas, *I Rode with Stonewall*, 59; Robertson, *General A. P. Hill*, 108; Jones, "The Old Virginia Town," 19; Bean, *Stonewall's Man*, 88.

39. R. Toombs to A. Coward, July 7, 1862, in *OR*, ser. 1, vol. 11, pt. 2, p. 698; Daly, *Alexander Cheves Haskell*, 100; Howard, *Recollections*, 271, 273; Von Borcke, *Memoirs*, 111–12, 114.

40. Pierre Gustave Toutant Beauregard, *A Commentary on the Campaign and Battle of Manassas of July, 1861. Together with a Summary of the Art of War* (New York: G. P. Putnam's Sons, 1891), 44.

41. W. H. Taylor to Bettie Saunders, Apr. 3, 1864, and Aug. 15, 1864, in Tower, ed., *Lee's Adjutant*, 148, 182.

42. Alexander, *Military Memoirs*, 44.

43. Ibid., 36; Von Borcke, *Memoirs*, 86, 171; Douglas, *I Rode with Stonewall*, 175–76, 306, 296, 294; Caldwell, *History of a Brigade*, 105; Sorrel, *Recollections*, 202–3; Alexander, *Military Memoirs*, 505; "Obituary of Capt. Murray F. Taylor," *Confederate Veteran* 18 (Feb. 1910): 82; Stiles, *Four Years*, 280–83; Gill, *Reminiscences*, 113–14.

44. Alexander, *Military Memoirs*, 40, 570; J. E. B. Stuart to R. H. Chilton, Feb. 28, 1863, in *OR*, ser. 1, vol. 12, pt. 2, p. 735; Longstreet, *From Manassas to Appomattox*, 250; McKim, *Soldier's Recollections*, 151; Theodore Stanford

Garnett, *Riding with Stuart*, 20; Sheeran, *Confederate Chaplain*, 8–9; Long, *Memoirs*, 192; Hennessy, *Return to Bull Run*, 113.

45. A. R. Chisolm to P. G. T. Beauregard, Aug. 1, 1861, in *OR*, ser. 1, vol. 51, pt. 2, pp. 207–8.

46. S. W. Ferguson to P. G. T. Beauregard, Aug. 4, 1861, and J. Heyward to P. G. T. Beauregard, Aug. 10, 1861, in ibid., vol. 51, pt. 2, pp. 212, 227.

47. Confederate States of America War Department, *Regulations, 1863*, 73, 253; HQ Light Div. unnumbered G.O., June 24, 1862, in *OR*, ser. 1, vol. 11, pt. 3, p. 616; ANV G.O. #94, Aug. 11, 1862, in *OR*, ser. 1, vol. 12, pt. 3, p. 928; for medical planning, see Cunningham, *Doctors in Gray*, 113–16; Sorrel, *Recollections*, 90–93.

48. Imboden, "Confederate Retreat," 3:422; Cunningham, *Doctors in Gray*, 121; Hunter H. McGuire, "General T. J. ("Stonewall") Jackson," 25:101.

49. See report of Richard S. Ewell, 1863 [Gettysburg report], in *OR*, ser. 1, vol. 27, pt. 2, p. 451; S. G. Welch to wife, Sept. 3, 1862, in Welch, *Confederate Surgeon's Letters*, 23; McClellan, *Life and Campaigns*, 133; Von Borcke, *Memoirs*, 236.

50. Confederate States of America Ordnance Bureau, *Field Manual*, 141–42.

51. James M. Garnett, "Diary," 27:5–6; John William Jones, "Gen. A. P. Hill, Partial Sketch of His Thrilling Career," *Confederate Veteran* 1 (Aug. 1893): 235; McKim, *Soldier's Recollections*, 184–85.

52. Grady McWhiney and Perry D. Jamieson, *Attack and Die: Civil War Military Tactics and the Southern Heritage* (Tuscaloosa: University of Alabama Press, 1982), 143–69, 160; Wert, "The Tycoon," 14; Kenneth C. Allard, *Command and Control and the Common Defense* (New Haven: Yale University Press, 1990), 59.

53. S. W. Melton to J. A. Seddon, Nov. 11, 1863, in *OR*, ser. 4, 2:950.

BIBLIOGRAPHY

Published Works

Alexander, Edward Porter. *Fighting for the Confederacy: The Personal Recollections of General Edward Porter Alexander.* Edited by Gary W. Gallagher. Chapel Hill: University of North Carolina Press, 1989.
————. *Military Memoirs of a Confederate.* 1907. Reprint, with introduction by Gary W. Gallagher, New York: Da Capo Press, 1993.
Allan, William. *The Army of Northern Virginia in 1862.* 1892. Reprint, with introduction by John C. Ropes, Dayton, Ohio: Press of Morningside Bookshop, 1984.
Allard, Kenneth C. *Command and Control and the Common Defense.* New Haven: Yale University Press, 1990.
Bean, William Gleason. *Stonewall's Man: Sandie Pendleton.* Chapel Hill: University of North Carolina Press, 1959.
Beauregard, Pierre Gustave Toutant. *A Commentary on the Campaign and Battle of Manassas of July, 1861. Together with a Summary of the Art of War.* New York: G. P. Putnam's Sons, 1891.
Betts, Alexander Davis. *Experiences of a Confederate Chaplain, 1861–1864, by Rev. A. D. Betts, Chaplain 30th N.C. Troops.* Edited by W. A. Betts. 190?. Reprint, Ann Arbor, Mich.: University Microfilms, 1973.
Blackford, Susan Leigh Colton, comp. *Letters from Lee's Army; or Memoirs of Life in and out of the Army in Virginia during the War between the States.* Edited and abridged by Charles M. Blackford III. 1894–96. Reprint, New York: C. Scribner's Sons, 1947.
Blackford, William Willis. *War Years with Jeb Stuart.* New York: C. Scribner's Sons, 1945.
Boswell, James Keith. "The Diary of a Confederate Staff Officer." *Civil War Times Illustrated* 15 (April 1976): 30–38.
Caldwell, James Fitz John. *The History of a Brigade of South Carolinians Known First as Gregg's and Subsequently as McGowan's Brigade.* 1866. Reprint, Marietta, Ga.: Continental Book Co., 1951.

Bibliography

Chamberlayne, John Hampden. *Ham Chamberlayne—Virginian: Letters and Papers of an Artillery Officer in the War for Southern Independence, 1861–1865.* Edited by Churchill Gibson Chamberlayne. Richmond, Va.: Press of the Dietz Printing Co., 1932.

Chisolm, Julian John. *A Manual of Military Surgery for the Use of Surgeons in the Confederate States Army: With an Appendix of the Rules and Regulations of the Medical Department of the Confederate States Army.* 1861. Reprint, with introduction by Ira M. Rutkow, American Civil War Surgery Series, no. 4, San Francisco: Norman Publishing, 1989.

Coddington, Edwin B. *The Gettysburg Campaign: A Study in Command.* New York: Charles Scribner's Sons, 1968.

Confederate States of America Ordnance Bureau. *The Field Manual for Use of the Officers on Ordnance Duty.* 1862. Reprint, Ardentsville, Pa.: D. S. Thomas, 1984.

Confederate States of America War Department. *Army Regulations Adopted for the Use of the Army of the Confederate States.* Atlanta: Gaulding and Whitaker "Intelligences" Press, 1861.

———. *Regulations for the Army of the Confederate States, 1862.* Richmond, Va.: J. W. Randolph, 1862.

———. *Regulations for the Army of the Confederate States, 1863. Corrected and Enlarged with Revised Index (the Only Correct Copy).* 1863. Reprint, Harrisburg, Pa.: National Historical Society, 1980.

———. *Regulations for the Army of the Confederate States, 1864. Third and Only Correct Edition, in Which Are Corrected over 3,000 Important Errors Contained in the Edition Published by West and Johnson.* Richmond, Va.: J. W. Randolph, 1864.

———. *Regulations for the Army of the Confederate States for the Quartermaster's Department Including the Pay Branch Thereof.* Richmond, Va.: Ritchie and Dunnavant, 1862.

Connolly, Peter. *Greece and Rome at War.* Englewood Cliffs, N.J.: Prentice-Hall, 1981.

Cooke, John Esten. *Outlines from the Outpost.* Edited by Richard Harwell. Chicago: R. R. Donnelley and Sons, 1961.

———. *Wearing of the Gray: Being Personal Portraits, Scenes, and Adventures of the War.* 1867. Reprint, Gaithersburg, Md.: Olde Soldier Books, 1988.

Craighill, Edward A. *Confederate Surgeon: The Personal Recollections of E. A. Craighill.* Edited by Peter W. Houck. Lynchburg, Va.: H. E. Howard, 1989.

Cunningham, Horace Herndon. *Doctors in Gray: The Confederate Medical Service.* Baton Rouge: Louisiana State University Press, 1958.

Cutrer, Thomas W., ed. *Longstreet's Aide: The Civil War Letters of Thomas J. Goree.* Charlottesville: University Press of Virginia, 1995.

Dabney, Robert Lewis. *Life and Campaigns of Lieut.-Gen. Thomas J. Jackson.* New York: Blelock and Co., 1866.

Daly, Louise Haskell. *Alexander Cheves Haskell, the Portrait of a Man.* 1934. Reprint, with introduction by Lee A. Wallace Jr., Wilmington, N.C.: Broadfoot Publishing Co., 1989.

Davis, Nicholas A. *The Campaign from Texas to Maryland with the Battle of Fredericksburg.* 1863. Reprint, Austin, Tex.: Steck Co., 1961.

Dawson, Francis W. *Reminiscences of Confederate Service, 1861–1865.* 1882. Reprint, edited with introduction by Bell I. Wiley, Library of Southern Civilization Series, Lewis P. Simpson, editor, Baton Rouge: Louisiana State University Press, 1980.

Douglas, Henry Kyd. *I Rode with Stonewall.* Chapel Hill: University of North Carolina Press, 1940.

Dowdey, Clifford, and Louis H. Manarin, eds. *The Wartime Papers of R. E. Lee.* Boston: Little, Brown, and Co., 1961.

Early, John Cabell. "A Southern Boy's Experience at Gettysburg." *Journal of the Military Service Institution* 43 (January–February 1911): 415–23.

Early, Jubal Anderson. *Lieutenant General Jubal Anderson Early: Autobiographical Sketch and Narrative of the War between the States.* Philadelphia: J. B. Lippincott Co., 1912.

———. *A Memoir of the Last Year of the War for Independence in the Confederate States of America.* Lynchburg, Va.: C. W. Button, 1867.

Evans, Clement Anselm. *Intrepid Warrior: Clement Anselm Evans, Confederate General from Georgia.* Compiled and edited by Robert Grier Stephens Jr. Dayton, Ohio: Morningside Bookshop, 1992.

Formento, Felix, Jr. *Notes and Observations on Army Surgery.* 1863. Reprint, American Civil War Surgery Series, no. 9, San Francisco: Norman Publishing, 1990.

Freeman, Douglas Southall, ed. *Lee's Dispatches to Jefferson Davis, 1862–1865. From the private collection of Jones de Renne.* New York: G. P. Putnam's Sons, 1915, 1957.

———. *Lee's Lieutenants: A Study in Command.* 3 vols. Charles Scribner's Sons, 1942, 1970.

Fremantle, Arthur James Lyon. *Three Months in the Southern States, April–June 1863.* New York: John Bradburn, 1864.

Fuller, John Frederick Charles. *The Generalship of Alexander the Great.* 1906. Reprint, New York: Da Capo Press, 1993.

Gabriel, Richard A., and Karen S. Metz. *From Sumer to Rome: The Military Capabilities of Ancient Armies.* Contributions in Military Studies, no. 108. New York: Greenwood Press, 1991.

Gaddy, David Winfred. "William Norris and the Confederate Signal and Secret Service." *Maryland Historical Magazine* 70 (summer 1975): 167–88.

Gallagher, Gary W. *Stephen Dodson Ramseur, Lee's Gallant General.* Chapel Hill: University of North Carolina Press, 1985.

Gallaher, DeWitt Clinton. *A Diary Depicting the Experiences of DeWitt Clinton Gallaher in the War between the States while Serving in the Confederate Army.* [Charleston, W.Va.?]: privately published, [1945?].

Garnett, Theodore Stanford. *Riding with Stuart: Reminiscences of an Aide-de-Camp*. Edited by Robert J. Trout. Shippensburg, Pa.: White Mane Publishing Co., 1995.

Georgia. *Regulations for the Commissariat of the State of Georgia, 1861*. Milledgeville, Ga.: Boughton, Nisbet, and Barnes, State Printers, 1861.

———. *Regulations for the Quartermaster's Department of the State of Georgia, 1861*. Milledgeville, Ga.: Boughton, Nisbet, and Barnes, State Printers, 1861.

Gilham, William. *Manual of Instruction for the Volunteers and Militia of the Confederate States*. Richmond, Va.: West and Johnston, 1862.

Gill, John. *Reminiscences of Four Years as a Private Soldier in the Confederate Army, 1861–1865*. Baltimore: Sun Printing Office, 1904.

Goff, Richard D. *Confederate Supply*. Durham, N.C.: Duke University Press, 1969.

Goree, Langston James, ed. *The Thomas Jewitt Goree Letters*. Volume I. *The Civil War Correspondence*. Bryan, Tex.: Family History Foundation, 1981.

Grant, Ulysses Simpson. *The Personal Memoirs of U. S. Grant*. Edited with notes by E. B. Long. 1952. Reprint, with introduction by William S. McFeely, New York: Da Capo Press, 1982.

Grimes, Bryan. *Extracts of Letters of Major-General Bryan Grimes to His Wife*. Compiled by Pulaski Cowper. 1884. Reprint, edited by Gary W. Gallagher, Wilmington, N.C.: Broadfoot Publishing Co., 1986.

Hardee, William Joseph. *Rifle and Infantry Tactics; for the Exercise and Manoeuvres of Troops when Acting as Light Infantry or Riflemen*. Philadelphia: J. B. Lippincott, 1860.

Haskell, John Cheves. *The Haskell Memoirs*. Edited by Gilbert E. Govan and James W. Livingood. New York: Putnam, 1960.

Henderson, G. F. R. *Stonewall Jackson and the American Civil War*. Introduction by Field Marshal Viscount Wolseley. 1898. Reprint, with preface by Walter Bedell Smith, New York: David McKay Co., 1961.

Hennessy, John, Jr. *Return to Bull Run: The Campaign and Battle of Second Manassas*. New York: Simon and Schuster, 1994.

Herzog, Chaim, and Mordechai Gichon. *Battles of the Bible*. New York: Random House, 1978.

Heth, Henry. *The Memoirs of Henry Heth*. Edited by James L. Morrison Jr. Contributions in Military History, no. 6. Westport, Conn.: Greenwood Press, 1974.

Hittle, James Donald. *The Military Staff: Its History and Development*. 3d ed. Harrisburg, Pa.: Stackpole Co., 1961.

Hotchkiss, Jedediah. *Make Me a Map of the Valley: The Civil War Journal of Stonewall Jackson's Topographer*. Edited by Archie P. McDonald. Dallas, Tex.: Southern Methodist University Press, 1973.

Howard, McHenry. *Recollections of a Maryland Confederate Soldier and Staff Officer*. 1914. Reprint, Dayton, Ohio: Morningside Bookshop, 1975.

Humphreys, Andrew A. *The Campaign in Virginia of '64 and '65.* New York: Charles Scribner's Sons, 1908.

Imboden, John Daniel. "Stonewall Jackson in the Shenandoah." *Century Magazine* 30 (June 1885): 290.

Johnson, Robert Underwood, and Clarence Clough Buel, eds. *Battles and Leaders of the Civil War.* 4 vols. New York: Century Co., 1887.

Joinville, François Ferdinand Philippe, Prince de. *The Army of the Potomac, Its Organization, Its Commander, and Its Campaign.* Translated by William Henry Hurlburt. New York: Anson D. F. Randolph, 1862.

Jones, John William. *Christ in the Camp, or Religion in Lee's Army.* Richmond, Va.: B. F. Johnson and Co., 1887.

———. "Gen. A. P. Hill, Partial Sketch of His Thrilling Career." *Confederate Veteran* 1 (August 1893): 233–36.

———. "The Old Virginia Town, Lexington." *Confederate Veteran* 1 (January 1893): 18–20.

———. *Personal Reminiscences of General Robert E. Lee.* 1874. Richmond, Va.: U.S. Historical Society Press, 1989.

Keegan, John. *The Mask of Command.* New York: Penguin Books, 1988.

Kinsolving, Roberta Cary Corbin. "Stonewall Jackson in Winter Quarters: Memories of Moss Neck in the Winter of 1862–63." *Confederate Veteran* 20 (January 1912): 24–26.

Lee, Charles Henry. *Judge Advocate's Vade Mecum.* 2d ed. Richmond, Va.: West and Johnston, 1864.

Lee, Robert E., [Jr.]. *Recollections and Letters of General Robert E. Lee.* Introduction by Gamaliel Broadfoot. Garden City, N.Y.: Garden City Publishing Co., 1924.

Lee, Susan Pendleton, ed. *Memoirs of William Nelson Pendleton, D.D.* 1893. Reprint, Harrisonburg, Va.: Sprinkle Publications, 1991.

Long, Armistead Lindsay. *Memoirs of Robert E. Lee: His Military and Personal History.* New York: J. M. Stoddard and Co., 1887.

Longstreet, James. *From Manassas to Appomattox: Memoirs of the Civil War in America.* Philadelphia: J. B. Lippincott Co., 1896.

Luhn, Edgar Ray, Jr., ed. *Luhn's Edition, C.S. Army General Orders.* Newville, Pa.: Civil War Source Book Publishers, 1992.

———. *Luhn's Edition, C. S. Army Special Orders.* 3 vols. Newville, Pa.: Civil War Source Book Publishers, 1992.

Luvaas, Jay. "Lee: A General without Intelligence." In *Intelligence and Military Operations,* edited by Michael I. Handel. Portland, Oreg.: Frank Cass, 1990.

———. *The Military Legacy of the Civil War: The European Inheritance.* 1959. Reprint, with new introduction by the author, Lawrence: University of Kansas Press, 1988.

———. "The Role of Intelligence in the Chancellorsville Campaign, April–May 1863." In *Intelligence and Military Operations,* edited by Michael I. Handel. Portland, Oreg.: Frank Cass, 1990.

Lyman, Theodore. *With Grant and Meade from the Wilderness to Appomattox*. Edited by George R. Agassiz. Originally published as *Meade's Headquarters, 1863–1865*. 1922. Reprint, Lincoln: University of Nebraska Press, 1994.

Mahan, Dennis Hart. *An Elementary Treatise on Advanced-Guard, Out-Post and Detachment Service of Troops and the Manner of Handling Them in the Presence of an Enemy*. New York: John Wiley, 1861.

———. *Summary of the Course of Permanent Fortifications and of the Attack and Defence of Permanent Works for the Use of the Cadets of the U.S. Military Academy*. Richmond, Va.: West and Johnston, 1863.

———. *A Treatise on Field Fortifications: Containing Instructions on the Methods of Laying out, Constructing, Defending, and Attacking Intrenchments: With the General Outlines Also of the Arrangement, the Attack, and Defence of Permanent Fortifications*. 3d ed., rev. and enl. New York: John Wiley, 1862.

Matthews, James M., ed. *Public Laws of the Confederate States of America*. Richmond, Va.: R. M. Smith, Printer to Congress, 1862–64.

———, ed. *Statutes at Large of the Provisional Government of the Confederate States of America*. Richmond, Va.: R. M. Smith, Printer to Congress, 1864.

Maurice, Sir Frederick, ed. *An Aide-de-Camp of Lee: Being the Papers of Colonel Charles Marshall, Sometime Aide-de-Camp, Military Secretary, and Assistant Adjutant General on the Staff of Robert E. Lee, 1862–1865*. Boston: Little, Brown, and Co., 1927.

McCaw, James B., ed. *Confederate States Medical and Surgical Journal*. Vol. 1, nos. 1–12, vol. 2, nos. 1–2 (1864–65). Reprint, in one volume with introduction by Ira M. Rutkow, American Civil War Medical Series, no. 12, San Francisco: Norman Publishing, 1992.

McClellan, Henry Brainerd. *The Life and Campaigns of J. E. B. Stuart, Commander of the Cavalry of the Army of Northern Virginia*. 1885. Reprint, Little Rock, Ark.: Eagle Press of Little Rock, 1987.

McKim, Randolph Harrison. *A Soldier's Recollections: Leaves from the Diary of a Young Confederate*. New York: Longmans, Green, and Co., 1910.

McWhiney, Grady, and Perry D. Jamieson. *Attack and Die: Civil War Military Tactics and the Southern Heritage*. Tuscaloosa: University of Alabama Press, 1982.

Moore, Jerrold Northrop. *Confederate Commissary General Lucius Bellinger Northrop and the Subsistence Bureau of the Southern Army*. Foreward by Lynda L. Crist. Shippensburg, Pa.: White Mane Publishing Co., 1996.

Neese, George Michael. *Three Years in the Confederate Horse Artillery*. New York: Neale Publishing Co., 1911.

Nichols, James Lynn. *Confederate Engineers*. Confederate Centennial Studies, no. 5, William Stanley Hoole, general editor. Tuscaloosa, Ala.: Confederate Publishing Co., 1957.

———. "Confederate Map Supply." *Military Engineer* 46 (January–February 1954): 28–32.

———. *The Confederate Quartermaster in the Trans-Mississippi*. Austin: University of Texas Press, 1964.

Nine, William G., and Ronald G. Wilson, eds. *The Appomattox Paroles*, April 9–15, 1865. 2d ed. Lynchburg, Va.: H. E. Howard, 1989.

"Obituary of Capt. Murray F. Taylor." *Confederate Veteran* 18 (February 1910): 82.

Owen, William Miller. *In Camp and Battle with the Washington Artillery of New Orleans*. 1885. Reprint, Gaithersburg, Md.: Butternut Press, 1982.

Paxton, Elisha Franklin. *The Civil War Letters of General Frank "Bull" Paxton, CSA, a Lieutenant of Lee and Jackson*. Edited by John Gallatin Paxton with introduction by Harold B. Simpson. Hillsboro, Tex.: Hill Junior College Press, 1978.

Pender, William Dorsey. *The General to His Lady: The Civil War Letters of William Dorsey Pender to Fanny Pender*. Edited by William Woods Hassler. 1965. Reprint, Gaithersburg, Md.: Ron R. Van Sickle Military Books, 1988.

Porcher, Francis Peyre. *Resources of the Southern Fields and Forests, Medical, Economical, and Agricultural: Being Also a Medical Botany of the Confederate States with Practical Information on the Useful Properties of Trees, Plants, and Shrubs*. 1863. Reprint, with introduction by Ira M. Rutkow, American Civil War Medical Series, no. 4, San Francisco: Norman Publishing, 1991.

Price, Channing. "Stuart's Chambersburg Raid, an Eyewitness Account." *Civil War Times Illustrated* 4 (January 1966): 8–15.

Priest, John Michael. *Before Antietam: The Battle for South Mountain*. Introduction by Edwin C. Bearss. Shippensburg, Pa.: White Mane Publishing Co., 1992.

Radley, Kenneth. *Rebel Watchdog: The Confederate Army Provost Guard*. Baton Rouge: Louisiana State University Press, 1989.

Ramsdell, Charles W. "Lee's Horse Supply, 1861–1865." *American Historical Review* 35 (1929–30): 758–77.

Ratchford, James W. *Some Reminiscences of Persons and Incidents of the Civil War*. 1909. Reprint, Austin, Tex.: Shoal Creek Publishers, 1971.

Rhea, Gordon C. *The Battle of the Wilderness, May 5–6, 1864*. Baton Rouge: Louisiana State University Press, 1994.

Richardson, James D., comp. *Messages and Papers of the Confederacy*. 2 vols. Nashville, Tenn.: U.S. Publishing Co., 1905.

Robertson, James I., Jr. *General A. P. Hill: The Story of a Confederate Warrior*. 1987. Reprint, New York: Vintage Books, 1992.

Roman, Alfred. *The Military Operations of General Beauregard in the War between the States, 1861 to 1865, Including a Brief Personal Sketch and a Narrative of His Service in the War with Mexico, 1846–48*. 2 vols. New York: Harper and Brothers, 1883.

Romero, Sidney J. *Religion in the Rebel Ranks*. Lanham, Md.: University Press of America, 1983.

Scheibert, Justus. *Seven Months in the Rebel States during the North American War, 1863*. Edited with introduction by William Stanley Hoole. Translated by Joseph C. Hayes. Confederate Centennial Studies, no. 9. Tuscaloosa, Ala.: Confederate Publishing Co., 1958.

Schuppert, M. *A Treatise on Gun-Shot Wounds*. 1861. Reprint, American Civil War Surgery Series, no. 9, San Francisco: Norman Publishing, 1990.

Seddon, James A. *Report of the Secretary of War, April 28, 1864*. Richmond, Va.: n.p., 1864.

Sheeran, James B. *Confederate Chaplain: A War Journal of Rev. James B. Sheeran, c.ss.r., 14th Louisiana, C.S.A*. Edited by Joseph T. Durkin. Preface by Bruce Catton. Milwaukee, Wis.: Bruce Publishing Co., 1960.

Sifakis, Stewart. *Compendium of the Confederate Armies: Alabama*. New York: Facts on File, 1992.

———. *Compendium of the Confederate Armies: Virginia*. New York: Facts on File, 1992.

Smith, Everard H. "Chambersburg: Anatomy of a Confederate Reprisal." *American Historical Review* 96 (April 1991): 432–55.

Sorrel, Gilbert Moxley. *Recollections of a Confederate Staff Officer*. Introduction by John M. Daniel. 1905. Reprint, with introduction by Neil C. Mangum, New York: Bantam Books, 1992.

Southern Historical Society Papers. 52 vols. 1867–1959. Reprint, Wilmington, N.C.: Broadfoot Publishing Co., 1990–92.

Stiles, Robert. *Four Years under Marse Robert*. New York: Neale Publishing Co., 1903.

"Stonewall's Commissary General, Maj. Wells J Hawks." *Confederate Veteran* 34 (August 1926): 286–87.

"Surgeons of the Confederacy: Dr. Hunter Holmes McGuire, of Virginia." *Confederate Veteran* 34 (April 1926): 140–43.

Taylor, Charles E. *Signal and Secret Service of the Confederate States*. 1903. Reprint, Harmans, Md.: Toomey Press, 1986.

Taylor, Walter Herron. *Four Years with General Lee*. 1878. Reprint, with introduction by James I. Robertson Jr., Bloomington: Indiana University Press, 1962.

———. *General Lee, His Campaigns in Virginia, 1861–1865*. Brooklyn, N.Y.: Press of Braunworth and Co., 1906.

Tower, R. Lockwood, ed. *Lee's Adjutant: The Wartime Letters of Walter Herron Taylor, 1862–1865*. Columbia: University of South Carolina Press, 1995.

Trimble, Isaac. "The Campaign and Battle of Gettysburg." *Confederate Veteran* 25 (May 1917): 209–13.

Trout, Robert J. *They Followed the Plume: The Story of J. E. B. Stuart and His Staff*. Mechanicsburg, Pa.: Stackpole Books, 1993.

Bibliography

U.S. Department of the Army. *Field Manual 101–5: Command and Control for Commanders and Staff.* Coordinating draft, July 1992. Washington, D.C.: Headquarters Department of the Army, 1992.

U.S. War Department. *List of Field Officers, Regiments, and Battalions in the Confederate States Army, 1861–1865.* 189?. Reprint, with introduction by John M. Carroll, Bryan, Tex.: J. M. Carroll and Co., 1983.

———. *List of Staff Officers of the Confederate Army, 1861–1865.* Washington, D.C.: U.S. Government Printing Office, 1891.

———. *The War of the Rebellion: A Compilation of the Records of the Union and Confederate Armies.* 128 parts in 70 vols. 1880–1901. Reprint, Harrisburg, Pa.: Historical Times, 1985.

Vandiver, Frank E. *Plowshares into Swords: Josiah Gorgas and Confederate Ordnance.* Austin: University of Texas Press, 1952.

———. *Rebel Brass: The Confederate Command System.* Baton Rouge: Louisiana State University Press, 1956.

Viele, Egbert Ludovickers. *Handbook for Active Service; Containing Practical Instructions in Campaign Duties for the Use of Volunteers.* NewYork: D. Van Nostrand, 1861.

Von Borcke, Heros. *Memoirs of the Confederate War for Independence.* 1867. Reprint, Gaithersburg, Md.: Butternut Press, 1985.

Von Borcke, Heros, and Justus Scheibert. *The Great Cavalry Battle of Brandy Station, 9 June 1863.* Translated by Stuart T. Wright and F. D. Bridgewater, with foreword by Bell I. Wiley. Winston-Salem, N.C.: Palaemon Press, 1976.

Wakelyn, Jon L. *Biographical Dictionary of the Confederacy.* Frank E. Vandiver, advisory editor. Westport, Conn.: Greenwood Press, 1977.

Wallace, Lee A. *A Guide to Virginia Military Organizations, 1861–1865.* Rev. 2d ed. Lynchburg, Va.: H. E. Howard, 1986.

Warner, Ezra J. *Generals in Gray: Lives of the Confederate Commanders.* Baton Rouge: Louisiana State University Press, 1959, 1993.

Warren, Edward. *An Epitome of Practical Surgery for Field and Hospital.* 1863. Reprint, American Civil War Surgery Series, no. 6, San Francisco: Norman Publishing, 1989.

Warthen, Harry J., Jr., ed. "Family Ties: Letters from J. E. B. Stuart." *Civil War Times Illustrated* 22 (October 1983): 34–35.

Winert, Richard P. *The Confederate Regular Army.* Shippensburg, Pa.: White Mane Publishing Co., 1991.

Welch, Spencer Glasgow. *A Confederate Surgeon's Letters to His Wife.* New York: Neale Publishing Co., 1911.

Wert, Jeffry D. *General James Longstreet: The Confederacy's Most Controversial General.* New York: Simon and Schuster, 1993.

———. "The Tycoon: Lee and His Staff." *Civil War Times Illustrated* 11 (July 1972): 10–19.

Williams, T. Harry. *Lincoln and His Generals.* New York: Alfred A. Knopf, 1952.

Bibliography

Wise, Jennings Cropper. *The Long Arm of Lee: The History of the Artillery of the Army of Northern Virginia*. 2 vols. 1915. Reprint, with introduction by Gary W. Gallagher. Richmond, Va.: Owens Publishing Co., 1988.

Worsham, John H. *One of Jackson's Foot Cavalry, His Experiences and What He Saw during the Civil War, 1861–1865*. New York: Neale Publishing Co., 1912.

Yadin, Yigael. *The Art of Warfare in Biblical Lands in the Light of Archaeological Study*. 2 vols. New York: McGraw-Hill Book Co., 1963.

Youngblood, William. "Personal Observations at Gettysburg." *Confederate Veteran* 19 (June 1911): 286–87.

Unpublished Sources

U.S. Army Military History Institute, Carlisle Barracks, Pennsylvania
  Braxton Bragg Papers
  Robert L. Brake Collection
  Civil War Miscellaneous Collection
  Civil War Times Illustrated Collection
  Harrisburg Civil War Roundtable Collection
  Daniel Harvey Hill Papers
  Lewis Leigh Collection
  Wiley Sword Collection

INDEX

335

Index

Index

343

Index

Trimble, Isaac R., 185, 273
Tucker, George W., 214
Tupper, Samuel, 181
Turner's Gap, Md., 265
Tyler, John, 8, 127

University of Mississippi, 155
University of Virginia, 93, 204, 206
Utah, 157

Vauban, Sebastien le Prestre de, 112
Venable, Charles, 67, 124, 174, 177, 179, 193, 237, 238
Verdiersville, Va., 252
Viele, Egbert L., 161
Virginia, 19, 23, 29, 31, 46, 49, 61, 63, 65, 70, 76, 101, 107, 114, 115, 126, 138, 152, 169, 189, 194, 215, 224, 229, 240, 256, 257
See also Army of Northern Virginia; battalion; cavalry; infantry; regiment; University of Virginia; Virginia Military Institute/VMI
Virginia Military Institute/VMI, 5, 151, 158
Von Borcke, Heros, 121, 156, 170, 208, 214, 220, 253, 259
in battle, 261, 264, 271, 272
on chief of staff, 14–16
on headquarters life, 195–98, 223, 224
on staff officer equipment, 200–202

wagon, 40, 45, 47–49, 51, 55, 61, 62, 65–67, 69, 76, 89, 98–101, 104, 111, 138, 200, 215, 216, 232, 276, 278
for headquarters and staff, 38, 61, 92, 192–94, 196, 198, 199
trains management, 94, 95, 163, 230, 268
See also transportation
wagon master, 6, 10, 11
Walker, John G., 11, 12
Walker, R. Lindsay, 85, 218
Walton, James B., 82, 86, 88, 164

Walton, Thomas, 128, 155, 170, 179, 259
War Department (Confederate), 3, 6, 17, 29, 37, 38, 52, 53, 77, 86, 102, 142, 227, 232, 236, 247, 254
Warren, Edward, 160, 161
Warren, Gouverneur K., 262
Washington, D.C., 114, 119, 121, 172, 194, 250, 251, 254, 255, 273
Washington Artillery, 81, 164
See also artillery
Washington College, Va., 174, 204
Watts, Thomas H., 132
Waynesboro, Va., 101
Welch, Spencer G., 217, 220
Wert, Jeffry D., 263
West Point, United States Military Academy at, 67, 150, 151, 156–58
West Virginia, 51, 55, 63, 190, 195
Wharton, R. W., 144
White, Thomas, 203
Whiting, William H. C., 171, 172, 257
Wickham, William C., 273
Wigfall, Louis T., 135
Wilbourn, Robert E., 118
Wilcox, Cadmus M., 105, 243, 261, 267
Williamsburg, Va., 14, 150, 211, 243, 264
See also battle, Williamsburg
Williamsport, Va., 11, 51, 273
Willis, John, 195
Wilmington, N.C., 97, 136
Winchester, Va., 31, 48, 49, 51, 63, 76, 77, 99, 106, 107, 126, 168, 194, 200, 201, 220, 231, 246, 272, 277
Winder, Charles S., 181, 199, 246, 258, 269
Winthrop, Stephen, 128
Wofford, William T., 273
Wolseley, Garnet, 190, 192
Wright, Ambrose R., 250

York, Pa., 51
Young, Henry E., 129
Young Men's Christian Association, 138

352